T0298498

Throughput Economics

Throughput Economics

Making Good Management Decisions

By Eli Schragenheim, Henry Camp, and Rocco Surace

Routledge
Taylor & Francis Group

A PRODUCTIVITY PRESS BOOK

First edition published in 2019
by Routledge/Productivity Press
52 Vanderbilt Avenue, 11th Floor New York, NY 10017
2 Park Square, Milton Park, Abingdon, Oxon OX14 4RN, UK

© 2019 by Taylor & Francis Group, LLC

Routledge/Productivity Press is an imprint of Taylor & Francis Group, an Informa business

Fisrt issued in paperback 2021

No claim to original U.S. government works

Printed on acid-free paper

ISBN-13: 978-0-367-03061-2 (hbk)
ISBN-13: 978-1-03-209202-7 (pbk)
ISBN-13: 978-0-429-02012-4 (eBook)

This book contains information obtained from authentic and highly regarded sources. Reasonable efforts have been made to publish reliable data and information, but the author and publisher cannot assume responsibility for the validity of all materials or the consequences of their use. The authors and publishers have attempted to trace the copyright holders of all material reproduced in this publication and apologize to copyright holders if permission to publish in this form has not been obtained. If any copyright material has not been acknowledged please write and let us know so we may rectify in any future reprint.

Except as permitted under U.S. Copyright Law, no part of this book may be reprinted, reproduced, transmitted, or utilized in any form by any electronic, mechanical, or other means, now known or hereafter invented, including photocopying, microfilming, and recording, or in any information storage or retrieval system, without written permission from the publishers.

For permission to photocopy or use material electronically from this work, please access www.copyright.com (http://www. copyright.com/) or contact the Copyright Clearance Center, Inc. (CCC), 222 Rosewood Drive, Danvers, MA 01923, 978-750-8400. CCC is a not-for-profit organization that provides licenses and registration for a variety of users. For organizations that have been granted a photocopy license by the CCC, a separate system of payment has been arranged.

Trademark Notice: Product or corporate names may be trademarks or registered trademarks and are used only for identification and explanation without intent to infringe.

Library of Congress Cataloging-in-Publication Data

Names: Schragenheim, Eli, author. | Camp, Henry (Henry Fitzhugh), author. | Surace, Rocco, author.
Title: Throughput economics : making good management decisions / Eli Schragenheim, Henry Camp, and Rocco Surace.
Description: New York, NY : Routledge, 2019. | Includes bibliographical references and index.
Identifiers: LCCN 2018059463 (print) | LCCN 2019001464 (ebook) | ISBN 9780429020124 (e-Book) | ISBN 9780367030612 (hardback : alk. paper)
Subjects: LCSH: Industrial management—Decision making. | Production management—Decision making.
Classification: LCC HD30.23 (ebook) | LCC HD30.23 .S374 2019 (print) | DDC 658.4/03—dc23
LC record available at https://lccn.loc.gov/2018059463

Visit the Taylor & Francis Web site at
http://www.taylorandfrancis.com and the Productivity Press Web site at
http://www.productivitypress.com

Contents

Tribute to Dr. Eliyahu M. Goldratt, 1947–2011

The authors dedicate this book to the memory of the person who inspires us and thousands of other people all over the world to do whatever we can to draw the most from ourselves and our businesses, and for our clients.

Dr. Goldratt has propounded the Theory of Constraints (TOC), as a pragmatic theory to run organizations, based on scientific rules and logic.

He was the author of a number of books that explain his Theory of Constraints, applied in different contexts: *The Goal: A Process of Ongoing Improvement* (1984), 2nd Rev edition (1992) and 20th Anniversary Edition (2004); *The Race* (1986); *Essays on the Theory of Constraints* (1987); *What Is This Thing Called Theory of Constraints and How Should It Be Implemented?* (1990); *The Haystack Syndrome: Sifting Information Out of the Data Ocean* (1991); *It's Not Luck* (1994); *Critical Chain* (1997); *Necessary but Not Sufficient* (2000); *Production the TOC Way* (2003); *The Choice* (2008) and *Isn't It Obvious* (2009). He set forth the comprehensive TOC Thinking processes and published dozens of magazine articles, white papers, videos, strategy and tactic trees, and even a theatrical play.

His contribution to the world is only partially recognized today. This book is part of wider efforts to gain more and more value from his legacy.

Foreword

"Don't stand in my shadow, stand on my shoulders."

These were the last words Dr. Eli Goldratt shared with me. It was June 2, 2011. Only days later, on June 11, 2011, the bigger-than-life Dr. Goldratt sadly passed away. These words both inspire and haunt me every day. His instruction was very clear: do not allow inertia to stop the development of the body of knowledge he called "Theory of Constraints" (TOC). Dr. Eli Goldratt was not only the creator of TOC and the author of a number of bestselling books, including *The Goal*, he was also the creator of Throughput Accounting.

Throughput Accounting was designed to help managers make better management decisions. Decisions like how to judge the performance of a specific product, customer, or department; whether to invest in new equipment; how to judge the organizational impact of a change; whether to buy or, rather, produce a certain product; whether it is wise to accept a particular customer's order, when it is not clear if there will be sufficient capacity; whether the price per unit the customer is prepared to pay more than covers the total marginal cost per unit.

Since the death of Dr. Goldratt, there have been a number of exciting new developments to expand the TOC body of knowledge and specifically related to decision making. As CEO of Goldratt Research Labs, I have aimed to stand on Dr. Goldratt's shoulders to advance the knowledge on making one of the most challenging types of decisions—qualitative decisions that require our judgment. When we use our judgment, we are prone to mistakes due to many cognitive biases and limiting beliefs. Dr. Goldratt made two valuable contributions in this field with the creation of his Evaporating Cloud and Change Matrix methods. To maintain the benefits while addressing the limitations of these two methods, I created and have been field testing the five-step ProConCloud method over the last decade.

The three authors of this book have aimed to do the same in the complex field of Throughput Economics, a more quantitative management decision making methodology. Throughput Economics was designed to maintain the benefits of Throughput Accounting, and at the same time, address some of its inherent limitations.

Why did Dr. Goldratt originally invent Throughput Accounting?

When managers use traditional Cost Accounting, it can often cause managers to do the opposite of what is good for the organization as a whole. It can result in outsourcing products or services that increases, rather than reduces the total cost of the organization. It can cause management to close down a division that is still making a positive contribution to overhead and profits. It can even cause management to focus on cost cutting and downsizing—change initiatives with a relatively small upside if they work and a big downside if they fail. It is no wonder then that the first implementations of TOC clashed with Cost Accounting. Dr. Goldratt realized quickly it was critical to develop an alternative. He developed Throughput Accounting as a practical alternative to allow managers at all levels to make decisions that would benefit the organization as a whole.

Despite its benefits, unfortunately, Throughput Accounting also had a few limitations. For example, it does not provide any real guidance on how to consider the likely future demand variability when making decisions. And for organizations that have relatively balanced capacity profiles with moving bottlenecks, following Throughput Accounting's "Maximize Profitability by using the Product Mix with the highest Throughput per Constraint Minute" could actually result in reducing rather than increasing profitability.

I have known the three authors of *Throughput Economics* for over 20 years. All three were also with me in Israel at that last meeting with Dr. Goldratt in his home. They also heard those inspirational words and took the message to heart. With this book the three authors are also aiming to stand on Dr. Goldratt's shoulders and to take his Throughput Accounting to the next level. They have accomplished this by expanding the scope of Throughput Accounting to assist with additional quantitative strategic and tactical decisions in a way that maintains the simplicity and benefits of Throughput Accounting, while addressing some of its key limitations.

We know that the success and failure of organizations are governed by the quality and speed of the decisions made by managers within these organizations. To improve the quality and speed of decisions, we have to understand and address the root causes of decision mistakes and delays at all levels of management.

I believe this book is a must-read for managers for three reasons.

First, it was written by three authors whose combined real-world business experience exceeds 100 years. Their different positions and perspectives within business cover three key dimensions that were needed to expand the scope of Throughput Accounting to an even more holistic quantitative decision-making framework. There is the management consultant, strategic advisor, and educator (Eli Schragenheim), the business owner, CEO, and investor (Henry Camp), and the certified public accountant and financial advisor (Rocco Surace).

Second, the book makes an important contribution by providing a powerful yet relatively simple framework for decision making within a complex world. The authors have used a number of case studies that, even though fictional, allow the reader to put themselves in the shoes of a manager facing real world decisions. Each chapter in this book touches on a different scenario that illustrates a dilemma managers may encounter in their business or organization.

And finally, in the age of Artificial Intelligence, more and more decisions previously made exclusively by managers will be automated. However, the type of decisions that will remain the responsibility of humans are those that are subjective by nature, which requires a combination of hard data, intuition, and a practical way to consider uncertainty and risk.

In an increasingly complex and uncertain world where managers need to decide where and how to invest their scarcest resource—their limited attention—, I believe Throughput Economics provides a step forward in each of these three factors.

I hope you enjoy this book as much as I did. The authors aimed to share their insights, not only to provide readers with a practical decision-making framework they can apply to making challenging decisions, but to trigger new questions that need to be answered by you, the next generation of managers.

We can see further, by standing on the shoulders of giants.

Dr. Alan Barnard, CEO
Goldratt Research Labs

Introduction

The Ultimate Task of Every Manager is to Make Good Decisions

Decisions often must be taken when time is pressing, when a lot of the relevant information is unavailable and complexity coupled with significant uncertainty make it hard to choose the right way. Improving the quality of such decisions would have a dramatic impact on the bottom line of an organization. This is what we, the three authors, are aiming at: improving the overall performance of organizations, by guiding their managers to make superior decisions.

It is true that there are also several other expectations of a good manager beyond making the right decisions at the right time. Such expectations include inspiring a sense of purpose in their subordinates and giving them an environment in which they can find the motivation to do whatever is required to move the company ever closer to its goal. Not less important is the ability to exert the right efforts to ascertain and act on that which needs to be done, *and* find the wisdom and control to ensure that what does not need to be done is *not* done. Both of these are required for sustainable success. It is critical for every manager to focus effectively to enable holistic, synchronized actions that result in exponential financial growth and stability at the same time. Another key task is to identify opportunities and emerging threats. These elements together support managerial decisions, the quality of which results in a new level of success for the organization to become ever-flourishing.

Humankind, working together, is an incredible and accelerating force for innovation. Think computer chips, transportation, communication, food production, energy, engines. This is business. We have made extraordinary progress as a species. As just one example, think about oil exploration. From the 1930's, experts in the field have been calling for "peak oil," the point at which the rate of consumption starts to deplete the known world oil reserves.[1] And, they were all correct. If you look at the known oil reserves, at any point in time, and subtract extrapolated consumption of oil for a decade or two, the oil reserves are exhausted. The reason peak oil hasn't occurred is due to the money and innovation expended to discover more oil, which has been steadily happening faster than the rate of consumption increases. When you consider that oil and gas extraction was only 1.236% of the total business production in the United States in 2017,[2] it puts in perspective how huge the challenge is for business innovation.

---

[1] Bryce, Robert (2014). Smaller Faster Lighter Denser Cheaper: how innovation keeps proving the catastrophists wrong. New York, NY: Public Affairs. See pages 180–181.
[2] Source: Bureau of Economic Analysis, U.S. Department of Commerce. https://bea.gov/

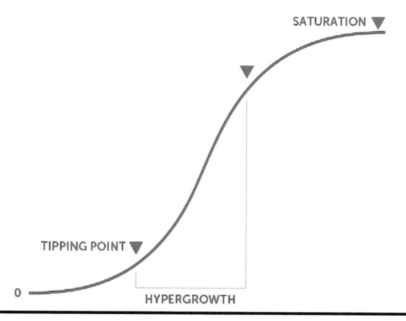

Figure 0.1   The progressive adoption of any innovation.

It is also true that innovation seldom moves steadily. Like biological evolution, there are periods of relative stability punctuated by disruptive change. We authors believe that an explosive improvement in business process has already begun, starting in the mid-1980s. It is following the normal process of adoption along an s-curve, as shown in Figure 0.1. It is a new way of thinking to manage companies.

The methodology we offer is built upon the legacy of Dr. Eliyahu M. Goldratt, the developer of the Theory of Constraints (TOC), and the author of the best-selling business novel, *The Goal*, as well as nine other books on the subject, many papers and presentations, and numerous videos. We, three disciples of Dr. Goldratt, stand on his shoulders to look even further into the basic struggle of predicting the future in order to do what is right, in spite of the complexity and uncertainty that are natural characteristics of the reality with which every organization must contend.

This book focuses on making superior managerial decisions when the situation is both complex and uncertain. To do that, we have to be aware of what prevents good managers from making the right decisions on behalf of their organizations.

Eli Goldratt had the rare gift of powerful intuition, combined with disciplined thinking, which allowed him to see through apparent complexity and uncertainty directly to extraordinary opportunities through deep experiences. However, we find that most of us require a more explicit explanation to be able to discover a quick path to vast improvements which are always possible in every situation.

Are the Current Decisions Commonly Made by Top Management that Bad?

The simple answer is *yes*; many managerial decisions are basically flawed. It is possible to prove this claim in a rational way by pointing to many decisions that are currently made which necessarily lead to inferior results. This can be demonstrated, even when we take into account the limited information available at the time the decision was made.

Note that very few companies succeed in increasing their profit every year for five consecutive years. Something must be preventing managers from identifying the good and safe schemes to do better and better.

Being accountable for their decisions, top managers are wise to be especially careful. Rejecting an idea which contains good promise but might end with less than expected results is personally much safer than forging ahead. Whenever such an uncertain idea is adopted, some other people in the organization may bide their time until the actual outcomes become clear. When the results are not fully satisfying, then the manager is blamed for making the wrong decision. This results in too many managers not taking actions they should, because failing to act risks much less after-the-fact criticism when the consequent undesired effects are much less obviously connected to the avoided actions. Actually, only an ultra-negative outcome might raise criticism about refraining from taking an action.

The unavoidable result is that too few ideas are accepted, only those which seem very safe. Even so, there are too many major blunders committed because of the flaws of some of the currently accepted methodologies, such as the use of cost per unit and local efficiencies. On top of many wrong decisions, there are a huge amount of different potential ideas that should have been considered and accepted based on their potential rewards, and the available capacity of the key resources, but are not even considered.

Opening the door to carefully check a much wider flow of ideas, coming from all over the organization, is both motivational and, even more, a practical way to strive to significantly and consistently improve the performance of the organization. What makes it practical is the methodology of revealing both the risk and potential of any idea very quickly, while also combining intuition with data coming from different functions within the organization.

This methodology is what this book is all about.

In the writing of the book, we have combined three very different perspectives.

The first is the perspective of a management consultant and educator, an "outsider" to any specific organization but one who has a very wide view of many different organizations. One characteristic of a consultant is that the burden of responsibility and accountability is relatively light since the consultant is not the one who dictates the final decision. This aspect has two major ramifications. On one hand, such a person can easily afford to be open to new ideas. Moreover, having been exposed to different organizations brings the benefits of gaining ideas that have been proven to work well in other environments. Having been exposed to the Theory of Constraints directly by working closely with Dr. Goldratt for many years adds another source of insights that can be used in many different cases. On the other hand, an outsider cannot see all the details that are unique to specific organizations. And, of course, not carrying the full responsibility might prevent the consultant from recognizing the inherent risk, even a threat, that bold ideas might present. Co-author Eli Schragenheim has this perspective. However, the perspectives of the other co-authors become especially useful and truly needed.

The second perspective is from a CEO and owner of several companies ranging from distribution to manufacturing to logistics to software development to trading. For someone who has, in the past, actually made decisions according to the same commonly used practices that this book was written to prove are flawed, admitting these flaws is quite painful. For this reason, many managers prefer to ignore the rationale against their own past practices. Henry Camp decided to recognize and admit his past mistakes in order to move ahead to a better framework, despite its less broad acceptance. The constraints viewpoint is specifically the method Henry uses to create value in his companies.

The third perspective is again from an outsider, but one from a service area which every significant company is required to utilize. This is the perspective of a very experienced certified public accountant (CPA), Rocco Surace, who has not only been exposed to the actual performance of many organizations, but also advises management teams on some of their major decisions, and even offers the service of helping his clients implement improvements. He has seen the consequences of more mistakes than the other co-authors combined.

Our Perspective

There is a common practice of differentiating between long-term decisions–so called strategic decisions–and short-term or tactical decisions. Actually, the two categories should be closely related and, in too many cases, the short-term is more influential in establishing global strategy. The methodology presented here is targeted at both categories of decisions by connecting them through understanding the relationships between short-term opportunities and their full potential over the long-term.

Revealing the level of uncertainty behind various ideas is absolutely essential for sound decision making. Reducing the natural personal concerns of key executives in handling uncertainty makes it possible to manage and even navigate the uncertainty to further improve performance, while keeping the organization safer. This is a way to become antifragile,[3] which is the focus of the methodology we describe in this book and the reason we wrote it.

---

[3] Antifragile is a term coined by Nassim Taleb in his eponymous book. He points out that an antonym for fragile does not exist in the English language. Fragile means a shock can destroy something. Robust is not an opposite since it only means that a shock has no effect. Antifragility is the characteristic of actually improving from a shock. Since you can't engineer out all types of shocks, isn't this what you want for your company and yourself?

Chapter 1

Overcoming Distortions Resulting from "Cost per Unit" Accounting— Daily Bread, Part 1

Concepts are abstract guidance for understanding reality. The true test of any concept is to apply it in a specific case and find out how effective the actions derived based on the concept are in the particular case. This is where we start our journey to evaluate the existing guiding concepts in organizational decision making by examining a fictional, but realistic, case to find out where the general concept leads us.

A Decision to Make

Daily Bread is a medium-sized producer of bread and other bakery products. The company sells to supermarkets, bakery shops and hotels. Daily Bread just received an interesting business offer. Events to Remember wants to use Daily Bread products for all their events. Events to Remember runs three different events every day. These include conferences, luxurious weddings and special organizational events. The stumbling block is that Events to Remember is willing to pay only 60% of Daily Bread's list price! The average margin of Daily Bread products, based on their recent calculated cost of production, is 27.8%.

Considering the quantities Events to Remember requested in their offer and using the standard cost-per-unit means a loss of $3K per month, based on the assumed daily income of roughly $491 instead of $818 from selling the same quantities at regular prices. The CFO claims that his intuition is telling him that the above calculations might not reflect the real picture; the actual loss could be smaller and it's even possible that the move could lead to a minor profit. Still, the level of concern is high. Worries are compounded by the production manager's warning that the additional quantities might, from time to time, overload the ovens and the packaging line.

However, having Daily Bread's products served at all Events to Remember's events could have a considerable impact on the market, boosting Daily Bread's reputation in the high socio-economic segment, because Events to Remember is willing to allow Daily Bread to visually identify their brand with the products served during the events. Consequently, Marketing and Sales are pushing to go ahead with the deal.

Is the Decision Clear-Cut?

The CFO has already expressed a certain hesitation. On one hand, it seems quite reasonable to accept that a 40% reduction in price would result in a loss. The official cost accounting figure for the margin is 27.8%, which means that price reduction of 40% would definitely generate a loss. On the other hand, the CFO is fully aware that some of the costs allocated to the cost-per-unit of the products might not increase proportionally, if Daily Bread decides to accept the offer. Therefore, it could be that accepting the Events to Remember deal would not actually cause a loss. The CFO's doubts that the calculated $3K monthly loss is real come from recognizing that the cost of labor might not change due to the additional orders and, even more certainly, most of the other fixed costs, like management, rent, and depreciation would not increase due to the additional production. Most CFOs are quite aware that full absorption costs are not precisely accurate in such a case, but many managers and employees do not understand it at all.

Then, there is another issue—how beneficial is the marketing impact of Events to Remember promoting Daily Bread's products to wealthy potential customers?

What Additional Information Is Required to Make a Good Decision?

The basic idea of cost accounting, which was developed over a century ago,[1] is that effective cost allocation methods produce a reliable estimate of the cost per unit. Harsh criticism of its being too simplistic for modern times opened the way for the emergence of Activity-Based Costing (ABC), which requires additional efforts to identify all the cost drivers and their related activities leading to detailed cost calculations, per unit, per client, per deal, per invoice and even per line item on an invoice.

Does All the Extra Information Gathered by ABC Support Better Decisions?

Let us first check the impact of a basic assumption behind ABC, that **every use of capacity costs money!** Activity-Based Costing identifies every activity and captures each of their costs. The implied assumption, which is generally accepted, is equivalent to "there are no free lunches."

Is it always true that every use of capacity generates cost? Let's examine several examples that raise some doubt:

1. **Using a very expensive production line at night.** If overtime is paid to operators or an additional shift is required, additional costs are generated. However, consuming the capacity of the production line at night adds no cost. It may be argued that any additional usage

---

[1] The timing is pertinent because, a century ago, a higher percentage of the expense to make most products was labor and the means of compensating people was piece-work. Workers only received good wages if they produced at a consistently high level. Under such a model, the cost of labor per unit is defined by the piece-work rate, which was known exactly. Once the dominant methods of compensating employees became hourly and salary, the direct connection between a product's cost and the labor component of that cost was broken.

of the production line shortens the life of its machines and equipment. However, the vast majority of the line's components require replacement because of new innovations delivering greater speeds or quality long before their true end-of-life arrives.

2. **A waiter in a restaurant at an off-peak time.** A couple comes in and asks for the menu. There are no extra costs for wait staff due to this request.

3. **The headquarters of a company uses the entire floor of a building.** One room is left empty because no one has found a use for it and the company chooses not to rent it out. When someone suggests using it, there is no additional expenditure beyond what is already being spent.

What makes it often possible to use capacity for free is that, in most cases, **capacity can only be purchased in significant minimum amounts.** For instance, employing an operator for 40 hours every week means that if that operator only performs 34 hours of work in a given week, he still gets full pay.

Machines, equipment and space in buildings are purchased with certain capacities. It does not matter how much of the capacity is used in a specific period—the cost remains the same. Only very few resources are truly sold per unit consumed: electricity, water and some IT resources. Yet, even electricity is effectively paid for whether it is needed or not; the lights may be on and the air conditioning active regardless of the amount of work going on in the building.

To satisfy their desire for efficiency, some economists, accountants and business people adopt the convenient belief that **it is possible to match capacity to demand.** In other words, they choose to believe an organization can get reasonably close to utilizing every machine fully and every employee for their full 40 hours per week, excluding time allowed for approved breaks. Consequently, they believe it is a reasonable managerial target and their duty to avoid wasting any available capacity of any resource. Many employees truly seem to work throughout their 40 hours. But, if you examine their productivity it will indicate very significant fluctuations, meaning in some months that their actual output will be considerably lower than in other months. Employees know just how to look busy when they are expected to be busy. It does not mean they can't do (much) more whenever they want to, for example, if allowed to go home early with full pay as soon as their work is complete.

A funny incident happened in one of the TOC conferences. The following question was asked: *"In my organization, the demand fluctuates heavily between months; however, the amount of overtime is relatively consistent throughout the year. Can you explain to me why?"*

The audience reacted with loud laughter, which was not very polite, but expressed a simple truth that somehow escaped the person who asked the question. People know how to adjust their workload in order to be busy enough to maintain their incomes. The conclusion was that at peak demand there was enough capacity, including the overtime, to process and deliver all the demand. During the off-peak time the workers know what to do to get their overtime.

In reality, **there is no way to load any resource, human or machine to its limits without creating impractically long delivery delays.** Imagine a rush job that needs to be completed right away, but there is no available capacity. The choice is either to delay the rush job, which is clearly going to cause a problem, or interrupt the fully loaded resource which postpones what that resource is currently working on. The only way to avoid delays is to maintain a certain level of spare capacity. The important concept of "protective capacity" means a level of spare capacity that is absolutely required in order to ensure good delivery performance. We'll deal with the concept of protective capacity in more depth later in this book.

Machines cannot fake being busy and can operate 24/7 when you include time for setup and maintenance.

The inevitability of maintaining significant excess capacities on most resources is partially due to having to purchase capacity only in chunks. There are two additional reasons for the excess capacity every organization requires.

The first is **the need to reliably deliver value to clients within a reasonable time frame.** Promptly delivering value to clients requires synchronization among several resources. This creates dependencies between the resources which comprise the system. Every resource is impacted by internal fluctuations. The combination of dependencies plus foreseeable fluctuations results in a greater negative impact than either contributor alone. This is another core TOC insight.

Demand behavior is the other cause of the necessity for excess capacity. In almost all environments, fluctuations in demand are both frequent and unpredictable. There is no practical way to match the available capacity to the demand quickly enough to avoid losing some orders when demand increases and wasting some capacity when it declines. Of the two forms of waste, losing orders is far more damaging to current and future profitability than wasting capacity. Thus, the available capacity must be enough to respond to peak demand. This necessarily requires maintaining considerable excess capacity during momentary and often even prolonged off-peak periods.

What Happens When One Resource Runs Out of Capacity?

It does not matter how much capacity is still available from all the other resources; as long as just ONE resource is a bottleneck, the full market demand cannot be met, thus, disproportionately impairing profitability. Most companies experience periodic overloads of some of their resources. Temporary bottlenecks mean that the whole system is blocked from being productive for as long as the resources are overloaded. The inevitable consequence is that some sales are lost. There is insidious damage, since it is not always possible to be certain that sales were lost. For example, if a customer calls and asks when they can get an urgent order, customer service cites two months, the caller thanks the person and hangs up, there is no way to know that they needed three weeks delivery and have moved on to their next most favored supplier. In other words, management has never experienced their company's true financial potential and, as such, have learned to accept their circumstances as much closer to optimal than they actually are.

In the case of Daily Bread, a concern that either the ovens or the packing line would become a bottleneck has to be verified; otherwise, some of the company's clients might react in a very unfavorable way to sudden shortages of their supplies. The fact that accepting the order from Events to Remember does require additional capacity is not enough to determine whether one of the resources might become a bottleneck. If it does, then more decisions have to be made to deal with this situation. Management has just three options when they have a bottleneck:

1. Allow the market to become grossly dissatisfied. If the organization is a true monopoly or government regulations support the behavior, customers have no alternative to waiting. However, even so, the delays necessarily result in lost opportunities for customers, which translate into lost business for the company.
2. Reduce the sales of some products or services that utilize the capacity of the bottleneck resources. It is usually difficult or impossible to ensure that curtailing certain sales does not cause collateral damage.

3. Find ways to increase capacity quickly using overtime or outsourcing. There are two problems with this option:
   a. It is not always possible.
   b. **Additional capacity is typically purchased at a premium.** Not to mention, it may only be possible to buy significantly more capacity than is required.

This could be a relevant question for Daily Bread, if adding Events to Remember's demand turns one or more resources into bottlenecks. The next question is whether the capacity of the ovens and packaging line can be expanded. If there is such an option, what will it cost?

Our analysis fully reveals the flawed assumptions behind all cost accounting, Figure 1.1 demonstrates the non-linear behavior of the capacity cost and the actual demand for capacity. The complete new realization is:

The cost of capacity is not linear!

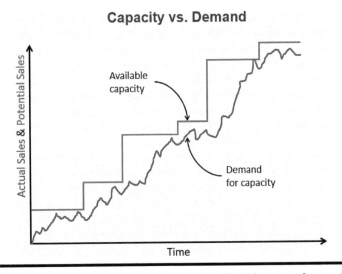

Capacity vs. Demand

Figure 1.1   **When expected upward variations in demand might exceed capacity, the capacity must be increased or some customers may not be served on time and in full.**

This means that the cost of producing 1,000 widgets is seldom equal to 1,000 times the cost of producing one.

Note: buying widgets is usually linear. Most of the time, buying 110 widgets costs 1.1 times the price of 100. Exceptions are getting a quantity price break and paying a less-than-minimum-order surcharge.

However, **when it comes to producing widgets, the cost-per-unit varies in a non-linear fashion.** The cost of capacity of almost every single resource varies in a step function and each resource has a limit beyond which increasing the capacity in the short term is impossible. For some resources, capacity can only be purchased in huge amounts. To achieve any further increase in capacity could be significantly, even prohibitively, expensive (i.e. having to buy a whole new production line or plant!). On the other hand, as long as the existing system has enough capacity to cover all the demand, changes in actual production have a limited impact on overhead costs. Exceeding a production line's capacity limit, however, could double the expense, even though market demand might only increase incrementally. Other resources, such as manpower, are purchased in progressively smaller steps as the company grows and employs more and more people. Still, when a company only has one of a certain skill of employee, adding another means doubling the cost of that resource. For this reason, especially in smaller companies, employees often end up wearing many hats. Again, the total cost of capacity is a non-linear step function with many steps of different sizes which can be surprisingly difficult to extrapolate.

How Should Management Decide Whether to Invest in Purchasing an Additional Production Line When, at Best, the Sales Would Go Up by 15%?

Can the decision be based on the margin calculated by the expected selling price minus the cost-per-unit?

The cost-per-unit calculation includes not just the cost of the production line plus materials, but also the capacity cost of every other resource required for producing and selling 15% more products, whether these resources actually have the required capacity or not.

Let us evaluate a simpler and more common decision: A potential client wants 100 widgets every week. The client is willing to pay $1,000 for this weekly supply regardless of the fact that the list price varies between $11.50 and $13.00.

The practical questions are:

1. **If management accepts this order, will the company earn more net profit?**
2. **Are there other positive and negative long-term ramifications?**
3. **What is the risk of compound interactions due to the decision?**

The first question is usually the key. If analyzed properly, it certainly includes checking the possibility of running out of capacity—if the additional 100 widgets, on top of the existing demand, would turn even one resource into a bottleneck. The second question requires considering possible long-term ramifications, especially regarding the impact on the future market demand and the potential for price erosion due to market recognition of discounting, as well as reactive price reductions by competition. The third one requires ascertaining the impact of uncertainty related to the previous questions.

The three vital questions above are relevant to all the examples used so far, including the case of Daily Bread.

The most important insight is to view the organization as a system which is paying for a set of various resources, each with a fixed level of available capacity: space in its buildings, management attention, access to raw materials, utilities, equipment and employees with the requisite skills.

Maintaining this set of resources and their respective capacities comprise most of the expenses of the organization. Options for quickly increasing capacity, when necessary, should be evaluated well in advance of the expected need, taking into consideration their actual absolute added cost.

Can Current Methods and Accounting Tools Provide a Satisfactory Answer to These Important Questions?

If the answer is no, then we must seek alternative tools. Furthermore, if we are wise, we should identify the invalid assumption(s) that lead to unsatisfactory answers and, thus, ensure we aren't making more mistakes. Lastly, we should fully understand the needs that are met by the current approach, which led to its adoption. Those needs still must be met. However, the methodology may no longer be relevant given the new reality.

The big advantage of cost allocation methods, yielding the cost-per-unit, is that they simplify decision making at all levels. What makes the cost-per-unit measure easy to use is that it does not require consideration of the size of the decision at hand. However, when such a useful simplification leads to very serious distortions regarding the actual ramifications of larger decisions, then we should identify the simplest alternative that captures the true impact of the potential effects. Abandoning the cost-per-unit approach is unfortunately necessary.

In the quest for a better decision-making process, we first need to understand conceptually the actual cost of a decision and its impact on sales and gross margin. In order to do so, we should evaluate the true added value of selling one additional unit of a product. But, before that, let's present a glimpse into a generic idea about what effective decision-support of managers should look like.

Chapter 2

A Conceptual, Yet Natural, Way to Make Decisions

Suppose a company is evaluating an idea to launch a series of new products. Two broad ways to conduct the analysis exist.

Current Practice: Focus on the Merits of the Proposed Idea

The analysis concentrates just on the characteristics of the opportunity itself by considering its pros and cons. The first action is to estimate the potential sales of each of the new products and their associated costs. The simple decision criterion is that the revenues should cover all the costs and result in an acceptable overall margin. There are commonly many such opportunities vying for management's attention with different impacts on sales and costs, each carrying its own degree of risk. We can easily calculate the margin per unit of product. This allows us to prioritize ideas and make sure we don't spend too much for a margin that is too thin. A common practice is to decide upon a minimum margin per unit as a threshold for acceptance.

What Critical Information Is Lost by This Approach?

As we saw in the first chapter, we typically lose sight of the impact on the capacity at hand. As we demonstrated, the cost of capacity is not linear. When a new idea is considered, it is possible to consider the truly variable costs of implementing the idea. It is also possible to evaluate the capacity required from the key resources. However, will the consumption of that capacity add cost? This depends on whether all the other requirements for capacity, coming from all the current orders the organization is already committed to deliver, leave enough excess capacity to process the activities for this new idea. If this is the case, then no additional cost above the current cost of maintaining the capacity is required. But, if the additional activities require capacity beyond what is currently available, then the impact on cost cannot be easily determined.

Another potential obstacle stemming from the current practice is that interdependencies between the new idea and the existing activities might be missed. Launching new products could easily impact the sales of current products, for good or ill. Concentrating exclusively on the new idea blinds decision makers from these indirect impacts and can lead to disappointing financial results overall. Furthermore, ambiguity regarding the cause of an outcome is likely because, while the sales of the new products could be fine, overall sales might be depressed by the change.

Yet another downside to the current practice of thinking about new ideas separately should be considered. A new idea's net impact on the holistic performance of the organization can be quite significant or very small. When many opportunities result overall in some small improvement and also overload management attention, then a stream of insignificant ideas might prevent management from dealing with a few ideas that could yield much bigger impact globally.

A Holistic Approach: Adding the Proposed Idea to the Overall Current State

Our suggested new practice is to check the new idea by effectively evaluating its addition on top of all the current activity. This way, if we have the capabilities to process all the required information, we gain the full impact of the proposed idea.

Such an approach always should have been the normal way to make decisions. However, as it turns out, we human beings prefer shortcuts to avoid straining our brains.[1] And, the shortcuts usually work well enough but can fail when we consider new opportunities in isolation. Therefore, by far the most conceptually **simple** way that actually works[2] is to add the impact of the new idea to the current load. After all, what is simpler than a straightforward and reliable approach that analyzes a new idea's actual impact on the bottom line?

The reason this approach is counterintuitive is that it seems too complicated. Because of this, people sense that it is too slow to truly support real-life decision-making.

Everything in this book is meant to demonstrate a viable way to make our approach reasonably easy to implement, allowing you a simple, truly superior decision-making mechanism. The first realization concerns the question of "information," which is required to make a superior decision, in addition to what is available to support such a decision. Eventually, we'll need to ask ourselves the question:

> **Given that some of the truly required information is not available—how can we still come up with a superior decision?**

---

[1] Please don't think we are being silly. There is significant evidence that humans evolved their significant forebrains at a time when it was not at all certain that there would always be enough food for fuel. Consequently, as a survival mechanism, we evolved an unconscious preference to act on quick intuition instead of thinking things through slowly and deeply.

[2] This is a good time to explain Camp's Law: *"When in doubt, choose a less efficient route."* In the final accounting, there is nothing more efficient than being effective. Before we blunder, the same intuition we prefer to use sends us a message. How many times have you derided yourself saying something like, *"I knew that wasn't going to work."* When you send yourself this message in the future, slow down and check before you continue your train of thought. The slight amount this slows you down is far less than the time it takes to repair the damage.

Chapter 3

Information Is Derived from Hard Data, Intuition and Assessment of Uncertainty

Managers need to make many decisions. Since the opportunity to improve is limited by the amount of attention available to consider and implement the improvements, managers are under constant and intense time pressure. In order to make good decisions, they require relevant information.

Three Different Types of Information Required for Making Good Decision

1. **Hard data.** This is the easiest type. It consists of accurate numbers or facts that can have an impact on the decision.
2. **Intuitive assumptions about reality.** They may not be proven in any way but they come from the life experience of a person. Usually, they are approximately correct but occasionally are not only wrong, but persistently wrong, even when held by experienced experts.
3. **Assessment of uncertainty and risk.**

These three types of information, while drawn from the past are assumed to be relevant, at least in the near future, and yet they support decisions that always look into the future. It is a matter of judgment, based on circumstances, how far into the past supporting information remains pertinent.

The search for relevant information and then its use to make a decision is quite different for each of the three types of information. The following is an example of a typical decision, which will be used throughout this chapter to highlight the differences between the types of information supporting the making of a business decision.

A large chain of drugstores considers discontinuing the sale of the Brand C electric shavers. The reason given is that the sales of Brand C are slow relative to the two leading brands and the margin of Brand C is lower.

Table 3.1   Current Sales Data for Brands A, B and C

Brand	Sold/mo	Price/unit	Cost/unit	Margin/unit	% Margin
A	1,000	$100	$60	$40	40%
B	850	$90	$50	$40	44%
C	420	$130	$105	$25	19%

The above numbers, Table 3.1, are hard data—accurate numbers that represent the recent past.

It seems obvious that Brand C is much less desirable than the other two brands, but what positive financial outcome is expected from dropping it? Are the costs of keeping Brand C on the shelf higher than the total margin generated from offering that brand?

What Information Is Necessary to Check the Argument?

Many times a decision to stop selling a product is based on saving costs. Are the costs always saved? The answer should specify what costs could be saved and then whether a specific decision, such as no longer selling Brand C, truly leads to reducing these costs.

Handling inventory requires some capacity of purchasing agents, transportation, space in warehouses and load on the warehouse employees. Chapter 1 taught us about the non-linear behavior of capacity, which is certainly valid here. Discontinuing Brand C would definitely reduce the workload of purchasing people and free up some space in the warehouses, but, even if true, it does not mean costs will be saved unless a warehouse is closed, enough people are fired or overtime is reduced. Finally, to the extent the savings are real, are they more than the lost gross margin?

Only when storage space is truly limited to the point that aisles must be blocked with products, perhaps then reducing the inventory of Brand C might lead to a dip in overtime due to less shuffling of products to gain access. There might be minor cost savings due to less overall transportation and finance costs due to reduced inventory. But one-time losses from disposing of residual inventory could be more significant. On the other hand, if the last of its inventory is to be sold before Brand C is dropped, to avoid any shrinkage losses, then what management attention will be required and at what opportunity cost?

The information above is hardly completely reliable data. Data on the detailed capacity utilization of people is seldom collected because it is almost impossible to trust. Thus, intuition about whether the load on a specific human resource is too high, while not absolutely reliable, is better than trying to actually measure it. Accurate utilization of space is also seldom collected because it is not truly useful, often changes and it requires a lot of work. In other words, a space can be observed to be full, so the intuitive information is good enough when the cost of obtaining precise facts is too high.

Under Activity-Based Costing (ABC), information on the capacity required to handle Brand C products could be collected but the point is that this capacity utilization, in the vast majority of cases, does not generate any real additional cost. The intuitive information is good enough to answer the question of whether giving up Brand C would beneficially reduce the cost of purchasing agents and warehouse space.

Assuming there are no real savings of purchasing costs and space is not truly limited, then basing the decision only on the hard data, which does not include any cost savings, management should reject the idea. Eliminating Brand C lowers gross profit by $10,500[1] every month, which is much greater than any apparent cost savings.

To rationally continue considering the suggested action, there must be a claim that this move would lead to additional sales of other existing products. In this case, since the gross margins on Brands A and B are 60% higher, it is not necessary to gain as many sales of A and B as will be lost by dropping Brand C. Once Brand C is gone from the shelves, as long as customers buy at least 263 more units of Brands A and B combined,[2] more gross margin is produced than was lost from the discontinuation of Brand C. However, any claim that consumers will behave in this fashion is purely based on intuition.

The Value and Limitations of Intuition

Could it be that **without Brand C on display, more of Brands A and B will sell?** The first possibility is that most buyers who prefer Brand C would substitute Brands A and B instead of looking for an alternative to Brand C elsewhere. Another option is that, when the shelf space is dedicated to just Brands A and B, the simpler product offering is more effective because potential buyers are less overwhelmed by the available choices. This line of reasoning suggests that when the level of variety is decreased, then customers will be less confused and buy more electric shavers.

The above assumptions are anything but hard data. They are not stored in any computerized database and are absolutely not certain. They are based on employing an intuitive sense of cause-and-effect logic, meaning detailed connections between causes and effects are not consciously articulated. Such a supposition might also include a rough idea of the net impact. When such arguments are brought forward by people who have rich experience in the relevant area, their off-the-cuff estimations are often, quite appropriately, treated as valuable information. They are plainly relevant, even though they are also uncertain, and it remains possible that such assumptions are largely wrong. These are the characteristics of intuition.

Until artificial intelligence is far more developed. Management is ill advised to ignore informal knowledge based on people's experience and opinions, in spite of the risks involved with relying on intuition. Actually, there are even risks inherent in relying on what is considered hard data.

In this example, there is a chance, though usually slim, that one or more of the data elements is grossly in error, for instance, due to a typing mistake. It is clear that such an incident is relatively rare,

---

[1] 420 units × $25/unit
[2] 420 units × $25/unit /$40/unit

but it is still part of the overall inherent uncertainty. Or, it could be that some specific cause has just changed market demand for better or worse and the historical data do not yet fully reflect the change.

Intuition Springs from the Knowledge and Areas of Expertise of Specific People

Suppose that, while the above intuitive assumptions are directionally correct, the impact on sales of Brands A and B is limited, for example, to 10% more sales of both brands, which results in an additional $7,400 in gross profit.[3] However, this increase fails to cover the planned gross margin loss of $10,500 of Brand C. While the intuition of the salespeople is correct that the sales of Brands A and B would increase, their intuition regarding the extent of the financial benefit might not be good enough.

The importance of intuition should not be doubted. However, one should also consider the known weaknesses of human intuition. Three areas in which intuition may be problematic are:

1. The most obvious weakness is that **intuition is truly personal,** thus, subject to the basic characteristics and intelligence of the person. An optimist would have a natural tendency to see the best-case scenario, ignoring or underestimating the risk of undesired outcomes. Personal biases go directly into one's intuition for good or ill.
2. Intuition is not fully verbalized in one's mind. Therefore, **it is difficult to communicate it to others.** It is a poor way to convince others since the complete rationale may not be entirely clear, unless the others share the same deep understanding of the subject matter. Some personalities are particularly reluctant to express their intuition, exactly because they themselves feel they are not certain enough. Others are quite content to share, if only for the pleasure of hearing themselves speak.
3. **Intuition is typically built slowly,** thus, is difficult to change. So, when the relevant area is going through or has relatively recently undergone a change, intuition based on the past might be far from current reality.

Yes, intuition cannot be relied on but, in most cases, it is "about right," which can be quite valuable. It should be viewed as basically unreliable, thus, intuition contributes to the overall inherent uncertainty. Yet it is far more valid than knowing nothing! This is part of the challenge of living with uncertainty.

Considering Uncertainty and Potential Risk

Inherent uncertainty, including the part contributed by intuitive information, has a huge impact on every single decision we make. To be clear, the decision-making process should distinguish between two different circumstances of uncertainty:

1. There is a broad spread of possible outcomes but, reasonably speaking, even the worst is tolerable.
2. There is a possibility of **disaster!**

---

[3] 10% × (1000 A's × $40/A + 850 B's × $40/B)

The second category consists of **outcomes that should be avoided** at practically all costs—no matter that with just a little bit of luck, huge benefits might materialize. An example is a decision to put all of the company's money and efforts into one deal, which if lost, would cause immediate bankruptcy, but if won, would cause huge profit. What makes such a decision unusual is that the negative side becomes the only factor influencing the decision. The damage of bankruptcy is far greater than what the actual loss in dollars represents (except when bankruptcy is already imminent, in which case, the added risk may be seen as relatively insignificant). Most decisions considered seriously by management lack this live-or-die characteristic; even though they remain highly uncertain, they do not risk the entire organization.

The assessment of risk should always be taken in context. If the company is already in imminent danger, the comparative difference in downsides may be negligible.

To differentiate between the two types of uncertainty, we use the term "risk" to mean "a reasonable possibility for a significantly worse situation."

The term "reasonable" is important because people and management alike often consider many decisions that have an **ultra-small chance of causing a disaster.** After all, most people, including the most important people in the organization, take airline flights and live under constant, albeit minimal, threat of a lightning strike, heart attack or terrorism. By being "reasonable," for this definition of risk, we add a certain human judgment to ignore a very rare chance for something catastrophic to happen.

Coming back to the specific example of the drugstore, the realization is that cutting one of its product brands, which is relatively slow moving and has low margins, shouldn't have a destructive impact on overall performance, so it is not a significant risk.

There are two exceptions to the expectation of limited negative impact. One is a situation where the availability of that particular product is what brings customers into the store even though they typically buy other products. This happens when the product has a strong and widespread reputation, novelty value or feeds a desire to show it to and amaze friends, though most people cannot afford it. The other case is when certain products are very important to just a few customers, but those customers are disproportionally good ones who also buy many other things as well. Thus, if that particular product is no longer available, the risk is that those customers will find another store which still carries it and make all their purchases there. Losing those customers completely might be too heavy a blow for the organization to withstand.

How Do We Know Whether Some Particular Action Embeds Considerable Risk?

Again, two alternatives to consider are the amount of uncertainty and an estimation of the actual damage that represents the risk:

1. **Use statistical models** to estimate the average, distribution and standard deviation of the key variables to decide when the possible outcomes include situations that should be avoided. Estimate the probability that a highly problematic situation might actually happen and decide whether this probability can be considered "reasonable."
2. **Use human intuition to define the reasonable worst-case scenario** and decide whether such an outcome is too damaging to be tolerated.

These two broad approaches are an integral part of decision making, even when risk is not involved. When the reasonable possible negative outcomes are not dramatic, it might still be negative enough to eventually result in rejection of the suggested idea. In order to come to a sound conclusion, the decision maker should also be aware of what is the reasonable best case—meaning the likely potential positive outcome.

Living in an uncertain world means being ready to deal with a variety of possible outcomes regarding everything we do. Actually, we also need to be ready for developments in reality over which we have no control, but to which we are nevertheless exposed. Some examples are the sudden emergence of a new competitor, an alternative product or a change in tax laws or import/export tariffs.

The basic mathematical model for considering uncertainty, assuming knowledge of the probabilities of all possible outcomes, can produce an average result, called "the expected value," which considers all the impacts (such as the change in sales and costs) together with their relative probabilities. The mathematical model also yields a standard deviation—letting us understand the likely spread of the possible results. These two critical parameters allow us to establish a "confidence interval" of possible results of the expected value plus and minus enough standard deviations to satisfy us, with a high enough probability, that the actual result will fall within that range.

The main problem with a mathematical approach is that the reality of managing organizations means accurate probabilities are almost never known. It is sometimes possible to use statistics to assess the expected value and standard deviation based on past data. In the vast majority of cases, the problem is that there is insufficient truly relevant data for any such statistical model because of the likelihood of sudden deviations, like the emergence of new products and competitors, disappearance of competitors and customers, changes in regulations, and so on.

A more practical way to create an effective confidence interval, based on intuitive assessment of uncertainty is by carefully building a **reasonable pessimistic scenario** and a **reasonable optimistic scenario.** These scenarios define the reasonable range of likely results, summarizing the focused information of the impact of uncertainty that should be considered by the decision maker. Being "reasonable" is based on human judgment to contain the range of possible results, ignoring potential scenarios that seem too remote to be practically considered.

A Full Analysis of the Case

The considered decision: Dropping the current monthly sales of 420 units of Brand C, which has $25 margin per unit.

The consequential direct loss of margin is: $10,500.[4] A reasonable assessment of the costs savings, mainly financial gains from lower overall inventory and minor savings in transportation, is between $1,000 and $1,500 per month.

Pessimistic assessment of increased monthly sales of Brands A and B: Half of the current units of Brand C sold will be converted to sales of A and B together. This rough intuitive assessment claims that it is unlikely that more than 50% of the current customers of Brand C would look elsewhere to buy either Brand C or an alternative not offered by the company.

The intuitive sense is that the absence of a "perfect" choice of electric shavers will not impact any other sales. This is based on the feeling that electric shavers are not the typical type of drugstore products that customers expect to find in high variety. It is also a product group from which typical male customers, who do not use razors, only purchase once every two or more years.

---

[4] 420 C's × $25/C

Based on these pessimistic assessments, the total change in contribution to net profit amounts to: −$1,100.[5] So, according to the pessimistic assessment the decision would create a small loss.

Optimistic assessment of increased monthly sales of Brands A and B: The vast majority of Brand C's customers, say 90%, would buy from the company's offered alternatives. On top of these sales, Brands A and B would yield an additional 20% of their current sales due to greater exposure on the shelf and diminished confusion among shoppers.

The change in profit is $20,920.[6]

Back to the Decision

Any actual result within the range of −$1,100 to +$20,920 is reasonably possible[7]. This is the best available supporting information the decision maker can get. Had both assessments been positive, there would be no doubt about accepting the proposed decision. If both outcomes were negative, the decision would have been even more straightforward. Often, some doubts remain and management is forced to make what they hope is a sound judgment. Practically, the information suggests that the whole issue is not truly important, since its predicted impact on the bottom line is too small to make a substantial change in the overall organizational performance. Could the managers seek a bigger move with more significant impact, preferably one with no reasonable doubt that it should add a good contribution to the bottom line?

A Summary of the Key Insights

These insights guide us on the way forward, so it behooves us to repeat them in short format:

- There is a real need for a structured decision-making process combining intuition with analysis of hard data, while also considering the impact of uncertainty. Only the combination reveals the full scope of the ramifications.
- The analysis should consider intuition, in spite of its limitations, because it balances the lack of enough relevant and reliable hard data.
- Intuition should be translated into logical rules and/or numbers.
- Intuition should be confined to the area in which it has proven to be or can be expected to be effective. For instance, rely on salespeople for valuable intuition about the market, but not necessarily on the consequent financial impacts.
- Intuition, as well as any forecast, is much more effective when a reasonable range is provided instead of a single number, which may evoke confidence that it is exact when, in fact, there is no likelihood of it being so. For instance, my intuition in assessing the time it takes to

---

[5] −$10,500 lost margin on C + $1,000 low cost savings + 50% × 420 units × $40 per unit

[6] −$10,500 lost margin on C + $1,500 high cost savings + 90% × 420 units × $40/unit + 20% × (1000 A's + 850 B's) × $40 per unit

[7] To help the reader understand the calculations, we have retained full precision and not rounded the results to the nearest thousand dollars, which might be reasonable given the uncertainty of the inputs. Perhaps it is easier for people following our advice to simply bear in mind that they can't know the precise upper and lower thresholds for pessimistic and optimistic. In other words, claiming that the range is −$1,000 to +$21,000 makes sense or cautioning people to consider the lower and upper boundaries approximate are both valid. As we cautioned in the introduction, there is no certainly on which to rely, just a probable range.

reach the airport from my home is 25 to 50 minutes. This range is considerably more valuable when it comes to increasing the chance that I will make my next flight than either "on average it takes 35 minutes" or "I can usually get there in 30 minutes."

■ In order to handle inherent uncertainty, decision makers should go through a process of generating two different scenarios. One is a reasonable pessimistic scenario and the other a reasonably optimistic scenario.

■ In all cases, cost allocations make it considerably more difficult, if not impossible, to arrive at good decisions.

Chapter 4

Throughput—a Key Concept Pointing in a Sensible Direction— Daily Bread, Part 2

Daily Bread, the same company mentioned in the leading case of Chapter 1, has an opportunity to sell 800 donuts to Children's Hospital every day. Instead of the regular price of 78 cents per donut, the price every other customer pays, the hospital is only willing to pay 70 cents, a total of $560 per day.

A Consideration of the Change

Assuming that the additional 800 donuts do not cause any capacity problems for Daily Bread, **what does this new deal contribute to Daily Bread's bottom line?**

Baking 800 donuts requires raw materials purchased from suppliers. Let's assume that $220 is paid to suppliers for everything that goes into 800 delivered donuts. The costs of labor, equipment and space do not change due to this incremental deal since capacity is available. The slight increase in energy costs are included in the $220 sum, which comprises all the truly variable costs. The difference between the sales and variable costs is $340 per day,[1] which is the **added value generated by Daily Bread in accepting this deal.**

While common accounting methods also recognize an incremental impact, it is usually called the "contribution" of a particular deal. However, contribution margin is reduced by direct labor, which is not truly variable (as it was in the distant past) in almost all cases. "Marginal costing" is a cost accounting method for supporting decision-making regarding incremental and temporary opportunities. However, marginal costing is rightly criticized because of its focus on local contribution and short-term considerations only. A reasonable rebuttal points out that only considering variable costs might embolden salespeople to offer prices too low to reliably cover the fixed costs, which have not been considered at all in marginal costing calculations.

---

[1] $0.70 per donut × 800 - ($220)

The case of the drugstore chain in Chapter 3 scrutinizes the accumulation of the margins of three brands. In retail, the margin is usually based on the selling price minus the cost of purchasing the item. Since no other costs are involved, the margin is the added value of selling one item, such as the above example of Daily Bread selling donuts to a hospital.

Throughput (T) is a key concept in the Theory of Constraints (TOC). It is similar to "contribution," but its definition makes it more useful and broadly applicable, while addressing all the concerns regarding marginal costing. Throughput was defined by Dr. Goldratt as:

Throughput: The rate at which the organization generates "goal units"

For commercial organizations the definition becomes:

The rate at which the system generates money through sales, which is sales minus the truly variable costs

Goldratt's definition refers to the whole system, usually an organization. This marks a basic difference from "contribution," which focuses on a specific deal, item, product line or division. Although it is possible to calculate the sum of all contributions achieved over a time period, this is definitely not the common approach, especially not across the whole organization.[2] Instead, the most similar measurement is "gross profit," which also usually reduces sales by additional operational costs that are not certain to vary with each and every sale.

The emphasis on added value is a breakthrough insight. Of course, both the total expenses that do not vary with individual sales and the capital invested in all the assets should also be considered when assessing the performance of the organization as a whole. Yet, the trend of Throughput (T) over time is a most important holistic measurement, which provides an excellent indication of the direction in which the business is heading.

The above definition of T requires interpretation, especially the word "rate" which refers to the holistic Throughput measured over time periods, such as a month or a year. "Generates money" means the difference per chosen period between revenues and the Truly Variable Costs (TVC) without which those revenues could not have been produced. The adjective "truly" emphasizes that those costs occur with every sale, even the smallest of sales. Therefore, unless labor is paid per piece, we do not consider it part of the TVC. When a company brokers outsourced hours of human resources, such as in the case of programmers or service technicians, and pays those resources only for the hours they sell, then it is an example of labor being TVC. Now that piecework is seldom utilized, the most common example of labor being TVC is commissions paid to salespeople. Other than these exceptions, **the cost of labor is not included in the calculation of Throughput,** nor is the cost of overhead or management.

---

[2] Many years ago, one of us, Henry Camp, used his programming expertise to modify his company's ERP system to calculate and track net profit per invoice for several months. To his dismay, one month the sum of the thousands of estimations was low and the next month it was high. When it proved to be roughly accurate one month, he realized that it was simply a fluke due to sales being close to budget. Even in this relatively simple company, a distributorship with precisely known costs of goods sold, in a good month the sum of the profits of all the invoices was much lower than actual profits. In slow months, it was quite a bit higher than the accounting profit. Since sales varied +/–25% month to month, even without seasonality, Henry found the estimated net profit per item, per invoice and per customer completely useless. The following month, just by chance, he read Goldratt's novel, The Goal, and it changed his approach ever after. A properly conducted scientific experiment can be quite elucidating.

How should those costs that are not TVC costs be considered? It doesn't make sense to simply ignore them. The point is that for a very small increase or decrease in sales, we can assume that the change in the generated Throughput reflects the same change to the bottom line. This conclusion is a direct consequence of the basic definition of T and TVC. But, when more considerable changes in sales are evaluated, then there is no guarantee what would happen to the costs that do not vary with a single sale. The next chapters explain how all the other costs are considered as a part of the analysis which leads to predicting the full impact of a decision or any other significant move on net profit.

Back to Our Daily Bread Example

The monthly T for Daily Bread is the sum of all sales in that month minus the costs that truly vary with every sale. Assuming the ongoing activity of Daily Bread continues, the TVC includes the materials used for producing the products that Daily Bread sells, such as flour, butter, sugar, milk, packaging, and so on.

T is applicable to any specific item, as long it has a selling price. It is also easily applied generally to a customer, division or product line or more specifically to an item or deal. In the latter cases, the T is not per time, but per item or deal. The meaning of T per item or deal indicates that any additional sale of that item increases the monthly and annual T by that amount. Any change in T within a time period is designated as ΔT. Thus, in accepting the order from the hospital, Daily Bread increases its monthly T by $10,200[3].

Throughput (T) is *not* profit! The total T is not the profit and the ΔT per item is not necessarily the change in profit of the items sold. In order to generate T, the organization must spend money that is not TVC. On top of those truly variable costs is **all the money invested in the organization (Investment or I).** Think of this as the money tied up within the organization in the form of assets. All the other costs, the ongoing expenses required to make sure the organization is able to generate T, are denoted as **Operating Expenses (OE).** In other words, **OE is all the money the organization spends to generate "goal units."** Think of this as money spent to turn Investment into Throughput.

The connection between T, I and OE and the financial performance measurements of the organization is simple. Let's start with one with which everyone agrees:

$$\text{Net Profit}(NP) = \text{Sales} - \text{Expenses} \qquad (1)$$

In Throughput Accounting, expenses are split into two parts: TVC and OE. Therefore, by substitution, we get the following connection:

$$NP = \text{Sales} - TVC - OE \qquad (2)$$

since, by definition,

$$T = \text{Sales} - TVC \qquad (3)$$

therefore, by substitution into the formula (2),

$$NP = T - OE \qquad (4)$$

---

[3] 30 days/month $\times$ $340 ΔT/day

The money held in the organization, I, is part of the calculation of Return on Investment (ROI):

$$ROI = NP/I \tag{5}$$

Note: In Throughput Accounting, the term I means "Investment" from the company's or the system's point of view (not the point of view of the owners). Therefore, it includes all the assets of the company, not just those financed by the system's owners but also by any loans, whether from banks, other lenders, suppliers selling on terms (A/P) and service providers who do work before being paid (A/P or Other Current Liabilities).

The simple formulae above raise the question: **what is the advantage of using T, I and OE to calculate NP and ROI?**

It seems, at first glance, to be a trivial and even useless change. Why bother? The simple answer is that by separating the TVC from all other expenses and subtracting it from Sales, the relevant information reveals the value generated by the organization. This value, when compared to I and OE determines the current state of the organization, but it is clear that T is a critical element to support better decisions. The big difference between marginal costing and T, I and OE is that full attention is focused on the total value added (T), rather than just on individual sales and potential opportunities. This focus answers the question of what the total ΔT would be for the whole organization when a proposed opportunity is undertaken on top of everything else.

The convention of considering the total T of the organization plus the ΔT of a specific move supports the process of making a decision by accurately revealing the actual impact to the whole organization, rather than trying to estimate the net financial impact that stems just from the opportunity in question. It is obvious that the holistic analysis should also consider what happens to OE and I when the new opportunity is added to the current activities.

There are two explanations regarding the special power of T, I and OE information:

1. **Throughput informs us of the full value of sales.** There are many decisions that impact only sales and cause no change to the costs of maintaining capacity. In such a situation, the ΔT (the change in total T due to the decision) expresses the economic value of the decision. This is demonstrated by the decision of Daily Bread to sell the extra 800 donuts per day at a reduced price, without any impact on OE because no overtime or any other additional capacity is required, as is assumed in this case. The only other possible problematic factor is if the deal somehow affected other sales. For example, other clients, who become aware of the discount, may also try to gain price reductions or become annoyed enough to buy from a competitor. Such effects are due to dependencies between sales that occur when market segmentation is insufficient. Still, the question remains, what is the impact of the deal on the total Throughput? A clear distinction between the sales and expenses of the company allows focused questions to reveal relevant information required for decision making.

2. **At the same time, the role of OE is clarified.** OE comprises all the expenses that **do *not*** vary with every single sale, regardless of size, but are nevertheless required to maintain the available capacity of the various capabilities needed for the anticipated variety of sales. Every single expense included in OE is related to capacity. As examples, outsourced payroll, accounting and banking services are all part of the capacity of required capabilities for

generating Throughput, even though these services are very generic and not influenced by specific transactions or products.

As discussed in Chapter 1, the total cost of capacity does not vary in a linear fashion but is the aggregation of many step functions. This fact clarifies the behavior of OE when the level of sales fluctuates. Certain changes in sales might not cause any impact on the OE. In such cases, the decision depends only on the additional Throughput or ΔT. In other cases, the impact on OE might be quite significant, depending on the amount of additional load on one or more resources. To estimate ΔOE, we need to identify the resources from which more capacity is required and the cost of those increases, providing it is even feasible to do so within the necessary time frame.

The second insight above clarifies why OE is spent at all. Business operators spend OE only to generate T, now or in the future.[4] In other words, spending OE is good so long as it provides a greater amount of T. In such circumstances, the OE spent indirectly adds to the Net Profit.

The converse is often lost on business owners, operators and analysts who look for and applaud every announced cut. Sadly, cutting OE usually results in the loss of a greater amount of T, thus diminishing NP in the longer term. The only OE that can safely be cut is OE which produces less T, directly and indirectly.

We want to make clear another advantage of using T and OE. Both are flow metrics. T is the rate of flow of money into the company and OE is the rate that money flows out. NP is the net inflow to the company, over some period of time. Making a huge sale is wonderful. Earning a high margin on a product may be a feather in one's cap. But, every company's financial performance is measured against time—weekly, monthly, quarterly and annually. Increasing the profit of a particular order or the percentage that profit margin is of sales is not the goal of a company. **A company's goal is to make more and more money per period.** To do so means getting more flow of NP per time period. You must put big orders and high margin orders together with the rest of the more mundane sales to grow profits.

The usual "revenues minus expenses" approach, without distinguishing between TVC and OE, provides no hint about how to induce an increase in revenues. This often leads managers to focus on reducing easily identifiable expenses, like overtime and finding ways to curtail overtime hours, with little to no consideration of impairment to revenues. On the other hand, T and OE provide an easy-to-use framework for evaluating changes.

From the basic formula, $NP = T - OE$, it is possible to evaluate the net impact of one decision on the bottom line because it is also true that: $\Delta NP = \Delta T - \Delta OE$.

The range of ΔT that is considered possible is likely the outcome of a sales analysis, including all the dependencies among the different customers and individual sales. To calculate ΔT it is possible first to calculate the total T after the changes by converting every expected sale into Throughput by subtracting its TVC from the revenue and summing the total, which yields the total new T after all the changes. Then, subtracting from that the total Throughput before the

---

[4] A common exception is when a business operator is also the business owner and pays him- or herself more than the market would typically bear in an arm's-length agreement. Distributions of profits to an owner are another example of the same thing. These actions may not be at all good for the company but may be quite nice for the owner. In a public company, if an employee diverts funds to themselves, it is considered theft, even if that employee is an owner.

changes yields the ΔT. Alternately, calculate ΔT directly by considering just the additional T minus any T lost due to the proposed changes.

ΔOE is the change in the total OE, bearing in mind all the adjustments to the cost of capacity required for the considered opportunities. When considering an increase in sales, if spare capacity remains on all resources, then no expenditure is needed and ΔOE = 0.

Although it is not typical of the TOC approach, it is possible that there is an attractive opportunity to drop some portion of the existing OE that was required for sales that generate even less Throughput. Normally, that capacity should be retained and efforts to capitalize on it will happen later. Generally speaking, when capacity is cut, it is not as easy to bring it back when the market changes and requires that capacity. There are situations where adding capacity is impossible, too slow to benefit current opportunities or too expensive. The question then is whether the additional T that could thereby be captured is expected to be greater than the OE necessary to maintain the surplus capacity.

The wisdom of the Theory of Constraints (TOC) leads management to draw the best from the resource that lacks enough capacity. It can mean refusing to accept orders that do not exploit the capacity limitation of that resource. Such a state calls for very careful managerial judgment of both the state of capacity and the market perspective of the company's performance.

In the simple example of the deal between Daily Bread and the hospital, let us now consider an interdependency between that hospital and another customer, a smaller hospital, which buys 300 donuts daily for the regular price of 78 cents. Because of the discount now offered by Daily Bread, the pessimistic view is that the smaller hospital will, someday in the future, insist on paying the same price of just 70 cents per doughnut too. One can argue that a commitment to a larger quantity should yield reduction in price, but the smaller hospital might not accept the argument and threaten to approach other bakeries for which such a daily order is attractive.

Should this come to pass, the ΔT is the added daily Throughput of the new deal minus the lost Throughput from the old deal, which amounts to $316 per day.[5]

In considering ΔOE, suppose that producing the additional 800 donuts every day, on top of the current regular production, requires five hours of overtime, at a cost of $20 per hour. This means that accepting the deal would add, every day, ΔOE of $100 to the previous level of OE.

Under these assumptions, the deal with the bigger hospital, plus agreeing to give the same price to the smaller one, would bring an additional $216 per day[6] to the current net profits of Daily Bread, or $78,840 in NP for the whole year.[7] Even under these pessimistic assumptions, this is a good deal.

Is it at all possible that the same deal could cause a loss due to causes that are not part of the deal itself?

Lack of capacity could make a deal that seems to offer an attractive ΔT – ΔOE result in a loss. Consumption of capacity is due to all the existing demand, plus the added demand of the new deal being considered. It is enough that just one single resource lacks capacity to cause substantial delays in delivery to clients across the boards. If such a shortage of capacity persists, then loss of market demand will inevitably occur. Exhausting capacity anywhere creates interdependencies between any new deal and existing sales—an interaction between sales and

---

[5] $560 Sales - $220 TVC – 300 donuts × ($0.78/donut – $0.70/donut)
[6] $316 ΔT – $100 ΔOE
[7] 365 days/yr × $216/day

operations that takes on the characteristics of what is often called a vicious cycle. Deliveries become delayed, which results in a chaotic system, which causes more delays, ultimately resulting in lost orders and customers.

Let's check in more detail what can be done when one resource lacks capacity. One answer is to first consider and then do whatever it takes to more fully exploit that constrained resource and subordinate everything else to implement the plan. One way to exploit a constrained resource's capacity is to give up sales of products that generate less T per unit of that particular resource's capacity. Such an act might cause negative effects that have to be carefully evaluated. One possibility is losing more sales than is required to free the desired amount of capacity, for example, customers preferring another supplier who is willing to provide all rather than part of their needs. Such moves should be carefully considered by estimating whether the negative effects can be prevented or ensuring that the total potential loss of T is low enough.

When, as a result of positive word of mouth, effective marketing or a certain significant sale, total sales go up, there is a concern that more than one resource could limit the potential T. In this situation, there still remains the option of dropping certain sales, freeing enough capacity of the overloaded resources to enable operations to deliver reliably as required and still generate more T than the current state. Multiple and interactive constraints cause chaos much more devastating than a single constraint. Note that dealing with a capacity limitation by dropping certain sales focuses only on the T side since no change in available capacity is yet considered. When there is no need for a change in the currently available capacity, then there is no reason for a change in the prevailing level of OE.

There is an alternative approach: rapidly increasing capacity. However, this is not always possible. When it is possible to increase the required capacity within the necessary time frame, it drives up ΔOE. Although we might only need to increase the available capacity of a specific resource by 1%, the minimum possible rapid capacity increase might be 5%. For instance, an agreement with the union could allow overtime only when several employees stay on the job together. The objective result is expressed by $\Delta T - \Delta OE$; in order to improve NP, we require the difference to be greater than zero.

So far, we have dealt with only T and OE, which leads to the following question: **how do changes to "I,"** which may be required by a decision, **impact the company?**

"I" was originally defined by Goldratt as "Inventory" and was used to express all the money held within the organization. To avoid the confusion which would result from forcing a broader definition of "inventory" on an unaware general public, "I" was later defined as "investment." Like OE, "I" exists only to maintain capacity of resources. Investment in inventory of materials, plant and equipment required to generate Throughput should be viewed as a special type of capacity. Even though inventory behaves in a more linear way than most other resources in its consumption, its purchase still comes in chunks due to packaging, shipping considerations and, commonly, supplier pricing and policies. Of course, other investments, like a new production line or an additional store are also included in the definition of "I."

The difference between I and OE is the expected time frame for generating T. OE includes expenses that are required for generating T in each period. Expenditures that are expected to support generation of T in the future are considered investments. Such investments are made with after-tax funds, in most countries, subject to depreciation and, thereby, expensed over time. The standard treatment is to apportion these expenditures into periods, like months or years, over their expected useful lives. It is, thus, possible to treat an investment, such as the purchase of a production line, as a stream of annual expenses. Investment justification should compare the periodic depreciation of an investment, plus other required OE with the stream of T enabled.

Here again, we emphasize the especially pertinent value of focusing on T rather than on revenue. It is meaningless to use revenue to justify an investment. When the investment is stand-alone, then a projection of annual profits could be used. However, when the investment is part of the overall activity of an organization, then ΔI can only be compared to a new stream of ΔT less the possible ΔOE that is fully dedicated to the objective of that investment and is not any part of the capacity used for other activities.

The vital insight of this chapter is the simplification of dealing with two different aspects, the T side and the OE side of the net profit formula, $\Delta NP = \Delta T - \Delta OE$. There is a need to analyze both impacts together. Compared with traditional Cost Accounting and especially with Activity-Based Costing, the TOC approach, which focuses on changes to each component separately but then combines them together and evaluates the total impact. This approach vastly simplifies the evaluation process and enables accurate decisions based on direct impact to the bottom line.

To better understand the behavior of OE and how it supports generating Throughput, we need to dive into the issue of capacity. How much capacity do we need of various resources to support a certain level of Throughput generation? This is what next chapter is going to highlight.

Chapter 5

More on the Problematic Nature of Capacity

The fundamental rationale for both I and OE is to maintain necessary capacity. It is reasonable to claim that *all* organizational expenditures are used for providing available capacity. Even a narrow definition of resources would still demonstrate that the cost of manpower, offices, IT, plant and equipment are by far the major part of total costs.

The notion of capacity, the maximum pace available from the required resources over time, is most easily recognized in manufacturing. In some service businesses, like airlines, hotels and theaters, from time to time a clear internal constraint limits sales. In such businesses, the impression is that their product offerings are perishable, such as a seat on a flight, meaning that the opportunity for additional revenue is lost when they are not sold in time. Actually, **it is the capacity of the temporary constraint** that is perishable. It is the seats on a given flight, in the case of airlines, or the opportunity to sell a hotel room for the night that disappears next morning. So, when there is the potential for high demand, it should be management's focus to ensure that all rooms are occupied every night, and at the highest possible prices that don't engender ill will from those who pay them. Think of paying five times the normal rate, due to of a natural disaster.

While common sense informs us that any amount of lost time on any resource is lost forever, the more pertinent question is whether the time that might be wasted needs to actually cause a loss of Throughput. When excess capacity, such as an empty seat on a flight or an idle hour of a production line, can be turned into sales with positive T, then all the additional T goes directly to the bottom line.

For instance, selling tickets at attractive prices at the last minute or accepting a client's urgent request for a very small quantity that uses existing excess capacity definitely and disproportionally helps increase net profit. Even if the price of the cheap ticket is much lower than the average cost per seat required to cover the costs of the specific flight, getting money from those passengers is money that improves net profits (NP) on a dollar-for-dollar basis because costs remain the same, whether the seat is taken or not.

For a manufacturer, a new urgent order might require an additional setup and, because of that, cause the whole order to return less than the full absorption cost. This is more likely true when the order is a small one that requires its own setup. Some managers (particularly sales managers) claim that preserving a client is well worth the extra cost but this is a profitable action, even without the gratitude of the client! As long as the change in T is positive (additional revenue is higher than the TVC) and exceeds any related increase in OE, then NP improves.

With such a high combination of investment and operating expenses required to maintain the capacity of many different resources, the natural business desire is to spend less by trying to better **match the capacity, of all resources, to the actual demand.**

This is Utopia! Theoretically, it is possible but never found to exist in reality, as already mentioned in Chapter 1. We will explain further why this is the case. The difficulty of predicting demand is obvious. Yet, it is human nature to fear the unknown and, for some strange reason, a forecast allows people to rest easier and feel more confident, despite the fact that they are fully aware that every previous forecast has been wrong! In too many cases, determining the degree of capacity utilization is also difficult. Capacity is measured by its potential output over a long period of time, such as a month. This measurement leads to several complications:

1. Most of the time, several resources are required at the same time to accomplish a task. The overall time the task takes is dictated by the slowest resource. For instance, to send an email, one needs a computer, Internet connection, mail program and human being to type in the message. In the end, it is the speed of typing that dictates how many emails can be sent in an hour. The computer has the capacity to do more, but that is purely theoretical.

2. A similar, and potentially more devastating, complication is the dependency of one resource on the performance of previous operations. A machine that has the capacity of 1,000 widgets a day may only be able to produce 800 because a previous necessary operation has a limited capacity of only 800. However, when there is enough work in its queue to be processed, that machine can produce 1,000 but naturally this is not going to happen every day. Over the long term, the machine cannot average more than 800 per day. These dependencies, actually partial dependencies because of the role of work-in-process (WIP) inventory coupled with normal statistical fluctuations, inevitably lead to the conclusion that the chain of operations is limited by *one* weakest link. All the rest must have excess capacity; otherwise the system will produce at a rate *less than* the capacity of the slowest resource! Assuming there is demand for the capacity of the slowest resource, a balanced system will not be able to perform to its design capacity and provide acceptable performance to meet market requirements.

3. The capacity of human resources is especially tricky to measure.
   a. The true capacity limit of any human being depends a lot on their motivations: Does everybody want to be measured and have their real capacity revealed? When someone is forced to be measured, then it might seem attractive to that person to try to lower their measured capacity, as long as it still looks reasonable, so they aren't expected to work harder for the same pay.
   b. Another problematic aspect of human capacity is: Do employees prefer to work as fast as possible when there is no special need to do so? This means that it is difficult to judge capacity limits from daily actual performance. It might seem that the employee is working full time but, in many cases, this level of effort is significantly below their potential.
   c. Third, even when motivated and committed, human performance fluctuates profoundly, as is evident when we watch the performance of athletes and recognize the difference between good days and not-so-good days.
   d. Lastly, efforts to accelerate the pace of work beyond some point eventually results in a subsequent significant drop-off in pace because people need rest after they sprint, particularly if it has been for an extended period of time.

4. Setups complicate achieving good measurements because while they are being performed at the slowest resource, no output is produced for the whole system. The term "setup" is well known in manufacturing and unknown in other environments, even though it exists in services and is part of the devastatingly negative impact of bad multitasking[1] in human beings.

5. Most resources produce different types of outputs, which makes it hard to come up with a single measure of capacity. The maximum total output depends on the actual mix of the different types and varies considerably because of it.

6. Quality issues impact capacity directly and indirectly. Imperfect quality of an input might extend a task's touch time and require rework to fix the problem. Working on things that will be scrapped indirectly reduces the output of useful production. It is a fact that processing anything that will never be sold due to low quality or any other reason is purely a waste of capacity.

7. Specific resources have various complexities. Some resources process several outputs at the same time, such as ovens, chemical baths and classroom teachers. Another example is producing paper first as a very wide sheet, which is then cut into several different sized sheets. Some resources face sequence dependent setups that cause setup times to fluctuate widely depending on the particular sequence. As a clarifying example, imagine an extruder that is melting a polypropylene resin blended with a yellow colorant. It is fairly quick to change to blending in a green colorant; however, switching from a black to white colorant takes a very long time before the extruded plastic stops looking gray.

The complexity of measuring capacity has one, relatively simple consequence:

While measuring capacity is critically important, sometimes we must tolerate our inherent inability to measure it accurately.

The most decisive reason why matching capacity with actual demand is impossible comes from the inability to synchronize various forms of variation. Demand changes quickly and usually you do not know about the specifics of these changes in advance. On the other hand, increasing capacity takes time, often a very long time, and can require careful planning.

If the preferred approach is to maintain enough capacity for the periods of heavy demand, then it means having to tolerate a lot of excess capacity during market downturns. Trying to remove excess capacity as demand drops, usually losing money and expertise in the process, makes it hard to reacquire capacity, even when authorized to pay a premium for the skilled people who are in short supply. Part of the dilemma regarding how much capacity to maintain is the difficulty to assess the longer-term negative ramifications of being unable to supply all the demand at a given point in the future. Disappointed customers might look for viable alternatives and stick with them. In other cases, being "sold out" actually improves a reputation; when products, which are apparently in high demand, are offered again, customers will compete to get them before they are sold out once again.

Differences in the behaviors of both demand and capacity make capacity-matching a very costly and risky undertaking. The possibility of matching capacity to demand is a strategy that is

---

[1] Bad multitasking happens when working on several things contemporaneously. Jumping from one task to the other causes significant delays to all the missions. The recommended behavior is to focus and finish a task, bringing it to the state it can be continued by another resource, and then moving to the next task according to the global priority.

limited to situations when the trend is clearly known and not subject to market cycles. Even then, due to statistically normal fluctuations, there is no possibility, regardless of what you are willing to pay, to match all resources perfectly to the currently required load. In the real world, it can't be done.

When any particular opportunity is considered, the critical question is:

Do we have enough capacity, from every resource, to deliver the additional load?

When capacity measurements lack high precision, any answer should be a conservative assessment of capacity. This means that the protective capacity, the excess capacity that is required to protect delivery performance, must be enough to cover all combined uncertainties in operations as well as variations in demand. A simplifying insight is realizing that, practically, **only very few resources could run out of capacity due to an increase in demand.**

A potentially significant difficulty in dealing with capacity is understanding the instantaneous and also more prolonged ramifications to the timing of capacity consumption and the flow of products. The load on every resource varies over time, more so in some environments than others. It is possible that the varying demand on a resource always remains within the capacity of that resource, either because the resource has vast protective capacity or because the demand variation is relatively small. In other situations, peak demand may exceed the maximum capacity of a resource that is normally available or because the resource's ability to accomplish its work is temporarily diminished. In such cases, the temporary peak load delays some of the work.

Another difficulty in measuring monthly capacity is that it is quite possible to be inundated by peak loads within the month, where a specific resource temporarily lacks enough capacity to meet a sudden surge in demand, even though the monthly measurement indicates the resource is not even close to being overloaded. As the temporary peaks cause delays, the questions are how long these delays are and, even more importantly, what direct and indirect damage is caused by them.

In an arbitrary example, assuming the resource is not fully loaded, say it is loaded to 80% of its monthly available capacity, it can be safely assumed that most orders will be processed within one month or less. In many manufacturing organizations, delivery within one month is acceptable. In some service organizations, a delay of just one hour is intolerable and would result in a loss of some of the available market demand. Because of the criticality of being able to respond fast enough to needs, service organizations need much more capacity than their average load suggests.

The inherent difficulty of managing capacity is simplified by the recognition of the absolute requirement for a not insignificant level of excess capacity. In most services, this need is so obvious that there is no special emphasis on measuring capacity. After all, in an environment that needs, roughly half its average calculated capacity, what benefit comes from measuring capacity? For instance, the owner of a fashion shop won't measure the utilization of her salesperson, she just needs to validate that the salesperson is not occupied too long by a client while other clients have to wait.

This sensitivity to responsiveness to tolerance times is a complicating factor for managing capacity for manufacturing and many other environments where the enormous expense of providing capacity applies constant pressure to cut costs. The practical question is:

What is the maximum ratio of load to capacity that still ensures adequate performance to the market expectations?

Truly, it depends!

The Theory of Constraints (TOC) concept of the beneficial nature of maintaining protective capacity already highlights the basic advantage of knowing the highest appropriate ratio of load to capacity above which the risk of difficulty in responding to the market becomes unacceptably high. TOC does not provide a structured way to assess the required protective capacity. Instead it suggests the far simpler method of monitoring the effectiveness through a process of seeking feedback that looks for signals of high systemic pressure. The TOC mechanism of checking the actual performance and noting cases of extra pressure is called Buffer Management.

Buffer Management means monitoring the current state of the time or stock buffers planned and put in place to protect commitments to the market. These buffers are the protection mechanism against fluctuations that threaten the company's ability to its commitments to the market. Buffer Management issues signals when the remaining buffer seems too small. The last third of a buffer is colored "red." Red orders or inventory or projects are alerts for management, indicating a threat to the commitments made to the market. Too many "reds" serve as a warning that the protection mechanism, time, stock or protective capacity is imminently inadequate.

TOC time buffers alleviate the need to respond to temporary capacity shortages. A time buffer defines the upper limit for allowable accumulation of delays. Every resource should have enough protective capacity to be able to deliver all the demand within the period defined by the time buffer, despite variations in demand and internal fluctuations within operations.

The distinction between fluctuations in the market, which cause peaks of load, and internal variability implies the need for **two different stages of protective capacity.**

The weakest link in a chain of operational processes needs to be protected from incidental peaks in its load. A certain amount of protective capacity makes it possible to catch up during off-peak times. The rest of the resources must have even more capacity to be able to overcome the internal fluctuations that will eventually occur, sometimes simultaneously with surges in demand. As TOC taught the world, it is possible to highly utilize the weakest link resource—so long as all the others subordinate their operations accordingly. **The combination of minimal protective capacity on the weakest link and a higher level of protective capacity on all the rest is a good recipe for ensuring excellent performance** without falling into the trap of being forced to deal with the impossibly complex nature of individual resources with their interactive capacities that are continuously subjected to rapidly changing circumstances.

Let's make a distinction between the regular available capacity provided by relatively fixed costs and options that quickly increase capacity in smaller increments for a certain extra price. This is certainly relevant for manpower since overtime or using temporary workers is often possible. The use of extra man-hours may add considerable additional capacity to other types of resources, such as machines, equipment and space. Fixed assets are available 24 hours a day, seven days a week, but many times not fully in use.[2] When manpower is available, it is possible to utilize the unused capacity of a machine or the space of a meeting room as free additional capacity. The extra cost, ΔOE, is just the expense of the additional manpower yet, the additional production is across the whole system of other resources, buildings, equipment, utilities, management and support staff with enough capacity already. Outsourcing is another common option for quickly increasing capacity.

---

[2] Think of your own car. It is an asset that loses value over time almost regardless of how much it is used. If you drive 24,000 miles per year and average 40 miles per hour, a mix of city and highway miles, then you don't use your car about 93% of the year. In the future, expect better ways of finding immediate transportation on demand that eliminates the expense of such underutilized assets.

These options for quickly increasing capacity when needed represent a new kind of buffer called **"Capacity Buffers."**

Time and stock buffers use protective capacity to overcome both internal and external fluctuations. The effectiveness of a buffer depends on its amount of protective capacity. Capacity Buffers that are in place and ready supplant the need for the expense of permanent capacity, still allowing fast reaction to emergencies indicated by Buffer Management's red signals. Capacity Buffers often play a crucial role in enabling the acceptance of new sales and business opportunities, although typically requiring a higher rate of OE.

Managers driven by their perpetual desire to lower costs whenever possible, should evaluate Capacity Buffers as a valid solution. Not hiring more people and buying more equipment saves money for sure. Many times, overtime, temporary workers and outsourcing seem exorbitantly expensive too. When considering the benefits of Capacity Buffers, managers question whether paying more for extra capacity all of the time is better than living with the risk that there might be some damage done by minor delays in some tasks, until work can be delivered by the system's existing capacity. After all, they know well that surges of demand only temporarily overload existing resources.

Human nature is biased to avoid known damages more so than to strive for larger but less certain benefits.[3] People hate the thought of being blamed. So, using Capacity Buffers is an excellent solution to the dilemma between investing in more permanent capacity versus being able to respond to peaks of demand. Yet, since most managers have not yet experienced the benefits of broadly implementing Capacity Buffers, they quite humanly tend to estimate the financial improvements so conservatively that they feel more comfortable sticking with the status quo.

But, in the moment, any new trend looks exactly like a temporary surge. Who claims that the expected average demand is still valid? Is it wise to pay more or save some money? A structured decision-support mechanism where the actual extra cost, ΔOE, is directly compared with the ΔT that is at stake significantly reduces the pressure on managers. More important, it takes the decision-making process out of an emotional framework and puts it squarely into a logical one.

This book is about making both trivial and pivotal decisions in a superior way. How much capacity to maintain is a key ongoing decision. Uncertainty impacts both sides of the equation: The load from demand and the capacity level of various resources. The importance of rendering sound decisions makes the TOC concept of having protective capacity and monitoring it through Buffer Management extremely helpful.

Capacity Buffers Are an Important Tool for Dealing with Both Types of Uncertainty

It is a strategic responsibility to prepare and maintain ample Capacity Buffers. This raises the question: What is the right ratio between the available capacity within the organization and the optional capacity available soon enough but for some additional expense? The cost of optional capacity is usually considerably higher than the average cost per internal capacity unit. Certainly, the

---

[3] Kahneman, Daniel. *Thinking, Fast and Slow*. Loss aversion: pps 282-286, 288, 290-294, 296, 297, 300-309, 337-339, 349. Obviously, an important topic to the Nobel Prize laureate.

cost of one hour of overtime is higher than the base pay per hour. Relative to the regular available capacity, the proper size of the Capacity Buffer depends on:

- the minimum quantities in which regularly available capacity can be purchased,
- the size of expected peaks of demand and possibly also on the degree to which demand at the peak period can be delivered at a premium,
- other short-term market opportunities and
- the skills and capabilities required for the tasks at hand.

When the required resource is a highly skilled person, the minimum quantity that can be purchased is often a full-time employee. Using temporary workers depends on whether the required level of skills exists in the market and the confidence that, when required, the right number of temporary workers can be found. Sadly, when the economy is good there is a greater likelihood of needing a Capacity Buffer and less likelihood of finding temporary workers with the requisite skills. And, skilled temporary workers are often available during a down turn but the need for them is reduced. Beyond these specific questions lies the general query of whether or not the ratio between full-time employees and temps is about right. In general, deciding on the right ratio between regular available capacity and quick additional capacity is a key strategic issue for operations that has direct ramifications on what can be reliably offered to the market.

Using skilled freelance programmers is common enough to open the mind to other areas in which professional freelancers are used to dealing with surges of load on internal people. Thus, consulting companies, usually small ones, might collaborate to cover a temporary shortage of consultants. Airlines are used to renting aircraft, together with a full professional crew to deal with lack of availability of both aircrafts and pilots. Some airlines are also doing so to avoid or bypass internal strikes, quite a different type of uncertainty managed by the same solution, a Capacity Buffer.

In many other areas, the use of Capacity Buffers is much less than it should be. Determining and maintaining the right level of a Capacity Buffer relative to the regularly available capacity can be supported by simulation of various scenarios, where the simulation captures both the actual capacity utilization and the levels of T, OE and I. This way managers can get a glimpse of the immense hidden profits that can often be captured through the superior flexibility only possible with Capacity Buffers. It is exactly because the potential profits have never been identified, in other words, that the current level of profitability doesn't justify it that managers fail to place appropriate emphasis on developing Capacity Buffers of all necessary types. Later in this book, our examples will demonstrate some of their intrinsic power. However, only dedicated analysis of your actual case will truly reveal the potential you are currently overlooking.

Chapter 6

Analyzing a Simple Case—P&Q, Part 1[*]

The Fallacy of Cost Accounting

In order to prove the fallacy of cost accounting, Dr. Goldratt imagined a simplistic organization selling only two products, P and Q, produced by only four resources, named according to their colors: Light Blue, Blue, Green and Gray. To further simplify matters, the weekly demand is known and does not vary. Capacities are straightforward: every resource works precisely eight hours a day, not one minute less or more, five days a week. That means that the available capacity of every resource, regardless of its color, is 2,400 minutes per week. The total weekly cost of providing this capacity, excluding the cost of materials, is $6,000. Demand for product P is exactly 100 units and for Q it is 50 units. These will be the weekly sales, as long as the system is able to provide those quantities by week's end. There is no chance to catch up next week.

Figure 6.1 specifies all the details. The numbers in the colored ellipses denote the time it takes the resource to perform the task required for making P and Q products. There are no setup times. In the diamonds, the diagram shows raw materials and an outsourced part complete with purchase prices.

One simple question:

How much money does the organization make?

One approach, see Table 6.1, is revenues minus expenses. Selling 100 units of P for $90 per unit brings in $9,000. Selling 50 Qs for $100 brings in $5,000. Total sales is, therefore, $14,000 per week. According to this calculation, the weekly profit is $1,500.[1]

---

[*] *Warning: This chapter is full of very detailed calculations. There is a point to it all. The chapter tests several common approaches to cost accounting, proving them to be wrong. From this we should deduce that, if they are that wrong for a very simple case, they are certainly incorrect for more complex and realistic cases. Therefore, we suggest readers track the calculations in order to understand our claims.*

[1] $14,000 sales – $6,500 raw materials – $6,000 OE

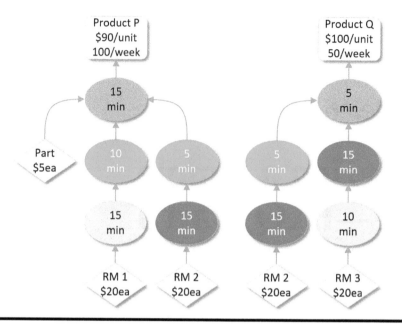

Figure 6.1   P and Q production diagram.

Table 6.1   P&Q Cost Accounting

Product	Units	Price/unit	Sales	RM/unit	RM Expense	Operating Expense
P	100	$90	$9,000	$45	$4,500	
Q	50	$100	$5,000	$40	$2,000	
Totals			$14,000		$6,500	$6,000
					Profit	$1,500

Throughput-based calculations result in the same profit. (See Table 6.2.) Good! We are all on the same page, so far.

Table 6.2   P&Q Throughput Calculations

Product	Units	Price/unit	RM/unit	Throughput/unit	Total Throughput
P	100	$90	$45	$45	$4,500
Q	50	$100	$40	$60	$3,000
Total					$7,500
OE					$6,000
				Profit	$1,500

What Are the Costs to Produce P and Q?

Weekly operating expenses (excluding material costs) are $6,000. The total available work minutes are 9,600.[2] Since every resource is paid equally, the cost of overhead per minute is $0.625.[3]

The cost of producing one unit of product P is $82.50.[4] P's price is $90, which leaves a net profit margin of $7.50 per P.[5] Selling 100 units of P generates $750 in weekly profit.

The cost per unit of product Q, according to this approach, is $71.25,[6] yielding a margin of $28.75 per Q that is sold.[7] Selling 50 units of Q yields a profit of $1,437.50.[8]

Based on margins per unit, total net profit comes to $2,187.50.[9] This approach results in a higher profit than the previous simple approach, which is only $1,500!

What happened? So, which one is right? What is wrong with the other calculation?

The first flaw is the hidden assumption that the company matches its capacity to the demand. This is neither the case here, nor in any other situation, except for hypothetical ones, as previously mentioned. Did we learn this in school? Did we forget such an important point?

In order to produce 100 of P and 50 of Q, we require less capacity than what is available and paid for. Producing 100 units of P requires 6,000 minutes.[10] Producing 50 units of Q requires 2,500 minutes.[11] Therefore, the company needs only 8,500 minutes each week, out of the available capacity of 9,600.

There are two ways to consider the wasted 1,100 minutes the company pays for without the benefit of any salable output.

1. Regular cost accounting claims that, since the required capacity is only 8,500 minutes, the cost per minute is ~$0.7059.[12] This makes the cost of one P $87.35.[13] The margin is $2.65,[14] which seems very poor indeed. The cost of one unit of Q is $75.30.[15] The margin on each Q sold is $24.70.[16] The overall profit, according to this approach is $1,500,[17] which is exactly in line with the first approach.

---

[2] 2,400 minutes/person/week × 4 people
[3] $6,000/week / 9,600 minutes/week
[4] $45 of P's raw materials + 60 minutes × $0.625/minute
[5] $90 price per P – $82.50 cost per P
[6] $40 of Q's raw materials + 50 minutes × $0.625/minute
[7] $100 price per Q – $71.25 cost per Q
[8] 50 Qs × $28.75 profit per Q
[9] $750 from Ps + $1,437.50 from Qs
[10] 100 Ps × 60 minutes per P
[11] 50 Qs × 50 minutes per Q
[12] $6,000 OE / 8,500 total minutes required
[13] $45 of P's raw materials + 60 minutes × $0.7059/minute
[14] $90 price per P – $87.35 cost per P
[15] $40 of raw materials + 50 units × $0.7059/minute. For those of you who are precision-minded, actually the cost of 50 Qs is closer to $35.29, the penny difference is just rounding error, since $6,000/8,500 is actually 0.705882352. Please don't fret about a penny over the sale of 50 Qs, cost accounting's problems are far worse than rounding errors, as you will soon see.
[16] $100 price per Q – $75.30 cost per Q
[17] 100 Ps × $2.65 profit per P + 50 Qs × $24.70 profit per Q

2. The Activity-Based Costing method would use the above cost/minute of $0.625 to calculate the cost of the waste: $687.50.[18] So, the total margin minus waste is $1,500.[19] Again, this approach also confirms the first calculations.

Beware! The above calculations only achieve a precise match between cost/unit and the simple straightforward calculations because of the use of the **actual units sold** and the **actual capacity used.** When the quantities produced and sold change, then the calculated cost of additional sales is again different from the actual additional cost. Recalculating costs after every change would make using cost accounting impractical to use. Consequently, the usual cost accounting procedure ignores changes in cost due to changes in sales; only adjusting standard costs annually or, at best, quarterly.

Since decision making is all about looking into the uncertain future, relying on cost/unit calculated according to the past is fundamentally flawed.

Accounting method aside, when the boss reviews the situation, it seems clear that Q is much more profitable than P. The key data regarding the two products that show the difference is presented in Table 6.3.

Table 6.3 P&Q Net Profit Contribution Study

Product	Weekly Demand	Price/unit	RM/unit	Minutes/unit	Throughput/ unit	Net Profit/ unit
P	100	$90	$45	60	$45	$2.65
Q	50	$100	$40	50	$60	$24.70

Really? Is Q Truly More Profitable than P?

Since the company only requires 8,500 minutes out of the 9,600 it purchases, no difficulty is anticipated in meeting the full demand from the market. Following the conclusion that the margin of P is much lower than Q would create the desire to expand the sales of Q, even if it means giving up some Ps. If almost any alternative could be found, such as coming up with some new product W, it would make sense to drop P from the product mix altogether, because P is a miserably unattractive product relative to Q. Therefore, almost any arbitrary W would undoubtedly yield a better margin than P. Both regular cost accounting and ABC would lead the owner to that seemingly trivial conclusion.

Actually, **this is a grossly flawed conclusion!** All the above calculations were made under two more hidden assumptions:

1. There is plenty of resource capacity.
2. The cost per unit of capacity is fixed.

The resources only need to produce at just under 89% of their capacity, a total utilization of 8,500 minutes out of the available capacity of 9,600 minutes. Everything seems fine. However, let's see what happens when we calculate the load on each of the four resources individually. (See Table 6.4.)

---

[18] 1,100 minutes × $0.625
[19] $2,187.50 − $687.50

Table 6.4   P&Q Resource Capacities

Resource	P Required Minutes/ unit	Q Required Minutes/ unit	Total Required Minutes per Week	Available Minutes/ week
Light-Blue	15	10	2,000 *(100 Ps × 15 min/P + 50 Qs × 10 min/Q)*	2,400
Blue	**15**	**30**	**3,000** **(100 Ps × 15 min/P + 50 Qs × 30 min/Q)**	**2,400**
Green	15	5	1,750 *(100 Ps × 15 min/P + 50 Qs × 5 min/Q)*	2,400
Gray	15	5	1,750 *(100 Ps × 15 min/P + 50 Qs × 5 min/Q)*	2,400

Oops! The Blue resource requires 3,000 minutes but has only 2,400 available. If there is neither the option to increase capacity, such as overtime, nor a way for resources to be cross-trained, it is impossible to fully satisfy the market demand.

There is a critical decision to make: **Which Sales Should the Company Give Up?**

The straightforward answer, based on the conclusion that Q is a much more profitable product, is to forego sales of P, as necessary, to shrink the amount of work to what can actually be accomplished.

The company wants to fully utilize the limited capacity of the Blue resource. Producing 50 units of Q requires 1,500 minutes of Blue's work,[20] leaving 900 minutes, which is enough to make exactly 60 units of P.[21]

The resulting profit is calculated directly: sales from 50 Qs is $5,000.[22] Sales from 60 units of P are $5,400.[23] Therefore, total revenues are $10,400. Material costs total $4,700.[24] Now, considering the fixed costs of $6,000 on top of the material cost, the Net Loss is $300.[25] **The company loses $300 every week. Ouch!**

If the generally accepted cost per unit method is correct, it is impossible to achieve better profit by producing some different combination of Ps and Qs. Furthermore, every minute the owner delays in closing the company means more losses.

People hate bad outcomes and are generally unwilling to leave any stone unturned seeking a better one. Out of desperation, the owner tries the direct method again modeling the opposite decision: selling 100 Ps and reducing the sales of Qs enough to completely utilize the Blue resource. Making 100 Ps uses up 1,500 minutes.[26] That leaves 900 minutes to produce Qs.

---

[20] 50 Qs × 30 minutes of the Blue resource per Q
[21] 900 minutes left / 15 minutes of the Blue resource per P
[22] 50 Qs × $100 price per Q
[23] 60 Ps × $90 price per P
[24] 60 Ps × $45 of raw materials per P + 50 Qs × $40 of raw materials per Q
[25] $10,400 − $4,700 − $6,000
[26] 100 Ps × 15 minutes per P

Only 30 out of the desired 50 Qs can be produced.[27] That combination also exactly matches the available capacity.

The NP for this decision is +$300! **What?**

$$\text{Revenues} = \$12,000 = (100 \text{ Ps} \times \$90 \text{ per P} + 30 \text{ Qs} \times \$100 \text{ per Q})$$

$$\text{Material costs} = \$5,700 = (100 \text{ Ps} \times \$45 \text{ per P} + 30 \text{ Qs} \times \$40 \text{ per Q})$$

$$\text{NP} = \$300 = (\$12,000 - \$5,700 - \$6000)$$

How can this improvement be possible?

It is a very troubling question. Based on the common and accepted algorithm, the best result should have been achieved by making Q highest priority and then complementing the sales by utilizing the remaining capacity available to produce P. However, this method would result in a loss, while the opposite alternative actually yields profit. **There is clearly a need to understand what went wrong with the cost-accounting approach.**

Do the math over again with close scrutiny to find some structural or conceptual flaw. It may even make sense to ask an expert to perform the calculations independently. After rigorous confirmation, the unescapable realization is that flaws are inherent in the very concept of "cost per unit!" Yet, cost per unit is currently taught in the world's most prestigious universities, generally accepted by accountants, widely used by top-notch businesspeople and touted by most consultants. This creates a potentially dangerous situation because revealing the extent of the flaws in "simplifying" decision making by means of calculating costs per unit risks insulting the intelligence of advocates, particularly powerful ones.

Even though the calculated margin for Ps is only $2.65 and the margin for Qs is $24.70, the correct decision is to produce Ps over Qs, as much as possible. Cost accounting not only let us down, it wasn't even close! The costs-per-unit in this example are off by an order of magnitude! The message is quite clear.

Costs of particular products cannot be calculated individually.

Instead, the whole system, including all of its products and the capacities of its resources must be considered together. This situation is exactly what cost per unit was developed to avoid.

This case was designed by Dr. Goldratt to demonstrate two erroneous ramifications stemming from cost-per-unit calculations:

■ Ignoring the lack of capacity of individual resources means that all cost calculations can be erroneous.
  - Translating overall capacity into cost is inappropriate. Such costs do not consider the critical limitation of available capacity of individual resources.
  - Neither ABC nor conventional cost accounting consider the available capacity per resource when analyzing the financial outcome of a managerial move.
    • Consequently, both may lead managers to exhaust capacity in their attempts to increase profit.
    • Worse, they blind management to the full potential of using additional capacity, even though it might appear to be quite expensive.

---

[27] 900 minutes / 30 minutes per Q

- Another serious failing is hiding opportunities to use available capacity for sales that appear unappealing but may actually boost profits nicely.
■ Cost per unit is unreliable in establishing the appropriate priorities between products.

While Product P requires more time and materials while commanding a lower price than Q, it has one critical advantage: **P requires only half as much of the only capacity constrained resource as Q.**

The P and Q case shows how far off any cost per unit calculation can be. Furthermore, the reader should take away that individual capacity limitations must be carefully considered, while surplus capacity can be utilized for free. An understanding emerges that Throughput per minute of the Blue resource leads to the correct relative priority between products.

The Throughput generated per minute of Blue producing Ps is $3.00.[28]

For Qs, the Throughput generated per minute of the Blue resource is only $2.00.[29]

The correct priority of P is fully 50% higher than Q. This explains why the producible product mix of 100 Ps and then 30 Qs is $600 per week more profitable than making 50 Qs and 60 Ps. Even if the price of Qs was increased from $100 to $125 per unit, the company would still perform better by producing Ps first, before making any Qs at all.

Think about that last sentence a little more. In most competitive markets, raising a price by 25% often renders buyers uninterested and the seller uncompetitive. Yet, as we have shown, modern cost calculations might lead a manager, salesperson or engineer to make a similar blunder, based on failing to consider the capacity of each individual resource and assuming costs per unit are fixed.

Is this insight a general principle? **Should we always follow the priority set by T/cu[30]?**

The answer is: **you need to be very careful to consider the context;** otherwise even T/cu can lead to faulty decisions similar to those made using cost per unit. Principally, to make T/cu applicable, there must be resource constraint which is truly active (the demand is greater than what that resource can process) both before and after the contemplated change. In other words, the change under consideration does not exhaust another resource(s) capacity or add enough capacity to the constrained resource to move the systemic constraint either externally or to another internal resource(s).

If the constraint is external to the system, there are three possible cases:

1. There is a supply constraint, meaning it is not possible to procure enough raw materials to meet demand.
2. There is a demand constraint (in other words, although availability of raw materials is satisfactory and there is enough internal capacity, there are too few orders to fully utilize the capacity of the system, despite the fact that there are enough orders in the whole marketplace to fully consume the system's capacity). In this case, the company is not preferred over its competitors enough to utilize all its capacity.
3. There is a market constraint, meaning the worldwide demand in the marketplace is insufficient to fully utilize the company's internal constraint (or bottleneck).

---

[28] $45 Throughput per P / 15 minutes per P
[29] $60 T per Q / 30 minutes per Q
[30] T/cu where "T" stands for Throughput and "cu" stands for constraint unit, in other words, the Throughput produced by utilizing one unit of time of the constraint's productive capacity.

There is an easy test to recognize internally constrained situations, such as the P and Q scenario where an internal constraint is definitely present. Every marginal increase in its capacity utilization improves the performance of the entire system. For business organizations, it means achieving higher profits to the extent that the additional flow generates T. For internally constrained systems, there are two critically necessary conditions for T/cu to yield effective priorities:

1. **There is one and *only* one active capacity constraint.**
   a. This view of a constraint as an active limit to selling more implies that there is no practical way to quickly increase its capacity (using a Capacity Buffer). When there are options, such as overtime and outsourcing, taking advantage of an option to sell more typically adds a certain amount of OE. As long as ΔT is larger than ΔOE, the limited standard capacity of that resource does not constrain the performance of the organization. Additional demand is still desirable. This point will be discussed further, later in this chapter.
   b. Note that capacity constraints are often only active at peak times. During off-peak times, T/cu should not be employed.
   c. When two or more capacity constraints interact, T/cu cannot be used.
2. **The decision being considered has a small impact relative to the residual capacity.**
   a. If you are focused on the short term, where the one active capacity constraint is unlikely to shift to other resources, then T/cu remains fully applicable. To avoid trouble, serious attention must be directed to always maintaining "protective capacity" of all the non-constraint resources. This helps keep the current capacity constraint as the focal point, so small changes in market demand do not result in the emergence of a new resource as the constraint. All the rules for exploiting the constraint and subordinating everything else to that decision have become habitual to the culture. Therefore, having to adapt to a new active capacity constraint would be disruptive to the company's "clock".[31]
   b. However, when major marketing and sales initiatives or acquisitions are considered, the possible increase in demand could result in the emergence of a new capacity constraint or even several. The situation of multiple interactive constraints is so chaotic and disastrous to performance that it guarantees a loss of business, to the point that the number of internal constraints eventually drops to one or even none.

Thus, T/cu may misdirect its users when there is either no current active capacity constraint, multiple active constraints or when the decision considered is significant enough to threaten current capacities of more than one resource.

The P and Q case demonstrates that subtracting cost per unit from price per unit to calculate net profit per unit sometimes leads to ghastly errors. So, **why do most managers continue to use cost per unit for their critical decisions?**

---

[31] If the reader is not aware of our reference to "the clock," it comes from the book *Built to Last* by Collins and Porras, see chapter 2. Here is an excerpt, used with permission of the authors:

"*Imagine that you met a remarkable person who could look at the sun or the stars and, amazingly, state the exact time and date. Wouldn't it be even more amazing still if, instead of telling the time, that person built a clock that could tell the time forever, even after he or she were dead and gone?*

Having a great idea or being a charismatic visionary leader is 'time telling;' building a company that can prosper far beyond the tenure of any single leader and through multiple product life cycles is 'clock building.' Those who build visionary companies tend to be clock builders. Their primary accomplishment is not the implementation of a great idea, the expression of a charismatic personality, or the accumulation of wealth. It is the company itself and what it stands for."

It is our sense that, while managers rely heavily on cost per unit to ensure that their prices leave enough profit, there is very little deep understanding of the erroneous nature of cost per unit. After all, as we have mentioned earlier, it is the nature of human beings to fear the unknown. It is this very fear that makes forecasts so popular, regardless of their eventual inaccuracy and the significantly negative effects on performance that stem from making decisions based upon them.

Furthermore, to the extent that there is some understanding that unused labor results in a too optimistic net profit per unit sold, then it pressures those who are aware to fully utilize their labor, thereby, limiting protective capacity. And, of course, exhausting capacity of normally non-constraint resources leads to chaos. In such an environment, employees are quite rightly reluctant to take on anything new. If you have ever noticed a general reluctance to change, even for the better, lack of protective capacity is an excellent and totally rational reason for it.

People who are overloaded are well aware that they will deliver projects late. Taking on something new will only exacerbate their lateness. They also understand that they may be blamed for delivering late. Enough blame may lead to termination. Who wants that?

Variation #1 of the Original P&Q Example

For the sake of simplicity, The P and Q case above ignored the option to increase capacity of the four resources. In reality, since non-human resources are available 24 hours a day, seven days a week, there are numerous practical ways to increase the capacity of the staff.

In the P&Q case, the average cost per hour of a person, along with related fixed costs, considering eight hours a day and five days a week, is $37.50.[32] Note, the hourly pay rate is less than $37.50, but including fixed costs results in this average hourly expense of each person.

What if we offer the operator of the Blue machine an additional $300 each week (an overtime rate of $30 an hour) in return for staying for two more hours every day? This would provide the owner 10 additional hours a week, precisely the amount of time required to produce the extra 20 units of Q, thus, fully exploiting the existing demand from the market.

The owner wonders fleetingly how will the other three operators will feel—those for whom there is no need to work overtime? While their agreement to work up to 40 hours a week remains in place, the higher utilization of the Blue machine operator forces them to work more than before. Is it fair that the lucky guy who operates the constraint makes more money while they aren't paid anything extra for working more than they have grown used to?

In order to keep a happy work atmosphere, the owner decides to compensate each of the other three workers with an additional $15 for every extra hour the operator of the Blue machine now works. This raises ΔOE for every extra hour of the Blue resource to $75, $30 for the Blue Machine operator and $45 for the other three operators.

Is it worthwhile? It seems to be a very high price, in fact, double the current $37.50 average cost per hour per person, loaded with fixed costs, like rent, utilities, maintenance, advertising, and so on.

---

[32] $6,000 per week / (40 hours per week × 4 people)

On the other hand, without the additional capacity, the performance of this company is a profit of only $300 per week. Selling the extra 20 Qs would generate $1,200 of ΔT.[33] The required ΔOE for 10 additional hours is $750. ΔT $-$ ΔOE $=$ $450.[34] The new weekly profit is $450, a 50% increase! For the owner who expected $1,500 per week, it is irresistible!

The above example demonstrates what is possible, even at exorbitant expense. There are other considerations of which we should be aware. For example, there is no guarantee that employees who are given hefty raises will happily revert back to their previous situation if, in the future, demand should drop enough to shift the constraint from production to a lack of orders.

When it is possible to maintain enough of a Capacity Buffer, such as the option to gain more production for $75 per hour, the notion that the Blue station is an active constraint collapses. It is the lack of market demand that limits the performance of the organization, so long as the ΔT of any new sales is larger than the relevant required ΔOE.

A Variation on the Variation

What happens if the worker at the Green station organizes the Light Blue and Gray workers to band together and threaten to quit unless compensation is paid out fairly? The owner may feel that the only viable option is to meet labor's demands. The only approach they find acceptable is to return to equal pay for all four workers. The workers all want to receive $30 per hour for two extra hours each day, even though some of them would have no work to perform. The ΔOE would then rise to an extra $1,200/wk.[35] If this decision were made, there would be no change from the original weekly net profit. The union (which excludes the Blue worker in its charter) understood the situation emotionally, but not so well mathematically, so they held out for all $30 or nothing, claiming *"It's the principal that's important here."*

They got nothing, in the end. Now, both sides are angry with each other and, again, there is no opportunity for overtime. The owner is back to being frustrated at achieving such a low profit of $300 a week, because customers are begging for more of Product Q than the company can make.

Variation #2 of the Original P&Q Example

A salesperson was asked by a new customer whether they can produce a product called W. This raised new thoughts. Making the new product requires the same resources, with the exception of the Green resource. The customer is willing to commit to a regular weekly delivery of 100 W units. It is up to the owner to decide, based on the following details, shown in Figure 6.2.

The attraction of the new product is its much better ratio of Throughput to constraint-units consumed (T/cu) which is $9.40,[36] much more than for either P ($3.00/cu) or Q ($2.00/cu). Using

---

[33] $60 T per Q × 20 Qs

[34] $1,200 − $750

[35] $30 per hour per employee × 4 employees × 5 days per week × 2 hours per day

[36] ($77 per W − $30 of raw materials) / 5 minutes of the Blue resource

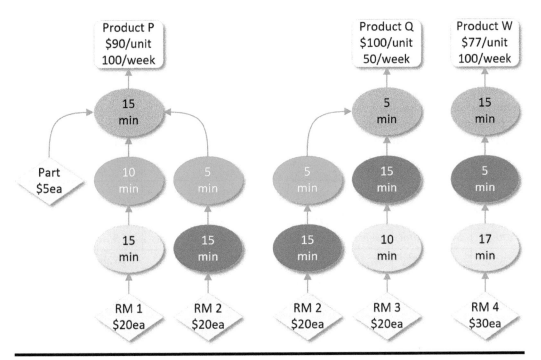

Figure 6.2   P, Q & W production diagram.

T/cu as guidance, the company decides to first satisfy all of the demand for W and then comple-ment it with P units as long as capacity remains.

Readers are suggested to stop here for a short while and use their intuition about what could be achieved with the addition of product W. Remember, currently the company makes a profit of $300/wk. How much more can be achieved without increasing the available capacity? Get a pencil, paper and a calculator or, if you prefer, fire up your favorite spreadsheet and calculate the new profit.

In your own business efforts, you will need confidence born of practice to use Throughput Economics to increase your profits. In fact, you would be correct to think that learning this well will (indirectly) pay you to do this exercise very carefully. Think about it, your goal is not to hurry along to fin-ish the book but, instead, to learn how to make more money without more guesswork!

If one proceeds as they have learned to, as most people do, consideration is given to the Blue resource. Producing 100 Ws requires a paltry 500 minutes, leaving 1,900 minutes for other products. As just proved, Ps are better than Qs at exploiting the Blue resource, so you might plan to make 100 Ps using 1,500 more minutes of the Blue resource. Fortunately, there are 400 minutes remaining with which we can make some Qs. How many Qs? Well, each Q requires 30 minutes of the Blue resource, so that leaves time for 13 complete[37] Qs.

Imagine how happy everyone is after this Friday afternoon's production planning meeting, when they consider the information shown in Table 6.5. This profit is more than double the $1,500

Table 6.5 P, Q & W Data Table

Product	Units Sold	Price /unit	Total Sales	TVC/ unit	Total TVC	Blue Mins Required /unit	Blue Resource Minutes	T/Minute of Blue	Throughput
W	100	$77	$7,700	$30	$3,000	5	500	$9.40	$4,700
P	100	$90	$9,000	$45	$4,500	15	1,500	$3.00	$4,500
Q	13	$100	$1,300	$40	$520	30	390	$2.00	$780
Totals			$18,000		$8,020		2,390		$9,980
OE									$6,000
								Profit	$3,980

they first imagined they could earn before the impact of the Blue constraint was recognized. It is only right to plan a company-wide celebration for later that evening with spouses at a wonderful restaurant. Hopefully, this will begin to repair the bad blood between management and labor that resulted from the extra pay offered the Blue worker. The owner also quietly slipped the salesperson an envelope containing a hefty bonus for bringing this great opportunity to the company.

What happens the following Monday when the production plan is put into effect? While the message that the new product W is the best, the production manager soon realizes that the complexity has grown and making a viable weekly production plan is not easy at all. He is clear that the Blue should work continuously without any idle time. This means the Blue resource cannot wait for the Light Blue to process one unit for W, which takes 17 minutes, and then process for only 5 minutes and then wait again. There should be no wait time for the Blue resource!

Thus, the Blue resource must start processing RM2 parts for P or Q. Since, Ps are the second priority, they let Blue work on that first. Only when there are enough parts for W in queue for Blue should the Blue operator switch to that work. Well, this is easy enough. Except, to process all the 100 units of P the Light Blue needs 1,500 minutes and processing the 100 W units the Light Blue has to dedicate 1,700 minutes during the week. At that point the production manager suddenly realizes that the Light Blue does not have 1,500 + 1,700 minutes to give in one week without overtime which contains only 2,400 minutes!

What happened here?

---

[37] Any fractional production which does not result in a complete saleable unit is ignored. However, in a real production environment, the partially completed unit remains in inventory over the weekend and could be finished the next week. For the sake of simplicity, we have intentionally ignored this possibility.

The Light Blue resource became a true bottleneck. Suddenly, it is evident that another constraint has emerged due to the addition of the new product W, which seemed so attractive. This is what you might call mental inertia. The attractiveness of product W was its low consumption of the Blue resource; however, W's introduction consumed all of the Light Blue resource as well.

This is exactly the type of difficulty that is often encountered when you continue to calculate T/cu on the constraint before making a significant change.

Neglecting to challenge the assumption that you are aware of which resource is actually the constraint is dangerous.

Dear reader, before you get worried that Throughput Economics is complicated, please relax. The real problem is trying to blend the conventional cost accounting in your mind with the Throughput accounting approach. Bear with us. This way not only produces reliable results, enabling better decisions, but is also easier, because in the end, it saves a lot of time and stress.

If you were one of the few that, after the break at the bottom of page 11, realized that there were multiple constraints, congratulations. Even one of the authors failed to realize it while checking the math. It caused him, who thought he knew better, to laugh loudly at his folly. (This author will go unnamed, though his last name does not begin with an S!) It just goes to show you that when you get your mind going on one track and look to finish it before moving on, you can find yourself quite reluctant to take the time to verify whether the circumstances have changed.

1. **IDENTIFY the system's constraint(s).**

2. **Decide how to EXPLOIT the system's constraint(s).**

3. **SUBORDINATE everything else to the above decision.**

4. **ELEVATE the system's constraint(s).**

5. **WARNING!!!! If in the previous steps, a constraint has been broken, go back to step 1, but do not allow INERTIA to cause a system's constraint.**

Figure 6.3   Goldratt's five focusing steps.[38]

This is what Dr. Goldratt meant when in Step 5 of his Five Focusing Steps, see Figure 6.3, he warned us ... warned us about letting **inertia** get in our way, blocking us from realizing that we should circle back to Step 1 whenever the constraint changes. In his initial articulation of the fifth focusing step in the second and third editions of *The Goal*, after the word WARNING, which preceded the instructions regarding inertia, Dr. Goldratt put four exclamation points and refused to relent when the copy editor objected. It is a major blunder to allow yourself to remain unaware that the constraint has shifted to a different resource. After all, how does the owner explain it to the salesman that she can no longer afford to pay the hefty bonus? Now, he may get mad, like the workers. Isn't that just perfect?

---

[38] This list is the Five Focusing Steps word for word as they were first expressed in Eli Goldratt's book *The Goal, 20th Anniversary Edition* (2004) page 307.

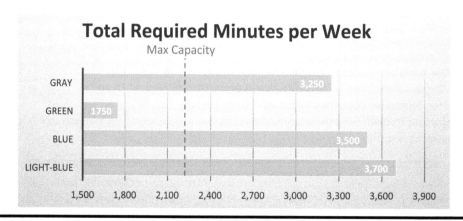

Figure 6.4 P, Q and W resource load chart.

The point is that adding a new product, opening a new market or making an acquisition is *not* a small decision. **The evaluation of potential constraints under the new decision requires a further analysis.**

Starting again from the beginning: the market has a steady demand for: 100 Ps, 50 Qs and 100 Ws. Translating all the demand into load per available resource gives us the data for the bar chart in Figure 6.4, which indicates that, given the new demand, Light Blue is the most loaded resource; however, the Blue and Gray resources are also loaded well beyond their capacities.

Looking for the optimal theoretical solution with multiple constraints requires using linear programming. The optimal theoretical solution for this variation of the original case is shown in Table 6.6.

Table 6.6 P, Q & W Linear Programming Optimized Profit Solution

Product	Price/ unit	TVC/ unit	Throughput/unit	Maximum Demand	Actual Sales	Throughput
P	$90	$45	$45	100	35	$1,575
Q	$100	$40	$60	50	49	$2,940
W	$77	$30	$47	100	81	$3,807
Totals						$8,322
OE						$6,000
					Profit	$2,322

Well, if you are still thinking like most people do, this is quite astonishing. The Q product was the worst from the perspective of a Blue resource constraint. It was the one we could most easily give up. From the Light Blue perspective, product Q is by far the best since the solution calls for producing all but one of the market's demand of 50 Qs.

The available capacity for this product mix is shown in the bar chart in Figure 6.5.

There are a number of reasons Figure 6.5 is labeled "Theoretical."

One is because, in reality, we must consider intra-day statistical fluctuations. Not only is real demand not perfectly steady, in the real world, a worker might sneeze, creating a momentary pause. If that happens at the resource preparing work for a constraint which is loaded to 100%, then it would be enough to spoil the theoretical solution.

Secondly, if two resources are loaded close to their limits, they will become interactive constraints. Statistical fluctuations will cause one of the fully loaded resources to waste the capacity of another, thus resulting in chaos! Nothing will happen according to any plan, no matter how well thought through.

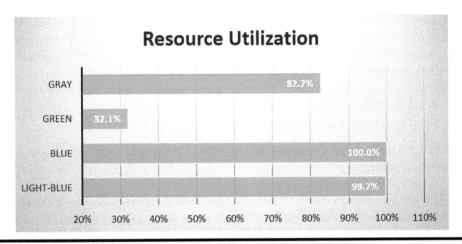

Figure 6.5   Theoretical load requirements for linear programming solution.

And, most importantly of all, the production diagram back in Figure 6.2 shows clear dependencies between the resources. For all but the first operations, the various resources must wait until the preceding resource finishes. To convince yourself quickly, you only need to look at the Light Blue resource, it has eight unused minutes per week. From the moment Light Blue finishes its last task, no matter which of the three it is, only eight minutes remain in the work week.[39] There is no way to complete the last product in process because either 20 minutes (in the cases of Q and W) or 25 minutes (in the case of P) are required of the subsequent steps. If you are still curious, try to see if you can find any scenario that uses all of the Blue and all but eight minutes of the Light Blue resource. Considering dependencies, the linear programming solution doesn't even work in theory.

Considering practical realities, seldom can any company dictate the exact number of units it wishes to sell. Even when the market demand is larger than what the company can comfortably commit to without significantly increasing lead times, there is no easy way to determine which client gets the desired production and which does not. Clients often wish to buy multiple products and it is not smart to limit those sales. Failing to sell what a customer requests is likely to lose the whole customer, not just the few products you prefer not to produce.

The above solution does not consider, for instance, whether the market for P is ready to accept only 35 units per week or if the market for W has a problem with just 81 units. In the real world, it could be the case that the customer will take either 100 units of W or 75—not 81.

Yet another unrealistic assumption is the lack of any setups. This is a huge simplification. The Blue resource only requires 5 minutes to process W but its predecessor, the Light Blue operation, requires 17 minutes per part; thus, it is wasteful to allow the Blue station wait for every piece coming from Light Blue. The Blue station should first process several pieces of RM2, using materials from the RM stock until there is work ready for W. Then switch to process that one piece for W, before going back to process more RM2s while Light Blue processes another piece for W. Such a scheme in which the Blue goes back and forth between two different operations lets the Gray process suffer much less from a waste of time

---

[39] Light Blue is loaded to 99.7% ~ 2,392 minutes—just 8 minutes less that the whole 2,400 available minutes in the workweek

at the beginning of the week. Otherwise, we might have the Gray station exhaust its capacity toward the end of the week, even though it does have, on average, enough capacity for processing the entire weekly plan. Had there had been some setup time, as in reality, such an approach would have been untenable.

Our conclusion is: The production lead time, based on the product mix determined by linear programming and the current capacities of the four resources, is longer than one week! Although those quantities cannot be delivered, the company could build up to a lower practical maximum over the period of several weeks but only by building work-in-process (WIP). The shop floor can achieve a steady state of production in which there is some WIP at the start of the week. Some of the initial work would be to finish the WIP from last week, and toward the end of the week the Light Blue and the Blue would process WIP for the following week.

The important lessons from the original case and its variants are:

1. Not only is the concept of **cost/unit** flawed, but also it **distorts understanding of the most beneficial priorities between products, deals and clients.** A product that initially seems more profitable is not necessarily so.
2. While it is *impossible* to match capacity to demand, **it is easy to capitalize on spare capacity to deliver huge improvements to the bottom line.** Utilizing protective capacity for what may even seem to be a less lucrative opportunity can be wonderfully beneficial.
3. Throughput per constraint-unit, T/cu, is a concept that requires serious analysis and care, especially when the moves considered are significant. **It is much safer to analyze various what-if scenarios and evaluate their net impacts on capacity and the bottom line,** instead of depending on "per-unit" measurements which require constant validation of the assumptions that underpin their use.
4. This chapter has been focused on an artificial example that exposes flaws in commonly accepted concepts. In the example, several resources are allowed to reach close to 100% of their theoretical capacity. In the real world, there is no way to implement such plans. We clearly understand that when Blue is 100% loaded, then the part that is completed at the very last minute still does not result in a completed product because it has to be processed through other resources.
5. Also, at the start of the week, it would have been utterly shocking to realize that relatively lightly loaded and, therefore, deprioritized resources, such as the Gray and Green (82.7% and 32.1%, respectively) would lose so many minutes waiting for work that they both ran out time.
6. If we consider realistic statistical fluctuations, then actual performance will always be somewhat worse that theoretical performance and occasionally much worse.

This example undeniably proves that the concept of cost per unit can result in distorted priorities and that economic predictions are untrustworthy. Nevertheless, our proposed approach must handle variations in the data and consider uncertainty in a more practical way.

The next chapters delve deeper into reality where uncertainty, inaccurate data, and non-linear behavior play a major part, causing management not just concerns but grave fears of making critical mistakes, while working hard to improve. It is these concerns and fears that make reasonable people seem reluctant to change. Dr. Goldratt always claimed that people are not unwilling to make big changes and pointed out that they often undertake serious and expensive decisions, such as marrying and having children! We agree.

It is truly a shame but no surprise that people are rightfully reluctant to plunge ahead with so-called 'improvements' at work. The rest of the book shows how to make changes that actually do improve performance, in spite of real-world complexity and uncertainty. The recommendations for which actions to take and what to stop trying reliably lead to much better outcomes, achieved in a reasonably stable way.

Chapter 7

Some Thoughts about Accounting Principles and Standards

So how did we get to this point, starting back when Eli Goldratt saw the need to address cost accounting in the first place in the early 1980s, right through to now, when we authors still perceive the strong need for this book?

Business accounting before The Great Depression of 1929 was like the Wild Wild West, virtually no rules or standards. After The Great Depression, what was then The American Institute of Accountants (now the American Institute of Certified Public Accountants), and the New York Stock Exchange started issuing accounting standards.

To oversimplify, the reasoning for this movement was the ambitious objective of assuring the investing public and banks that companies' financial reporting fairly represented the financial state of the company. To achieve that objective, companies were required to follow an established set of rules and standards in their financial reporting, which would eventually be audited by independent CPAs external to the companies themselves. Another by-product of the emerging accounting principles and financial reporting standards was to provide some level of comparability of financial results over time and between different companies.

Accounting and financial reporting rules, principles and standards were issued, re-issued, and issued some more. They continue to be issued.

Allow us to share some numbers to make a point:

- There are 44 issued International Financial Reporting Standards (IFRS), with their 10,000 plus pages of related guidance.
- The typical published GAAP (Generally Accepted Accounting Principles) Guide is at least 1800 pages.
- Since 1937, the SEC has issued hundreds of accounting pronouncements called Financial Reporting Releases (FRRs).
- From 1938 to 1959, American Institute of Accountants Committee on Accounting Procedure (CAP) issued 51 Accounting Research Bulletins (ARBs).

- The Accounting Principles Board (APB) issued 31 Accounting Principles Board Opinions (APBOs), four statements and several interpretations from 1959 to 1973.
- Since 1973, the Financial Accounting Standards Board (FASB) has issued 168 Statements of Financial Accounting Standards, and continues issuing accounting principle guidance in the form of codification position statements.
- Since 1984, the FASB Emerging Issues Task Force (EITF) has issued hundreds of guidance papers.
- Each year, hundreds to thousands of research, response, and opinion papers are published, peer reviewed, and vetted in any number of professional accounting periodicals and web sites.
- Tax law and regulations add a whole layer of complexity and required obedience to traditional accounting principles.

The list goes on.

> In all of this guidance provided over the last 90 years, not one page, not one paragraph, not one hint of a suggestion was ever made that any of these published principles, rules or standards should be followed within a company to determine product costs, product pricing or, in general, be used to determine management accounting performance measures.

Rules that were meant to bring consistency to financial reporting have been extended as 'rules' within companies' managerial systems.

The point is that the perspective of fair representation of the current financial state of a company might easily be at odds with what managers require to make good decisions. There are two major differences between the external requirements and internal ones:

1. In order to establish a good way for the government, banks, or investors to understand the basic financial state of a company, certain broad standards are necessary. However, from a decision-maker's perspective, these standards could be much too generic; even distorting key information items that are relevant to decisions at hand. A typical example is how finished-goods inventory is evaluated. External reporting standards have an assumptive reliance that generally accepted accounting principles were followed such that the reported inventory value includes all the deemed associated overhead costs. There are also rules that prevent inventory from being reported at more than its market value. While well intended, this concept is flawed, especially when historical margins are threatened. A decision maker might be aware that some inventory items face low demand and, thus, offering them at a significantly reduced prices could be the right decision – despite what the standard markup from the inventory's reported value seems to suggest.
2. External reporting cannot fairly evaluate the long-term opportunities that a specific company faces, definitely not its risks. The objective is to reflect the current status, with little reference to the future, certainly not the long-term. However, for the company decision-makers evaluating long-term prospects is a critical part of their responsibilities and they need to find the right performance measurements and indicators to aid in their consideration.

A few paradigmal considerations to think about:

- Are all costs created equally?
  - Isn't there a basic difference in the nature of the cost of an employee's salary and the cost for a temporary worker who is only called when truly needed?
  - Or, the cost of materials versus the cost of renting the headquarters' offices?
- How many individual line item costs immediately (or even eventually) adjust to changes in the overall demand?
  - For example, one doesn't expect salaries to vary because of changes in sales. However, the value of inventories that include overhead and labor allocations should react to fluctuations in demand but almost never do, in real-time.
- Do costs determine selling prices? Should they?
- Can you accurately allocate the purchase price of a building to a unit of production?
- Did the worker who produced 10% more today than yesterday at the same rate of pay, really cost you less because he produced more?

How many people believe in their company's daily approach to quoting to the extent that they blindly rely on their own internal cost structure and margin requirements to determine an appropriate selling price?

There have been many well vetted and intelligently developed cost accounting practices over the years in an attempt to build a better costing system. Some examples are:

- Standard costing
- Absorption costing
- Marginal costing
- Target Costing
- Activity Based Costing
- Various methods of overhead absorption costing

They were all developed based upon the recognition that better managerial accounting methods were needed to enable a company to manage better. Additionally, they all were attempts to discover the holy grail of an accurate product costing system.

Eli Goldratt did, at times, remind us that before answering a question, it is necessary to validate the question. A premise might be invalid; if so, any answer must also be invalid.

Such is the case with asking for accurate individual product costs. By the nature of what is involved, there can be only one circumstance under which truly accurate product costs are possible. When all a company does is buy the product, adds no value to it and resells it to a customer.

Other than that, there can be no "accurate" product costs.

Of course, there is the statistically supported argument that we often make in TOC, the answer is well "within the noise" or as one often says, close enough. But, BIG BUT, when is close enough good enough and when can it be misleading? If the desire is to determine an inventory "carrying cost", close enough will likely suffice. If it is to determine whether or not to accept an order, enter a market, decide whether to make or buy, the odds are overwhelming that any product cost analysis will be misleading.

We hope by now you agree, the previous chapters in this book having supplemented your clear understanding of this important principle.

A simple example: It is amazing to see how many times a decision is made to not take an order because the internal costing system says it will be unprofitable, while there is known unused (already paid for) capacity. These same people intuitively know it makes perfect sense to accept the order but they don't want to accept blame for taking an order that management reporting makes appear bad.

Okay, for the big picture understanding, let us play with another simple example.

Would managing performance be easier if everyone managed with data this simple?

The market will buy our widgets for $100 each

Our real variable costs of material and freight for every widget produced is $30

All of our costs to unlock the doors every morning and produce widgets is $1 million per year

Simply put, we must sell 14,286 widgets to break even *($1 million divided by $70)*

Let's take this example a little further. The simple details of the $1,000,000 in annual costs are shown on Table 7.1

Table 7.1 Annual Operating Costs

Production labor	$150,000
Production overhead	$550,000
Selling & Administrative overhead	$300,000

Total production costs are $700,000[1] plus $30 variable cost per unit produced. Still simple? I hope you think so. Now, let us enter the accounting world where 1 + 1 will never equal 2.

We already stated the simple math above showed we must *sell* 14,286 units to break even. That would likely be the minimum production budget which the sales department would be tasked to sell. What if we sold only 10,000 of those units?

10,000 units times the $100 selling price equals $1,000,000 in sales. Okay, we broke even because we also have $1,000,000 in costs. Or, do we?

We have 4,286 units unsold. They will be accounted for in inventory. The question is at what cost? At the variable cost of only $30 per unit, $128,580[2]? Or, will production costs be allocated to the widgets left in inventory? In its simplest form, the allocation would be according to Table 7.2.

Table 7.2 Inventory Value Calculation

Total units produced	14,286
Total production costs *($150,000 + $550,000)*	$700,000
Total production costs per unit *($700,000 / 14,286 units)*	$49
Amount in inventory *(4,286 units × ($49/unit + $30/unit Material & Freight))*	$338,594

---

[1] $150,000 of production labor + $550,000 of production overhead
[2] 4,286 units × $30/unit

Our simple math above showed without question that the company had to sell 14,286 units to breakeven. Let us now look at the traditional and alternative accounting for the year's activity as shown in Table 7.3.

Table 7.3   Alternative Accounting Treatments

	Traditional Accounting	Throughput Accounting	Cash Based Accounting
Sales	$1,000,000	$1,000,000	$1,000,000
Raw Materials Cost:			
Material & Freight	428,580	428,580	428,580
Production Costs:			
Labor & Overhead	700,000	700,000	700,000
Less Inventory	(338,594)	(128,580)	-0-
Net Costs of Production	789,986	1,000,000	1,128,580
Gross Margin	210,014	-0-	(128,580)
Selling & Admin. Exp.	300,000	300,000	300,000
Net Profit (Loss)	$(89,986)	($300,000)	($428,580)

In all three financial reporting alternatives, the company had the **exact same** operating results. The company produced 14,286 units and 10,000 units were sold. Each alternative presented materially changes the financial reporting of the exact same operating results.

If this were your company, you undoubtedly would want to report the traditional results to your bank, investors and, maybe, your parents. Moreover, there is nothing wrong with that. However, an intelligent manager, who wants to improve performance, would prefer the Throughput alternative, because it gives a more accurate picture of the true situation.

The managerial point is there are several issues to address; cash flow and the market for its products, to name a couple.

Conventionally, the typical immediate reaction would be to look at all costs. That is always something that should be managed. However, as has been proven time and again, a company cannot "cut costs" to sustainable profitability.

That is the relevance of this book.

Virtually all traditional methods of cost accounting, at the very least, distort profit-targeted decision-making and, at their worst, can significantly distort managerial performance measures that are so very important to making strategically important decisions.

We hope you are thinking about the relevance of this book to your business. We hope the simple examples in this chapter clearly demonstrate the need to understand the actual impacts of your decisions. From now on, we will deal with realistic cases and the truly relevant information for making good decisions, avoiding the distortions of using the generally accepted accounting principles, which were developed for quite different needs.

Chapter 8

A More Realistic Case—
Daily Bread, Part 3

Daily Bread's Top Management Meeting and Dilemmas

On Friday, March 17, at 6pm, the management team of Daily Bread (the same company mentioned in Chapters 1 and 4) assembled in a private room at a local hotel, close to the bakery, to discuss the offer from Events to Remember. Clark, the CEO of Daily Bread, intended to use the new offer as an example to enter into a strategic discussion about how Daily Bread might safely grow.

Clark reminded his staff that the offer is to supply a variety of Daily Bread products to every event organized by Events to Remember for prices that are only 60% of Daily Bread's list prices!

The company's CFO, Raphael, shared his initial data analysis of the quantities required by Events to Remember. At the reduced prices, it would mean an average daily revenue of $491.04, out of which $245.28 is the cost of materials. (Note: the detailed calculations from his analysis will be presented in a table later in this chapter.) Accordingly, the daily Throughput (T) would be $245.76. Also, on the meeting's agenda is the offer from the National Children's Hospital to buy 800 regular donuts every day but for only 70 cents each, instead of 78 cents, yielding $560.00 daily, of which $171.60 is the cost of materials. The resulting Throughput from this second deal is $388.40 per day.[1]

Linda, the VP of Marketing and Sales, explained the benefits of Events to Remember's offer. "This deal is not just about the money generated directly by the sales. I understand that sales at 40% off list price is not terribly attractive. The point is the exposure that Daily Bread will get at these events. Events to Remember is going to offer the entire variety of our products. At most events, there will be a stand with our products and a large sign with our logo and name. Small baskets of our products will be part of the decoration on every table. Each basket, which

---

[1] In Chapter 4 the deal with the children's hospital was analyzed but a certain complication was added, concerning another smaller hospital that might also demand the same reduction in price. We do not reuse that complication here. Instead we are dealing with two, seemingly independent opportunities which require the capacity of the same resources.

is a take-home gift, will carry our signage. I don't mean to be crass but its customers are rich, which is ideal for our future positioning. So, even if Raphael claims that the deal results in a loss, we should look at it more as an investment in advertising and marketing. I need that exposure in our best potential market! My intuition, based on my 14 years of experience in bakery products, tells me this will create a clear image of Daily Bread as THE bakery products for the high-end market."

Raphael, the CFO, clarified: "I didn't say the deal would generate a loss. If I considered full cost allocation, then it is a loss. From a marginal costing point of view, it yields a very small margin. I'm concerned because I think it is possible to get much better deals. For instance, the Children's Hospital deal yields much more even though we sell less. On the other hand, I see the advantage of receiving income instead of having to pay for a marketing campaign as a byproduct of the deal."

At that point, Clark pulled rank and took the lead in the discussion: "I'd like to get a good assessment of the potential for any loss on the deal, but it must be realistic and take into account our current state of fairly low profitability. If there is a possibility of a loss from the Events to Remember deal offset by huge benefits due to the indirect marketing campaign, then I'd like a conservative assessment of the potential increase in sales to evaluate the overall impact."

"Actually, Clark, you're going to need both a conservative, call it pessimistic, and an optimistic assessment to validate what might be the full range of impacts from such a significant decision." Raphael interjected. "Remember, we also have an offer from a large hospital where the price reduction is more acceptable than what Events to Remember is willing to pay. I believe Linda can win more deals like that."

Linda promptly characterized the second opportunity "Selling donuts to hospitals will not improve Daily Bread's image in the market. The food in hospitals is of the lowest level and everybody knows it! I'd prefer that no one knows that the donuts in the hospital are from Daily Bread. Personally, I believe that a low price to Children's Hospital would not impact the price to the other hospitals we already sell. But, if we start selling to hospitals more broadly, the lower price could undermine our prices to other major clients. The high socioeconomic market segment is the one on which we need to focus. This is a clear strategic opportunity."

Clark answered, "I understand your point; however, we need numbers to make a decision. Can you provide me with some?"

Robert, the VP of Operations, decided this was the appropriate moment to participate in the debate. "Before you go into just the financial aspect of those deals, the first question is: **can operations deliver?** I'm concerned that we might not be able to supply both Events to Remember and the new hospital simultaneously. I want to thoroughly check the volume from both deals. I intentionally keep some protective capacity to be able to withstand some incidental peaks in demand. We just need to make sure that none of our other clients is impacted. I want to be certain that our protective capacity is maintained."

Clark continued along the same line of inquiry. "I assume you are mainly worried because of the ovens. Can't we quickly gain capacity from Oven #2, which operates only 12 hours a day? Events to Remember mainly puts on their events in the afternoon or evening, while right now the pressure is on us to supply early in the morning."

Robert retorted: "Yes, but it could be expensive. We can definitely use more of Oven #2, which we are only using from 6pm until 6am. It is idle during the rest of the day. However, I'd need to hire another technician to ensure smooth operation of all the ovens. The cost of electricity will also go up; energy is a substantial expense, as you know. We need to take into account that Oven #2 is older and less efficient than Oven #1."

Robert continued to layout the picture from the angle of operations, "Now, we'd also probably need to employ a few more people to prepare the products before they go into the ovens. I know you all complain that the ovens' utilization efficiency is not high enough. The problem is, in order to get more product through, we need to maintain a smooth flow to and from the ovens and the pace is not all that uniform right now. We might have better overall utilization when Oven #2 becomes fully operational 24 hours a day, but don't expect miracles. Now, if the exposure from Events to Remember boosts sales from our regular market, then I'm really uncertain we'd be able to deliver, day in and day out, to the very high on-time standards our customers have grown to expect."

Linda said, "We spoil our customers and that's exactly what I want! Our competitors are all over the place on delivery timing, sometimes fine, but often quite late. I pick up a significant amount of ad hoc business because of it. It is often a reason we win new customers. They get sick and tired of the hassles. If we lose our near perfect on-time-in-full credentials, we'll be under pressure to differentiate on price; yet, everybody tells me we aren't earning enough as it is."

Raphael chimed in, "Actually, from the load numbers I have examined, my impression is that both opportunities can be undertaken. We might need a few more people. I'm not sure about it, but it could be very worthwhile. Several months ago, I was exposed to a somewhat different way of presenting the required information for such decisions. Let's give it a try."

He hands out a single sheet of paper to the rest of the management team. (Tables 8.1, 8.2 and 8.3 represent the contents of that piece of paper.) He continued, the Table 8.1 represents the margins when we subtract just the truly variable costs (TVC). The practical meaning of the Throughput, or T, is the money from sales that we get to keep offsetting the cost of running the bakery:"

"The average daily Throughput had better cover all the other costs of our operations, which I call Operating Expenses or OE. Our daily OE averages $16,872, so it leaves us with an average daily net profit before taxes of $427."

Raphael continued his explanation, "If you look at the Table 8.2 which shows the impact of the Events to Remember deal, based on predicted average quantities per day (without any boost to regular sales), it adds the following revenues and resulting Throughput:"

Table 8.1 Daily Bread Current Average Daily Production Load

Products	Price/unit	TVC/unit	Throughput/Unit	Daily Sales in units	Daily Throughput
Bread (basic)	$1.20	$0.3600	$0.8400	4000	$3,360
Bread (premium)	1.50	0.4500	1.0500	3000	3,150
Donut	0.78	0.2145	0.5655	6000	3,393
Donut (special)	0.81	0.2350	0.5750	4000	2,300
Roll	0.72	0.2200	0.5000	6000	3,000
Roll (special)	0.78	0.2560	0.5240	4000	2,096
Total					$17,299.00

Table 8.2 Anticipated Typical Daily Orders from Events to Remember

Event to Remember Products	Qty/day	Regular Price	Events to Remember Price	Revenue	Throughput
Bread (basic)	120	$1.20	$0.720	$86.40	$43.20
Bread (premium)	120	1.50	$0.900	108.00	54.00
Donut	160	0.78	$0.468	74.88	40.56
Donut (special)	160	0.81	$0.486	77.76	40.16
Roll	160	0.72	$0.432	69.12	33.92
Roll (special)	160	0.78	$0.468	74.88	33.92
Total				$491.04	$245.76

"Likewise, the National Children's Hospital deal adds the following financial impact, if you look at Table 8.3:"

Table 8.3 Anticipated Daily Orders from National Children's Hospital

National Children's Hosp. Product	Qty/day	Regular Price	National Children's Price	Revenue	Throughput
Donut	800	0.78	$0.700	560.00	$388.40

As Raphael explained the tables, Clark seemed downcast. Looking up from his calculator, he asked, "So, both deals only increased our daily Throughput by $634.16? It's just 3.7% more T. Somehow I thought the impact would be far greater."

Raphael answered: "Yes. But, assuming we don't need to spend more Operating Expenses, and this assumption must be carefully checked, then our daily profit would grow from $427.00 to $1,061.16. Therefore, the potential growth in profit, without even considering increases to our regular sales, is almost 150%!"[2]

Before this overwhelming news had a chance to sink in, Robert intervened again: "Wait a minute, don't get excited yet. This is only true if we have enough capacity currently, otherwise we'll need to activate Oven #2 for more hours every day and that's not cheap! I almost hate to point out here that we are looking at the sales of a typical day. However, there are days when demand is higher, such as Mondays. The protective capacity I maintain takes those normal fluctuations into account."

Clark responded, "Okay, we need to somehow evaluate our capacity boundaries and the cost of activating Oven #2 for additional time. Robert, can you explain how you calculate the capacity of the ovens?"

Robert responded, "My best assessment is we can produce a maximum of 50,000 regular donuts. That quantity would fill the ovens, using Oven #2 the way we currently do – only 12 hours a day. Now, to make our different products comparable, I translate all the other products into donut-equivalents. Regular bread, for instance, is equivalent to 3 donuts and rolls are 1.5 donuts each, from the perspective of their required space and time in the oven. So, our basic capacity unit is one donut. Every product's capacity requirement is expressed in those terms."

---

[2] $634.16 in added profit / 427 in current profit

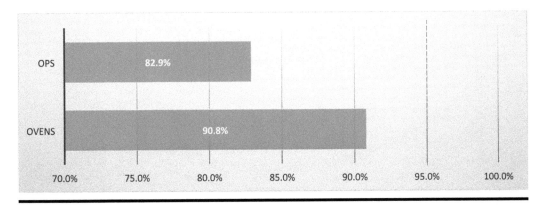

Figure 8.1   Current capacity profile for Daily Bread.

Robert went on, "Let me emphasize that we can NEVER reach that theoretical maximum of 50,000 units. I use a practical maximum planned capacity of 95% of the 50,000 donut limit, to make sure we can withstand any incidental fluctuations and maintenance problems, plus peaks in demand. After all, in our business and with our quality commitments, we just can't hold inventory for more than 24 hours. Even with 5% slack in our production capacity, I'm forced to crank up extra hours of Oven #2 periodically during the year to catch up. If I didn't have that option, I'd have to leave more like 15% to 20% spare capacity."

Raphael took over, saying, "Robert and I worked on the capacity data and it is represented here." He passed out a second sheet of paper to each of them with four capacity charts. Figures 8.1, 8.2, 8.3 and 8.4 represent the contents of that second piece of paper.

"This is the capacity profile of a typical day." Raphael said, pointing to the top chart on the second page. (See Figure 8.1)

Raphael went on, "As Robert told you, on Mondays, the load is higher but the ovens still don't penetrate the 95% limit as marked on the chart by the red dotted line. Most of our customers ask for a fixed quantity every day, so the daily fluctuations aren't bad. I wonder how Events to Remember's actual demand is going to fluctuate day to day. Anyway, Events to Remember is a small part of our overall production and their fluctuations should be easily handled by the protective capacity Robert maintains."

"You can see that operations – our direct labor – are less loaded than the ovens and they remain below the 95% line. We don't have much slack to play with here. Robert insists that the 95% limit should not be penetrated to ensure smooth feeding of products into the ovens. Otherwise, we'll end up wasting what capacity we have on the ovens."

Robert interrupted to reinforce what Raphael is telling them, "Please guys, don't forget Murphy's Law. Unless everything, and I mean everything, goes perfectly, we can expect total chaos in the bakery when our plan exceeds a 95% load on any resource group. Sorry to interrupt, Raphael, but I just can't emphasize enough the importance of dealing with reality and not theory for this decision."

With a nod of thanks to Robert, Raphael continued, "Now, let's look at that same chart, if we were to add the average daily orders we expect from Events to Remember and that is shown in the second chart." (See Figure 8.2.)

"As you can see, I'm showing the new demand from Events to Remember in orange and added that utilization onto our current loads. Now, all this additional load can be accommodated from our spare capacity. Thus, there would be no change in our operating expenses."

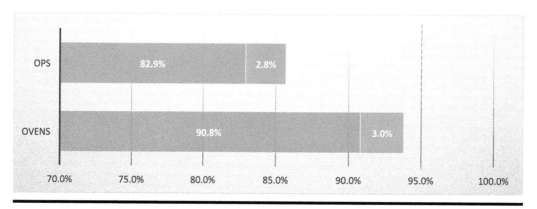

Figure 8.2 **Capacity chart showing current volume + Events to Remember.**

"Let's go on to look at the typical day's load, plus the 800 donuts for the hospital, for the time being, without the Events to Remember order. I want you to see that we can handle that additional order alone." (See Figure 8.3)

Clark added, "It is amazing to see what these relatively small orders do to our profitability and capacities. I had no idea that highly discounted orders, which I frankly thought would be real losers, actually make such a contribution to the bottom line. Does everybody find this kind of meeting where we review our opportunities against these capacity charts as useful as I'm finding it?"

There were general murmurs of assent. The members of the management team were nodding their heads and looking around at each other, seeing firm agreement.

Raphael continued his presentation: "As you can see from the first page, the one with the tables, selling an extra 800 donuts for just 70 cents brings more Throughput ($388.40 versus $245.76) and requires less capacity than the Events to Remember deal." (Refer back to Tables 8.2 and 8.3 together with Figures 8.2 and 8.3.)

Now, Linda interrupted: "But, the Events to Remember deal might result in more regular sales at our regular prices! How do you account for that?"

Raphael explained, "That is going to take a little more effort. There are a couple of caveats we need to check before we consider the increase in regular sales. Note that, if it is possible to accept both customers without having to increase capacity, then there is no point discussing which one brings more Throughput for utilizing the additional capacity from our key resources. We want

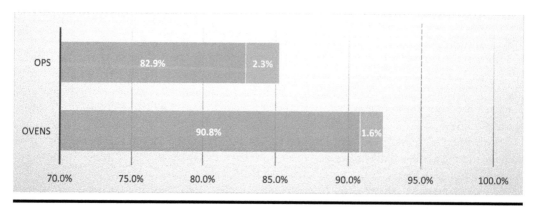

Figure 8.3 **Capacity chart showing current volume + National Children's Hospital.**

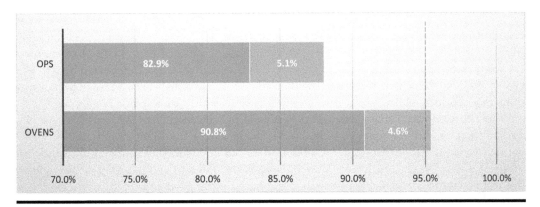

Figure 8.4 Capacity chart current volume + both new customers.

both orders, since both have a positive impact on the bottom line. It is only when we run out of capacity that we should check whether it is better to add capacity or raise our prices enough to curtail sufficient orders to remain within a load we can handle."

He continued, pointing at the last capacity chart, "If you will look at this chart, it indicates what both deals do to our capacity after handling normal daily sales." (See Figure 8.4)

"What we see here is that we are on the verge of a problem. While our staff is still capable of producing everything without overtime or additional people, the ovens have penetrated beyond the 95% line, although only by 0.41%."

Robert reacted to the precise calculations: "When you print out these charts with decimals and everything, they appear to be very precise numbers but they certainly are not! As I have explained, the capacity units I provided are approximations. These are a typical day's sales – averages. They fluctuate. And, the 95% line is my best guess but it is still just that."

"When the numbers on the production plan are just a little beyond my limit, I prefer to take a conservative approach and increase capacity by extending the hours of Oven #2. However, that means extra costs which offset at least some of the additional Throughput. Still, I'd rather avoid scrambling and having to make apologies to customers for late or missed orders. After all, we are talking about Daily Bread's reputation here! On the other hand, going barely past my admittedly arbitrary rule of thumb would probably not create a problem, with the exception of a few days each year. I just get nervous that you all will come storming into my office and blame me when your pet customer gets shorted."

Raphael carried on, "Right, this is a business decision that's above my pay grade too. Let me reinforce what Robert just said: adding capacity is only one way to deal with running out. The alternative way is to reduce the sales of products that yield less Throughput per capacity consumption of those resources that are exhausted. We can theoretically achieve a reduction in sales of specific products by raising prices, however, we can't be certain how successful that strategy will be."

"Even a small price increase may eventually cause too many customers to switch to a competitor but we won't necessarily know right away. As Linda pointed out to me a year ago, a lesson I still remember well, this is because we are not a really significant vendor for most of our customers. It won't kill them to just pay the increase for a while until they have the chance to evaluate alternatives. Worse, this also means that we wouldn't get the relief we were seeking right away on our constraint resources. It pays to be cautious here, because we necessarily rely on opinions that could easily be too conservative or not safe enough. That is why I like Clark's approach of utilizing a reasonable pessimistic to optimistic range for us to consider."

Linda responded, "What exactly do you mean by 'it pays to be cautious?' We always try to be as conservative as we can and still reality sometimes beats us. So, we need to be even more conservative? I see myself as a conservative and responsible marketing person. I hate to take chances unless I'm pretty darn certain. I don't want to drive any of my customers away. They are too hard to win over in the first place. That would put an extra burden on my salespeople. More importantly, I think they'd be demoralized if we drove away the customers they are so proud of winning."

Raphael responded, "Being cautious means carefully considering all the ramifications. No, we don't want to drive customers away, but we might need to consider such a move in order not to drive away ALL of our customers because we can no longer meet our commitments! All I suggest is to try to get a realistic picture built upon the opinions and intuition of everyone on this team that looks reasonably like what could happen, the good and the bad. We assess the range and then make the decision. As a finance guy, I want to translate the inputs and outputs into numbers. Recognizing that there is uncertainty leads me to look for a range of possible outcomes."

Clark jumped in as well, wearing his CEO's hat. "Guys, guys, I see what you are saying. We all should remember that we are in business to make money. We will listen to everybody and make as good an assessment as we can. But, our priority is to increase our earnings year after year. If necessary, those sensitive salespeople will have to learn to get sales at good prices and to understand the impact of any reduction in price on Throughput. The sales that don't produce enough Throughput across our most constrained resource are subject to being dropped anytime demand is greater than our safe capacity, even if that means losing those customers."

"Plus, I know how salespeople work. After all, I used to be a salesman myself! It is the customer who butters your bread. A smart salesperson goes to bat for their customers, usually by giving them the **best** possible prices and service. We don't know how elastic our current prices are. I'm game for testing the limits and I'll take responsibility for the outcomes."

Raphael nodded his agreement now that his boss had taken the risk of others being blamed off the table, he continued. "Good. Now, let's see what happens after taking these two deals when regular sales grow due to the fantastic exposure our products will get at occasions organized by Events to Remember. Linda, can you give us a reasonable pessimistic assessment of how much sales will increase?"

Linda: "I cannot give you a number. Any commitment to a specific number is almost certainly a lie. Let me only say that such exposure should give us, overall, at least 5% more sales after 3–6 months, unless we spoil our A+ reputation and ship half-baked rolls to a major conference or some other such disaster. On the other hand, if we make a favorable impression in the eyes of the highfalutin market segment, then our sales will grow nicely; say by more like 10%, again within 3 to 6 months."

Raphael seemed pleased with her answer: "That is good enough. When it comes to assessing the future, we've got to live with a certain level of vagueness when we make decisions. Linda's intuitive sense regarding increased sales is enough to outline the potential range of results, both financial and to our capacity status."

"To understand the overall impact of the decision on our financial performance, let's assume every product would increase its sales by 5%." Raphael walked over to his open computer and started typing. "Let me adjust the first table with the increased number of units sold. Hang on, this won't take a minute. I have it all set up and just need to input Linda's low and high side estimates."

They fell into chatting with one another while they waited for Raphael to adjust his spreadsheet and turn on the overhead projector that he had requested the hotel to provide in the meeting

Table 8.4 Both New Customers + 5% Sales Lift

Products	Price/unit	TVC/unit	Throughput/Unit	Daily Sales in units	Daily Throughput
Bread (basic)	$1.20	$0.3600	$0.8400	4200	$3,528
Bread (premium)	1.50	0.4500	1.0500	3150	3,308
Donut	0.78	0.2145	0.5655	6300	3,563
Donut (special)	0.81	0.2350	0.5750	4200	2,415
Roll	0.72	0.2200	0.5000	6300	3,150
Roll (special)	0.78	0.2560	0.5240	4200	2,201
Total	(Includes ΔT from + 5% Volume = $864.95)				$18,163.95
Added ΔT from Events to Remember					245.76
Added ΔT from National Children's Hospital					388.40
Total T					18,798.11
Less OE without added capacity					16,872.00
New Daily Net Profit					$1,926.11

room, so that each of them could see the impact. There was excitement tempered by anxiety that they wouldn't be able to say yes to the new business.

Raphael finished and duplicated his screen to share with them, saying, "This Table is the one you saw before with the added assumption of 5% more sales." (See Table 8.4)

"As you can see from the second to last row, our current daily Operating Expenses are $16,872. So, the potential exists for a daily profit of $1,926.11, if it is possible to contain Operating Expenses at that rate of daily flow?"

Robert is surprised and exclaims, "Wait a minute. No way! What about the materials we purchase? When we produce more, we need more raw materials. Then, with these volumes we would certainly need to add hours on Oven #2, which means more OE.

Raphael soothed him by saying, "First of all, we don't need to worry about purchasing more materials, because those costs are handled by the Throughput calculations and are not part of the operating expenses. Unless you tell me there is a problem increasing your purchases of raw materials – it's not an issue."

"Regarding the possibility of penetrating into the protective capacity of the ovens, and also that of direct labor, let's review the result of the detailed calculations. You can see it on this chart." He showed Figure 8.5 on the screen.

They all looked at the chart on the screen. Once everybody had a chance to review the update, Raphael continued his analysis. "Based on Robert's cautions, it is clear to us all that this load is unacceptable. If we can't resolve it one way or another, the quality of our products and mainly our on-time delivery performance to our clients, would take a severe hit. Generally speaking, there are two ways to resolve overloaded capacity.

He put his index finger up, "One – **produce less of some of regular products.**" He added a second finger for emphasis, making a 'V.' "Second: **quickly increase capacity.**"

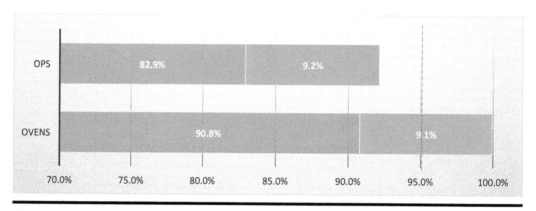

Figure 8.5 Current volume + both new customers + 5% lift.

"The option of limiting the sales of one or more products reduces the total Throughput, as well as the load on our resources. The right approach is to choose products that yield lower Throughput per oven-hour, thus, ensuring our total Throughput goes up, not down! I'm sure Linda can tell us more about the negative consequences of telling loyal customers that we are no longer able to supply them. Right, Linda?"

Linda's head dropped and it was a moment before she said anything. Finally, she raised her eyes and looked directly at Clark, not Raphael, and said, "Well, I'd like you to understand the possible ramifications on sales. This is a complicated topic. I'd love to dump one particular, relatively small, distributor. But, then we lose all the products that distributor is currently buying, not just the products we'd like to reduce. Actually, this is the same risk we face with curtailing sales of a particular product to any customer – the distributor or retailer might feel forced to look elsewhere and stop buying our other products as well."

Clark responded: "As we've discussed, a risky, but possible, way to reduce the demand for one particular product is to increase its price. As you say, we cannot know in advance the exact impact of a given price increase and, therefore, we don't know how much it should be. I'm aware that some customers claim that increasing the price even on just one SKU is unfair. But as demand increases, this is what usually happens – the price goes up – supply and demand." He crossed his forearms with his hands extended, making the familiar X-shaped supply and demand curves.

Clark continued, "I've been thinking about that issue for some time, because I feel our prices for regular bread and possibly donuts are too low. This is the main reason I wasn't happy with the offer from Children's Hospital. Still, I understand the merits of selling a large quantity that doesn't compete with our regular sales."

Raphael, who was still standing in front of them, said, "All right, let's see if we can avoid even a small risk of lowering our sales volume through price increases. First, let's analyze the option of adding capacity. We went through the cost of energy and included an additional technician for Oven #2. Robert, can you summarize what the union agreed to?"

"Sure," Robert replied. "When I approached the union leaders about the extra technician, they liked the idea but want it to be continuous scheduled time. Specifically, they want to avoid 15 minutes here and an hour there. They feel it isn't fair to a technician to have him sit around, not always being paid. If a guy drives in, it needs to be worth his while. I understood their issue and agreed but I told them I didn't want to be forced to always run Oven #2 for a whole shift as we've had to do in the past when we needed to catch up with demand.

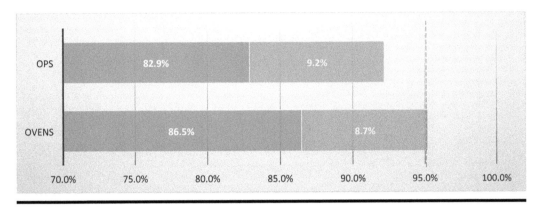

Figure 8.6   Current volume + both new customers + 5% sales lift with 2 extra hours on Oven #2.

After some discussion, we agreed to add the tech we need to operate Oven #2 in two-hour increments. Each block of two hours buys us 5% more daily capacity through the ovens, enough to bake up to 2,500 additional donut-equivalents." Robert looked at Raphael and nodded to let him know he was finished.

Raphael jumped right back in, "To add two hours of Oven #2, the additional expenses of the technician and power would be about $300, which does not include any overtime from direct labor. Here is the capacity chart after adding two more hours on Oven #2." All the eyes in the room darted to the screen to see what is presented here as Figure 8.6.

"While Throughput remains the same, expenses go up by $300. Still, the open question is whether the additional capacity is sufficient."

Robert's brow was furrowed. He spoke up. "I really don't want to be the one who always sounds pessimistic, but my main problem now is the load on my direct labor. Especially when the load on the ovens is also high, there is a need to guarantee smooth supply of ready-to-bake products. In other words, when the ovens are already heavily loaded, it pays to ensure we don't waste any critical oven time by not being ready to load and unload them. So, to be safe, we'll probably need some overtime to reduce the pressure on the direct labor to keep pace with the ovens. Guys, my experience is that if I take one resource to 95%, I better ensure the others are no more than 90%. It gets crazy if more than one resource gets overloaded. You don't want to see that, believe me."

Raphael responded, "OK, suppose we add 10 hours of overtime – say five people working two additional hours each. This would also cost $300." His fingers were flying over the keyboard on his laptop. In seconds, a new capacity chart was projected. "So, the daily net profit would end up at $1,326.11[3], a very nice growth in profit. Our current profit is only $427. The multiplication of profits by 3.1 makes our current $427 in daily net profit look downright puny! Here is the full impact of adding 10 man-hours of overtime on capacity." (See Figure 8.7)

Robert nodded. "This will do! I can manage the two new discount customers, plus an additional 5% of our regular load and still maintain our operational excellence. However, what if the increased regular demand is even higher given Linda's optimistic estimate? Then, the additional capacity might not be enough."

Clark commented, "Good thinking. I'd love to multiply our profit before taxes. For me, it is almost too good to be true. The fact that the Events to Remember deal does not cause an outright

---

[3] $1,926.11 potential net profit – $300 for 2 oven-hours – $300 for 10 hours of overtime

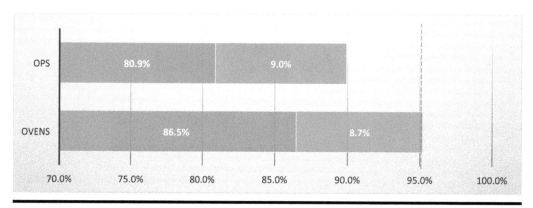

Figure 8.7 Current volume + both new customers + 5% sales lift with 2 extra hours on Oven #2 and ten hours of overtime.

loss is a huge comfort. With such a quick analysis of any idea based on the intuitions of both Linda and Robert, the picture of how our company actually works is much clearer. It helps me overcome my fears."

"Wait a minute." Linda interrupted them before they could move on by asking, "Robert can you help me out? I'm confused. It's probably something obvious, but why has the capacity needed for our regular business fallen? Look right here on the original sheet you handed out with the capacity figures." Her red fingernail stabbed at the original blue bars. "The capacities are 82.9% for operations and 90.8% for the ovens before the additional demand is considered. We haven't changed that basic demand at all. Yet, the blue bars on the screen now read 80.9% and 86.5%. Both are down. Why?"

Robert answered her. "Linda, you are absolutely right. The basic original load did not change at all. But, remember that we have changed the capacity by adding more time both in operations and on the ovens. The numerator stayed the same but the denominator got bigger. That accounts for the drop. Given our increased capacity, the old load uses up less of the total available capacity. Makes sense?"

Linda nodded. "Of course! Duh. I get it now. Sorry to slow everybody down. I was stuck on that point and I wanted to make sure I was with you before you went any further. Please, carry on, Raphael."

Raphael smiled at her, thinking to himself that he wished more people wouldn't pretend to understand finances, just to protect themselves from looking stupid in the eyes of others. He appreciated Linda even more for her bravery and self-deprecating humor. He glanced around the room, thankful to be a member of the top management team at Daily Bread. Then, he projected the updated profit calculations, as shown in Table 8.5.

Clark continued, "So, if we consider this as the pessimistic scenario, we also need to check the optimistic assessment. Robert needs to be prepared. What higher costs would be required to produce the optimistic demand?"

Raphael said, "Okay, let's check the load first this time. There is no point me projecting potential profits until we know if we can make it." His fingers clicked the keyboard of his laptop for a few moments. He quickly said, "Nope, the additional two hours of Oven #2 and 10 hours of overtime aren't close to being enough. Robert, come help me here."

Robert got up and walked over to where he could see Raphael's laptop. They collaborated, mumbling and pointing for a minute. Eventually, Robert nodded and returned to his seat.

Table 8.5 Updated Net Profits Based on Pessimistic Sales Lift with Added Capacity of Oven #2 and Overtime

Products	Price /unit	TVC /unit	Throughput / Unit	Daily Sales in units	Daily Throughput
Bread (basic)	$1.20	$0.3600	$0.8400	4200	$3,528
Bread (premium)	1.50	0.4500	1.0500	3150	3,308
Donut	0.78	0.2145	0.5655	6300	3,563
Donut (special)	0.81	0.2350	0.5750	4200	2,415
Roll	0.72	0.2200	0.5000	6300	3,150
Roll (special)	0.78	0.2560	0.5240	4200	2,201
Total	(Includes ΔT from +5% Volume = $864.95)				$18,163.95
Added ΔT from Events to Remember					245.76
Added ΔT from National Children's Hospital					388.40
Total T					18,798.11
Less Current OE plus 2 hours of Oven #2 plus 10 hours of OT					17,472.00
New Daily Net Profit					$1,326.11

Raphael quipped, "Yep, with 10% more business, the load on both the ovens and the direct labor force blew through Robert's capacity limits."

Nodding his agreement, Robert explained, "Okay, we know what we have to do here. We'll need yet another two hours from the oven and two more 10-hour blocks of overtime, bringing the required total OT to 30 hours."

As he said this, Raphael projected the now familiar bar chart shown in Figure 8.8 onto the screen.

"I can't wait to see how much we make under this scenario!" Linda said.

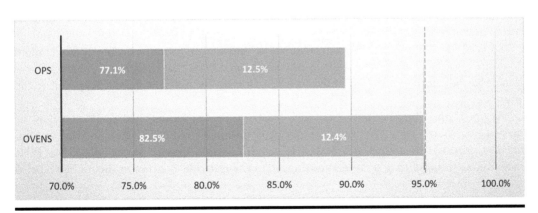

Figure 8.8 Current volume + 10% sales lift + both customers with 4 hrs of Oven #2 and 30 hrs of overtime.

Table 8.6   Net Profit with + 10% Sales Lift + Both Customers with 4 hours of Added Capacity on Oven #2 and 30 hours of Overtime

Products	Price /unit	TVC /unit	Throughput / Unit	Daily Sales in units	Daily Throughput
Bread (basic)	$1.20	$0.3600	$0.8400	4400	$3,696
Bread (premium)	1.50	0.4500	1.0500	3300	3,465
Donut	0.78	0.2145	0.5655	6600	3,732
Donut (special)	0.81	0.2350	0.5750	4400	2,530
Roll	0.72	0.2200	0.5000	6600	3,300
Roll (special)	0.78	0.2560	0.5240	4400	2,306
Total	(Includes ΔT from +10% Volume = $1729.9)				$19,028.90
Added ΔT from Events to Remember					245.76
Added ΔT from National Children's Hospital					388.40
Total T					19,663.06
Less Current OE plus 4 hrs of Oven #2 plus 30 hrs OT per day					18,372.00
New Daily Net Profit					$1,291.06

"Isn't this strange?" Raphael said with a puzzled look on his face, "Let me show you." And, with that he projected Table 8.6 on the screen for them all to see.

"A better response from customers of 10%, instead of 5%, makes the projected net profit **drop** from $1,326.11 to $1,291.06! While it is still much better than what we have today, I guess all that high-priced extra capacity uses up more OE than the T increases. That surprises me! Yep, the ΔOE for the optimistic evaluation is $1,500 per day[4], which is $900 more than the pessimistic ΔOE of $600. At the same time, the added T between the optimistic and the pessimistic is only $864.95."[5]

Raphael continued, almost as if he were speaking to himself, "The conclusion we can draw is that the current prices we charge don't always cover the ΔOE of extra hours of Oven #2 and the cost of overtime. Crap!"

Raphael realized he hadn't given them any sense of the other option, reducing demand, might do to the capacity problems they were facing. He decided to do that right away. Otherwise, how would they be able to develop any intuition about which of the different approaches to utilize and when?

As he finished his thought, Raphael looked up. Seeing he still had their attention, he carried on, "Now, I suggest we check into the option of reducing sales, instead of adding any capacity, to understand how that scenario would impact our results. This Table includes one column that is more important than the rest. The column in the middle labeled

---

[4] $300/2hrs of oven time × 2 + $300/10hrs OT of 5 workers per day × 3
[5] 19,663.06 of T with both new customers plus 10% sales lift − 18,798.11 of T with both new customers plus 5% sales lift

Table 8.7 Throughput Generators using Ovens (8 items)

Products	Throughput / unit	Oven Donuts	Throughput /Donut Eq.	Base Qty	Δ Qty	Throughput
Events to Remember	$245.7600	1,504	$0.1634	0	1	$245.76
Bread (basic)	0.8400	3.0	0.2800	4000	400	3,696.00
Roll (special)	0.5240	1.5	0.3493	4000	400	2,305.60
Bread (premium)	1.0500	3	0.3500	3000	300	3,465.00
Roll	0.5000	1.4	0.3571	6000	600	3,300.00
800 NCH Donuts	388.40	800	0.4855	0	1	388.40
Donut	0.5655	1	0.5655	6000	600	3,732.30
Donut (special)	0.5750	1	0.5750	4000	400	2,530.00
Total						$19,663.06

'Throughput/Donut Eq.,' shows the Throughput contribution from one standard capacity unit of the ovens, our most loaded resource." (See Table 8.7)

As they scrutinized this latest table, Raphael explained what they were seeing. "It is not surprising that the Events to Remember deal is at the top of the list of worst contributors since the 40% reduction in price provides a meager Throughput, while the load to produce those products remains the same. However, since that deal is the direct cause for the fantastic increase in regular sales, we'd be crazy to eliminate it. In the future, when we achieve a stable higher demand without being dependent on this kind of marketing, we should re-consider the role of Events-to-Remember, depending on our capacity profile at that time."

"The next best option is to limit the quantities of regular bread sold. If the combined quantity of regular bread is limited to 2,800 units, then my calculations confirm that the plant can handle both new customers, plus a 10% increase in regular sales of all other products. The capacity bar chart looks like this." (See Figure 8.9.)

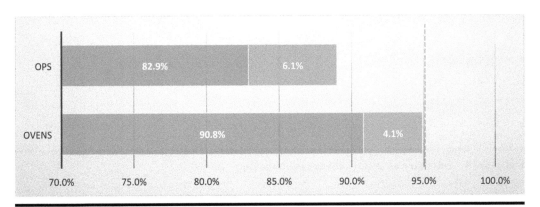

Figure 8.9 Current volume w/2,800 basic bread limit + both new customers + 10% lift (except basic bread).

"I've got good news and bad news. The good news is, if we ditch sales of just 1.200 loaves of our regular bread sales, and not accept any of the lift on that category that results from the Events to Remember exposure, from a capacity point of view, there's no need for any added Operating Expenses at all! However, dropping sales of basic bread by 1,600 units[6] reduces Throughput by $1,344.00[7]. This action drops total Throughput from $19,663.06 to $18,319.06. That's the bad news."

Raphael continued on, "Overall, in this scenario, the resulting net profit is $1,447.06[8]. This is the best profit yet, if we can hit exactly that amount. What these numbers are telling us is that our profit is quite sensitive to the number of loaves we sell."

Linda followed up on Raphael's caution, "So, resolving the lack of capacity by limiting the sales of bread is fully dependent on my team's ability (or lack of it) to sell 1,600 units, or any other number, less than the expected demand without collateral damage to sales of our other products."

Raphael went on, "I made a diagram of the options we just went over. Let me type in the net profit amounts. In each of them, ΔNP refers to the additional profit above the normal profit of $427." His fingers danced again over the laptop's keyboard for no more than a minute. "There you go. This is a summary of our six options:" (See Figure 8.10.)

Clark rose from his chair and dramatically bowed to his CFO. "Thank you, Raphael. I don't think I have ever had such great data presented quite this well." The rest murmured their assent, as Raphael sat back down in his chair, waving his hands at them to stop.

Once they quieted back down, Clark's face became much more serious. He looked around the table, catching each person's eye, one by one. Then, he said, "Friends, we are now in a situation where we should check our pricing." They all looked around at each other, wondering where that

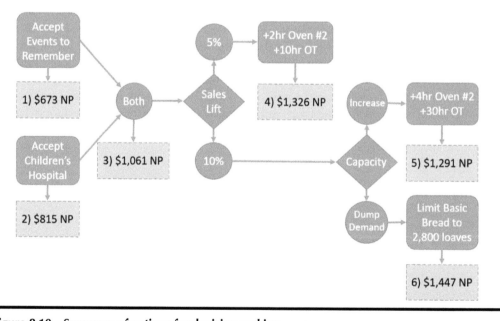

Figure 8.10   Summary of options for decision making.

---

[6] 400 units of lift + 1,200 units already being sold
[7] 1,600 units of dropped sales × $0.84 T per unit
[8] $18,319.06 of T − $16,872 of OE

comment had come from and what he meant. After all, company profit was going to increase dramatically, so why delve into pricing issues now?

Clark went on, showing them his ability to think out into the future, by saying: "The goal of this company is to make more and more money as time passes. We can't do that without growth in our revenues. Actually, now that I know what it is, I prefer to look at our growth in Throughput. Now, we have to ensure that our Operating Expenses (OE) do not grow even faster. This beautiful decision diagram is warning us that we have to be very careful."

He continued, "I mentioned to you before that I sensed our price on basic bread, one of our staples, is too low, of course given certain reasonable assumptions about the potential impact of a price increase on the demand. For the first time, I have seen the data that proves it." He turned directly to the CFO and said, "Thank you, again for such a clear presentation, Raphael!"

As he looked back at his team, he could see that they didn't fully understand him. So he explained: "One reason companies go out of business or stagnate is because, to grow revenues, they feel compelled to first buy new capacity, taking on OE. Until they gain enough new T to become a larger, more profitable entity, they don't earn enough T to support their expenditures. We are flirting with that situation right now! We make less money with ten% sales lift than we do with five%. This means that the cost of adding extra capacity isn't covered by the Throughput we gain from the additional sales. Now, this does not mean all our sales generate insufficient T to cover the cost of extra capacity. Therefore, we should focus our price analysis on the products that yield the least T per capacity of our ovens and our operators."

"If our customers like our products and service, we owe it to them to find a way to satisfy their demand, even if we are forced to use expensive added capacity. However, we have to insist on gaining additional profit for our greater efforts, meaning that the ΔT must be bigger than the ΔOE for the extra capacity. When we have enough confidence in our ability to attract more demand, we will be able to add the appropriate man-hours at our regular pay rates and then operate the ovens for only the cost of the energy required. In other words, once we know the true sales lift, we'll hire more people. We need to be careful that every increase in OE is eclipsed by the increase in Throughput it makes possible. Raphael's new process we went through plus the supporting tools to visualize the loads and the profitability scenarios allow us to be both daring and yet check carefully the ultra conservative side."

Clark continued to explain his vision. "If the demand were to persist at higher prices, then we'd be able to afford maintaining more manpower than we need on average, provided we still have extra oven-hours to run when there is high side fluctuation. This situation is especially handy when lucrative new short-term opportunities are identified. It is cheaper, also better for most of our people, to work regular hours rather than be expected to do overtime on top of their regular hours."

Robert interjected, "You are right Clark. It is not always easy to find volunteers for even one or two hours of overtime at strange hours. At first people jump on it to give them the money to do something fun or special but it becomes a burden after a short while. If we do it a lot, I'm worried about turnover."

Clark nodded and resumed his train of thought. "Our basic bread is the natural first candidate for a price increase. If the maximum capacity of our ovens is 50,000 donuts per day in 36 oven-hours[9], then in one hour we can do 1,389 donuts[10] or 463 regular bread loaves[11]. Given that the

---

[9] Oven #1 for 24 hours per day and Oven #2 for 12 hours per day

[10] 50,000 donut-equivalents per day / 36 hours per day

[11] 1,389 donut-equivalents / 3 donut-equivalents per loaf

T per loaf of bread is 84 cents, the T we generate from baking regular breads for one hour in one of our ovens is $389[12]. Raphael, what's the extra cost of an oven-hour plus the overtime needed to flow products through it?"

His CFO was ready with the answer, which showed he was tracking Clark's line of thinking. Raphael said, "It is $375 per hour[13]. However, let me warn you, that amount is only correct if we use all the extra hours for baking. Any unused hours would raise our effective cost per hour of premium capacity."

"You see?" Clark asked them. "*At best*, $375 of ΔOE per premium hour is too close to $389 in ΔT per hour from producing bread. If the exact quantity we need is somewhat less than what can be in produced in two or four oven-hours the ΔOE might not be covered by the ΔT."

Raphael provided some perspective by adding, "Clark, 'might not' might not be strong enough." He smiled at his pun and continued, "If we waste more than 3.6% of any block of premium capacity, we will lose money on any regular bread we make during it and sell![14]"

Robert was scratching his head as he said, "Wow. That really puts what you were saying into perspective, Clark."

Linda added, "Yeah, all these numbers are great but what I want to know is, do I tell my salespeople to put on the brakes with regard to selling bread or what?"

Clark smiled at her and responded, "Thank you. That is a great question you asked, Linda. It challenges us to break our inertia around our main staple, bread. Before we had the insights from Raphael's new process, we would have just earned less money than we could have and been blissfully ignorant. This new knowledge gives us a target to improve the T per loaf of bread and find less expensive ways to temporarily increase capacity. I think we should raise the price by 15 cents and see what it does to demand. We might want to also increase the price of the premium bread to keep the relative price difference between the two the same. He turned to Linda and asked, "Linda, what do you think? Will it work?"

Linda digested his words for a minute. She continually suffered from salespeople who promise the moon and then deliver much less. She had sworn to herself that she would not become one of them. Finally, she said, "Boss, the market has a lot to say about prices. Our customers are aware that we are not the only bakery they can use. That being said, it is my sense that raising prices today from $1.20 per loaf to $1.35 would not cause much of a negative reaction from customers. We haven't raised prices on bread for years. My market surveys from the salespeople indicate that competitor prices range from $1.25 to $1.45 on basic breads. We have been aggressive on bread pricing. On the premium breads, I'm comfortable, for now, with going up 20 cents per loaf. I expect these price increases will have a limited impact on the demand – maybe the demand would remain the same, instead of increasing by 5% or 10% like I previously suggested."

Raphael was ready to check the ramifications of increasing the prices on both categories of bread, assuming the original quantities of bread would remain stable – up because of the Events to Remember marketing and down an equal amount due to price competition. He asked Linda, "What do I do about the bread prices for Events to Remember?"

---

[12] 463 loaves × $0.84 of T per loaf

[13] For example, they required 4 extra oven-hours plus 30 hours of overtime to accept the two new customers and the optimistic sales lift. The added cost for the premium capacity per hour was ($300 per 2 oven-hours × 2 + $300 per 10 hour block of overtime × 3) / 4 hours.

[14] 100% − $375 ΔOE per hour of bread produced / $389 ΔT per hour's worth of bread sold

Table 8.8   The Impact on NP of Price Increase Plus 5% Sales Lift

Products	Price /unit	TVC /unit	Throughput /Unit	Daily Sales in units	Daily Throughput
Bread (basic)	$1.35	$0.3600	$0.9900	4000	$3,960
Bread (premium)	1.70	0.4500	1.2500	3000	3,750
Donut	0.78	0.2145	0.5655	6300	3,563
Donut (special)	0.81	0.2350	0.5750	4200	2,415
Roll	0.72	0.2200	0.5000	6300	3,150
Roll (special)	0.78	0.2560	0.5240	4200	2,201
Total	(Includes ΔT from +5% Volume = $539.45)				$19,038.45
Added ΔT from Events to Remember					270.96
Added ΔT from National Children's Hospital					388.40
Total T					19,697.81
Less Current OE plus 2 hours of Oven #2 plus 10 hours of OT					17,472.00
New Daily Profit Net Profit					$2,225.81

She responded, "My deal with Events to Remember is 40% off our list prices. So, if we go up, they go up. No way am I going to argue to hold their prices."

After a short break of 10 minutes Raphael was ready with the figures: "Let's start with the price increase on the two breads and sales lift of 5% except on the bread. Here is the overall impact." He projected what is shown in Table 8.8.

"Assuming the sales of the two bread items neither grow nor drop, due to the price increase, the resulting T goes up significantly because every dollar of the price increase goes directly into the T. As we have learned, it is important to see the capacity profile including the additional capacity:" See Figure 8.11, which he then showed them.

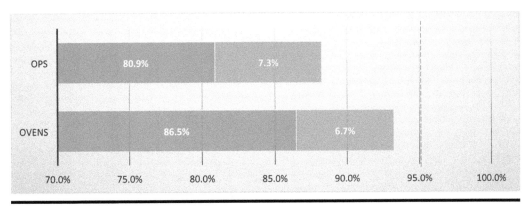

Figure 8.11   The plant load after a price increase on breads and 5% sales lift on other product categories.

Table 8.9 The Impact on NP of Price Increase and 10% Sales Lift

Products	Price /unit	TVC /unit	Throughput /Unit	Daily Sales in units	Daily Throughput
Bread (basic)	$1.35	$0.3600	$0.9900	4000	$3,960
Bread (premium)	1.70	0.4500	1.2500	3000	3,750
Donut	0.78	0.2145	0.5655	6600	3,732
Donut (special)	0.81	0.2350	0.5750	4400	2,530
Roll	0.72	0.2200	0.5000	6600	3,300
Roll (special)	0.78	0.2560	0.5240	4400	2,306
Total	(Includes ΔT from +10% Volume = $1078.9)				$19,577.90
Added ΔT from Events to Remember					270.96
Added ΔT from National Children's Hospital					388.40
Total T					20,237.26
Less Current OE plus 4 hrs of Oven #2 plus 20 hrs OT per day					18,072.00
New Daily Profit Net Profit					$2,165.26

"As we see both the ovens and our people, with 10 hours overtime every day have plenty of protective capacity. Ready to see the impact of sales lift of 10%?" Seeing heads nodding, Raphael projected Table 8.9 on the screen.

Raphael explained what they were seeing. "Once again, what we see here is that the Throughput from the increase in sales fails to cover the cost of the further increase in capacity, both the oven and the manpower. But, have a good look on the capacity profile after adding the 4 oven-hours and 20 hours of overtime." He displayed the bar chart shown in Figure 8.12.

"In order to process the additional sales lift on the four non-bread product categories, it requires a second block of 2 hours of the oven and also a second 10 hour chunk of labor at overtime rates,

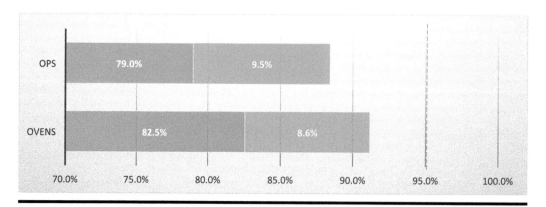

Figure 8.12 The plant load after a price increase on breads and 10% sales lift on other product categories.

however, barely so. Had we kept it at one block of extra oven time, the load was 95.5%, barely over Robert's 95% utilization limit. With the extra block of oven time, the load is only 91.17%. Really, it is almost the same story with the labor. We can almost do it with only one ten-hour block."

Clark beamed "That's good for now. It will be hard to hit the 10% sales lift figure anyway. If we do come up a little short, we'll get away with only an extra two hours using the oven and ten hours of overtime, plenty of extra T and a huge net profit. If we do happen to hit the +10% high side target, Linda, can you lose the few loaves of bread necessary?"

"Now, you are talking!" Linda said. "I know exactly how to reduce bread sales by small amounts, like a few hundred loaves. Remember the distributor I mentioned before. They could find themselves on allocation during heavy production days. That's easy peasy!" She was smiling contentedly.

Clark pointed at her with a smile and said, "Yep, you're on it! We'll also have to check our assumption that the impact of the price increase on the bread products will be limited. Maybe there will be some lift after all."

Robert chimed in, "Eventually, we'll come to better, more flexible, arrangement with the union. They wanted a block of time to make it worthwhile for the employees to stay over. It doesn't make sense that we can ask five people to stay for an extra two hours but not give them thirty minutes more once they are already there. The same thing for the tech that supports the oven. Why wouldn't he prefer the extra half an hour too, right? I'll talk it over with the steward. When we get to the point of needing to hire more full-time employees, the cost of such capacity increases will be at much less of a premium."

Clark followed that by commenting, "As I said, we definitely know what to do now to continue improving. Raphael will you please show an updated version of that awesome decision diagram, so we can see the big picture?"

Raphael responded, "Aye, aye, Captain. As you wish." Almost immediately, Figure 8.13 appeared on the screen.

Clark spoke up again, "Great work, Raphael! I'm impressed all over again."

Raphael felt he should use an abundance of caution and reiterate a point that was now obvious to him but he wanted to be sure the others really understood, so he said, "Please remember that, since OE increases in stairsteps, there will be places along our path between these numbers with

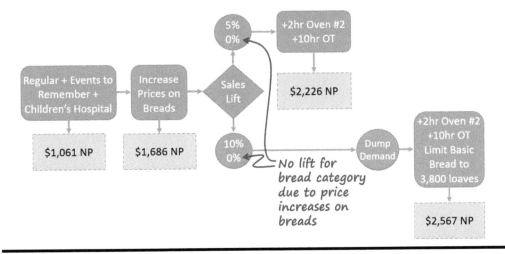

Figure 8.13   Summary of options for decision making including price increases on breads.

higher and lower profitability. The point is, we shouldn't focus on finding little niches of maximized profitability. We ought to be thinking about continuing our growth."

Clark carried on with, "I agree. Thank you for making that clear."

"Well, it's obvious that we want both deals. Keep in mind, as good as Linda is, even she can't accurately guess how much the demand will grow due to the deal with Events to Remember. Furthermore, once we start to supply their events, the boost in sales won't be sudden. We can wait and see how much the demand actually grows. Robert, be ready to add capacity when necessary. You better get ready to add the first two hour block on Oven #2. Then, the necessary man-hours to maintain the smooth flow through the ovens. You understand the implications of our fluctuations in demand better than anybody else and how to maintain a Capacity Buffer to protect the flow of our products. You are authorized to use overtime at your discretion, without the normal approval from me."

"Linda, I want you to stay on top of how our price increases are impacting sales and whether there is any unexpected impact on the sales of other products. I don't want to be caught by surprise here. As soon as you become aware that some of our assumptions are incorrect, call for a meeting so we can all review it."

"Raphael's what-if scenarios taught me that unless we get enough Throughput from our products, we are in danger of being unable to maintain profitable growth through this ungainly phase in which we must rely on very expensive emergency capacity. We shouldn't limit the sales of a product that is important to our good customers but I want more than enough Throughput from it to cover the costs of premium OE!"

Clark continued. Speaking to them all, "I'm very encouraged. It seems our little bakery is going to make much more money. I'd like everyone to be on the lookout for more opportunities like these in the future. We now know how to obtain pertinent information, including reasonable uncertainty levels and how to analyze any idea, no matter how crazy it seems. After all, I never expected those two opportunities would have such an impact on our bottom line. And, if you think about it, **the new opportunities were not actually the big contributors. It was the indirect benefit of the analysis that helped us finally raise prices that haven't made sense for years!**"

"I have a wild idea that I'd like to check with all of you soon – to offer daily direct-to-home delivery of our products very early in the morning. Nobody is offering such a service in our city. We'd probably need to use a third-party logistics provider for such a move. The question is: will the approach increase our bottom line or decrease it?"

Chapter 9

Using What-if Analysis to Support Mutual Decisions

We are all used to making decisions based mainly on intuition. We support them with certain measurements that tell us how good the decision will be. For instance, we intuitively recognize the need to come up with more attractive services. Then, we must determine pricing for the new services. We expect calculations, such as the difference between our cost and the selling price, to tell us whether the impact of our new idea will be accretive to profits. The most relied upon metric which commonly results in distortions is cost per unit, a main topic in the previous chapters. More sophisticated calculations might come up with a weighted number that represents the relative cost-benefit of every alternative.

One perilous flaw of using a single weighted metric to make a decision is that it usually only factors in parameters stemming from that particular idea or decision itself. Holistic side effects are typically ignored, such as the possibility of negatively impacting other sales or opportunities. Perhaps worse, decisions based on a single metric can inadvertently impinge on the protective capacity required to avoid chaotic operations and its cascade of negative symptoms. Thus, the same decision could yield an excellent outcome in one case and produce a devastating loss under different circumstances.

Sadly, this realization is not widespread. As mentioned in Chapter 2, the usual approach is to evaluate the proposed idea in isolation, while ignoring its holistic ramifications. Even if there is an awareness of the potential for blunders, decision makers may lack a process to consider interactions and global consequences or find such considerations too unwieldy to be practical at the pace with which their decisions are required to be made. How would a typical management team evaluate the Events to Remember offer? It seems reasonable that they would evaluate two cascading decisions:

1. As a relatively unattractive business proposal, the CFO or a delegate would have the key role. Using the difference between the offered price and unit cost, it is likely the proposal would be rejected, because they (perhaps inaccurately) conclude it would lead to a loss.
2. As a marketing move, is it worth the potential loss? In many cases, the decision would be turned over to the VP of Marketing to decide whether the 'loss' added to the marketing budget is worth the predicted outcomes.

The Daily Bread case, and its detailed analysis, demonstrated that there are two critically important variables that impact the bottom line: the whole organization's expected Throughput and the capacity required to deliver the entire demand relative to the total available capacity. Lack of capacity could turn an apparently good deal into a miserable one. Having available capacity could make a seemingly unattractive deal a real gem that adds substantial profit.

Uncertainty is another, not less important, aspect. How should one evaluate the probability of a loss versus the possibility of significant profit? There is no way that a single number, no matter how it is determined, can support an effective decision-making process. Uncertainty means there is always a range of various organizational and personal ramifications. Mathematics uses two parameters, at the very minimum, to describe any stochastic function. This was a particular hot-button of statistician and management guru W. Edwards Deming.

The previous chapter demonstrated a very different way of making decisions. Here are several key points of this decision-making process:

Decisions are made by the top management team through direct interaction during a meeting, NOT by the most relevant executive who makes the decision and possibly shares it with other executives for feedback. The full analysis should consider the impact on the organization as a whole. To do so, it must be evaluated by the entire top management team, relying on their intuitions, which are typically most effective in their specific areas of responsibility. The idea behind the proposed decision may have been initiated by lower level people but then it is the responsibility of the executive to bring the idea for analysis by the whole executive team.

The decision under consideration is put into the context of all the currently expected activity of the organization. Only then is it possible to ask: how does the decision impact the goal of the organization? Practically, this means maintaining sales and capacity profiles that represent the current reality of the organization, before new decisions are contemplated.

The use of Throughput rather than sales is a vital factor. Wide acceptance that Throughput (T) is what truly represents the added value created by the organization is absolutely necessary for every organization. The generated T should be higher than the necessary operating expenses (OE) required for providing the available capacity. The T over some period of time should be used to judge any return on investment (ROI).

Changes in Operating Expenses (ΔOE) resulting from the decision at hand should always be due to penetration into the protective capacity of one or more resources, thus requiring a quick increase in these capacities. Facing the increase in demand, due to Daily Bread's exposure of during Events to Remember occasions, required greater utilization of the second oven, including additional man-hours and energy cost, which constitute the ΔOE of the decision to accept the Events to Remember offer.

What-if scenarios that consider the whole organization are the core direction for any good solution. Analysis of these scenarios predicts what might happen when that decision is implemented on top of the regular activities. For instance, the idea of the hospital asking for a reduced price was translated into a what-if scenario in which it was added to the current situation to evaluate the changes to T and OE. Later, that decision was combined with another decision to accept the offer from Events to Remember. This was only decided after determining and carefully checking the combined effect, including the prediction of T growth from current customers. Similarly, any new suggestion, such as buying a competitor to laying off a team of operators who produce seemingly unprofitable specially customized products to small clients, can be presented as a scenario in which that decision is added to or subtracted from the current state.

Dealing with significant uncertainty requires TWO what-if scenarios for every decision to be analyzed. One is based on a **conservative** (reasonably pessimistic) assessment, while the other is a reasonably **optimistic** assessment of the possible outcomes. Both scenarios are absolutely required for decision making. Each scenario should be reasonable, meaning that it's not exaggerated by including overly rare cases that the planners should ignore. By developing both scenarios, each one based on reasonable judgments, it defines a boundary of the area where we **know we don't know.** The range between the reasonable extremes are totally realistic, even though we have no idea exactly what will happen. When we expect market demand to be above a certain level, yet not higher than another level, then our best expectations are that the actual market demand will fall between these values. We had better be prepared to satisfy any level of demand within that range. Both scenarios are translated into numbers, reflecting the financial and capacity ramifications of undertaking the decision on top of the regular activities. Depending on the resulting capacity and possible changes to the offering which are required because of lack of capacity, a realistic scenario and its range of bottom-line outcomes are defined. This range of possible results reflects the best available information.

This process typically leads to checking various **COMBINATIONS of potential decisions.** Each opportunity should first be individually checked as additions to the current sales and capacity profiles. In this process, some might be rejected. Then, it is imperative to check the **combination of the plausible decisions since** every action has an impact on capacity. Thus, the total impact is verified again against the possibility that several of the opportunities might have to be passed over. There may be advantages to substituting something new for less attractive current sales and adding more capacity of certain resources.

Be aware that outside the likely range are extremes where we know we don't know. There are more possibilities where we don't know we don't know – surprises. It could be the case the outcome lies beyond the reasonable range defined. We simply need to be mentally ready for such circumstances and accept them as an infrequent part of the reality in which we live. If the vast majority of our decisions lead to results that lie within the expected range and the consequences of the rare outliers are not catastrophic, then we are in the best situation that our capabilities allow us.

The key takeaway is that **the true contribution of an opportunity can only be checked when it is combined with everything else the organization is doing.** First of all, we have to check the impact of the decisions under consideration, on top of all other current activities, on the total sales, also taking into account the impact on sales beyond the considered decisions. This check should yield the contribution of the opportunities on the total Throughput. Then, the total impact on capacity is carefully checked, making sure that enough protective capacity is still available. This is absolutely necessary in order to check whether Operations has the available capacity to deliver.

This is quite a different process from the norm today. It is imperative that all the proceedings are prepared and every top manager is aware of what is expected.

Preparing for a Top Management Session

There are two major preparation efforts for these periodic meetings. One is to **compile the data based on the expected sales before any new decision is made.** This data should include the capacity consumption of current sales, which constitutes the **"reference profile."** The available options for adding capacity, along their associated costs, are important, if there is a chance of exceeding the current protective capacities when more opportunities are revealed. The load and economic impact of every plausible opportunity is added on top of the reference levels. Blended results are compared to the status quo, checking whether or not the idea improves the bottom line.

Another advance effort aims at having a ready list of new possibilities to be checked and discussed at the meeting. It requires a junior person to approach every top executive, get the descriptions of new ideas to be discussed in the meeting and make sure all the required data for each idea is captured. Every idea for which demand is uncertain must include two reasonable expectations from the proposal – a conservative assessment and an optimistic one. Each idea requires calculations to provide the initial net impact of the idea on both Throughput and capacity.

The Daily Bread example had two major opportunities: The Events to Remember opportunity and the Children's Hospital order. The expected numbers for both ideas were prepared prior to the meeting. The hospital deal had fixed quantities for a given price; thus, there was no need for two assessments.

The required data, drawn mostly from the organization's existing database, is used to build the reference profile. In simpler cases, a spreadsheet or paper, pencil and calculator may be enough. For a more user-friendly approach try an appropriate software package[1].

Every proposal should be presented in a standard template, so it can be readily added to the reference profile. Usually, such an idea involves only a few SKUs, their expected sales together with Truly Variable Costs (which are used to calculate T) and consideration of their indirect effect on the sales of other items. The Events to Remember offer involved an expected impact on ALL items sold, but this is uncommon.

The Meeting and the Analysis Discussion

1. Every opportunity is first checked on its own terms – does it generate positive T or significantly reduce OE? If this condition is not met, there is no reason to consider the idea further.
2. Next the idea is checked regarding its impact on other sales and the combined impact on the Throughput. Events to Remember's offer yielded little added Throughput on its own but its positive impact on other sales and the resulting additional T made the deal lucrative. In other cases, the secondary impact on other sales could be negative. For example, offering a customer a discount, which eventually forces competitors to offer lower prices, undermining a portion of a marketplace. When the resulting change in Throughput is negative, the idea should be rejected unless it allows a reduction in OE that is greater than the lost T.
3. The next step is evaluating the total capacity profile. If, and only if, the protective capacity of even one resource is penetrated, then the participants in the meeting should either find ways to add or free up capacity or reject the idea.

As was demonstrated in Chapter 8, there are two broad ways to deal with lack of sufficient capacity. One way is to free capacity by reducing some existing sales, by either increasing the price or limiting the quantity to a specific customer or market. The other way relies on increasing capacity within the relevant timeframe.

It is certainly possible to combine both approaches. These actions should be discussed and decided upon during the meeting itself since the knowledge of the relevant managers is necessary to confirm that such a move is possible in the specific case and to identify any ramifications on other areas.

As such decisions are carefully reviewed, the final phase of the meeting is dedicated to checking the feasibility of accepting the combination of **all** the decisions that passed their individual

---

[1] DSTOC, Decision Suppose in the TOC Way, developed by Vector Consulting Group from India, is such a software package, developed according to the specifications of Eli Schragenheim.

plausibility tests. The procedure for dealing with a lack of capacity is considerably more challenging. At this stage, freeing capacity can be done by giving up one or more of the new opportunities, even though they passed the ΔT - ΔOE first and second checks. The option to reduce sales of other products is also open. Then, all the options for adding more capacity, which increase costs, should be evaluated as well. The range of outcomes between the conservative and optimistic scenarios might compel the management team to take certain calculated risks.

Eventually, a set of decisions, both on Sales and Operations, are made. Management must agree on their risk tolerance, assuming the outcome will be somewhere in between the combined conservative and optimistic scenarios.

Frequency of Meetings and the Role of an Appropriate Decision Timeframe

Top management shouldn't meet too often, certainly not daily. Significant new opportunities do not usually appear that often. Even if they do, there is typically time to digest the implications and prepare the data for analysis. A monthly meeting seems appropriate, which can be canceled if there is nothing new to consider and capacity remains sufficient. If the company is overly busy, especially then, it is short sighted to cancel the meeting, because a new opportunity could possibly be far better than the current ideas. It might be a shame to delay a new game changing idea, as difficult as reversing previous decisions is for many. Generally speaking, those meetings should not take too much of management's attention capacity. The benefits of identifying potential new opportunities can be huge.

Another related topic is the time horizon over which a decision is contemplated. The Daily Bread example has some uncommon characteristics that make checking the capacity profile simpler than in many other manufacturing environments. Analyzing the demand and capacity for just a typical day is appropriate for Daily Bread, but not for most other organizations. The reader understands the decisions Daily Bread management discussed were not for the short term, certainly not for one day. Both decisions were for the mid to long term. But, for Daily Bread, daily operations match daily demand simply because the option to hold finished goods inventory is limited due to the speed with which baked goods become stale. Therefore, in Daily Bread's case, the analysis of the reference profile of a typical day is good enough to realize how the organization would address the new deals on top of regular sales, including the predicted increase of demand of regular sales. In a short lead time situation, such as daily production that fluctuates heavily, the analysis should have identified a reasonably heavily loaded day as a reference. It might be a strategic issue to decide how much to produce for a certain day of the week, if it seems consistently different from other days. Certainly, the weekend days and Monday might have consistently different demand than the other days.

Most manufacturing and service organizations have more flexibility in planning their weekly or monthly operations. Typical production lead times can range from a few days to many months. This may mean that the routine horizon of the decision-making meeting evaluating the desirability of short-term opportunities has to include a whole month, or even a quarter, in order to properly consider changes in the offerings to the market and changes in capacity.

New opportunities and other ideas that impact longer time frames, such as a year or more, as well as decisions requiring substantial investments should be analyzed based on demand and capacity data over more lengthy time periods. Normally, the uncertainty of expected demand over the long term is much greater than over the short term. Consequently, it is natural that the range of outcomes that are considered reasonable is much broader, making decisions more difficult with non-trivial chances of producing a loss. Still, the process provides the best available information at the point in time at which the decision was adopted.

The Critical Difference between the Throughput Economics Approach and Detailed Production Planning

The analysis shown in Chapter 8 is basically different from the need to plan every day exactly what should be produced that day, including the exact use of each resource and the sequence of work. The decision support mechanism demonstrated in Chapter 8 does not go into detailed production planning. Naturally, that plan would vary from one day to the next. The conclusion with regard to Daily Bread showed that it is worthwhile to accept the two offers that were on the table: both the daily delivery to the hospital of 800 donuts, and also the offer from Events to Remember, which on top of the quantities required for the events is expected to increase regular demand. The analysis presented the required additional capacity according to conservative and optimistic scenarios and also validated a very significant increase in the profit.

The case also considered the impact of price increases on two product groups, revealing that, as long as the price increase does not impair current demand by too much, the impact on the bottom line is bigger than intuitively expected. The case reveals that the translation of an idea into T and OE is always enlightening and frequently surprising.

Daily Bread still needs to evaluate every single day what needs to be produced. We assume that the daily sales are produced that day, in order to ensure freshness. In such a case, the daily firm orders must be collected as early as possible. They may also produce to stock, assuming unplanned demand may occur during the day. It requires the production planner, together with the sales team, to decide on the quantities and sequence of each product. They also need to determine whether additional hours on Oven #2 are required and, if so, how much more manpower to deploy that day. The analysis considered the level of protective capacity, including the Capacity Buffer which could be required. This book does not go into the detailed daily production planning practices that should ensure fast and reliable flow to deliver all the demand.

The Impact of the New Process on the Behavior of Top Managers

In almost every company, there is a significant gap between actions actually taken and what should have been undertaken. Adopting new rules for making key decisions has important ramifications on the desired behavior of the decision makers. We expect every top manager to actively peer into the future and frequently discover moves that help the company's overall performance improve continuously. This is the essence of the duty of every executive in the organization.

Does this behavior actually occur? If not, what are the core reasons?

The commonly prevailing approach of measuring performance against specific targets is focused on the recent past. Thus, the metrics themselves shift the behavior of top managers to focus disproportionately on the short-term and even to limit improvement initiatives, in order to demonstrate stability and reliability, as opposed to periodic leaps in performance. It seems that sudden improvements frighten board members and shareholders much more than it makes them happy.

The suspicion is that any sudden improvement is accomplished at the expense of the future and that the instability, positive as it seems to be, is deemed too risky. This perception and the managers' own worry that they may run out of big ideas, compel many managers to be overly cautious.

Our suggested decision-making process exposes actual risks by presenting both reasonable scenarios, circumventing fear of risk. This clarity of awareness of inherent uncertainties reduces the possibility and the impact of an unwelcome surprise.

The mutual decisions of management can be easily documented so that even relatively extreme results are, to a certain degree, expected and well understood. Individual executives may fear that after-the-fact analysis, using hindsight made clear by an outcome which is viewed as negative, might endanger his or her career. Our mutual decision-making process, especially when the risks are calculated according to the information available at the time, vastly reduces the concerns of managers regarding their own personal risk of blame.

Moreover, the approach creates a (sadly) rare culture that encourages taking actions that bring value, even though the pessimistic assessment occasionally materializes. Not less importantly, it also prepares all the managers for the possibility of significantly higher demand, along with its own challenges, such as a failure to meet commitments to the market, which can endanger the company's reputation. Making mutual decisions with a fully cross-functional team that considers likely low and high extreme outcomes provides the managers time to prepare for any reasonable scenario.

The top sales executive should be expected to actively develop new opportunities through the sales team. The ability, in the monthly top management meeting, to quickly assess all the ramifications of every opportunity, certainly the impact on capacity and finances, opens the door to a flood of alternatives to consider. Being exposed to the range of possible results and involving both Operations and Finance encourages raising any potential opportunity for discussion and eventually reaching a decision via consensus.

The operations executive should seek the best options to deal with fluctuations in demand. Maintaining Capacity Buffers and the option to deploy additional manpower are two important mechanisms to stay in sufficient control of both costs and newly identified opportunities.

The CFO is the ideal person to lead preparations for the meetings and then also be in charge of the analysis. Looking into the future and letting people express their intuition and encouraging them to translate that intuition into conservative and optimistic assessments may seem atypical for a CFO. The ability to lead the discussion on strategic issues, consider intuition and uncertainty while understanding the nonlinear behavior of capacity costs, should be the criteria for that job. When a CFO is not capable of leading such a discussion with the other top managers, then the CEO should take the lead.

Chapter 10

T-generators and Critical Resources—Two New Required Terms

The terminology used by the Theory of Constraints (TOC) community is quite unique and requires explanation, because the terms used are not to be found in a regular dictionary. The TOC terms used thus far are Throughput and Operating Expenses. As this book expands the scope of the current TOC body of knowledge, advancing "Throughput Accounting" into "Throughput Economics," some new generic terminology is necessary. This chapter introduces two additional terms and explains why they are necessary.

Critical Resources

Every organization is made up of resources with required capabilities and finite capacity. It is quite common to make a distinction between direct and indirect labor. It is certainly possible to do so when "direct" means drawing a straightforward connection between a specific customer's order and the capacity required from a specific resource. Somehow this distinction is applied to human resources but not to equipment and buildings.

Is it Helpful to Utilize this Categorization?

Even for a direct-labor worker, such as the operator of a machine, it might be difficult to quantify how much net capacity is consumed by a specific workorder, because many times the operator is simultaneously watching several workorders going through the same or different processes. The capacity of every indirect resource, such as the IT person who supervises the ERP system, is absolutely required to generate the Throughput. When the quantity of different products, and the number of work orders, significantly increase, that IT person or the whole IT department might run out of capacity, causing chaos throughout the shop floor. Alternatively, the IT staff might, in a different situation, be able to easily handle a doubling or tripling of the volume of work.

Another example is the people managing the raw materials warehouse. They are certainly not strictly impacted by a specific production workorder but they are affected by the total amount of inventory required and the number of different SKUs needed. It is absolutely impossible to allocate the load exactly against the available capacity of **every** resource. Thus, we don't see any benefits of making a distinction between direct-labor and all the rest of the required human resources. Since direct-labor fails to fluctuate directly with changes in production volumes, it is obvious that so called 'indirect-labor' does not lend itself to any form of allocation.

Do We Need to Monitor the Predicted Load against the Available Capacity of Every Resource?

Theoretically, since every resource has finite capacity, any resource might run out of time to finish its work. Thus, it seems we must monitor all resources to identify not only situations in which there might be a lack of capacity but any penetration into some resource's protective capacity, which might cause chaos in operations and the delivery of products and services.

In reality, because of the ultra-complicated and highly sensitive nature of any network of resources and workorders, **organizations simplify the operation of their internal systems by tolerating a high level of excess capacity.**

There is no practical way to keep adequate control of such an interconnected and interdependent system, like a company, without significantly wasting capacity. While it is theoretically possible that every resource could become a bottleneck,[1] practically speaking, the vast majority of resources cannot become bottlenecks without other resources becoming bottlenecks first. In practice, only a scant few resources might limit the creation of Throughput when a certain event or random cause occurs that puts too much load on that specific resource.

Even though organizational culture promotes efficiency, reality forces the management of organizations to tolerate excess capacity as long as it isn't flagrant. However, the common desire of management is to work towards very high utilization of all resources, which causes a chronic conflict between the drive for efficiency and the realistic understanding that excess capacity is necessary to achieve adequate delivery performance to customers.

Pressure is mainly applied to human resources, especially what is called direct labor, because when they seem 'underutilized' the situation is often interpreted as laziness, incompetence or lack of motivation. Low efficiencies are considered equivalently to wasting of money. It comes as no surprise then, that a special talent of employees is looking busy even when they are not. By that means, they avoid criticism, added workload and even layoffs – most of the time.

The perception of waste is felt especially strongly when expensive machines are idle for a significant period of time. Again, the blame is usually directed at the designated operators, less so toward the planners. This is why operators try their best to manage the pace of work so that their machine doesn't appear idle too long or they deliberately process more than planned, producing inventory that does not increase Throughput. Don't think this doesn't also happen in service industries but, in that case, the inventory is the largely invisible open tasks that have been started but seem to take forever to finish.

---

[1] A bottleneck is a resource that faces more work than it can process. In other words, the load relative to its available capacity is greater than 100%.

Dr. Goldratt, the developer of TOC, argued for many years about the need to recognize the simple fact that excess capacity on the vast majority of the resources is a must. He pointed out that pushing to improve local efficiencies results in inferior systemic Throughput and much lower profitability.

The term "constraint" is applied to the resource that most limits the performance of the whole organization. Every organization has only very few constraints. The term refers mainly to three possible types of constraints: raw materials, internal resources and market demand.

When demand from the market is the constraint, it means that the organization can easily serve more clients. Thus, it is clear that every internal resource has excess capacity.

It is relatively rare that some raw material is so scarce that the organization is unable to get enough of it. TOC does not treat the failure to buy enough material as a constraint; it just advocates identifying an effective procedure to eliminate that occurrence.

A resource within the company might become the constraint of the organization when some demand is not met due to the lack of sufficient capacity. A constraint is not necessarily a bottleneck; overall it might have enough capacity to process all the demand but not enough to deliver everything in the time frame expected by customers. The organization could have a capacity constraint loaded only to 80% on average, yet the organization still loses sales because that resource is not always able to respond, due to lack of capacity in the required timeframe.

A related term is "the weakest link" – which refers to the most loaded resource. The weakest link is the first place to become a constraint but remains a non-constraint when demand is lower than what its capacity can deliver. As a simple example of the weakest link, consider the number of seats in a theater. When a show is very popular, the number of seats are the obvious constraint. When most people who are interested in the show have already seen it, there will be unoccupied seats – seats are still the weakest link, but not the constraint.

Does TOC Claim that only ONE Resource Can Constrain the Whole Organization?

In an organization it is possible, actually rather common, that several different operational lines, which are responsible for different families of products and services, are each constrained by a separate resource, so long as they have very little direct interaction. In his book, *The Haystack Syndrome,* Goldratt analyzed the situation of **interactive constraints** and came up with a detailed and relatively complicated solution. The problem with interactive constraints is that oscillations of the actual load between them cause a waste of capacity due to "starvation," which causes instability in the time needed to deliver. The solution proposed by *The Haystack Syndrome* is just the least bad way to handle such a situation. Maintaining a reliable delivery of all the company's commitments to the market requires that no capacity constraint interacts with any other constraint.

What Happens when there is a Sudden Significant Increase in Sales?

The second variation on the P&Q example, in Chapter 6, showed that any significant change, such as the launch of an additional product, might disrupt the existing situation where one specific resource is the constraint and all others are non-constraints. A significant change might cause some current non-constraint to penetrate into its protective capacity and by that become a second constraint. If one constraint is an aid to focusing, two, or more, active constraints make managing nearly impossible, at least until bad service curtails customer demand enough to return the circumstances to one of a single active constraint.

This is especially true for new marketing and sales initiatives which impact the product-mix for meeting the new demand. Depending on the resulting mix of products, an emerging most-loaded resource might be different than the current profile. It is protective capacity that prevents small changes in product mix from causing the constraint to move unexpectedly.

When such a change in constraints takes place, the organization is under pressure to adjust very quickly. This suggests the need to closely monitor capacity utilization of all the critical resources that might penetrate their protective capacity profiles and have, at the ready, effective mechanisms to rapidly respond to the situation. As we have already covered, there might be more than one alternative solution. Thus, management has to be prepared to make an effective choice.

What Are the Criteria for Placing a Resource under Tight Capacity Control?

The first criterion is the probability of that resource having its protective capacity consumed. The following observation is an important consideration:

Organizations cannot afford to have too many resources likely to run out of capacity

This understanding clashes with pushing to achieve higher local efficiencies. Every time a resource causes trouble by dissatisfying customers, there is pressure to add capacity. If the cost of increasing the capacity is reasonable, then it may be authorized. However, when increasing the capacity of a resource is quite expensive, then operations is expected to tolerate the uncomfortably high load and find ways to reduce the consequences of occasional overloads, mostly by limiting the demand from the market. This can be achieved by increasing the quoted lead-time, but such a move might have future negative consequences.

Resources whose capacities are relatively expensive to expand have a higher chance of experiencing capacity limitations that impair reliable delivery. Many of those resources have enough excess capacity but others could be exposed to temporary peaks that use all their available capacity. It is important to monitor their capacity and check whether the predicted load might penetrate into their protective capacity.

There is another group of critical resources whose load has to be constantly monitored: **resources that are normally fully utilized, supported by an easy and affordable method to utilize external temporary capacity whenever necessary.** For example, there may be many freelancers or temporary workers available, or companies who provide outsourcing of a certain capability, such as transport services. When such resources are available, the concern is not running out of capacity, but controlling the expenses of utilizing the extra capacity.

Those two groups comprise the set of **critical resources.** It is important for any manufacturing or service company to have good enough information on the available capacity of every critical resource for every likely future load of products and services. The vital assumption is that by checking available capacity against the predicted load on these critical resources, decision-makers have the relevant information on what is possible and what is too risky to even attempt.

The ΔOE that our proposed process calculates only considers these critical resources. If there is certain knowledge of other resources that may require extra additional capacity, then that

ΔOE should be added to the cost of required additional capacity of these critical resources. In one of our next examples, we will evaluate such an expense when an export move is considered, which requires paying for offices and personnel at the export site.

T-generators

A straightforward scheme for a manufacturing company is to offer every product for a fixed price. Service companies also price their services without regard to who buys them or how much they buy. The same applies to retail where every product for sale has its own price. This approach is beneficial because of its basic simplicity and visibility. It is easy to calculate the sales for a mix of items since the total sales equals the sum of those of the individual items times each one's price.

Some wonderful opportunities for better business are lost this way. Maintaining fixed prices allows customers to pay just that price, even under circumstances when they are ready to pay more. Customers who can't afford a price or perceive the product offering to be of too little value avoid buying it.

Several business sectors use dynamic pricing schemes, selling the basic item, in various ways for different prices, thus enabling them to reach a wider market. Airlines, for example, developed a complicated scheme for selling tickets for their flights using a wide range of prices for an equivalent seat on the same flight. On the other hand, there are serious consequences from pricing in a way that is perceived as too opportunistic. Providers can generate ill will if their customers feel that the pricing model is unfair – by taking advantage of circumstances to force them to pay more while others pay less. Certainly, customers are encouraged to actively look for ways to pay lower their price. It creates a relationship that legitimizes cheating and negatively impacts the image of the airlines. Such practices can make customers vindictive – looking to settle the score and inviting the emergence of a competitor who radiates openness, visibility and fairness.

Most businesses try to find a "good enough" compromise between fixed prices and unscrupulous market segmentation that enables price differentiation for very similar products and services without causing animosity. Here are some broad guidelines to achieve effective market segmentation:

1. Selling the same items in relatively distant geographical locations. For instance, exporting the items to another country makes it possible to use different prices without affecting the prices in the domestic market.
2. Price reductions for large quantities. This includes rebates, when the quantities purchased by a client within an agreed period of time are above a certain level. Very large or high profile clients often get unconditional special prices.
3. Special sales for limited time periods after which the original price is restored.
4. Making small changes to a basic product, such as different product numbers, labeling, packaging design or using different brand names (like OEM's do) to misdirect consumers or justify various pricing models.
5. Combining several items together and pricing the package differently than the sum of the list prices. This includes offers things like a "baker's dozen" – selling twelve units and giving the thirteenth free or including a 'free' gift for orders over a certain size or buy one get one free.
6. Bundling services, such as an extended warranty or transportation, to create different offerings to clients for the same item.
7. Rush service for a higher price is another generic approach to price differentiation.

The variety of approaches to pricing the same or similar items **makes it necessary to differenti-ate between what is produced and what is being sold.** The word "product" is widely used for both purposes. The problem is that it creates a mental "box" where the norm is simply to sell the produced item as is. From time to time, there is a need to cause the market to draw more from a product, by using a reduced price applicable to all clients. By thinking out of the box, many oppor-tunities can be found to achieve price flexibility. Some ideas to penetrate a new market segment, usually with lower prices which may be viewed as unattractive to the seller, but depending on the available capacity, could be quite profitable.

There are marketing and sales people who are capable of thinking creatively. However, when management includes new approaches as an integral part of the organizational culture, then **it becomes the norm to consider many more options for selling the same basic product for dif-ferent prices, thus increasing Throughput considerably.**

Let's call the basic **output of operations: products.**

What is sold will be referred to as Throughput-generators (T-generators).

A product is either produced internally or purchased to be sold. Either way services can be bundled with the products or not. Basic information needed for any product is the truly variable cost of the raw materials that go into the product and the concurrent capacity requirements from the needed internal resources.

A T-generator includes, at the very least, a single unit of one product. The basic structure of a T-generator is a list of its raw materials and their quantities to the unit. For example, a laptop computer can be sold as the laptop alone or as a package that includes several accessories sold together as one T-generator. Such a package could include one unit of the specific laptop, one unit of a docking station, two units of an external 27" monitor and one unit of an external mouse – five items and four different products sold in one sale with one price.

Every T-generator also needs a price tag. Sometimes there is a need to consider additional truly variable costs (TVC) that are required by the T-generator, such as the TVC of special packaging required by the T-generator or the cost of additional services, such as home delivery and instal-lation. Also required for decision support is the sales forecast for each T-generator as a necessary input to assess the total expected Throughput and load on the resources.

A product can be a part of many T-generators. Each T-generator may include many different products and related services. This is a typical many-to-many relationship, where every product could participate in many T-generators, and every T-generator may include many products.

For instance, a regular donut is a basic product of a bakery. The cost of materials that go into one donut is the central element of the TVC of that product. Producing a donut requires capacities of both ovens and manpower.

A T-generator consisting of just one donut is certainly commonplace. The price tag for that T-generator minus its TVC yields the Throughput for each donut sold. Then, the bakery might have a package of six donuts, sold for 5% off the regular price for six donuts. A client, such as a hospital, might ask for daily delivery of 800 donuts and demand a price reduction of 12%. This is a separate T-generator, not 800 units of the regular donut, because it carries a different price. A significant client might order a mix of different products for an overall price; in this case, it is a T-generator built from the required mix of products with one price tag for the whole mix.

The current sales profile consists of all the T-generators and their forecasted sales for the time horizon over which the new opportunities to be considered are going to be analyzed. The horizon can be a week, a month is quite common but it could also be a quarter or a whole year. Determining the most appropriate time horizon is the first step, which dictates what data is required, such as the predicted sales for every T-generator for the entire period. It makes sense to use the average forecast for every T-generator in building, the sales profile, which serves as the reference context for every proposed idea. To achieve the objective of having a reference for judging the economic contribution of variety of ideas, it is not necessary to consider the pessimistic and optimistic estimates for each T-generator. The reason is that the important information conveyed by the reference is the average total Throughput and the resulting average load on the critical resources.

The inherent inaccuracy of capacity consumption does not grossly distort the results when one focuses on differences in T (ΔT) and the utilization of the protective capacity of every resource. Both inputs are aggregations of many individual items, hence, they are reasonably close to the actual total T and total load on the critical resources. A computer program, such as a dedicated one or simply a spreadsheet, can quickly calculate the overall load from a sales profile on the critical resources. The overall load relative to the available capacity of those resources over the time horizon is the current capacity profile.

New decisions may either change the parameters of several existing T-generators, such as the price and sales forecast, or require the creation of new T-generators. Of course, newly introduced products become new T-generators. New T-generators can also be just different combinations of existing products and services. Emphasizing an interest in new T-generators as a method for price differentiation and their impact on the capacity of the key resources can encourage the flow of new ideas from employees, especially from marketing and sales people.

The idea of packing products in various ways as a legitimate means of attracting demand and to charge different prices is a useful insight for any business organization. The advantage of packages in getting overall high T for moderate capacity of the truly critical resources is demonstrated later in this book with the help of a specific case.

Chapter 11

Finding More to Sell— Choco-for-You, Part 1

Many Small Decisions Constitute a much Bigger Impact

Creation of the new term "T-generator" is aimed at opening the mind to a variety of options. This means that growth in sales is not necessarily the result of introducing new products. Of course, we all know about promotions as a key mechanism to increase sales and there are many more options. Some of them are built from a combination of many small ideas. One lesson, which Clark of Daily Bread learned in **Chapter 8**, *is that a small increase in sales can lead to a significant change in Throughput and an even greater impact on the bottom line. Another lesson is that while every such small idea can be beneficial, it is imperative to check the combination of such ideas. Here is another case, which is somewhat more complicated than either Daily Bread or the P&Q, that evaluates some simple means to increase sales and the estimated impact on net profit.*

We humbly suggest that the reader tries to see the forest not the trees. We present quite a few numerical details about each alternative, the needed capacity and the various ways to free capacity. In the end, we show the simple, straightforward approach of looking at ΔT - ΔOE of both the pessimistic and optimistic scenarios.

Choco-for-You is a producer of chocolate in a small country. Its products are highly thought of and substantially more expensive than their competition. Jon, the CEO of the company and a major shareholder, is determined to dramatically grow the business of Choco-for-You. He is aware that substantial growth is risky, so he wants to identify a growth path which keeps the risks well within reason.

Like every single organization anywhere in the globe, Choco-for-you appears quite complex. It produces four different families of products, each manufactured by a dedicated production line. Yet, all of the products are packaged by a common packing line, which is the most loaded resource and considered Choco-for-You's capacity constraint.

However, this is not the full picture regarding the packing line. The old packing line, which was replaced only a year and half ago, is still in a good enough state to be used but is slower than the new line. It also emits a loud noise persistently that irritates the operators. In addition, the quality of the packing for the high-end products is also inferior relative to that of the new line.

The old line is kept in working condition so it can be used when there is higher than normal demand. Because of the noise and the difficulty meeting the quality standards, the union demands operating the old line for a full 24 hours, thus, ensuring good compensation for its operators. As a result, using the old line is relatively more expensive, but it reduces the concern that the packing line might become a bottleneck that disrupts the stable delivery to the clients and risks permanent damage to the long-term reputation of the company.

There is one more serious complication. Cocoa is a basic raw material used in chocolate production. Their country does not grow its own cocoa; it is being imported from Central and South America. There is only one local importer of cocoa that has an agreement with the government to subsidize a certain annual quantity of cocoa, keeping the price relatively low to support the country's chocolate industry. Three years ago, Jon signed an agreement with the importer, committing annually to purchase a fixed amount of cocoa every month at an attractive price. If Choco-for-You can't sell enough of their chocolates, they must take the remainder of the contract at year's end.

Due to all the other agreements the importer has made with other clients and in order not to exceed the subsidized amount of imported cocoa, the overall quantity held at the local importer is limited.

Alex, the VP of Operations, who is also in charge of purchasing the materials, is well aware that there are incidental losses, either in the warehouse due to damage or spills during production. These amount to 2 to 4% of cocoa used in a year, which could endanger delivery. So, Alex fought for and eventually succeeded to get the importer to agree that Choco-for-You has the right to buy up to an additional 1.2 tonnes, in special purchase orders of 100 kg at a time, above the committed annual amount per year. This additional raw material availability is 5% of the annual commitment of Choco-for-You.

Bill, the VP of Business Development, has also been worried that cocoa might become a constraint, thus preventing him from taking advantage of new business opportunities. Fortunately, he secured a source in Brazil who is ready to sell cocoa to Choco-for-You but, with shipping, customs and without the subsidy, it is more than double the normal price. As a result, Sherry, the CFO, hates the idea.

At the current average pace of production, cocoa use is about 96.5% of the basic commitment to the importer, not including the scrap. This percentage does not include the option to buy an extra 5% from the importer, if and when Choco-for-You needs it.

Another complication is that production line 2, which produces the most popular product family, is loaded up to almost 85% of its theoretical available capacity limit. Alex made it clear to the production planners that the 85% threshold is the absolute limit for planning line 2's capacity. The reason for that limit is to allow the packing line, which packs all the products, including line 2's, to be planned all the way up to 90% of its theoretical load limit, so delays are avoided. One must bear in mind that it is quite impossible to even approach theoretical limits anyway. Alex has discovered the hard way that he can't drive the work centers and the operators to higher overall utilization without damaging delivery performance, which is critical to keep the variety of clients loyal to Choco-for-You. Thus, Alex is quite pedantic about not loading the production lines higher than his 85% limit, as long as the packing line is planned even close to 90%.

This is the current regular load situation versus the available capacity:

Looking at Figure 11.1, recall that the packing line is the most loaded resource and it is very close to its limit, as defined by Alex. There is a delicate balance between the packing line, production line 2 and the limited availability of cocoa. The other three production lines currently have plenty of protective capacity but could also become critical, should demand shift. This is the core of the complexity in running the plant.

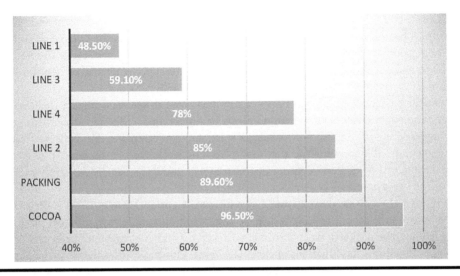

Figure 11.1   The normal average capacity load on critical resources.

Does this fact that lines 1, 3 and 4 have excess capacity point to new opportunities?

Jon had an idea, which he presented to his team: "Let's come up with different combinations of two products, maybe several units of each, into packages with a price that is 7 to 12% lower than the current prices combined. I'm thinking mainly of choosing products from different lines, one item that is a good runner and another item that is a slow mover. Maybe we can encourage customers to buy more products from us. Today, most customers buy sometimes from us and sometimes from our competitors. The price reduction for a two-product package would attract customers for whom our products are too expensive but only marginally. They may use the discount as an excuse to treat themselves. Other customers will buy exactly the products they like in the quantities they prefer and still pay the full price."

Jenny, the VP of Marketing and Sales, seemed a little hesitant. "A good idea but is also a little risky. I have learned my lesson that reducing the price by 10% reduces T by much more than 10%! When we sell discounted packages, the full-price sales of those component items will decrease but I don't have a clue by how much."

Bill, the VP of Business Development, laughed loudly, which seemed impolite, but that's typical of Bill's character. He said, "Really? You don't have a clue? You must have some idea. Most of those packages would reduce the component T-generators sales – so the reduction in sales will be more than zero. The reduced sales cannot be more than the original sales. We have to come up with reasonable pessimistic and optimistic assessments."

Jenny became irritated. She retorted, "To say that sales will decrease between 0% and 100% helps nothing. The real impact is unknown to us. I think I have very good intuition on what's going on in the market but I cannot provide a good prediction on a hypothetical move I've never experienced before."

Jon rushed in to calm the debate: "**We have intuition, which is our biggest asset, even more so than our logical brains.** I understand that trying a new strategy is subject to much less precise assessment than a known one. So, we should try it on a relatively limited scale at first and improve our intuition as we observe the ramifications. What I want from you, Jenny and Bill, is to come up with six different pairings together, along the lines I have described. For each coupling, suggest a price and give me your consensus estimations of reasonable pessimistic and optimistic forecasts both for the sales of the package and the negative impact on the sales of the individual items. I hope you can do that in two or three days. Once you have it, please give the numbers to Igor in IT to make sure one of his wunderkinds will feed the supporting load estimation program with this data."

Jon concluded the meeting: "Let's meet again next week to see what impact this small move has on our company. OK?" Seeing them nodding, he proclaimed, "Meeting adjourned."

Six suggestions for combination packages were duly prepared for the consideration of the management team of Choco-for-You that took place one week later. Jenny, the VP of Marketing and Sales, explained the general concept of relatively big packages, usually containing five pieces of each of the two products.

"We thought, on one hand, we should give reductions in price due to quantity – such as buying five pieces and, on the other hand, we wanted to offer a combination of two different products that would generate some curiosity from customers. I asked for and got some data from cashiers about customers purchasing a combinations of chocolate items. Don't ask who gave me such confidential data. I called in some favors. Anyway, Bill and I agreed that the six packages are a good sample for a test. I want to emphasize that we are treating it as a test. One package is small, built of 1&1 items, four are 5&5 items and the last package is 3&3. Let's see how many packages are sold and what the actual impact on the normal sales is."

Sherry, the CFO, intervened: "Test or not, we must judge the impact on our profitability. In the past, we have evaluated such ideas in isolation – without comparison to our current state. We now are aware that we better use the current performance as a reference. So, I have collected the necessary reference numbers that define the company's current profitability. Here are the key figures for next year, assuming no new decisions are made. (See Table 11.1.)

Table 11.1   The Current Financial Situation of Choco-for-You[1]

Sales	TVC	Throughput	OE	Profit
133,268,604	68,269,080	64,999,524	63,480,000	1,519,524

Sherry continued, "First, I need to emphasize a technical point. The TVC does NOT include the cost of the cocoa. Alex and Igor decided to treat cocoa as a resource, because of the commitment to buy a certain quantity and the limitations on buying more."

"Back to the numbers, you can see that our overall margin is only 1.14% of the sales. This is **not** good enough. We have barely been keeping the company above breakeven over the last four years and it is not safe. One little unforeseen problem or a dip in demand could ruin us. This is why I take such a personal interest in figuring a way to boost profits without taking too many risks. So, I'm anxious to see Jenny's and Bill's predictions and the ramifications on our financial status."

Just to emphasize the current state of reference, Jon, the CEO, asked to quickly calculate the baseline ratio of T to OE. "After all, we want to grow T faster than OE," he added.

T/OE is 64,999,524/63,480,000 = 1.024

---

[1] Permit us to remind the reader that the currency is whatever is used in the country where Choco-for-You resides. Thus, we don't use any sign for a specific currency.

Igor, their IT guy, led the analysis of each one of the six packages, each had two different scenarios. The first suggested package as shown in Table 11.2, was:

Table 11.2 Composition of Package 1

Product ID	Quantity	Regular price/unit	TVC/unit	Throughput/unit
PL118	3	30.00	16.00	14.00
PL412	3	45.00	17.00	28.00

Package 1 is a new T-generator, TPL118412. The product number has been chosen to reflect that it is built from two specific items: 118 from line 1 and 412 made on line 4. Packaging the new T-generator requires an additional TVC of 10.00. Following the idea of offering a reduced price, the suggested price is 210, while the aggregated regular price of the products in the package is 225. The price reduction is about 7%. Package 1, at its new price and with the added TVC, generates 101.00 in T.[2] Selling the items individually would generate T of 126.[3]

According to the pessimistic scenario, as predicted by Jenny and Bill, 400 of Package 1 (TPL118412) could be sold every month, or 4,800 units per year. However, the pessimistic prediction also assumed that **all clients will switch to the package.** Thus, the sales of the current items, with their higher prices, would drop to zero! But, the overall quantity of 400 packages, each containing three units of two different products, generates considerably more than the current individual sales.

All of the management team looked shocked, when considering what we show here in Table 11.3. If the above calculations are true, then offering the package, relying on a very conservative assessment, would increase overall profits by 10%.

Table 11.3 The Pessimistic Impact of Introducing Package 1

T-generator	Price	TVC	ΔTVC	T/Unit Sold	Predicted Sales quantity	Predicted loss of sales units	ΔT
TPL118412	210.00	99.00	10.00	101.00	4800		484,800
TPL118	30.00	16.00		14.00		5,280	−73,920
TPL412	45.00	17.00		28.00		9,240	−258,720
						Total ΔT	152,160

Except, this is only accurate when there is no ΔOE increase, which would only occur when no addition to the readily available capacity is required. That assumption has not been validated so far. In most TOC analyses, the cocoa would have been part of the TVC and, thus, the ΔT would have been smaller. In this case, as mentioned above, there is already a commitment for a certain amount of cocoa, whether the sales that would consume that cocoa materialize of not. Therefore, the entire cost of buying cocoa is considered OE. Like other OE, you buy capacity and use it or lose it. Cocoa has the advantage of failing to expire, as an employee's workday does, but

---

[2] $210.00 - 3 \times (16.00 + 17.00) - 10.00$
[3] $3 \times (14.00 + 28.00)$

is equivalent to office supplies or payment for a job in progress – what hasn't been used delays a future payment.

Igor went on checking the load on all critical resources. The impact of the new package, built from two existing products (out of a total of 80 products), is not dramatic. The additional consumed capacity from lines 1 and 4, which produce the two products, is available. Even the packing line does not penetrate its theoretical limit of 90%. In other words, **the required extra capacity is free!**

The additional cocoa required is still within the minimum commitment to buy from the local importer. Thus, there is no concern. This means all the ΔT, 152,160 from Table 11.3, would directly increase the profit before tax.

So far, the management team has analyzed the conservative scenario, still yielding very nice growth of profit. What if reality turns out to be closer to the optimistic scenario? Certainly, sales will be higher but it might also require much more capacity.

Igor went on with the evaluation of the optimistic scenario for the new T-generator called TPL118412. The following Table 11.4 uses the optimistic predicted sales, which impacts the T generated by the package and the reduced sales of the two items that comprise TPL118412:

Table 11.4 The Optimistic Impact of Introducing Package 1

T-generator	Price	TVC	ΔTVC	T/Unit Sold	Predicted Sales quantity	Predicted loss of sales units	ΔT
TPL118412	210.00	99.00	10.00	101.00	6000		606,000
TPL118	30.00	16.00		14.00	1680	3,600	−50,400
TPL412	45.00	17.00		28.00	2040	7,200	−201,600
						Total ΔT	354,000

The optimistic assessment predicts higher sales of the package and that some of the original items will still be sold, although much less than before the introduction of the new package.

The capacity bar chart for the optimistic scenario are shown in Figure 11.2.

The packing line slightly penetrates the 90% utilization limit Alex has set for production planning. The detailed new load on the packing line is 90.14%. Is that serious?

This is a question for Alex to answer since the 90% threshold expresses his best intuition of the maximum needed protective capacity to ensure smooth delivery to all clients.

What would be the cost of freeing some capacity on the packing line?

One way to free capacity is to reduce some of the existing sales. The packing line, the weakest link of Choco-for-You production floor, is the only resource penetrating into its protective capacity. Igor presented the following table – sorting the products based on the ratio of T per minute of the Packing Line. The T-generator that yields the least T per minute of the packing line is TPL211, which yields only 0.25 per minute – much less than all other T-generators. Its sales quantity for the whole year is only 9,240. See Table 11.5.

What if Choco-for-You stops selling this product?

The impact on the load of killing TPL211 is shown in Table 11.6.

Eliminating TPL211 has solved all Alex's concerns. Jenny, the VP of Marketing and Sales declared that getting rid of this relatively slow mover would not create any problems with any of her clients. "Actually, I already was thinking that TPL211 is a product nobody really cares about.

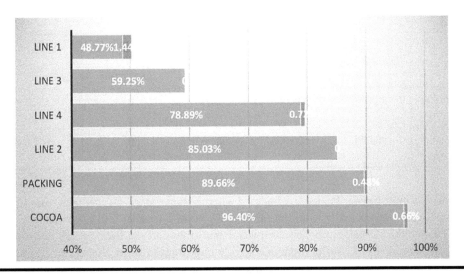

Figure 11.2 The optimistic capacity load on critical resources after launching Package 1 (TPL118412).

Table 11.5 Worst T-Generators in Terms of T per Constraint Unit (Packaging Line Minutes)

T-generator	T	T/Minute	Current Sales in units	Total T
TPL211	4.00	0.25	9,240	36,960
TPL213	5.00	0.31	228,000	1,140,000
TPL115	4.00	0.33	31,680	126,720
TPL120	4.00	0.33	13,200	52,800
TPL207	6.00	0.38	26,400	158,400
TPL212	6.00	0.38	44,400	266,400
TPL110	5.00	0.38	39,468	197,340

Table 11.6 Freeing Capacity Under 85% and 90% Thresholds by Dropping TPL211

Resource	Current Load	New Load
Line 2	85.03%	84.53%
Packing Line	90.14%	89.91%
Cocoa	97.06%	96.82%

Table 11.7   Final Range of Outcomes Considering both Scenarios

	New sales of TPL118412 in units	ΔT from new sales	ΔT lost due to reduced sales	ΔOE: the cost of adding capacity	ΔNP = ΔT − ΔOE
Pessimistic scenario	4,800	484,800	−332,640	0	152,160
Optimistic scenario	6,000	606,000	−288,960	0	317,040

Since line 2 is most heavily loaded, I wondered whether some other T-generators from line 2 are really necessary. I was actually thinking of TPL207. Now, I see that TPL120 would be a better choice. I know that TPL213 provides even less T per minute of the Packing line but there is no way to compromise TPL213 sales. That one is truly important to many clients and customers."

The optimistic financial impact of Package 1 is:

> The ΔT from the optimistic case, before eliminating the TPL211, is: 354,000
>
> Loss of T produced by the now eliminated TPL211 is: −36,960
>
> The new calculated ΔT for the optimistic scenario would be: 317,040

A summary of the results for launching the TPL118412 is shown in Table 11.7.

Jon explained his thoughts after the complete check of package 1, "Package 1 definitely brings considerable value, boosting our current profit between 10 to 20%. What we don't know though is whether we will need to eliminate TPL211 or not. Giving up that slow-mover is only required if the sales of the package are way up there, close to the optimistic end of the scenarios."

"We do not have to make that decision now! We'll know more a few months after introducing the new package. Since even the pessimistic assessment boosts NP nicely, there is no doubt we should introduce the package. It is rare to find opportunities without real downside risks. It seems to me, we should now look attentively at all the rest of the proposed packages. I hope our bottom line increases even more significantly, assuming we don't face more capacity problems."

The other five packages were analyzed. Two of them were rejected because the pessimistic assessment showed a loss. The ΔT lost from current sales were more than the ΔT from the expected sales of the packages, given the added TVC on those packages and the reduced prices.

Jon led the continuation of the analysis: "We are now coming to the significant decision. We rejected two of the six new packages we evaluated. So, we have four good new T-generators. **Can we handle all the four?** As is, each of the remaining four packages alone adds to our profits. Obviously, the combined ΔT is positive but do we have enough capacity for all four? If we need to add capacity, is the required ΔOE significantly less than the expected ΔT?"

"Igor, will you add all four packages to the current reference state, reflecting the reduced sales of the individual items that are part of the packages? I want one combined scenario presenting the pessimistic and optimistic assessments. Igor, I'll also ask you to explain the hidden assumption behind the combination of the four different decisions."

Igor was keen to show his knowledge in handling uncertainty. He said, "From a purely statistical approach, merging all the pessimistic and the optimistic in order to have the total pessimistic and optimistic results, would yield exaggerated aggregated assessments. While every individual assessment may reasonably be either low or high, when we aggregate several independent assessments, which are all on the low side, the result is too low. We get an analogous outcome by aggregating the high-end assessments – we'd get too high an assessment. The reason is that the probability that reality will behave according to all pessimistic assessments or all optimistic ones is vanishingly small."

"However, in this case we feel certain the resulting range between the pessimistic and the optimistic is good enough. First, we are considering just four different items. Second, since the assessments were done by the same people, they are subject to the same personal bias. Consequently, shrinking the aggregated assessment range might be too risky. Therefore, reasonable outcomes remain within the ranges suggested by the aggregated pessimistic and optimistic assessments. If the results of both scenarios turn out to be positive, there is little doubt that the decision will improve profits."

The following Table 11.8 shows the initial Throughput analysis of the combined four packages, including dropping TPL211:

Table 11.8   Impact on Profit due to ΔT Compared to Baseline (Pessimistic Scenario)

T-generator	Price	T/unit	Baseline Sales in units	Predicted Sales in units	ΔT compared to baseline
TPL118412 Package 1	210.00	101.00		4,800	484,800
TPL117305 Package 2	295.00	85.00		6,000	510,000
TPL206104 Package 3	250.00	100.00		3,600	360,000
TPL411318 Package 4	285.00	90.00		12,000	1,080,000
TPL104	24.00	11.00	10,164	2,964	−79,200
TPL118	30.00	14.00	5,280	0	−73,920
TPL412	45.00	28.00	9,240	0	−258,720
TPL117	31.00	7.00	39,732	28,932	−75,600
TPL305	33.00	17.00	13,332	3,732	−163,200
TPL206	32.00	18.00	106,656	97,056	−172,800
TPL411	31.00	14.00	144,000	114,000	−420,000
TPL318	34.00	14.00	10,560	5,760	−67,200
TPL211	24.00	4.00	9,240	0	−36,960
				Total ΔT	1,087,200

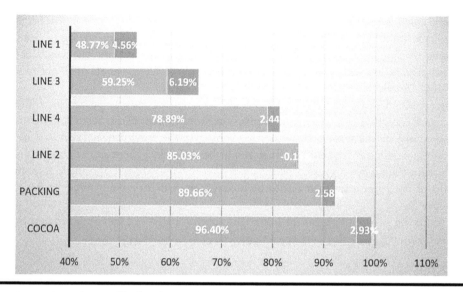

Figure 11.3 Capacity profile for the Pessimistic Scenario.

Igor explained, "The total ΔT represents the additional T due to the sales of the new T-generators minus the T lost from reduced sales of the old T-generators, which are parts of those new T-generators. Plus, you can see at the bottom of the table, I already eliminated TPL211, as we discussed earlier."

"Remember, we needed to drop all TPL211 sales just to allow Package 1 to be introduced. What we don't know yet, is whether eliminating that product alone releases enough capacity. Now, here is the total impact on the capacity." He showed them the chart in Figure 11.3.

"The packing line is over its limit of 90%. line 2 seems to cross its 85% limit by 0.03% but there is a tiny reduction, due to dropping TPL211, of just 0.13% which you can hardly see on the chart. The total utilization of line 2 on my computer shows 84.90%. So, we are good there. Cocoa, is now 99.33%. Considering our typical scrap rate, it is obvious that more cocoa will be required."

Igor was shaking his head, as he said, "Eliminating the sales of TPL211 is not enough to settle all the capacity issues. Both the requirements for cocoa and the capacity of the packing line penetrate into their protective capacity limits."

Igor suggested adding capacity to both. The result of his check was purchasing an additional 600 kg of cocoa, fortunately, still within the quantity the agreement with the local importer allows and at the good price of 30,000 per 100 kg. On top of that, an additional 10 days using the noisy old packing line costing of 9,000 per day had to be added to the OE.

The resulting financial impact of the changes is:

ΔT due to introducing the four packages:[4]	1,087,200
ΔOE for extra capacity:[5]	−270,000
ΔProfit (ΔT − ΔOE):	**817,200**

---

[4] See Table 11.8
[5] 600 kg of cocoa × 30,000/kg + 10 days of the old packing line × 9,000/day

Table 11.9   Expected Financial Performance Based on the Pessimistic Scenario

Sales	TVC	Throughput	OE	Profit
137,345,844	71,259,120	66,086,724	63,750,000	2,336,724

Igor said, "Given the above changes, the predicted overall financial performance would be ..." and he showed the information in Table 11.9. "... there you go. The baseline T was 64,999,524 and we added 1,087,200 to that. Also, OE increased by 270,000 for operating the old packaging line and the extra cocoa we'd have to buy. That explains the increase in OE from 63,480,000 in the baseline."

> *The reader can refer back to* Table 11.1 *at the beginning of the chapter as a reference to the baseline financial performance.*

Igor continued, "T/OE has changed from 1.0239[6] to 1.0367.[7] And, profit grows from 1,519,524 to 2,336,724.[8] That's more than a 53% increase in profit!"

"This is just the impact of the pessimistic assessment!" said Igor.

Alex was quick to respond, "I want to see the impact on the capacity of the critical resources of the optimistic one! The question is whether we'd face such a load that we wouldn't be able to function properly."

Igor immediately showed the capacity profile for the optimistic assessment. (See Figure 11.4.)

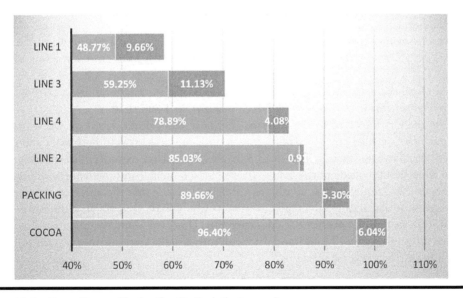

Figure 11.4   Capacity profile for the Optimistic Scenario.

---

[6] 64,999,524/63,480,000
[7] 66,086,724/63,750,000
[8] 1,519,524 + 817,200

Igor announced, "There is no point in showing you the can't-be ΔT, since you can see for yourselves, we don't have nearly enough capacity. First, let's figure out *if* we can do it and, if so, how much OE it will cost us. That way, if we end up dropping products, I can show you that all together in one table."

Jon asked the group, "Well? Can we do it?"

Igor answered him. "As you know, we have no mechanism to increase the capacity on line 2 and eliminating TPL211 alone is insufficient to bring line 2 back below our 85% limit. Can we reduce demand for some products in the line 2 family, Jenny?"

Jenny seemed to be troubled by the option of reducing the sales of other T-generators without cutting them totally from the product mix. She argued, "That might be really hard. Let's say I keep certain distributors from buying a product or two. How could I explain it, when they will inevitably see the product still available from other distributors? Alternatively, if I put all the distributors on allocation, then I have them all mad at us, not just a few. We should be very careful before taking such onerous actions."

Igor shrugged and said,

"Jenny mentioned eliminating TPL207, which would reduce the load on line 2 to 84.6%. TPL207 is the fifth lowest T contributing product. If it's our preference to drop a product from the company's offerings completely, rather than limiting the sales of a product, this is the most logical choice. However, it means that, under the optimistic scenario, TPL211 NO LONGER needs to be eliminated. Only TPL207 should be withdrawn from the product mix of the company."

Jenny agreed that it was a valid option and the one she preferred.

Igor carried on, "On top of eliminating 207, we'll need the whole 1.2 tonnes of additional cocoa from importer to deliver the optimistic scenario. Packing will require 19 days of the old packing line throughout the year to deliver everything to all customers on-time. Here is the graph of our capacity after the elimination of TPL207:" He showed them Figure 11.5.[9]

The additional utilization of the capacities of lines 1, 3 and 4 do not necessitate any ΔOE. However, due to the self-limitation of sales, Choco-for-You loses the Throughput of the 26,400 units of TPL207. Every unit of TPL207 generated 6.00 in their local currency, all of which are now lost.

Based on all the detailed calculations, Bill presented the summary results of introducing the four new T-generators in both scenarios, which is shown in Table 11.10.

Sherry, the CFO, reacted to the analysis, "So, next year's profit, based on the introduction of the four new packages and also taking into consideration changes to both sales and capacity levels, will be anywhere from: 2,331,924 to 3,167,244. You claim that it is quite unlikely to get a better or worse result outside of this range. I have had too much bad experience with predictions and forecasts. So, Alex, allow me to ask you this: Are you sure that the operators won't demand more overtime or that additional temporary workers wouldn't be needed? We currently pay about 300,000 every year just for overtime of floor operators. Don't you think we might need more overtime once the pressure rises? Lines 1 and 3 are currently usually working only two shifts. Will we need a third shift under these scenarios?"

---

[9] Just a reminder: Attentive and persevering readers may notice that the baseline bars for cocoa and the Packing Line in Figure 11.5 dropped from the previous baselines shown in earlier Figures. This occurs, as we explained in Chapter 8, because adding capacity resets the 100% capacity to a new higher level. Therefore, the baseline load consumes less of the new higher capacity.

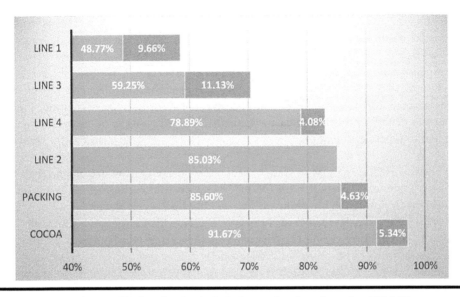

Figure 11.5 Capacity profile for the Optimistic Scenario after dropping TPL207.

Alex responded to her challenge: "It is possible that, in the future, we should include manpower in the calculations and assess how many more overtime or special unplanned shifts we might need. But, I don't foresee a significant impact."

He followed up with, "When lines 1 or 3 need a third shift, we just add one additional operator. All the other crew are required anyway for line 4 and mainly for line 2. Some of my people are used to be consistently paid for overtime every month. I assume they know how to manipulate our system to get the paid the overtime they need. Maybe overtime might go up by 10%, max. I looked very carefully at the capacity chart – I'm confident it won't be more than that. So, yes, you can include in your calculations an additional expense of 30,000 per year for extra overtime but only if the optimistic scenario or something close to it happens."

Table 11.10 Summary of the Reasonable Range of Financial Results for Both Optimistic and Pessimistic Scenarios

	Revenues from New Packages	Throughput from New Packages	Throughput Lost from Lower Sales	ΔOE: the Cost of Added Capacity	ΔNet Profit ΔT − ΔOE	Total Net Profit
Pessimistic scenario	7,098,000	2,434,800	1,347,600*	270,000[A]	817,200	2,331,924
Optimistic scenario	11,772,000	3,954,000	1,775,280†	531,000[B]	1,647,720	3,167,244

* Includes lost sales and the elimination of TPL211
[A] Buying 600 kg Cocoa and 10 days of Old Packing Line
† Includes lost sales and the elimination of TPL207
[B] Buying 1.2 tons Cocoa and 19 days of Old Packing Line

Sherry commented, "Okay, I hope your intuition is close. It's clear that additional overtime of 30,000 for the whole year won't change our decision. I also have our credit line with the bank in mind. If we have to use more of it, because of the expected higher level of inventories, then our interest expense will go up. This doesn't threaten the endeavor either. We have about 6 inventory turns right now, so the increase of a little 4 million in sales, according to your optimistic scenario, would mean about 20,000 additional financial costs,[10] not a big deal, I have to admit. I just think we all need to be on our toes to validate that the ΔOE is not going to be more than we expect. I would like to supervise the impact on the cost very closely. Overall, I still think we should go ahead."

Jon wanted to stress the point. "Yes, it seems clear to me that we are on the right track. I accept Sherry's offer to closely watch the OE for expenses we didn't consider in these calculations. We don't know by how much the profit will increase but I do expect the profits to soar. A critical decision we'll have to face is whether to eliminate TPL211, which is the easier choice, or TPL207, which we should eliminate only if the sales of the packages and other products are closer to the optimistic assessment. I assume we'll be able to delay this decision until a couple months after launching the four new packages. There is no need to make that decision now. We'll also activate the old packing line only when we have to. We know what to expect."

"It seems to me we have great expectations. It is now time to make it happen."

---

[10] Since TVC is about ½ of sales, 4 million in sales means 2 million of TVC. 2 million of TVC divided by 6 turns per year gives 1/3 million of new inventory on-hand on average. If bank interest rates are 6%, that times 1/3 million gives 20,000 in added annual interest expense.

Chapter 12

Evaluating the Next Leap in Performance and Its Required Investment— Choco-for-You, Part 2

The previous chapter dealt with a combination of several small-scale decisions. The range of expected outcomes seem quite impressive, we think you will agree, even according to the pessimistic extreme. Is this enough for a company? Should they rest on their laurels, occasionally adding more packages or is it at all reasonable for management to think about prospering to a much greater extent?

This chapter leads us to the next level of achievement. Here, we consider a much more daring step, requiring a substantial investment. This second improvement takes place after the company has absorbed the first step change. It is our assumption that their current reality after the last change has now, once again, stablilized.

The small steps taken by Choco-for-You's management were not intended or expected to cause a massive disruption to their business operations. Six months after the launch of the additional four packages, sales increased to a level between the pessimistic and optimistic assessments. This change required an increase in OE of 357,000. The significant new numbers for the next twelve months are shown on Table 12.1.

Table 12.1   Choco-for-You's new financial baseline

Sales	TVC	Throughput	OE	Profit
138,818,064	72,302,500	66,515,564	63,837,000	2,678,564

Just as a reminder, just six months ago, their annual performance measurements were according to Table 12.2.

Table 12.2 Choco-for-You's Previous Financial Baseline Six Months Earlier

Sales	TVC	Throughput	OE	Profit
133,268,604	68,269,080	64,999,524	63,480,000	1,519,524

Sales have increased by 4.16%. The associated increase in T of 2.33% is more moderate due to the impact of the reduced prices and the lost sales of full-price items.

Both cocoa and the packing line had become too loaded to support reliable delivery performance. The consumption of cocoa required purchasing an extra 100 kg from their importer, every month and a half. They run the old packing line about one day every 4 weeks, to keep from falling behind on their deliveries.

Neither the increase in Sales nor T look all that impressive. OE went up by just 0.56%. The T/OE ratio improved from 1.024 to1.042. The profit, however, dramatically increased by 76%! This occurred because the T increased much more than the OE. It is important to note that the initial T and OE were relatively close. The net profit return on sales ratio was only 1.14%. Therefore, the impact of the increase in T relative to the OE made for a jump in the profit. The new return on sales is 1.93% – still low. So, management fervently hopes there remains room for much more improvement.

What can the management of Choco-for-You do now?

It is certainly possible to continue with the basic idea of preparing other similar packages. There is no doubt that Jenny and Bill should come with a plan to extend the use of packages. However, this move concentrates on their current local market for chocolate and on the same four lines of products. If Choco-for-You wants to grow dramatically, then new strategic directions should be evaluated.

What if Choco-for-You actively identifies ways to increase its market through new products or by starting to export the current products to neighboring countries?

Coming up with new products that truly expand the customer base is a risky move involving substantial investment in R&D and then in marketing the new products. Moreover, it is very difficult to predict when a customer, who likes a new product, simply stops buying the old one in favor of the new. Instead, let's analyze the potential economic impact of opening an export market.

Such an effort might involve a substantial increase in OE, such as opening an office, hiring several people to handle the orders from local distributors, advertising costs and rough estimations of flight and lodging expenses for key people in Choco-for-You to travel back and forth to the export market.

There are also obvious additional truly-variable-costs for export items, such as tariffs used by the other country to protect its own manufacturers. In addition, there are transportation expenses for moving the goods to either a central warehouse or directly to the distributors. As the idea of maintaining fast flow to ensure availability without too high stock leads to transporting a relatively low quantity of items. In such cases, treating transportation costs as TVC makes sense.

In the end, Choco-for-You's team made the simple decision to consider shipping costs to the new market as additional TVC, which boiled down to an average estimation of 3.00 (in their local currency) for every unit of an exported item.

Jon, the CEO, Jenny, the VP of Marketing and Sales, and Bill, the VP for Business Development, together estimated the content of exports for the first year. The reasonable annual cost of maintaining the infrastructure for the export plan is 1,000,000 in their home currency. This can be treated as ΔOE, since it is largely independent of the volume exported.

A significant initial decision was to price the exported items the same as in the domestic market. Since every exported item includes extra TVC, the T is less for each item than when it is sold in the domestic market. The three also unanimously agreed not to export any of the products made on line 2 because that line is fully loaded. It did not make sense to load it with more T-generators that yield less T per unit.

At first, Jenny tried to claim that it was important to penetrate a new market with the full selection of Choco-for-You's best products, several of which are produced on line 2. Jon and Bill eventually convinced her that a satisfactory assortment from the other product families was good enough for the first year. They chose ten products from each production line, other than line 2, as the initial product mix for export. The decisions were largely based on intuition about what the export market might see as "worthwhile to try."

The real difficulty was to estimate the pessimistic and optimistic sales. Even though Igor, the IT guy, searched up a lot of statistics on sales of chocolate in their chosen export market, they all had the sense that the uncertainty was very high. Finally, Bill was the one that pushed his colleagues to come up with a broad generic approach. The breakthrough solution was to assume the pessimistic assessment would be 12.5% or one eighth of the domestic sales. The optimistic figure they settled on was three times that amount.

Bill explained his thoughts by saying, "This is not a normal forecast. We know that, over the first three months, we'll have low sales and that they will grow. I don't think we should go into detailed month-to-month assessments, because it won't improve our decision. All we want is what we might eventually see as annual sales. Six months after we begin exporting, we'll certainly know more. One thing we do know is that we had very low sales of the new packages in the first two months after their launch. Now, we have learned that we made the right decision. Thus, all we need is a very rough idea of sales and capacity both according to our current very limited intuition."

He lectured on like a professor, "We should offer the export market a mix of thirty T-generators. Each of them should be similar to the corresponding domestic T-generator, with the same price, even with our awareness that TVC is higher due to tariffs and transportation. As every new T-generator generates positive T and its sales in the export market do not impact domestic sales, it is certain that we'll get positive ΔT. The question is how positive the ΔOE will be, including both the extra OE due directly to the export market and the cost of the additional capacity we'll need. Will it exceed the ΔT? I want to emphasize that, for now, we are not going to expand our production lines. We will just use whatever we currently have, including the old packing line." With that, Bill nodded to Igor.

Igor said, "Figure 12.1 shows the reference load versus the available capacity, with the additional 13 packing days and 800 kg of cocoa, which are now required just for the increased domestic market. The sales of one T-generator (TPL207) has already been halted, in order to free capacity for line 2, so the current reference load does not include that particular item."

Igor followed that with, "The predicted consumption of cocoa for the next 12 months is about 97% of the total commitment to the local importer plus 800 kg additional cocoa. Taking into account scrap losses of material between 2–4%, this seems reasonable. We still have the option of buying 400 kg of additional cocoa from the importer."

"Remember, I found a way to import even more cocoa ourselves, if necessary," Bill bragged. Sitting behind him, Jenny rolled her eyes.

Igor seemed confused. Was Bill's comment somehow funny? He said earnestly, "I think that may be a big help, Bill. Because, with the addition of the export market, using Jenny's and Bill's pessimistic assessment, for 30 items of lines 1, 3 and 4, at the level of 12.5% of those item's current domestic sales, here is the load I calculated." He showed them Figure 12.2.

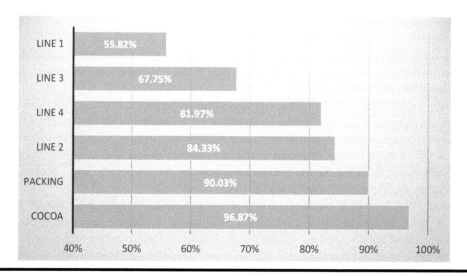

Figure 12.1   The new baseline capacity profile of the stable state after the successful launch of the four packages.

Igor plunged ahead with his analysis, "Given our scrap rate, we will have to buy more cocoa. It is now at 99.68%. This chart shows that activation of the packing line is beyond Alex's limit of 90%. We'll need to activate the old line to reduce that 92.32%. That is all straightforward. However, line 4, which has always been a non-constraint, is now above Alex's 85% level. At 86.13%, it threatens smooth operations of the packing line. This must be resolved. But, how? I'm afraid I don't know!"

Alex explained, "The idea behind my protective capacity limits is that I have found it is possible to allow one resource, the weakest link in the production floor, to reach the 90% of their capacity, provided that none of the rest are loaded beyond 85%. The weakest link needs protective capacity of 10% to recover from temporary peaks in demand as well as occasional quality and technical

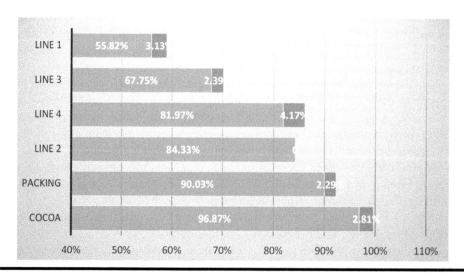

Figure 12.2   The capacity profile using the pessimistic quantities for export added to the new baseline.

problems on the floor. However, all the rest need to have even more flexibility to avoid wasting the critical capacity of the weakest link. If the buffer of work-in-process in front of the weakest link is ever exhausted, it weakens that key resource even further. One thing leads to another and matters just get more chaotic until I start running us short of inventory of our finished goods. Then, it is just a matter of time before some customer doesn't get their full order on time. Soon, it becomes a group of customers who have persistent backorders. This situation persists until demand drops off."

Bill wryly added, "Yeah, I call those drop offs *self-inflicted wounds*. Customers, who get shorted inevitably start looking for alternatives. Our competitors have cheaper ones. All it takes is for some rookie buyer to taste their dark chocolate and think to himself, 'This isn't so bad. Who will notice? And, maybe I'll get credit for a cost savings!' Poof! I'm battling a market-share erosion that we caused ourselves! That's crazy. It is far more difficult to recover the business at higher prices that it is to sell a story of a premium image in the first place. But, that's why I'm worth my salary!" Jenny rolled her eyes, again at his braggadocio.

Igor, who saw things in black and white, completely agreed with Bill's comments. He, for one, was damn glad that this man could get lost customers back. That was something he couldn't imagine being able to do. He liked their high-end chocolate but tried to imagine what he would do if he had a chance to buy a competitor's cheaper and almost-as-good alternative. He finally decided that it was his job to make sure they never ran out. That was the best way could contribute. So, he got back to making his quantitative contribution, saying, "In this specific case, two resources other than cocoa are above 85%: the packing line at 92.32% and line 4 at 86.13%. The difficulty is that while the capacity of the packing can be increased by more frequent activation of the old line, the capacity of line 4 is truly limited. What can we do there, Alex?"

Alex replied, "There are two ways to deal with the situation. One is to continue to keep the packing line as the weakest-link by eliminating one or more of the products that are produced by line 4. The other is to add much more capacity to the packing line, so its load drops below 85%, making line 4 the weakest-link."

"First, let's analyze reducing sales from line 4 product family. Here is the list of the worst T-generators on line 4. The first three are clearly slow movers. Note that any T-generator that is for export has an 'e' as the last character on its T-generator ID."

After Igor had shown them the information in Table 12.3, Alex continued his explanation with, "The assumption that limiting the sales of an existing T-generator but keeping it alive with

Table 12.3   Worst T-Generators in Terms of T per Constraint Unit (line 4 minutes) and an 'E' Suffix Designates an Export T-Generator

T-generator	T	T/Minute	Current Sales in units	Total T
TPL406e	10.00	0.45	495	4,950
TPL405e	11.00	0.50	2,558	28,138
TPL406	13.00	0.59	3,960	51,480
TPL405	14.00	0.64	20,460	286,440
TPL411	14.00	0.64	105,000	1,470,000
TPL410e	17.00	0.81	26,160	444,720
TPL411318	90.00	0.82	15,200	1,368,000

lower sales, would cause problems resulting from picking favorites between distributors, leads us to look for one or more T-generators that can be completely eliminated. The natural candidate for freeing enough capacity of line 4 being eliminated is TPL405, the fourth item in the list above. Its annual sales of 20,460 units significantly utilizes line 4's capacity. The second one in the list is TPL405e, which is based on the same product, but intended for export. Thus, it delivers even less T per minute of line 4's capacity. However, its predicted sales are low (only one eighth domestic sales). It makes sense to eliminate both of them. If we do, the resulting load on line 4 drops to 84.52%, which gives me sufficient protective capacity."

Igor took over saying, "Let's see …" He clicked his laptop's keys for only seconds and continued, "… removing those two T-generators would reduce T by 314,578.[1] It also lessens, to a certain extent, the consumption of cocoa and the load of the packing line but not enough to keep us from needing more of both."

"The new export market, even according to the pessimistic forecast, will require 500 kg of additional cocoa to stabilize production at the 97% level. This is on top of the 800 kg, already being purchased beyond our minimum commitment, which includes what we need for our now successful packages. The importer agreement only allows us up to 1.2 tonnes above the basic commitment. Thus, it is possible to purchase additional 400 kg of cocoa from the local importer for the sum of 120,000.[2] The last 100 kg we'll need we will have to import ourselves for the shocking price of 70,000. All these extra purchases of cocoa raises ΔOE to 190,000."

"The higher load on the packing line will require an additional eight days of packing with the old line, on top of our current requirement for 13 days. That's a total of 21 days using the old packing line during the year. This requires a ΔOE of 72,000.[3]"

Igor took a breath and continued. "ΔOE needs to include the annual costs involved with exporting that are estimated at 1 million. The total cost of the decision to export, according to the pessimistic scenario, is: 1,262,200.[4]" (See Table 12.4.)

Jon looked at the summary and said, "The result is positive, even if the whole effort makes a relatively small impact on profit, bringing it from 2,678,564 to 2,841,326, an increase of 6%."

Table 12.4 Financial Results from Exporting (Pessimistic Scenario) Restricting Line 4

	Revenues from New Export Sales	Throughput from New Export Sales	Throughput Lost from TPL405	ΔOE: the Cost of Added Capacity	ΔNet Profit ΔT − ΔOE	Total Net Profit
Pessimistic scenario	4,083,849*	1,711,202*	286,440	1,262,000†	162,762	2,841,326

* Without exporting TPL405e
† Includes 1m fixed cost annually + 400 kg at regular price + 100 kg at 70,000/100 kg + 8 days of old packing line

---

[1] −28,138 of ΔT from TPL405e − 286,440 of ΔT from TPL405
[2] 30,000/100 kg × 4
[3] 9,000/day of the old packing line × 8 days
[4] 1,000,000 export investment and other costs + 190,000 additional 500 kg cocoa + 72,000 old packing line for eight days

Alex cautioned them, "A lot of intuition went into the numbers, so we absolutely cannot ignore the possibility that the first year of export might end with a loss if the pessimistic forecast is simply not pessimistic enough. However, the above analysis was based on the alternative of reducing sales from the line 4 family in order to expose enough capacity from line 4 to maintain the packing line as the weakest link."

"The alternative I mentioned before is to choose to sell both those two T-generators, allowing line 4 to be loaded up 86.13% and meanwhile reduce the load on the packing line to 85%, so it's no longer the weakest link. We'll certainly get a different result – better or worse. To do this, 35 additional days of the old packing line (on top of the 13 days required now – before exporting) would be required. That's a total of 48 extra old packing line days. In this case, the financial results would be as I am showing here:" (See Table 12.5)

Table 12.5 Financial Results from Exporting (Pessimistic Scenario) Adding Packing Capacity

	Revenues from New Export Sales	Throughput from New Export Sales	Throughput Lost from TPL405	ΔOE: the Cost of Added Capacity	ΔNet Profit $\Delta T - \Delta OE$	Total Net Profit
Pessimistic scenario	4,183,611*	1,739,340*	0	1,645,000†	94,340	2,772,904

* Including exporting TPL405e
† Includes 1m fixed cost annually + 400 kg at regular price + 300 kg at 70,000/100 kg + 35 days of old packing line

Igor was smiling as he said, "Interesting, under the scenario in which we eliminated TPL405 and TPL405e, we only needed 500 kg of additional cocoa and 400 kg of that was bought at the subsidized price. Only 100 kg carried the full cost of direct-import. Now, with both T-generators still part of the active product mix, the extra cocoa required is 700 kg, which means buying 300 kg at the high price of 700 per kg. This, plus the extra days of the old packing days this an inferior choice."

Jon nodded, "Yes. I agree completely with Igor. However, to have the full information we need for making the decision about exporting, we must analyze the optimistic scenario."

Alex said, "The impact on capacity will definitely be much more significant."

Igor spoke about the logic of their decision, "There are two possibilities in evaluating the optimistic side. One is that ΔOE might be bigger than ΔT, especially because of using more expensive cocoa. The second is that the optimistic situation might be impossible to resolve capacity-wise. For instance, if the load on one of the production lines is too high. We have no means to raise capacity on the production lines, unless we consider buying a whole new line. The only valid alternative is cutting existing sales. This might reduce ΔT too much or, even more devastating, have negative implications on other sales we didn't intend to cut. Carefully checking the optimistic scenario is absolutely necessary even when the pessimistic one seems good."

With that said, he showed them the capacity chart for the optimistic scenario that identified for them where they'd need to add capacity.

Referring to the information in Figure 12.3, Igor reminded them, "This graph already factors in the additional 800 kg of cocoa required for the domestic market, as well as using the old packing line for 13 days. Therefore, the blue bars represent the situation without the export market, and the orange color shows the additional load due to exporting."

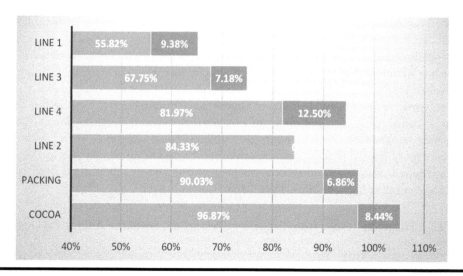

Figure 12.3 The capacity profile of the optimistic scenario before adding more capacity or reducing sales.

He was looking at his laptop and seemed to be speaking the thoughts that came into his mind without being aware of the others in the room. He said, "line 4 now penetrates almost 10% past the 85% limit. Without a Capacity Buffer for line 4, the only option is to reduce sales of the line 4 family to under 90% but then, we'd need more days to bring the overall packing line's capacity down to 85%. This would make line 4 our new weakest link. This would be the more reasonable course of action because line 4 cannot be elevated in the required time frame."

"Still, the pressure on line 4 necessitates a considerable cut of the line 4 family of products. Eliminating just TPL405, TPL406 and their export equivalents is not enough because export demand would keep line 4 above the 90% limit. Should we risk the ability to maintain delivery performance of the line 4 family of T-generators?" Without giving anyone time to answer, he rushed on.

"The next T-generator that yields the least T from line 4's capacity is TPL411, which is one of the faster runners in the line 4 family. If TPL411 is eliminated, then the total load of line 4 drops down below 85%. The relatively good news is that the packing line can then remain the weakest link. That way additional packing days can be used to bring packing just below the 90% threshold.

Table 12.6 Financial Results from the Optimistic Export Scenario

	Revenues from New Export Sales	Throughput from New Export Sales	Throughput Lost from dropping	ΔOE: the Cost of Added Capacity	ΔNet Profit ΔT − ΔOE	Total Net Profit
Optimistic scenario	12,196,146*	5,118,578*	1,807,920†	1,860,000^	1,450,658	4,129,222

* Not exporting TPL405e or TPL406e
† Losing T from TPL405, TPL406 and TPL411
^ Includes 1m fixed cost annually + 400 kg at regular price + 800 kg at 70,000/100 kg + 20 days of old packing line

Igor spoke but it was almost as if his laptop was speaking through him, "ΔOE consists of the basic 1,000,000 annual cost of making the exporting possible, then paying 680,000 for additional quantities of cocoa, plus adding 20 days of the old packing line, costing 180,000.[5] The total ΔOE is 1,860,000."

"The optimistic NP is 4,129,222. As appears in Table 12.6."

The Debate within Choco-for-You's Management Team

Viewing the two very different scenarios, the pessimistic as well as the optimistic, naturally led to more discussions within the management team.

Igor presented the predicted range of assessments: The profit due to the decision to export between 28-30 items is predicted to grow between **162,762** and **$4,129,22**.

Jon opened the discussion: "It is not surprising that taking a bold step to enter a new market leaves us with a wide range of possible results. The issue of exporting relates to our growth strategy. It raises the question regarding how much risk we are ready to undertake. We certainly need to look beyond this specific plan to export thirty or so items. If that move is successful, meaning much better sales than the pessimistic assessment, then the export move heralds new opportunities for the future."

Sherry, the CFO, wanted to explain her understanding of the information: "On the face of it, the numbers tell us we won't lose. This is **not** necessarily true."

"As I have commented before, the calculation of the operating expenses ignores some ΔOE, especially overtime and financial cost. The additional operating expenses would require paying extra interest expense to the bank. However, those expenses are admittedly not consequential. I mention them, because the pessimistic scenario might struggle to cover them."

"That said, I think the high profit predicted by the optimistic scenario is unrealistic, because the actual ΔOE would be larger, say by at least 200,000 based on my reasonable assessment. Such an increase in sales has an impact on the capacity of many resources, which are not included in the above calculations. Still, these added costs change the overall picture only slightly; the ΔNP, including the ancillary increases in costs, would still be well above 1 million."

"Overall, we have a chance of doing a lot of work for nothing or taking a chance of gaining one million plus. My Question is: **Is this the only serious proposal we should contemplate before making such a strategic move?**"

Bill felt the need to intervene: "The main point is that the risk is low! I don't care if the range is wide, as long as there is no serious chance of losing money. Now, once we are in the export market, we'll have so many new opportunities to explore, the sky's the limit! We can then vastly optimize our product mix, eliminating items with low T because we can tap into huge markets for the best items we can make. If the investment in starting to export doesn't threaten our current profitability, then we should simply go ahead."

Jenny had to express her reservations: "I feel uncomfortable with the possible cut of three T-generators from line 4. I don't care much for the two slow movers. However, TPL411 is not just a fast runner but also is an important feature in our offering. Basically, it is directed at young people between fourteen and eighteen. We have only twelve T-generators for this age group and this product is one of three from the line 4 family. I don't know how the distributors are going to react. This is of a major concern for me. I wonder, isn't there some other way? For instance, we

---

[5] 9,000/day of old packing line × 20 days

might consider increasing the price per unit from 31 to 34 or even 35, because this would probably reduce demand without us risking too much."

Bill responded: "We'd only give up TPL411 only if the sales in the export market are truly great. Anyway, I think that slightly increasing the price on TPL411 is a good move even if our export reality is closer to the pessimistic scenario. It'd give us the opportunity to test the true price sensitivity of that item."

Igor remarked that it is pretty easy to carry another 'what-if' scenario to check how a small increase in price for TPL411, resulting reduced demand, would impact the bottom line. But, it seemed that the management team felt this is would go into too much detail, while the direction to move ahead seemed clear enough already.

Alex felt he had to add another perspective: "**Our true blocking factor is the lack of potential to increase the capacity of each of the four lines.** We are already limited by line 2, so we had to give up TPL211, because of the domestic market. Now, we are contemplating a strategy of export, which would cause the capacity of line 4 to become a CCR. What would happen when the export market demands some of the line 2 T-generators? Notice what a relief it is that we kept the old packing line. Remember the pressure I was under to remove the old machines in order to free more space? Now, you see how right I was not to allow that to happen."

"Since we are already speaking about future strategies, then we need more options for adding capacity. The opportunities Bill speaks about require being able to respond fast enough to the new demand. This necessitates more capacity, not just for the added demand but also to not compromise the markets in which we already operate. I understand that to buy another line 4 or line 2 is a much bigger investment than just opening an export market based on the existing production capacity. So, let me propose something 'crazy.' B&G is a bitter competitor. We are much better than them, especially regarding their versions of the line 2 family. The result is that their equivalent of line 2 is most definitely not fully utilized. I heard that they operate it for only one extended shift a day and close it down for the whole weekend. What about offering them an attractive fee to use their line occasionally during the two days of the weekend? This would enable us to offer the export market some of our line 2 T-generators as well."

They were all clamoring at once. Everyone seemed in a rush to break into Alex's flow of thought. Jon reestablished his authority by asking everyone to be quiet for just a minute. "We should not let our emotions against B&G block our thinking. Alex has touched on an open nerve. We are ultimately constrained by four huge resources that are very difficult to enlarge. I want to think more about his proposal. It would be better if we could use also their equivalent line 4 capacity. Maybe we can think through such an offer."

Jon turned to Igor: "Igor, suppose I put a proposal for B&G on the table, without sending it to them yet. It would be just be an internal document for us to review before taking any action. Then Jenny and Bill will come up with an alternative extended export scheme, assuming we can use the capacity at B&G. We'd need to also consider the cost of the logistics between us and B&G. How long would it take you to model the pessimistic and optimistic scenarios so we can form our opinion?"

Igor shrugged, "It would take me just a few minutes to upload the supporting program with the data."

Jon now approached all the team, "OK, this is what I want you to work on during the next three days. Then, we will meet again here and discuss the new information."

"Jenny, please come up with two additional proposals for the first year of export. One where you choose different T-generators from line 4 that would still be effective as an introduction of Choco-for-You in the export market. Discuss with Alex which products use less capacity from line

4 that might still be appreciated by the export customers. The other product mix proposal should include several items from line 2 as well, again, assuming we'd be able to use B&G's capacity."

"Alex, we'd need a specific suggestion to B&G for using their capacity over the weekends. I would like to see the analysis, if such a proposal is economically viable, meaning ΔOE will be still considerably less than ΔT."

"Bill, extend your vision beyond the first year of export. First, define the minimum potential financial outcome of the export move. If the actual export ΔNP in the first year is below that line, we'll discontinue the endeavor; above that line, we should continue. Based on the various potential results, propose the next steps we'll have to take. My key interest is to check at what point in time we'd need to buy another line 2 and line 4. Such an investment must be planned in advance since it takes time to actually get a new line ready for work."

"Alex, I'll need you to determine the time it takes to buy and install such new lines, until we achieve full capacity from them."

Jon summarized the meeting: "I'm very encouraged by this meeting, even though we still don't have a clear decision on the proposal that we put on the table. It seems to me we are definitely going to export. The question is just with which choice of T-generators to start. Second, I can see how the shared information brings the best from each of us. I can say I'm much more optimistic now about the future of Choco-for-You than I was before this meeting. I was concerned about the limit of the domestic market as our constraint for growth. Now, I feel we might have the right answer to elevating that limit. Thank you all and I'll see you in three days."

Chapter 13

Analyzing the Significant Decisions as Explored in the Choco-for-You Case

Evaluating important decisions should involve raising various options and opinions in order to eventually reach the best result safely. It should seem natural that our analysis of such a major new move, such as going into a new export market, has ended with three critical insights:

1. Overall, the opportunity looks good despite certain minor risks. It seems the risk of losing money from exporting is very small. Even if that risk materializes, the losses would be small and short lived. This is an important aspect to recognize. Certainly the chance to make much more money is what led management to accept the idea, given the necessary condition that the conservative scenario wasn't awful.

2. The many details require a considerable amount of searching and checking, which is appropriate for such a big undertaking.
   a. Being able to perform the 'what-if' scenarios quickly is a practical requirement. A relatively simple computerized algorithm can show the optimum solutions in just seconds.
   b. It is possible to use an optimization algorithm as part of the supporting software to come up with the best choice. For instance, evaluating the pessimistic scenario of exporting required comparing two alternative approaches;
      i. either to free capacity through eliminating T-generators or
      ii. to add a lot of capacity to the packing line.

      There is a need to check combinations of the two alternatives. The difficulty is that such a computerized process might end with options that have further negative ramifications in reality, especially those that might disrupt the company's reputation in the market. A computerized algorithm cannot evaluate dependencies for which it is not defined to check.
   c. Perhaps, machine learning will allow that capability in the future. The question is whether AI could learn all the dependencies that human intuition and knowledge can spot. For instance, can a certain T-generator be eliminated from the domestic

market without causing negative reactions? Many times, it is not problematic to stop offering a particular T-generator but there are certain items whose absence from the product mix would result in significantly reduced sales of other products. Thus, every option must consider the intuition of the managers and get the consent of the key people that no other impacts are expected. We assume that machine learning might be utilized, in the near future, to uncover initial propositions for superior moves, based on learning from the actual results. This could allow the computer to suggest moves that are in line with reality. Still, the management team should carefully check the suggested initiatives: are they are realistic and do they avoid overwhelming negative ramifications.

3. The insight of Capacity Buffers is clearly explored in the case. The difference between Lines 2 and 4, which lack any Capacity Buffer, and the Packing Line, which has this option, has demonstrated the huge value of being able to quickly increase the capacity. This option is valid, even when the considered utilization is very expensive, such as 100kg of cocoa being directly imported without subsidies.

It is customary to categorize decisions as 'strategic' or 'tactical.' An accepted meaning of the former is having a big impact on the long-term, while the latter is a short-term opportunity usually with a smaller impact. As has been demonstrated already, some seemingly small opportunities have significant impacts on the bottom line. We think that strategic planning, aimed at achieving a superior state in the future, should lead to the pursuit of both short and longer term opportunities.

Having a clearly defined process to determine whether opportunities will result in significant financial improvements, while keeping stability and safety under good control. Thus, there should be constant pressure to discover short-term ideas that improve the current state, while still moving in the general direction of the long-term plan. It is definitely important to validate that short-term ideas do not block the long-term agenda. So, there is a need to identify short-term opportunities and be able to quickly and comfortably analyze the possible consequences as an integral part of the overall planning.

One might evaluate the idea of creating different packages from the organization's basic products as a short-term initiative. Simultaneously, it remains an ongoing project to improve the state of the organization by better exploiting current markets in which the organization is active. These efforts should never end. It is an integral and absolute necessity to constantly improve the flow of value. A huge number of possible ideas should all be aimed at this objective:

Extracting more from the current state of demand and capacity

It is the duty of top management to constantly strive for a stream of ideas to exploit the current situation. Every idea that might be considered short-term in some particular circumstance is actually a candidate for repeating over and over, when the appropriate conditions exist. For instance, a two-week promotion, when it is truly effective at bringing in new customers, can be repeated when enough excess capacity allows. Moreover, such conceptual ideas can be expanded into a long-term initiative, after the short-term has revealed its potential. If a promotion works very well in bringing new customers, it means there is a bigger market for cheaper prices. Ideas for segmenting the T-generators, by offering cheaper prices on some and higher prices on others, aim at different market sectors that look for better value and are ready to pay more, could be a significant strategic step.

Export is just one way to elevate the flow of value to a new level. The generic idea is finding a new market segment for the existing products by creating new T-generators with, potentially, different content of products and prices. Another way is creating truly new products aimed at either the same market segment or new market segments. We are combining here two different ways of elevating the flow of value: better exploitation of the current capacity and adding new markets. Both may be required for achieving a leap in the organization's performance.

One of the insights provided by Dr. Goldratt was:

Segment your market, not your resources

This important insight encourages us to identify opportunities provided by the current excess capacity of the resources, as long as there remains enough protective capacity to support flow of value. Discovering new markets is a huge opportunity to achieve a highly profitable state between demand and capacity.

Another way of elevating the flow of value is by offering a new means of delivery or a new method of pricing. For example, offering a faster response service for a certain markup creates new T-generators based on the same basic products but delivered to meet an unmet customer need and priced accordingly to their value saved or created. Thus, we aim at a more specific market segment for which the speed of delivery is of special value.

Another example is leasing relatively expensive equipment, which are used as resources by other businesses, as a very different method of earning payment. A similar idea is charging per use of the equipment by the client, instead of selling the client the equipment outright. A good example of this was Xerox placing their copier at the client office and charging per copy. This approach is now widely used for software which exists in a cloud and is charged by actual usage. A last example is providers of commercial aircraft engines charging for power-by-the-hour – once the airline starts the engines, billing begins. You have no doubt noticed on a sunny summer day that you might sit in a very hot jet waiting for ground control to release the plane for taxi. You can feel good that your sweat saves the airline TVC.

Strategic decision makers have to struggle with much greater uncertainty because of two different causes:

1. The further into the future one must peer, the higher the level of fluctuations. This uncertainty impacts both sales and capacity requirements.
2. Any decision that results in a deviation from the current state, is also a move away from the current comfort zone. As people get further outside their comfort zones, their level of intuition decreases dramatically. This has a large negative impact on the experts' ability to properly assess the degree of uncertainty.

The combination of larger fluctuations and less confidence in the assessment itself causes people to shy away from even attempting to make an assessment. Being required to estimate the potential demand in a new export market puts a lot of pressure on the shoulders of the relevant executives. However, the most damaging response is saying "I don't know," as this claim only supports no decision. The jeopardy is estimating too wide of a range but even a wide range is better for making decisions, because it leads to better understanding of potential losses and successes, while highlighting operational challenges.

The debate on the specific export proposal also raises awareness of the need to check more than just one alternative. Suppose Choco-for-You had two different valid options for export. The state of current capacity, on top of recognizing that there is a minimal product mix for every export market to be viable, makes it practically impossible to attempt both options simultaneously. It is simply too difficult to take two big steps at one time. Generally speaking, big moves should be taken one-by-one in order not to exhaust the capabilities and capacities of management to manage the transition.

After each step, there is a Transition Period. Managing the flow of a new volume of products while also having to deal with novel issues that are unknown today, adds considerably to the load on the limited capacity of management attention. Management attention is a kind of resource that requires special monitoring because when it is needed, it must be available or significant damage can result.

When two alternatives compete with each other, the decision-making process should go through the same procedure of creating the two scenarios, both conservative and optimistic, for each of the two alternatives. In the vast majority of the cases, the two conservative scenarios reflect the risks, while the two optimistic ones represent the chance of having significant leaps in performance. The choice is usually clear for the management team, once the full information is clearly placed on the table.[1]

Another topic mentioned in this case is **the possible treatment of materials as resources.** The practical differences between materials and resources correspond to two aspects:

1. Purchased materials behave in a linear way with few exceptions. It is possible, in most cases, to buy exactly the required quantity. Capacity, on the other hand, is usually purchased in minimum chunks, thus, creating very substantial differences.
2. Capacity is consumed per period of time. **The capacity that is not used in one period is lost forever.** The next day, that capacity is available again but we cannot redeploy the capacity of yesterday. Materials behave very differently. Once they are consumed, they cannot be re-consumed later. However, materials that were not consumed today can be consumed tomorrow, unless a very strict expiration date is applied to those materials.

The above differences make it necessary to treat the cost of materials and of capacity differently. The cost of materials is embedded with the sales. It becomes part of product that is sold to generate Throughput, making its use linear.

There are cases in which the purchase of some materials is definitely non-linear. It happens when a material is scarce enough to force commitments to purchase a certain amount per period of time. In such a case, any additional purchases are much more expensive and sometimes impossible. The use of natural gas by power-stations could pose such a situation, since the alternatives to gas, like oil or coal, are much more expensive.

---

[1] Please note a risk that exists in many companies due to their cultures. Some companies foment a sense of competition between employees. If true, an employees may support choices that elevate them but are not the best for the company. We council that this culture is universally bad. Any competition should be between a company and its competitors, not internally. Internal competition, for promotion, raises and assignments, is an obsolete notion. Where it remains, it still exists due to an erroneous assumption that we authors have worked to dispel with this book. The erroneous assumption is if the performance of each individual resource is maximized, it maximizes the results of the company. Yet, intuitively, you know that employees who compete against each other are not working synergistically and, even more, are they unlikely to be willing to subordinate to the weakest-link or the constraint of the whole company. Even those who agree with us, may find they still harbor some old thinking. This is one that is best purged. Don't let mental inertia allow these habits to remain!

Another example is the size of a container for supplies that are shipped by ocean, sea and river. Sometimes this minimum amount serves a whole year of consumption. This situation is similar to capacity but the difference is still that materials which are not consumed today remain available tomorrow, again, unless there is an applicable expiration time on the use of the materials. A short useful life makes materials more similar to capacity. In reality, there is always some finite useful life for materials, either because the quality deteriorates or because new and better products become available obsoleting the older offering. Practically, the question is whether there is a pressure to use the materials soon or no such a pressure.

Another case is when a manufacturing company owns the materials and uses them for production. This is typical for production based on agriculture. For instance, wine producers commonly own the vineyards. Decisions regarding how to grow the grapes are part of the overall strategy of the wine maker. Once the actual quantity of the crop becomes known, it is like having a capacity resource constraint. It is desirable to use the entire crop, as long as there is enough capacity of all the other resources, such as barrels. With wine, which can be sold several years later and, in some cases, even benefits from more barrel age, the common assumption is that the whole quantity will be sold for a good enough price.

A kind of twisted case is the production of meat. The special situation is that the main material serves many different end products. When the producer owns the farms for raising the cattle, then the similarity to managing resources is striking.

The company buys an animal and considers it as raw material. This means it is treated as a truly-variable-cost (TVC) and, thus, part of the sale that produces Throughput. The practical problem is how to divide the cost of the animal between the different T-generators produced from it. Any split of the cost to the various parts that go into different end products is clearly arbitrary but it could easily impact selling decisions on the T-generator level.

Suppose that some parts of the animal go into a relatively cheap T-generator with very little Throughput per unit. Any small increase in the TVC of those products could turn the T per unit negative. When this happens, should the company stop selling those cheap T-generators? The point is that any artificial cost allocated to any particular cut is not real. Thus, it should not be treated as TVC (truly variable costs). The company is buying and raising the animals mainly for the specific parts intended for much more profitable T-generators. If the company can't process the less profitable parts or make them into lower level products, sold as cheap T-generators, then those leftover parts will become scrap.

The straightforward business question is which alternative is better: producing and selling cheap T-generators as a separate line from the higher quality meat of choice or dumping them?

Only a complete check of both options can reveal the actual impact on the bottom line. The simple way to check both options is to model the animals as several resources based on the parts that go into specific products. Each of the parts has a certain available capacity determined by the total number of the animals. All the animals that were raised on the farms should be considered OE, supplying various amounts of capacity of the various parts. When more capacity is required, maybe for just one T-generator with more available demand than available capacity, then there could be two different ways to get that required quantity. One is to find sellers that agree to sell just that part. The other is buying whole animals, which also increases the available capacity required for the other T-generators as well. This raises the question: can we use the additional lower-demand parts to generate more sales of the cheaper lines of T-generators? The answer might be positive when the additional cheap sales, usually aimed at lower socio-economic market segments, do not disrupt the prices in the main markets.

The impact of these decisions should be evaluated only through the holistic analysis of the available options.

The impact of costs that behave linearly or close enough (materials) and other costs that vary in step-functions (resources) is determined by their characteristics. The modeling approach can easily be adjusted to be practical. But, remember, there is no way to be truly optimal. It is simple to reach the condition of having a good-enough model that leads to good decisions. Our requirement for a good-enough solution for decision-making is that it effectively highlights the likely range of reasonable results. Would the considered initiative increase the current bottom line or decrease it?

Chapter 14

The Role of Time and Timing in Decision Making

What is the appropriate horizon for checking the possible ramifications of a decision?

So far, the decisions have been analyzed according to a specific time period. It makes perfect sense that short-term decisions should use a monthly time period, or even weekly, to examine the relevant immediate ramifications. A top management meeting evaluating the market and new opportunities, as well as their ramifications on capacity, should be conducted every month to stay vigilant about what else can be done in the short term to improve.

The current capacity profile of the critical resources should trigger thinking about possible ideas to use the spare capacity that is well below the rough estimation of the protective capacity. View again the starting load chart of Choco-for-You as shown in Figure 14.1.

Traditional Theory-of Constraints (TOC) thinking focuses on the current constraint which appears to be the Packing Line. Focusing just on the packing line and evaluating the T per Packing-Line-Capacity for every T-generator would lead the management to put extra efforts towards searching new opportunities to sell more T-generators that deliver a high rate of T through that line. However, this can only be done at the expense of other T-generators, presumably ones with lower T per Packing-Line-Capacity. For such actions to increase profits, all four of the following necessary conditions must be met:

- The Packing Line doesn't have the capacity to supply all the demand, plus the new sales. If the Packing Line is capable of everything, then there are no trade-offs. Profits will definitely increase. If it is possible to add capacity to the Packing Line for a price, then the only question is whether ΔT is greater than ΔOE.
- Limiting the sales of lower T per Packing-Line-Capacity T-generators is enough to free the required capacity from the Packing Line and prevent crossing its protective capacity limit.
- The market will accept limiting the sales of the least contributing T-generators without causing a further reduction in sales.
- The additional sales of high T per Packing-Line-Capacity products don't push another resource to penetrate its protective capacity limit.

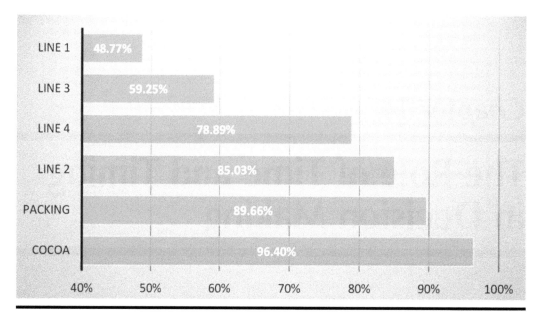

Figure 14.1 Starting capacity utilization for Choco-for-You.

When all four conditions apply, then ΔOE is 0. In such cases, all the ΔT goes directly to the bottom line.

However, the possibility of quickly adding capacity in fast micro-elevations of the constraint(s), is not typically checked by the traditional TOC tools. We are taking a much wider view of the existing options and offer a valid way to check the outcomes.

The load-profile of Choco-for-You, as shown above, points to additional options. The fact that there is a lot of excess capacity on three production lines tells us that any additional load on these lines would not cause any ΔOE. This is quite a valuable insight to guide our thinking toward hidden possibilities. Of course, any significant sales growth might cause the Packing Line to penetrate into its protective capacity envelope, which is something we should avoid. We may need to add capacity to the Packing Line, which does generate ΔOE of the direct costs of utilizing the old Line. However, the extra load cannot be allowed to push other resources past their protective capacity limits. The conclusion is that, while the current situation points to a good chance of being able to generate much more Throughput, we can't be certain unless the whole scenario is analyzed holistically.

Presenting the situation to the sales people could even lead to new ideas about T-generators that do not require packing, such as chocolate that is sold in bulk, by weight. When a hypothetical opportunity is well verbalized, new ideas will be raised. Even when just the short-term is considered, without any big investment in new equipment or development of new products, the possibility of a significant improvement in short-term profits is high.

Making efforts like these is what is implied by the second step of the TOC Five Focusing Steps: "Decide how to exploit the system constraint(s)".

Realizing the role of total Throughput, Capacity Buffers and the need to check the total load versus the protective capacity, is a guide for management to constantly look for better and better exploitations of both the market demand and the capacity limitations of very few resources.

However, when a very substantial opportunity is put on the table or a big move involving a substantial investment is considered, it is necessary to use longer-time frames, such as a quarter, a year, or even several years, to check the full ramifications. It also makes sense that some decisions have a considerable impact on the short-term and also over the longer term. Therefore, it is a necessity to check the same decision from both perspectives. For instance, offering new packages of basic items as new T-generators could be done relatively quickly but the intent is to continue to offer them in the long term, maybe even offering a much larger variety of packages.

We have already mentioned the following important assumption about the capacity used for decisions over a period of time:

> **The capacity utilized in the previous period for satisfying demand in this period is about equal to the capacity invested in this period for next period's demand.**

This means we assume that, in order to deliver the demand during the period under analysis, we better have enough capacity to process all the demand.

Do we lose accuracy because of this approximation? In other words, are there cases in which this inaccuracy might lead management to make the wrong decision?

There are two cases in which this approximation might distort the decision.

The first case is when there is an expected significant change in the demand between one period and the next. Seasonality and very large future orders are two examples. Promotions are self-induced peaks of demand that create a period of higher demand followed by a period of lower than normal demand.

The second case results in the intentional buildup of stock, for instance of new products, and consuming stock without the intention of replenishing it. This also happens when products are replaced by newer versions. In such a case, the capacity required by the demand for this particular period is NOT equal to the actual capacity required for the previous period. More capacity might be needed to build initial stocks that will hopefully support sales in later periods. On the other hand, less capacity may be required, because of sales of products already available on-hand that are not going to be replenished. There is a need for a special procedure to account for the stock produced or sold that will not be replenished.

The important realization coming from the seasonality case is the need to carefully consider the appropriate time horizon over which the decisions on the table should be evaluated. When the demand during a certain period differs from the adjacent periods, then a longer-time horizon must be used to assess even short-term decisions.

For instance, within a peak demand period, the amount of sales might hypothetically require double the available capacity of the weakest-link resource during that time period. When the situation is recognized early enough, then using excess capacity over several previous off-peak periods, it may be possible to produce enough stock before the peak season. Such a solution is relevant only for standard products, which can be produced without a specific client order. Therefore, the decision to produce is based on forecast. Note, the overproduction of several standard products is not for replenishing the stock, but rather is a way to not have to quickly replenish within the peak. The key idea is to free the capacity of the critical resources during the periods with much higher than normal demand.

There are several variations to building stock during off-peak periods in order to reduce the capacity pressure during the high season.

The key decision concerns the specific products to be produced to stock before the peak. The idea is that it is enough to prepare stock of only several fast runners, in order to free enough capacity during the peak.

Another required decision is to determine the amount of stock needed at the start of the season and what to leave for production in-season when the actual demand becomes clear. The stock of the chosen products at the beginning of the peak period should cover the expected demand throughout the peak itself. The overall available capacity during this extended horizon, which covers the low season, during which the stock is produced, and the high season, must cover the expected demand according to the optimistic scenario. The analysis has to ensure that while building the stock of the chosen items, the extra production does not interfere with supplying all the demand prior to the peak. And, when the high season arrives, there is enough stock to cover the difference between demand and available capacity.

Another aspect of the decision is to consider the scenario post-peak, when the demand goes down and the remaining stock might still be excessive. This is relevant mainly for the pessimistic assessment. The question to be analyzed in planning is how much stock might be left over for the subsequent lower demand period and what can be done with it? A key question is how long it might take to sell the surplus stock before resuming normal replenishment procedures. An option to consider is dropping the price of some of overstocked items to encourage their sales. Special care is required to account for the impact of reduced prices on the sales of other T-Generators. Sometimes, the best option when too much stock remains is fully disposing of the goods or dumping them in remote markets.

To properly analyze the impact of a peak of demand, where the actual capacity of the critical resources might be insufficient, the conclusion is that one should include an immediately prior off-peak period as well as the peak itself, considering the optimistic scenario. The pessimistic scenario should be used to clearly outline the full financial results over the whole timeframe from preparing stock for the peak, the peak period itself, and stabilizing inventory levels after the peak.

Determining an Appropriate Time Frame for a Specific Decision is Essential

Some decisions cause different effects on the short-term than on the longer-term. Therefore, the analysis must consider more than one timeframe.

For instance, a long-term deal with a big client could be great for the short-term, if the company has a lot of excess capacity but over the long-term that deal might block other more lucrative opportunities.

Another example is investigating the financial ramifications of a three-week long promotion, which requires evaluating two different timeframes separately. The analysis should focus on the capacity profile prior to and during the promotion, considering all the demand, not just for the promoted items. The other evaluation focuses on the full financial impact that includes the reduced sales immediately *after* the promotion. This check looks at the total T generated throughout the whole period, ensuring the overall T - OE is higher than it would be without the promotion.

A point to notice and understand is that when the use of extra capacity before a promotion is a must, it is in no way offset by the surplus capacity after the promotion. Do not rely on having enough capacity 'on average' – more is needed at certain times and much less at others. Thus, both horizons plus the period in question should be carefully evaluated, both before and after the promotion as well as the high-demand period itself.

Generically, the impact of time on decisions is much greater than what the above examples have exposed. Many key decisions are intended to achieve their objective over the long-term – many months or even years. There are three different factors that cause an inherent difficulty to assess probable impacts over longer terms.

The Special Difficulties with Long-Term Decisions

The first factor is **the impact of uncertainty,** which becomes much worse the longer one looks out. This inherent characteristic of uncertainty has a major impact on the ability to define a practical, yet reasonable, future range of demand.

The second factor concerns **the value of money.** It is obvious that the value of one dollar to be received ten years from now is lower than its value today. Beyond the diminished value due to uncertainty or inflation, another relevant reason is the inherent advantage of using the money now, which can be spent or invested to create more value in the future. For example, when we loan money, we expect to be compensated for that transfer of value, even when we are certain the loan will be repaid in full. This is the core of the concept of "the value of money," which is composed of two parameters: risk and potential value created. The price of money is commonly denominated as a certain interest rate per period of time.

The third factor is the **impact of the exact timing on capacity.** When a lead time is reasonably short, such as between a few minutes and several weeks, then the impact of the exact timing of either the cash transactions or the capacity utilization is typically immaterial to decision making. One exception is when cash is a constraint, threatening the survival of the organization. In that case, the exact timing of the cash transactions becomes critical. (More on cash in the next chapter.) Another exception is when tremendous leverage is used to gain a return. The problem with tremendous leverage is that it can work tremendously against the investor, under circumstances believed to be so rare they can be ignored.[1]

However, when lead times are longer than a few weeks, timing has more considerable effects; it could become critical. A relatively simple check of the predicted changes in T, OE and on the average capacity of the few critical resources might not be enough.

In such situations, even the question of the timing of the additional Throughput (ΔT) becomes meaningful for good decision-making. First of all, T is the difference of two different flows of money: Truly Variable Costs are usually spent before the revenues from the sale arrive. Accrual accounting whether Throughput Accounting or GAAP, calculates Throughput and gross profit, respectively, ignoring the difference in timing between paying for TVC and collecting revenues. When the difference in time is significant, the financing costs – the relevant interest rates rise. This interest is part of the OE.

For some ΔT generating decisions, especially when the flow of T generated is a small percentage of the flow of sales, the impact on ΔOE due to a higher level of financial costs might be significant enough to make a difference on the chosen direction, when factored in to the calculations. An example might be a commodity business, such as trading coal or soybean futures.

There are more cases where the TVC is not the only dedicated short-term investment for generating Throughput. There is also a need for ΔOE, when the regularly available capacity is too little. Assuming revenues are received much later than when the capacity is consumed, then the

---

[1] Read *Antifragile* and *The Black Swan*, by Nassim Taleb and Michael Lewis' *The Big Short* and *Bubbles, Booms, and Busts: The Rise and Fall of Financial Assets* by Donald Rapp. All expose the consequences and folly of massive leverage. It is only a question of who will suffer the catastrophe and when.

financial impact of the difference in the timing is even more significant. This situation is common for projects in which the lead time is between a few months and several years. Many times, projects require the purchase of materials, dedicated equipment and outsourcing certain tasks to subcontractors. These expenses can be categorized as either TVC or ΔOE. That distinction does not truly matter much, because every project deserves to be checked for its own ΔT - ΔOE, being the expected contribution of the project to the organization. We expect that the reasonable pessimistic estimation would address that situation, so all top managers are exposed to this information, including the financial impact on cash and the cost of money.

The Impact of Time on Capacity Calculations

The timing of capacity needs is a tough issue over longer timeframes. The important question we should consider is whether one or several critical resources could exhaust their regularly available capacity. This is a necessary aspect of validating the full ramifications of the decision. Even a temporary lack of capacity in a multi-project environment might either cause substantial delays on several projects or cause considerable ΔOE due to the urgent need to increase capacity. The concern, when we consider longer timeframes, is that the overall load on any critical resource will be problematic due to the impact of uncertainty, during a certain week or month way out in the future.

When enough additional load is placed on a resource, the unavoidable result is that some orders or projects are delayed. The critical question is how damaging are these potential delays?

The following examples demonstrate when there is a real problem and when there isn't a problem.

Suppose a manufacturing job-shop is producing to the specifications of their customers so that every order is fully customized and, thus, has to be produced from scratch per special order. The weakest link resource is, on average, loaded to 75% of its available capacity. How long might an unlucky order be delayed? Assume that a good enough priority mechanism is being applied. Theoretically, such an order might wait for the weakest link for three weeks. However, that assumes all the monthly orders arrive at the same time. Given that this is not typical, it seems reasonable to expect the longest delay, due to a temporary peak load, might be two weeks.

The relevant question now is: **how long of a delay is tolerable?**

When the standard response time, from the placement of an order until it is delivered, is significantly longer than two or three weeks, there should be no problem. However, when the market expectations are for a maximum wait before delivery of three days, then even one resource loaded to 75% on average might result in frequent delays. This means that, for a very fast response time, it is necessary either to produce to stock or to maintain very high protective capacity. Most service organizations maintain a lot of protective capacity of which management is only partially aware.

A similar situation happens, strangely enough, in multi-project environments, where the average lead time of a project could be between six months and several years. What happens in projects is that the "touch-time,[2]" comprises a significant portion of the lead time of the whole project. The ideal situation, in projects, is that the touch time along the critical-path or the critical-chain[3] is equal to the project lead time. Practically speaking, this does not happen very often because tasks in projects frequently wait for resources, because the needed resources are busy working on other projects

---

[2] The net actual work time done on the longest chain of tasks.
[3] The Critical Chain is the TOC re-definition of critical path so that not just the longest sequence of events but also resource dependencies are accounted for as well.

or tasks. Delays of the whole project due to unavailability of a specific resource could be substantial even though *every* specific resource has excess capacity when viewed throughout a whole year.

What makes multi-projects environments different than manufacturing and services stems from the following complicating characteristics:

- A single task in a project takes much longer time than regular tasks in both manufacturing and services. The ramification is that when two tasks compete for the capacity of the same resource, one task must wait until another is finished. Because such a delay could put a whole project on hold for a long time, there is a common tendency to multitask, allowing resources to work on multiple tasks at the same time or switch back and forth between them. This has a very significant negative impact on the timeliness of projects in a multi-project environment, to the extent that severe damage can be experience by clients.
- In a typical manufacturing environment, there are many open orders, say between 20 and 500, competing for capacity of the same critical resources. In typical multi-project environment, there might be three to twelve active projects competing for resources at the same time. A higher quantity of orders mitigates natural fluctuations in the load on the manufacturing resources. In a multi-project environments, on the other hand, the fluctuations are considerably larger. Practically, this means that the production manager in manufacturing has more flexibility to deal with temporary peaks than his equivalent in the multi-project environment.
- Human beings and expensive equipment are the key resources in projects and manufacturing, respectively. It is far more difficult to measure the capacity of humans. An engineer might look busy all the time but is still able to do more work, when necessary. We know how to control the pace of what we do depending on the degree of pressure we are under. Usually more pressure can result in more work but, beyond some limit which is different for each individual, more pressure results in less output. Additionally, people often undertake extraordinary efforts to hide their true capacity. So, although most human resources have considerable excess capacity, it is difficult to measure it.

Prior to this chapter, the analysis of decisions was focused on estimating ΔT and ΔOE, in addition to validating that all the key resources have adequate protective capacity. The impact of uncertainty, mainly around the demand, is handled by checking the reasonable pessimistic and optimistic scenarios.

When the decision on the table requires long-term analysis, a pertinent question is whether it is absolutely necessary to include the timing of both money transactions and capacity consumption. We should consider two different ways to deal with the timing issue:

1. Following the similar route already described.
   The simpler way is just to include a rough estimation of financial costs as additional ΔOE spent. Cash is a critical resource in long-term moves. Thus, it should be carefully monitored. The investment itself is usually not included. The objective of the calculations is to establish the return itself. The ROI can be calculated based on it. The scenarios must deal with the range between the reasonable pessimistic assessment and the optimistic one, while also considering the higher level of protective capacity required to cover for the possibility of temporary peaks and inaccurate estimations of capacity requirements. This certainly is an approximate analysis. In most cases, it is good enough to determine the risk of losing money versus the probability of a considerable gain. It is important to realize that

all calculations based on intuitive input cannot be precise, even for short lead-times. The objective is to gain a better understanding of what *might* happen. Since all decisions are based on predictions, mostly intuitive predictions of the future, there is no way to get accurate results.[4] The focus of the analysis is to reveal with reasonable confidence whether ΔT less ΔOE is greater than zero. When the pessimistic scenario predicts that this difference is less than zero and the optimistic suggests an amount much greater than zero, then management needs to decide whether the risk is worthwhile.

2. A more detailed analysis

   The objective of getting into more detail for the longer term is to gain a tighter range of possible outcomes. The big question is whether this objective is practical, since the impact of uncertainty of the details is usually much higher. A more sophisticated analysis considers the predicted timing of the investment, including materials and Capacity Buffer consumption, in addition to the timing of the revenues. This would enable a more precise estimation of the financial costs. The timings of the detailed capacity consumption are included in order to validate that no serious peaks of load would cause too much damage. Such an approach requires the calculation of the Net-Present-Value (NPV) of the money transactions, in addition to using the algorithm of the 'drum', a part of the TOC Critical Chain Project-Management (CCPM) to simulate the overall capacity and timing ramifications of all the projects.

The more complicated approach must face the challenge of considering situations in which the predicted load penetrates into the protective capacity at specific periods along the timeline. How should one treat a situation in which a specific resource is loaded to 110% in one period but the next period is loaded only to 60% the next, followed by only 50%? How should one measure the requirement for protective capacity in such a case? When there is a temporary peak, the lowest priority tasks are typically delayed. Using buffer management priorities should reduce the probability that the whole project is significantly delayed. Therefore, there is a good chance that the impact of the delays overall would be minimal.

Does Added Sophistication Lead to Better Decisions?

Since uncertainty is relatively high in the second case, it seems to us that the first way is a good enough way to present the available information without misleading the decision makers, in the majority of the cases. Certainly, more real-life experience would highlight whether the somewhat higher complication adds enough real value to be worth the trouble. People often fool themselves on this score. The fear of uncertainty is common, unless one has practiced a simpler way long enough that it becomes habit. Be careful!

Another topic to be considered is how to determine the strength of the **project portfolio** of a multi-project organization as a whole. This book is about evaluating every individual decision based on its impact on the total activity. This means that every single project is analyzed based on its impact on the portfolio, as well as on all other activities of the organization. The impact of adding one project to an existing portfolio should include its effect on the total risk the organization is facing.

---

[4] Statistically speaking, it is wise to round final figures, depending on how much uncertainty is expected. However, mathematically inferior results result if one rounds the outcomes of interim calculations. Wait until the end and make $1,314,237 into $1.3 million, as an example.

We already mentioned that every project is risky. Having a portfolio of many projects should reduce the overall risk. When we add a project to a given portfolio, we should assess the individual risk of the project and also check whether the overall risk of the whole portfolio is rising or falling. Overall risk is a serious factor to consider, enabling us to assess whether the survival of the organization is at stake.

The difficulty in evaluating the overall portfolio risk lies in the level of dependency between different projects. Dependency means the likeliness that any two or more projects will succeed or fail together. When both projects have the same end customer, the same professional team and very similar technical challenges, the overall risk is not reduced. It might pose too much of a gamble for the organization to undertake.

On the other hand, when projects are independent, the overall risk is reduced. In reality, certain dependencies always exist, when projects are performed by the same organization. Usually, these dependencies are only partial, meaning that the overall risk is reduced by the portfolio but the reduction is less than what would be expected from mathematical formulas that assume complete independence between variables.

Another important lesson is the strategic preference to have as much independence between projects and initiatives as possible to control the risks.

The foregoing discussion about project environments also applies to service providers, not-for-profit companies, retail, distribution and manufacturing, whether making finished goods for inventory or making products directly to customer orders. Simpler, as long it is good enough, it is actually better because it is less sensitive to small inaccuracies of data and the implementation is much more robust!

Lastly, bear in mind that companies should always be seeking to improve. These improvement initiatives are projects. Some are short-term, medium-term and others are long-term projects. So, the warnings and ideas expressed in this chapter apply no matter what the type of business.

Chapter 15

Cash as a Special Critical Resource

An Unexpected Problem with Cash

When Philip ran his weekly cash-flow forecast for the next two months, he flushed and his heart skipped several beats. He had not expected cash to drain so fast. Philip, the CFO of Adar Industries was aware of the extraordinary expenses of the advertising campaign and its impact on the working capital but he did not expect the extent of the sudden increase in inventories due to new products. He remembered how he had protested launching both new product lines intended for new market segments at the same time. However, even the pessimistic forecast of the potential ΔT of entering both new segments exceeded the expected ΔOE, while the capacity of the critical resources in manufacturing seemed under control, even with significant overtime, depending on actual sales. So, both ideas were accepted according to the growth strategy for the company. Now, he found himself wishing that he had stuck to his guns.

Philip felt that his warnings fell on deaf ears, based on the favorable business results revealed by the analysis. Now, the steady sharp growth of inventory and overtime expenses resulted in a deep penetration into the credit line and the first invoice from the advertising company had just arrived. Yet, sales of the new products were two months off and collections against those sales at least another month away. He remembered that Lora, the VP of Sales, had glibly advocated for the mutual introduction of the two product families and she also added that it'd take between four and six months before sales reached her expected levels.

In retrospect, Philip felt like he should have predicted that such a decision would have temporarily threatened his available cash position. Now, it is imperative to increase the credit line as fast as possible. Doing so is not going to be easy.

During an emergency meeting in the CEO's office, both surprise and tension are expressed. David, the CEO, who was the main figure in convincing the bank to approve the current credit level was uncertain whether there was a reasonable chance to increase the credit line still further. Even if this could be done, the interest rate would be significantly higher to cover the higher risk that the bank would need to account for.

Lora emphasized that the timing of the two launches is critical, because targeted distribution chains are imminently considering their options for next year. She has already succeeded to get them truly interested in the two new product families.

> *"It is inconceivable to delay the actual launch of either of the two families. We'll lose the respect that the three largest distributors have for us. Both product families suit them very well. If we can't deliver on time and in full, they would have to sell a competitor's products instead. Come on! This could be the breakthrough we have been seeking for so many years."*

Dmitry, the VP of Operations was truly agitated, "We have signed contracts with a dozen suppliers to make sure we get all the materials, for our existing products and the new ones. We brought back twenty retired operators to allow us to use the amount of overtime required to build the needed inventory of the new products. We included the initial stockpiling of inventory in the analysis, so what's wrong now? We cannot tamper with these plans without paying significant penalties. We carefully chose this off-peak timeframe, because we have enough free capacity of our critical resources to build the required inventory. We cannot stop now or even delay one family. The peak season hits in three or four months. When else could we launch the family Philip suggests we have to delay?"

David concluded, "Okay, we need more cash, as soon as possible. If we survive the tough period in which we are truly pressed for cash, then in six months the problem will disappear, because our new revenues and profits will persuade any bank to give us the credit line we need."

David paused for a while and then said in low voice and with deliberate emphasis, "I hope we all learn a lesson from this surprising situation."

What Can We Learn from the Above Story?

Critical resources have either been defined by being close to running out of capacity due to increased demand from the market or as resources where quick increases of temporary capacity are possible whenever necessary but at significant expense.

The trouble with cash is that there is either enough of it and we think of it only when we face a very substantial expense or it is not available, making it the crucial issue for every choice no matter how small. This chapter deals with the special resource called cash and when we must deal with cash as a critical resource.

The Special Type of Resource Called: Available Cash

Organizations need available cash to support the operations they require to earn more money. There is a significant difference between making money, meaning having revenues significantly greater than expenses and maintaining enough cash to pay for operations. One reason is the timing difference between regular expenses, such as purchasing materials and paying the salaries, and the time when revenues are finally received. The story above demonstrates a case in which a significant move with the intention of making much more money requires raising much more cash to support existing and new operations for a long period of time. Generally speaking, making profit does not mean that the organization is able to cover the cost of its operations in the short-term. Lack of cash could easily and almost immediately disrupt the future of that organization. How immediately? How long will suppliers keep shipping when they aren't being paid for previous shipments? How long will employees work for free? How long will the utility leave the electricity on? That's what we mean by "almost immediately."

When an organization is on the edge of survival, then cash is not just a critical resource. It is the single active constraint. No other critical resource or other critical issue is as important, at such a time. Being broke means that every action, opportunity or threat, must be analyzed on just two criteria:

1. How much available cash is required to maintain activities that generate more cash in the near future and
2. How quickly these activities generate the cash required to continue.

No other factors are relevant at this stage. This is a special situation that is outside the scope of this book.[1]

However, cash is a critical resource in many other situations in which the organization is not under imminent threat of survival. In many on-going businesses, the available cash is not a factor in the daily decision-making. Thus, in such situations, it should not be part of the critical resources group. However, there are also situations in which any initiative to improve profitability must be very carefully checked for its impact on the available cash. Its early cash ramifications are quite different from the initiative's future impact on profitability.

Distribution organizations that purchase a huge number of different products from many suppliers, transport, store and eventually sell and deliver them have lots of cash tied up in inventory. Their capital requirements are higher than in most other business sectors. Such organizations must exert constant control on their investment in inventory. Frequent and significant changes in sales or the mix of products might have a significant impact on the inventory investment, calling for urgent management intervention. When the level of cash drops sharply, penetrating deep into the line of credit due to an increase in the level of inventory, management must consider whether or not to restrain their overall level of activity and, by doing so, harm Throughput generation. Alternatively, they can seek more sources of financing to support the higher level of activity. Adding ways to generate available cash, which is the same as adding capacity to a resource, should consider higher costs of money and other short and long-term impacts on the available cash that directly impact purchasing and all other operations.

When long-term ideas are analyzed, then cash might easily become a critical resource, certainly when ideas requiring significant investments are considered. On top of the investment, once the idea becomes operational it might require a constant stream of ΔOE. Both types of additional requirements for money might threaten the credit of the organization and require special financing, which almost always increases the cost of money used by the organization.

When several such ideas are considered together, the combined analysis, done in the way described in the previous chapters, should also evaluate the amount of $\Delta Cash$ required due to the new financial situation and additional ΔOE. It is especially vital to look into whether that level of cash can be maintained, if it needs to be maintained. Loans and other forms of

---

[1] An important work on the situation of dealing with a 'cash constraint' for survival and applying the TOC logic to that situation was done by Ravi Gilani from India. The interested reader might like to watch the following video: https://vimeo.com/233884445 dedicated to that topic. An article by Ravi Gilani and Eli Schragenheim, one of the authors of this book, can be found at: https://elischragenheim.com/2017/05/11/evaporating-an-active-cash-constraint/. Another resource that treats the cash-constrained condition is a set of PowerPoint Slides created by Henry Camp from Ravi Gilani's work. Here is a link to download the PowerPoint from Dropbox: http://bit.ly/2AH9KZs The slides pertinent to a cash constraint are slides 71 through 85. However, the metrics suggested within are applicable to every company and, again, beyond the scope of this book.

financial aid are means to increase the required cash analogous to overtime as a means for increasing capacity of other human resources. Any ΔCash causes ΔOE due to the interest rate charged by the lender.

The key point for inquiring how certain actions impact cash resources is to recognize that it is *not* enough to maintain detailed cash control. It is easy to reject offers for increasing the available cash, such as taking a loan from an expensive mezzanine lender. But, if the extra cash is required for special actions which are expected to lead to higher profits, the high cost of financing might be attractive overall. In other words, as we have said throughout, management should consider the predicted ΔThroughput generated from those actions and compare it against the full ΔOE, including the high costs of the required financing. The outcome defines the return on investment required for the move.

Both the pessimistic and optimistic scenarios should include cash as a critical resource when long-term decisions are considered. Such long-term decisions have to be evaluated through two different time horizons.

1. The first horizon includes the period required for preparing and implementing the initial phases of the considered move. This is a relatively short-term horizon and the objective of the evaluation is to ensure there are no serious negative ramifications on the overall activities of the organization. The initial impact of the various investments on the financial stability and the state of the cash flow should be examined, making sure there is enough cash for operations. A concern is that the investment might drain the cash to the level that it becomes an active constraint. This situation threatens the survival of the organization. Another aspect of the short-term check is to evaluate the impact of the implementation process on the capacity of other critical resources, including the available capacity of the relevant managers who must lead the transition until the overall activity of the organization again becomes stable. The outcome of this check does not focus on the ΔT in the short-term, because it is just a side effect. The real focus should be on the resulting ΔT in the long-term. However, this effort will be more effective at revealing ΔOE that might be required and to ensure there is enough cash to pay for it. Lastly, make sure that no impending capacity shortage will harm the existing generation of T.

2. The second horizon looks out further into the future to allow evaluating the returns from the idea after the company reaches its new the steady state. At that point in time, the resulting ΔT and ΔOE of the new idea should be verified and the difference in profit over the timeframe can be considered as the return to be compared with its investment. The check, of course, considers all the other activities of the organization, in addition to the new idea considering possible changes indicated to the other activities, if required.

The obvious problem with cash, when treated as a resource, is that it is not just a resource, it is money, which is the key metric used to accept or reject any decision under consideration. This duality of cash, being a resource on one hand, and the metric of the goal on the other hand, might be confusing. Management need to note that the main performance operational measurements, such as T, I and OE, lead management to maximize the profit. However, when it comes to available cash, the need for protective capacity, meaning holding enough cash above what is required on average, should be addressed like any other resource. It is important to remember that examining cash as a resource is only one aspect in the decision but it is a truly critical one: **Does the organization have enough cash to perform all the activities necessary to generate the desired T - OE over the time horizon being considered, without limiting future performance?**

When there is enough available cash to cover even unplanned events and unexpected needs that might occur, then cash is not a major factor in the daily life of the organization. However, when the available cash resource penetrates into its own protective capacity, then the questions are: **Can the organization get more cash fast enough? If so, how much it is going to cost?**

The answers should be used when calculating the ΔT minus ΔOE of the activities that consume more cash than the status quo.

The cost of funds is interpreted as part of ΔOE, while the cash itself is just a resource required to generate the T. It is tricky but absolutely necessary to keep in mind that we treat money as two different entities: what we want to maximize and what we need for generating more money.

Securing Cash in Context

Even in first-world countries, where capital is readily accessible, running short of cash is far more likely to block a good idea for new ΔT than the ΔOE required for financing costs. In the rest of the world, capital is far less available, making it even more important, regardless of cost. The authors agree that "cash is king." Having access to cash means a much broader range of initiatives can be seriously considered.

In this chapter, we hope to help you avoid letting the need for cash take the company by surprise. We thought it best to make the point by using a specific scenario.

An Example to Explain How Serious a Constraining Factor Cash Can Be

For instance, imagine you want to start up a new company and it will be a distributorship. The same calculations apply, if you already operate as a distributor and look to add an additional product line of the same magnitude. To make it easy, let's say you have a group of customers willing to buy $30 million per year. How much capital is necessary to finance the operation of this company or to add the new operation to your existing company?

As a distributor what do you do? You buy finished goods in bulk, warehouse them until needed by your customers, resell them (generally in smaller quantities) and deliver, typically on your own fleet of trucks.

If you are conventional (unaware of the TOC's distribution solution) you might have (to make the math easy) 3.65 inventory turns per year.[2] Assume you are able to be competitive when you mark up your TVC for the products you buy by 20% and that your customers pay you in 1½ months after a sale.

First, you need money to buy inventory. You can probably get terms, for example, a 1% discount for paying in ten days. That discount adds 5% to T, so you wouldn't want to miss out on it. You have 100 days' worth of inventory but 10 days' worth will always be pending payment to your suppliers. So, you must finance 3 months' worth of TVC.[3] Add to that, 1.5 months' worth of sales, for which you are still awaiting payment. As they taught us all in grade school, you can't add apples and oranges, in this case numbers denominated in terms of TVC and sales. However, we know that sales are just undiscounted TVC marked up by 20%. Therefore, the 3 months of TVC

---

[2] Inventory turns of 3.65 means: the average on-hand inventory investment, in terms of the local currency, will be sold 3.65 times during the year. Another way of saying it is the expected TVC for the year is 3.65 times the average inventory on-hand. And, yet another way is to say that you hold 100 days of inventory.

[3] 100 days of inventory − 10 days inventory in A/P = 90 days or 3 months.

that is stuck in inventory is equivalent to 2 ½ months of sales.[4] In total you must have 4 months' worth of sales[5] or one third of a year's new sales already in the checkbook before you can embark on your new business or expand your old one.

"Wait a minute!" you exclaim. "You mean if I want to start a small $30 million in sales distributor, I have to already have $10 million?" The answer is, no, not exactly. Where capital markets allow it, you can borrow some of that money from a bank and put that into your checkbook. How much? Lets's check that.

Usually, for a new company, the bank will demand collateral and a personal guarantee.[6] The collateral can be the assets owned by the company. That is four months' worth of sales, as we just calculated. But, wait, the bank does not see all collateral as equally valuable.

They typically prefer Accounts Receivables from your customers more than inventory. The reason is, if you prove to be a poor business person and eventually can't pay them back, the bank isn't in your business. They don't know and don't want to know how to sell your inventory and to whom. So, they rely on being able to quickly auction off your inventory to the highest bidder. What do they expect to get? They hope, something better than half of what you paid for it. Anyway, they will only allow you half of the value of the inventory as collateral.

In the case of your Accounts Receivables (A/R), after you go under, they might sell that too. They expect to either collect or sell the invoices due from your customers for 75% or more of their value, if they are lucky. They will be more concerned with speed than maximizing their collections. So, you'll typically get collateral equal to three quarters of your A/R.

(Remember, before it gets to this point, you decided to walk away, presumably losses had mounted and things looked hopeless. However, you are always better to be the one to wind the company down yourself than to allow the bank to do so. You'll be far better than them at getting value for your assets.)

All together they may lend as much as 75% of the 1½ months of A/R plus 50% of 2½ months' worth of sales that are stuck in inventory. That totals 2.375 months' worth of sales. So, you only need to come with the difference, 1.625 months' worth of sales.[7] For a distributorship that is expected to sell $30 million per year, will require *only* a little more than $4 million[8] out of your pocket to finance the assets you'll need!

You're not finished though. The other major requirement for cash in a startup is operating expenses until cash starts to flow in from operations, four months later, in this case. Assume that you expect to net $½ million per year in profits. That implies operating expenses are $4.5 million per year.[9] OE flows only out for the first four months, as we calculated above. Four out of twelve months is one third of the year. Therefore, you also need cash equivalent to one third of the year's OE or $1.5 million dollars[10] on top of the $4+ million to finance the assets the bank wouldn't.

---

[4] 3 months of TVC / 120% Sales per TVC = 2.5 months of sales.

[5] 1.5 months of sales in Accounts Receivable + 2.5 months of sales in inventory = 4 months of sales

[6] A personal guarantee means that, if you don't pay the bank back, they can come take all the things you own, house, cars, property and sell them to recover what they lent.

[7] 4 months' worth of sales required to start the distributorship less 1.625 months' worth of sales a bank in a first world country might lend.

[8] 1.625 months' worth of sales x $30 million is sales per year / 12 months per year = $4,062,500 from you.

[9] $30 million in sales per year less $30 million / 120% in TVC give $5 million in T per year. Since T − OE = $½ million per year, then OE must be $4.5 million per year. (If you are watching very carefully, the 1% discount will be captured in Other (Income)/Expense, where it offsets interest expenses. In Throughput Accounting this will be netted out of OE.)

[10] $4.5 million per year in OE x 1/3 of a year, while no money has yet started to flow in.

Add a little bit more so the checking account isn't overdrawn and to cover other purchases of the many smaller things the company requires before it can get started. Call it $5.6 million dollars, all in.

But, aren't you in high cotton now? You are making $½ million per year. If that is net profit after taxes, in just over 11 years[11] you'll have earned your money back and start to get ahead.

So, you see our point. For many companies their cash-to-cash cycle time is long enough to be a significant factor in their decision making. Don't forget to consider the impact a major initiative can have on cash. There are many templated TOC solutions for projects, manufacturing and distribution which, among other beneficial things, reduce the time from when a dollar is spent on inventory until it returns home, along with the profits it earned. The aforementioned TOC insights are beyond the scope of this book but there are many other books and public domain resources available that cover them in detail.

---

[11] $5.51 million invested/$0.5 million in return per year = just over 11 years.

Chapter 16

The Quality of Earnings—
From the Perspective
of a TOC Minded CPA

"A billion here, a billion there, pretty soon, you're talking real money."

The above quote is attributed to Senator Everett Dirksen of the United States Senate. The three-term Senator was observing how flippantly government can be in deciding on financial matters – from taxes to spending.

In managing our business, the impacts of decisions of a dollar here, three euros there, 10 pounds here, 20 yuan there or 1000 yen anywhere have exponential effects in more ways than you may immediately think about.

The senator was right, except rather than "pretty soon," to quote one of my favorite charities, "someday is today."

We have devoted the majority of this book to the development of a methodology to offer the business world a conceptual pathway to think about costing in a way that truly represents the reality of operations, which will then enable a company to grow its Throughput faster than its Operating Expenses, which in turn leads to dramatically improving profitability. This is TOC thinking in its purest form, very simple cause and effect.

This concept of looking at costs in a way that reflects actual operational flow has more far-reaching impacts than maximizing the profitability of a product line or managing operations for profitability rather than 'efficiencies.'

We would like to devote some thoughts in this chapter to the impact that cost accounting has on the value of your business. Equally so, how should it influence your view of a business you may be looking to acquire?

Let's start with a simple example to make sure we are at the same starting point to further our discussion.

You own a company that has annual sales of	$50 million
Your truly variable cost of sales are	$25 million or 50% of sales[1]
Operational expenses are	$20 million
Profit before taxes	$5 million
Inventory	$5 million
$25 million TVC/$5 million of Inventory	5 Inventory turns
365 days per year/5 turns per year	73 days of Inventory on hand
Maximum Order Lead time to replace Inventory	30 days

This business should and likely would create significant interest, if it were placed on the market for acquisition. What could be good prices from the perspectives of the seller and buyer?

If you were to look at this business with the analytical purpose to acquire it, standard due diligence would be to retain a professional expert who is experienced at performing what is called a "Quality of Earnings" analysis. The expert would evaluate the business from a financial sense from top to bottom. The analysis would very analytically address such areas as: the quality of receivables, searching for undisclosed liabilities, the reasonableness of expenses and compensation, depth of management, value of inventory (its ability to be sold), accounting methods in use and one-time expenses, among other items.

One of the primary goals is to determine the economically adjusted operating income. To calculate it, you need to adjust out any aberrations in the financials and, also, get the best idea of what it would look like should the interested buyer in fact acquire the company.

On top of carefully checking the current financial state, the buyer should carefully evaluate the robustness of the potential future profits. This requires looking for indicators of a possible drop or increase in demand in the near future, as well as checking options for saving costs by becoming more productive. For instance, when the intent is to merge the company with the buyer's organization, the merged operations can typically eliminate many redundant processes as well as leverage their shared customer bases to increase sales. Such opportunities may be lucrative.

There are very important perspectives that TOC would add to this analysis. You would want to know how much positive change is possible when converting to the TOC flow approach from the conventional approach that seeks to save all possible wasted costs by balancing capacities as much as possible but then pays extra to mitigate all the chaos that ensues.

One perspective is an evaluation of the operational performance of the business. You would want to know what their on-time delivery performance or on-time, in full rate is for customer orders. The TOC operational methods are capable of being much faster and much more reliable, usually without adding more cost or investment. TOC experts would analyze what comprises the lead time[2] to manufacture or fill a customer order and establish a range of potential improvement. In a manufacturing environment, a TOC expert would question batch sizes and whether efforts to minimize set ups have actually gone too far.

Applying the concepts of improving flow using TOC methodology will decrease lead times throughout the supply chain, increase on time delivery performance and improve fill rates, which will minimize lost sales.

---

[1] It makes no difference if you buy or manufacture the product.

[2] Lead time is defined as the number of days from when an order is placed until it is delivered to the customer.

Can you now understand what adding a TOC based analysis to a quality of earnings study will provide?

> From a seller's perspective, how much value is not being realized from the sale of the business?
>
> From a buyer's perspective, how much hidden value they will be acquiring?

Our example company gives us a great place to start this analysis. They have an average of 73 days of inventory on hand. They can replenish inventory in, at most, 30 days. Let's imagine that the average time to replenish is 20 days.

Again, it doesn't matter a bit whether that is the response time of the company's own manufacturing process or the time to get a delivery from an outside supplier.

The TOC guidance is that the most inventory the company might ever need is the amount that might be consumed over that 20 days it takes to replenish plus enough to last until the 30 days it takes after the longest replenishment delay. If it is possible to sell 40 days' worth in just 20 days, which is not at all uncommon, then any reasonable demand could be handled by 40 days' worth plus the 10 days' worth the replenishment might be late. That is 50 average days' worth of inventory. We TOC experts are not finished yet. We order daily what was consumed. Therefore, there will be fresh goods constantly arriving. At any given time, there will be an average of 20 days' worth of inventory ordered but not yet received. Therefore, under TOC, there would only be 50 days' maximum consumption within the safe replenishment time less the 20 which are consumed on average, but not yet received.

The TOC expert conclusion is that there are 43[3] days of surplus inventory, which means money and capacity are currently being wasted in order to abide by whatever purchasing based policies and decisions are currently in play.

This is a clear signal that there is a business opportunity of which the current owners and management are unaware!

Now for the added bonus in this brief analysis. Do you also realize that the example company has $5 million invested in inventory. Proportionally, the TOC replenishment solution would reduce that to $2.1 million[4]. Effectively, that reduces the buyer's price paid by the difference, $2.9 million, **at least**! Just think about it. The company, through wasting capacity, had accumulated at least $2.9 million in excess inventory. Managing flow, using TOC, will typically free up that cash within two or three replenishment times. In other words, free cash flow.

Let us state the obvious, this part of the Quality of Earnings analysis would not be shared with the seller. If you were the seller, would you knowingly hand over $2.8 million of the selling price to the buyer? Of course not.

The average time to replenish inventory is 20 days. If that average could be cut to 15 days and the number of days an order might be delayed is reduced, the eventual result would be even lower required inventory.

Our experience also tells us that there is a related increase in sales resulting from increased customer service levels of on-time performance and improved fill rates. Many of those additional sales will be due to being able to meet requested delivery dates previously thought impossible, as well as not losing sales due to stock outs.

---

[3] Currently there are, on average, 73 days of inventory, less the 30 days's worth that TOC would hold.
[4] $5 million in Inventory × 30 days of Inventory under TOC/73 days of Inventory currently = $2,054,795

This hidden potential of increased sales is the most important of all the gems revealed in a TOC based Quality of Earnings review.

Again, this is the positive upward spiraling effect from a TOC based focus on flow. This beneficial feedback loop of having happier customers, which leads to a better reputation, attracting more customers, thus increasing profits and opportunities. Again, this is TOC thinking in its purest form, very simple cause and effect.

Furthermore, the TOC thinking would be to construct a value-based offering, guaranteeing customers reliable delivery, with the option of an even faster response time, for a premium appropriate to the customers' benefits. Such an offer would increase sales, Throughput and profits even more.

However, putting the shoe on the other foot, if before the pre-sale value determination, TOC was applied, the wasted capacity used for building unnecessary inventory could have been exposed and you, not the buyer, would have pocketed the $2.9 million.

There is also a likelihood that your overall financial results would have been better, which would mean you would receive a multiple of these higher profits in the price for your business.

You finance inventory either by reinvesting profits or leveraged borrowing. If by reinvesting profits, think about the taxes you must have already paid to net the $2.9 million you used to buy the extra unproductive inventory. Ouch!

It is time to restate a key point of Throughput thinking applied in a Quality of Earnings analysis. A Throughput analysis would expose the 'efficiency performance metrics' which are locally focused that actually add days to lead time, resulting in later deliveries, excess inventories, lost orders and unhappy customers. Therefore, for a buyer who is familiar with the TOC methodology, the decision-making process makes the deal irresistible.

These deceiving efficiency metrics are entirely a result of the cost allocation practices of the cost accounting in place within the company.

As has been well demonstrated in other TOC books[5], if the efficiency measures in place focus on "local" performance, the flow of the whole operations will be impacted negatively. By local, we mean a department, a group within a department, a single person, a product line, a shift, and so on, anything other than the entire flow from the company that delivers what the customers want.

As we have shown in this book, the whole concept of 'cost per unit' is a local metric, as if the cost of producing one unit is not dependent on how many units the organization sells and how much capacity the organization maintains. Without the holistic view, the local picture distorts the big picture.

To understand the rationale of our claim that focus on local efficiencies reduces the global effectiveness of the organization, let us start with the following known effect in reality: People are driven to perform to expectations. If you work in a department where you are measured on the amount of output you produce, producing output is what you will do. You will be driven to produce as much as you can, even when the reasonable optimistic assessment of sales for next period is much lower or it is not the most urgent job right now. Until the company expediter

---

[5] Corbett, T., 1998 *Throughput Accounting*, North River Press, Great Barrington, MA.

Noreen, E., Smith, D., Mackey, J.T., 1995, *The Theory of Constraints and its Implications for Management Accounting*, North River Press, Great Barrington, MA.

Caspari, J., Caspari, P., 2004, *Management dynamics, Merging Constraints Accounting to Drive Improvement*, John Wiley & Sons, Inc., Hoboken, NJ.

Goldratt, E.M., 1990, *The Haystack Syndrome*, North River Press, Great Barrington, MA.

forces otherwise, you will not have any focus on what is needed to improve the flow of the entire production process.

In such situations, it will be commonplace to find that most, if not all departments, are operating at a high-level of efficiency. It would also be just as commonplace for there to be issues with on time and complete delivery to customers or the alternative of extending lead times so much that, while not technically late, orders are too often lost due to exceeding the customers' tolerance time for waiting.

Since meeting all these local measurements are thought to be desirable, the typical solutions are incurring overtime or outsourcing additional capacity or, the most expensive option, permanently deploying increased capacity, whether it be equipment or people.

We believe in the options of overtime and outsourcing because they are Capacity Buffers that allow more to be done, periodically as needed. However, these needs should be predicted and included in the decision-making process. More times than not they are not.

The reality is, if you were to total all the calculated benefits of meeting local performance measures, they always accumulate to far more than the actual total profit achieved by the whole of the company. In other words, actual results are always significantly less than the sum of all the calculated local performance improvements.

There is that key scene in *The Goal*, the famous bestselling book by Dr. Goldratt and still the recommended book for everyone interested in TOC: Alex Rogo, a plant manager, meets Jonah, the clever guy who guides Alex to recognize the true rules of his reality. Alex was bragging about how the addition of robotics had improved efficiencies by 36%. Jonah expressed amazement. Apparently, taking Alex at face value but, perhaps, employing a barb to drive Alex away from his flawed understanding, Jonah remarked to Alex that he wanted to learn more about these robots that could improve the company's net profit by 36%. Alex, worried that he had not been clear, clarified for Jonah that it was not the profit but the efficiencies of that particular operation that were up 36%. He also revealed that company losses were actually getting larger. Jonah's famous reply was that he couldn't understand how one could claim a 36% improvement while losing more money?

The global, company-wide result for Alex's company, Unico, was negative and definitely had not improved due to the rise in the efficiencies of the operations with the robots.

How many of these efficiency improvements have you experienced in your own career?

Since local measurements are not tied to the performance of the system as a whole, there is a danger that as local performance improves, system-wide performance will not be sufficient, which leads to wasted capacity and wasted investments to find more capacity.

A significant lesson to be learned is:

- If metrics are focused on local efficiencies and,
- if these measurements do not subordinate to measuring the Throughput of the entire system, then
- capacity will be wasted on producing things the market does not want (yet), some good opportunities will be rejected because they do not seem profitable enough, lead times will become too long and unappealing to customers and customer satisfaction will suffer, curtailing sales.

We hope by now you see the point that we have made that even financial due diligence can be severely limited and misleading when driven by traditional cost accounting.

Unfortunately, there are many cases of failed mergers and acquisitions. Most of them fail according to some studies. You can safely assume that most all of these deals survived an exhaustive due diligence process. So why do these situations fail with such a high caliber talent providing a very detailed analysis?

Two very likely scenarios are the cause.

One: in the situation where the acquiring entity is an investment firm, the focus of their analysis will be on what is needed to maximize Return on Investment (ROI) in a designated time frame. The primary measurement will be EBITDA.[6]

Without question, profitability is always the goal. In reality, profits are a result of achieving a series of intermediate objectives. It is the alignment of those objectives to best service markets that will raise profitability, in addition to EBITDA. Thus, instead of taking the current EBITDA as the basis for calculating the ROI, the potential EBITDA, when all the intermediate objectives are properly synchronized, should be the key information for making the investment.

In these environments, it is common to witness that investment world measures will dictate the actions taken. A solution would be to understand the missing links of the investment finance world metrics to the correct operational performance metrics. The best way to ensure this is to not replace the investment firm's primary global metrics, which are EBITDA and ROI based.

However, the concept of Throughput being focused on the profit and loss statements and not allowing costs to be deferred onto the balance sheet in the form of inventory must be well explained and demonstrated, particularly how it leads to enhanced sales, Throughput and profitability.

Good financial performance is the result of high performing operations. Therefore, it only makes sense to make certain that correct operational performance measures are in place. An important step for developing the correct operational performance metrics is that every one of them needs to align and be properly subordinated to improving total operational performance. Allowing local metrics to be independently enforced and, therefore, become dominant leads to the negative spiral addressed earlier. Interestingly, the common state for businesses around the world today is surviving and even thriving, to the extent that they do, in spite of being trapped within a negative feedback loop.

A simple example: if you measure a particular function by how well and how many of a part they produce, you are incenting them to produce as much as possible, which means over production with the typical justifications, like "we will need the parts eventually" or "don't we want to get the most out of a machine set-up?" The result of all departments behaving in this manner ultimately results in some parts which are needed within the flow of production will not be where they are needed when they are needed, leading to late deliveries and eventual loss of customers. This is true at the same time as overall inventories are much too high.

Conversely, if each particular function's metrics are subordinated to the flow of the whole organization, subordination would mean being measured by whether or not that function did its part to protect the promised lead time of the overall production flow.

Time now to discuss the "we are now going to do it our way" syndrome.

Unfortunately, in many of these situations, adjustments to operations are made with the good intentions to maximize EBITDA. The investment firm acquired the company because of its profitability. If the due diligence did not focus on what in the company results in that profitability, most

---

[6] Earnings before interest taxes and depreciation and amortization

assuredly cuts will be made that will impact future profitability. The most common cuts, which almost seem like common sense, are to lay off people in order to adjust the available capacity to the demand. What it actually does many times is significantly reduce the built-in flexibility and sprint capacity to handle sudden changes in demand and the ability to process urgent orders. The unavoidable result is less satisfied clients leading to lower demand.

When such cuts do not work, they typically lead to lower performance and more cuts. Each cut destroys ever more capacity, which lead to a rapidly accelerating negative profit spiral. When it becomes inevitable that ROI targets cannot be met, the decision may be made to cut losses and divest the company.

A second perspective is in the case of a strategically targeted merger or acquisition.

The same level of significant due diligence is completed. However, there will be an eye towards identifying strategic synergies, whether they be more capabilities or the elimination of duplication of costs.

What can happen is, in the efforts to realize the synergies, the advantages that made either of the original entities successful can be undermined. The root of the problem is that the moves that are made are decided upon from a top management position. What too often ends up being ignored is that the decision undermines the whole reason for an operation's existence as they lose their operational effectiveness. For instance, some middle-level managers who were good at their jobs but now are forced to work under new rules they are not used to, become much less effective.

A very familiar action is the elimination of what is perceived to be excess capacity. As discussed throughout this book, excess capacity is needed to protect the flow of value through the entire operation, as well as to support finding new opportunities that are especially lucrative. When decisions end up indirectly reducing the demand, there is often much finger pointing and blame, which leads to distrust, which hampers communication and another negative spiral begins.

Management triage events are typical, which often result is personnel changes. Yes, the same personnel, who were so successful that it led to the idea of this merger in the first place, are often moved or replaced.

At this point, you can ask, "Does understanding Throughput eliminate all these issues?" Surely, in this environment of high finance with such world-class expertise involved in all of these decisions, simply understanding Throughput cannot possibly be the magic pill to achieve the desired success, can it?

You would be correct to think it is not a 100% magic pill. However, it can be a significant inoculation against uninformed decisions that initiate what becomes negative spirals.

If the real issue is bad leadership or poor culture, unfortunately history dictates all of these companies will eventually fail.

Hopefully, by now, you have an understanding of the importance of measuring actual operations, as opposed to making the operational metrics fit traditional standard measurements thinking. In terms of operational performance, this is the proverbial square peg in a round hole.

We ask you to imagine being armed with information about how the company you are analyzing really does operate. How much more, based on your analysis, could the following areas be enhanced:

1. Risk assessment, both in specific areas and overall performance
2. Actual and potential capabilities of most areas under analysis
3. Understanding capacity

4. Understanding targeted markets by learning more of their buying behavior regarding differing levels of performance and costing
   a. This can be an especially revealing area if the analysis is driven to drill down to provide data that can be studied to determine if information can be gleaned on such matters as:
      i. Customer loyalty
      ii. Consumer risk management
      iii. Market perceptions
      iv. Improved assessment on what the merger or acquisition will mean in the market

It is our sincere hope that you do see that it would be severely limiting to think of cost accounting principles in the limited world of traditional methods, whether it be simple absorption accounting, the use of a standard cost system, using Activity Based Costing or, even marginal cost analysis.

Senator Dirksen was prophetically more relevant than he ever intended.

A TOC and Throughput-based look at a company can lead to recognizing a few nuggets here and a few nuggets there and pretty soon we're talking about a gold mine. Or, an already tapped out mine.

Either way, the conclusion is extremely valuable.

Chapter 17

Now it's Time for a Big Move—Daily Bread, Part 4

The purpose of this book is to offer a new process for top management decision making. Our process allows consideration of specific market opportunities and validates that the current available capacity, including Capacity Buffers, are adequate to accommodate the expected additional demand. We also expand the boundaries of current TOC decision making guidance beyond the direction provided by Throughput Accounting's focus on the flow of Throughput through the company's current constraint. Many top managers have risen to their places in their companies, and rightfully so, due to their capability to look out into the future to a greater degree than their cohorts, a subject we touched on in Chapter 13. The dizzying myriad possibilities of the distant future do not allow one to understand the details of future demand and capacities with any sort of precision. Choosing an imagined future and making it reality requires understanding systems, peoples' capability to accept change, weighing the necessary management attention required (Chapter 16) and recognizing when to start building which competencies for markets that may not yet exist but should. We find the strong need for understanding the relationships between the potential Throughput and the cost of maintaining enough protective capacity a necessary condition for having the required flexibility to manage uncertainty. This chapter explores the broader aspects of leadership of a CEO as he discovers and reveals his vision of a new and momentous strategic direction without losing sight of the critical details.

The Motivation and the Search

Raphael knocked on the doorjamb of Clark's office before walking in. "Boss, I think I found something for us," he said. He pressed on, "You know I've been getting potential acquisition targets from that business broker. Anyway, there is one that might work for us, here in the Midwest. Do you have time to hear about it?"

Clark, the president of Daily Bread, just nodded his head at his CFO, put down his pen on his desk, leaned back in his chair and laced his fingers behind his head. They had been having a number of these impromptu conversations over the last month, ever since Raphael had pointed out to Clark that serious money had accumulated in the company's checking account.

Table 17.1 Daily Bread Comparison of Three Years' Financial Performance

Daily Bread (thousands)	2 Years Ago	Last Year	YTD Projection
Sales	$6,542	$7,433	$7,841
Throughput	4,920	5,657	5,954
Ops Expense	3,235	3,664	3,836
EBITDA	1,685	1,993	2,118
Net Profit	776	932	970
Total Assets	5,296	5,842	6,817
Cash	146	1,094	2,042
Bank Debt	425	0	0
ROA	14.7%	15.9%	14.2%

Clark smiled as he remembered how amazing this cache of money would have been before Raphael had introduced the company to the Theory of Constraints a little over five years ago. Since then, they had made significant improvements to the company's bottom line. The regional bakery had been barely scraping by with fluctuating earnings varying from tiny profits up to $100k, in good years. In just six months, they had found new discounted markets that boosted the annual profits to $400k, even before the expected positive impact on the regular market. Those discounted sales had given them much needed exposure to a group of new customers with plenty of disposable income. Now, a few years later EBITDA[1] was over $2m per year. Recently, Clark had asked Raphael to answer the question of why were their return on assets falling, when profits were still rising. The development in Daily Bread financial results are shown in Table 17.1.

After reviewing the data, Raphael had pointed out to Clark that most of the fixed assets were depreciated. They had paid off all their bank debt and had accumulated $2m in cash. The more cash accumulated, the bigger the company's assets. Since profits were now growing more slowly than before the *return* was growing more slowly than the *assets*. While still very good, this answer had disturbed Clark for reasons he couldn't immediately articulate.

After sleeping on it for a few months, Clark realized that they were out of hot new ideas for continuing to improve Daily Bread. His idea for delivering their products direct to homes, like an

---

[1] EBITDA stands for earnings before interest, taxes, depreciation and amortization – a measure of a company's ability to generate cash flow from its operations. Multiples of EBITDA are commonly used as a basis for valuing companies. The idea behind excluding interest is to equalize earnings regardless of the owner's cash position. Leaving out taxes equalizes between companies so they are comparable across different taxable zones and the tax impact due to interest. Depreciation and amortization are removed, because they are non-cash expenses.

Net profit is more appropriate for determining how many years buyers are willing to wait to get a return on their investment or, from the other side of the table, how many years of net cash the owner will demand in order to prefer giving up their company.

So far in this book, we have used net profit as the main metric that shows how well the company is performing. EBITDA is a substitute that is more appropriate in the context of acquisitions. Using EBITDA instead of net profit requires a slight redefinition of OE. Should you choose to substitute EBITDA for net profit as the company's prime metric, you simply exclude interest, taxes, depreciation and amortization from the OE.

old-fashioned milkman, hadn't panned out. Except toward the most optimistic extreme of their expected range, it was simply too expensive to deliver relative to the T generated from the small amounts an average family might consume.

For his part, Clark realized that the declining return-on-assts (ROA) was a signal that he was overdue for a breakthrough they didn't yet see butthat was right there, hidden in plain sight. From experience he knew that sometimes people scrutinize their systems so closely that they can no longer see the forest for the trees. The prescription: back away, gain a broader perspective and consider something on a grand scale.

Clark's intuition was telling him that he should invest the cash that was accumulating. They had already done a lot of that. They had commissioned Oven #3 and were running it during the night shift, the normal work time for bakeries. That was in addition to operating Ovens #1 and #2 twenty-four hours per day, seven days a week. Moving to 24/7 on two ovens became less expensive than the overtime on which they previously relied, since they had needed to hire more employees anyway. Now, there was enough manpower to run all the shifts at regular hourly rates. With the capacity from the extra staff they had boosted their Throughput much more than the expense of the added people. They had upgraded other resources and added capacity in mixing, as well as increasing the square footage of the preparation area. Even after winning a major contract from the local public school system, there was more than enough capacity to support their customers reliably every day.

No further investment or expense made sense, unless they captured significant new demand, and this seemed to be ever more difficult to do with their current product mix. So, Raphael had started paying down the company's long-term debt. Today, the company was debt free and cash rich. That was when Clark considered that a possible course of action was to acquire another company.

Raphael had called a business broker with whom he had gone to college, who had identified a number of companies for sale. Clark had never been conscious of how many different types of companies there are. There was a marina and boat storage company, two e-commerce websites, a moving company, an office equipment sales company, a staffing company, a fitness gym, an insurance broker, a manufacturer of jewelry, a software development company, an HVAC contractor, an accountancy, a beef processing plant, an automobile body and paint shop, a manufacturer of chafing dish fuel and the list went on. He asked Raphael to inquire if there were any other bakeries or related companies for sale that could open a new market utilizing the current surplus capacity and possibly support adding more. However, that the broker was unable to discover any such companies for sale at that time.

Now, here was Raphael explaining that he might finally have a logical acquisition target. "What have you got, Raphael?" Clark asked.

Raphael said "There is a bakery for sale about four hours away in a town called Belleville, IL, a suburb of St. Louis. They are about the same size as us, but they have been losing money for the last few years. Their EBITDA is positive but they have a lot of debt, which interest and depreciation are wiping out. I think we can get them cheap. The owner is out of money and worried about his personal guarantee at the bank."

Clark wondered, "What kind of products do they bake?"

Raphael answered, "Dog biscuits, mainly."

Clark retorted, "Dog biscuits? Really? How would that work?"

Raphael said, "It would get us into a whole new set of customers."

Clark leaned forward in his chair and said, "But, we can't sell any of our products to buyers of dog biscuits and vice versa."

Raphael continued, "That is true but there might be significant economies of scale to us in accounting, personnel, baking know how and management, most of all."

Clark didn't reply directly. After a moment, he said "I tell you what. Let's convene the management group to get everyone's opinion. Together, we can do better than just you and me, don't you think?"

Raphael laughed and said,"That's the truth. I think we've proven that by now!"

A few days later, the whole management team got together at the hotel where they had gotten into the habit of going to find agreement on the improvements they had implemented.

Interestingly, in the last three years, they had agreed on fourteen significant moves. Of those, two had been failures and had been rescinded, after a month or two. Although these "mistakes" did not turn out to be improvements, in both cases there had been circumstances which had changed, causing slightly adverse outcomes.

However, there were two observations they had been able to make about these errors. First, without the benefit of hindsight, they could find no fault with the decisions they had made and, secondly, the exposure to the poor consequences was trivially short, especially compared to the continuing ongoing benefits of the twelve positive decisions. Essentially, there was no rational justification to call the two decisions errors or mistakes. They were just examples of random manifestations of uncertainties.

Clark was proud that unknowns hadn't paralyzed the team. They knew enough to expect such surprises and handle them quickly, as soon as they realized that reasonable assumptions had been invalidated by reality. Had they been afraid to act, they might now have only had a handful of successes instead of a dozen. Overall, their protective capacity, the capabilities of their people, including management and the right culture provided the flexibility and the means to take advantage of opportunities. This realization is expressed in one of the pillars of TOC as verbalized by Dr. Goldratt: "Never say I know" counterbalanced by, "Never say I don't know!" You always know something and never everything.

They had all survived a lecture from Raphael about statistical variation and the probabilistic nature of outcomes. The point being that, while a single decision has an unpredictable outcome, what they were trying to do was to establish, from a series of decisions, the efficacy of their new decision-making process. Raphael claimed that he was already more than 98% certain that they had discovered a truly better way to make decisions.

In other companies, it is typical for individuals to champion their own ideas. Still, one serious mistake and your career trajectory slows way down. Two mistakes of consequence and you're almost certainly fired. The problem is, any poor outcome could have been simply unlucky, even if the idea was a very good one that would have succeeded nine times out of ten. Environments like that squelch a manager's willingness to take a good chance. Consequently, only virtually certain opportunities are undertaken, causing the company to gain profits but so slowly that an agile competitor could pass them by, sort of worse-off safe and nevertheless sorry. This describes many older big companies.

Perhaps worse, the way to climb the corporate ladder in such single-advocate systems is to be the one who has the most successful ideas. For anybody to get ahead requires the support of many others, who are likely necessary to assist in making the implementation (the hard part) succeed. "But if that guy gets ahead, what about me?" That is a question on which competing managers are likely to stew. How many good ideas just happen to fail in implementation in a dog-eat-dog environment in which the most successful earns promotion, power and money? How many side deals must be made to get a good idea through? Are those side deals good for the company or just the dealmakers? Are they even good for them or are they just costly compromises?

Clark stopped his thoughts and brought the meeting together, "Guys, Raphael has an acquisition he'd like us to consider. I thought we could go through it together."

Linda asked, "Is it a talent agency?" Everybody laughed.

Raphael gave her the stink-eye and said very slowly with mock seriousness, "No, it isn't a talent agency." and then in a rush, "it's a chain of nail spas with tanning booths. ... Just kidding. It's a bakery."

This got them all interested.

Robert asked, "What kind of products?"

"Dog biscuits are 90% of their product line with the remainder being rendered products like pig's ears and rawhide treats," Raphael replied.

There was silence for a while, until Robert said "Damn, I was really hoping they'd bake donuts, bagels or even cakes or cookies. We couldn't bake those products in our ovens. The odor would transfer and ruin our products. And, if we kept their plant, the biggest synergy, consolidating production, would be lost."

Linda joined in nodding, "Yes, and I'd be surprised if our salesforce could handle their products. While we bake for a small region, those types of products would sell nationally and to a completely different customer base. I bet most of our salesforce wouldn't want to travel the whole country and be on the road much of the time. You know what?" She stopped a moment to think about it. "It's even worse than that. Forget the salespeople, would you buy a loaf of bread from the local dog food manufacturer? This is anti-synergy. It would make everything harder."

Raphael said, "There are some significant economies of scale. My initial numbers estimate that we could save 3 to 4% of their operating expense."

Clark made another point, "The thing I worry about is how much more complication we'd be undertaking. What would it take to merge the two companies together into one facility? Would we really lose synergy from their products and market? Another big question is how much extra management time and know-how will be necessary driving the transition and for how long? Does that make sense at all for 3 to 4% of their expenses? I think we should discuss these questions first, before we go to a deeper analysis of expenses and capacity."

The conversation died out. They all seemed to be thinking. Robert observed that no one was smiling. This idea for an acquisition left him cold. It seemed to him that it was just an acquisition for acquisition's sake, despite being a bakery with similar technology. He had nothing to add to the decision. It seemed like he should have important input. He expected that they would expand in a way that leveraged his skill set and everybody else's. With that thought, he knew the deal wasn't going to work, that it shouldn't work. Then, a new idea came to him which he felt compelled to share.

Robert broke the silence, "This deal is a non-starter, friends. None of us like it. The problem we have is that we want to make an acquisition but this company, which is probably the closest thing we've seen and can expect to see offered for sale, is not even close to something we could ever get excited about. I get excited when I see our business getting boosted forward. This one doesn't add enough value."

He could see they all agreed and were hoping he had more to say. Fortunately, he did and continued, "Logically, if there are no companies for sale that meet our criteria, we have to buy a company that isn't for sale. But, if they aren't for sale, how can we buy them?"

"That makes sense," Clark murmured.

Raphael jumped in, "Wait! If we go knocking on doors, won't we have to offer too much to get the owner to stop what he is doing and even consider it? We don't want to have to pay too much! Don't we need to strike a good bargain?"

Clark waved him to calm down. "Raphael, don't worry. We won't buy anything unless you like the deal. Let me ask you, did you think the staffing company your business broker friend brought was appropriate for us?"

Raphael sputtered, "Uh, … I … But, … Well, that wasn't his fault. That was just what was available, at the time."

"Don't worry, Raph. Just answer the question," Clark coaxed with an easy smile.

Raphael realized that his reaction was inappropriately defensive and apologized, "I'm sorry guys. I guess I'm feeling bad about suggesting we use my friend to help us find a company. I mean, with the benefit of hindsight, it would have been wild-ass luck if he had found a company that was even a good fit. I guess I was worried that you all would blame me, like I let us all down by bringing him in. Okay. Never mind. Back to Clark's question. No. The staffing company might have been a great deal for another company in that business or even an accounting firm that already provides administrative services but it would have been too hard for us."

"Why?" Clark asked him.

"Well, because we'd have had to learn a whole new industry."

Clark pressed further, "What's so bad about that? Aren't we smart enough to learn something new?"

Raphael was pulling on his salt-and-pepper goatee the way he often did when considering a problem. "No, I expect we would learn the staffing business but would that kind of business suit us? Would it help us be better at baking and selling what we bake? I don't think so and the opposite would also be true. There is nothing about our business that would help us in staffing. I wouldn't call staffing one of our core competencies. Even if we kept their people to cover our weaknesses, there would be few synergies between our two businesses. I guess what I'm saying is, the blended companies wouldn't be worth any more together than they were apart."

Linda said, "Obviously, we'll need to give an owner reasons to sell and that probably includes paying more money than the owner ever expected to see. My guess is that, for most owners, the sweetener—the necessary amount over the normal price—might be far less than the benefit of a really synergistic acquisition."

Raphael thought about what Linda just said. "You could have something there, if the combination is a good one, by that I mean, if the two companies together will be worth far more than the sum of the two companies individually. It just depends on what we find. Is the owner a compatible member of this team? Is he close to retirement but has just been putting off selling his company? Or, is he…"

"Or, she," Linda interjected wryly.

Raphael winced, "Right! Is *she* a young entrepreneur who might be interested in building something with us or maybe she wants the money to embark on some new venture? It all depends on what each side, the seller and we, would consider a bargain."

Robert, the quiet one, added, "I guess the meaning of 'bargain' for us is getting more than we paid for."

"Bingo!" Clark shouted, jumping up from his chair. "I couldn't have said it better myself. Thank you, Robert! A bargain from our point of view has nothing to do with the value intrinsic to the company. It is all about the value or even the potential value of the company to us."

Robert continued in that direction. "If the deal is a bargain because it is possible to generate synergy between the two companies, then the other company might see it as a bargain to buy us. I assume our new way of thinking is not too common and so they would probably not see it our way. If they do, then it could lead to an offer to merge the two companies based on re-distribution of shares. However, from our side we have extra cash that we want to invest. So, unless the merger itself benefits from that kind of investment, I don't see us agreeing to a deal like that."

"Also, realize our Capacity Buffer, Oven #3, is only working eight hours a day, meaning 29% of our utilized capacity could be added with just a few more employees or some overtime. Oven #3's potential is there for no further investment, other than a little operating expense. Our Throughput as a percentage of sales is high. Even a moderate increase in sales would throw plenty of T to our bottom line. This is a reserve for growth. We won't need to invest in capacity unless we tap into large new markets."

Clark remarked, "I want this team to be in control of a bigger company, so I want a purchase that adds synergy to Daily Bread. Although I own all of Daily Bread today, maybe five years from now, we will look for a strategic alliance as a good way to go to the next step, and it might be a good opportunity for me to consider retirement. After we have digested this acquisition, assuming we ever find a synergistic one, I'm going to be talking to each of your individually about your interest in buying in as shareholders."

This gave them all something to think about. Clark had never before mentioned the possibility of selling any of his stake in the company. They looked around the table to see if they could guess what the others were thinking but nobody gave any overt signals.

Robert threw out, "Well, if we want serious synergies the most effective way is to operate from one plant. If necessary, we can add new capabilities to it. Since it's us and we're here, the target company either has to be moved here or is already in the local area. The latter is better for us, because we'd probably lose too many of their experienced and skilled employees if we moved their company here from too far off."

"How important is it to operate from one plant, Robert, can you expand the point a little for us?", asked Clark.

It felt good to Robert to share his knowledge, "I want one plant because the logistics of deliveries to clients is simpler, the utilization of the trucks is better and there is less room for confusion on which plant serves which clients. We have enough space here that is not fully utilized and there is enough surrounding property to add on, if need be. It's another Capacity Buffer, you might say. We can absorb two or three new lines, including ovens, and still not be overly congested."

"Robert, those are excellent points you make. We would do better to target companies in our local area," Clark responded.

"Fortunately, we know the area well," Linda added. "Between us we know most of the relevant businesses in our area, those that are not too small or too big to even consider. When we see a company that might work, I bet we either know the current owner or know someone else who does. If so, it could give us a warm introduction to get the conversation started."

Clark added, "I can vouch for the importance of that. I get an email or a phone call every week from some unknown party asking if I'd be interested in selling. I bet my junk mail folder has two or three in it right now! I usually receive more before I even finish deleting them."

"I called one of them back once. It has been years ago now. The email seemed so personal, I decided to listen to what they had to say. When I called the 800 number and said my name, the person who answered had no idea who I was. They must send out 10,000 emails to get one reply. They couldn't have been interested, given the way they handled the call. It put me off – the fake intimacy of their approach. They expected me to prove that we qualified against their selection criteria, yet the email come-on pretended to be well aware of Daily Bread. I was disgusted. We will need every warm introduction we can get and we better do our homework to be sure as we can that we are interested long before our first overt contact."

After a few moments of silence, Robert asked "So, how do we know what local company to pursue? What are the initial requirements to make us truly interested?"

Clark shot back "You are going to tell us."

Robert looked shocked. "Who me?"

"Yep," Clark answered.

"Why me? I think I'd be the last one to decide," Robert retorted.

Clark smiled and said, "No. Think about it. None of the companies that are for sale right now are even possibilities. Raphael finally found one that is sort of close but that's no good either. We need you to focus us on possible ways to use our facility. What would work?"

"Oh, I get it," Robert answered. "Well, cookies, cakes, like I said, other types of bread, like baguettes, crackers, biscuits, English muffins, brioche and I guess we could easily sell dough for pizzas and the like—they'd probably want that frozen."

Linda chimed in "Hey, I'd love to have a frozen product that didn't spoil!" She went on. "Back to the question at hand, lots of those products that Robert mentioned, I bet I could sell to existing customers. Why haven't we done that already? We wouldn't even need to do an acquisition."

"Yes," Raphael agreed. "We'd need to do more setups, but since there is enough spare capacity making some crackers requires no ΔI or ΔOE, at least not for a while, until our capacity is finally used up again."

Robert's eyes floated up to the ceiling and he wistfully murmured, "That would be a lot of crackers!"

They all laughed at that. Robert looked back down and blushed. He hadn't meant to get so dreamy. Now, he was embarrassed as so often happened to him in group situations. Anticipating the reactions of others was not his strong suit. He became serious, as he thought was proper and said. "Well, Linda, we could probably make every cracker eaten in the whole city out of our surplus capacity, if you can sell them."

They all roared with laughter again, making Robert blush even more deeply, as he wondered to himself, "What the hell's so funny about that?"

Linda, the empathetic one, rescued Robert by saying, "Let me suggest this. I'll get a complete list from Robert of what we can make. Then, I'll give that list to the salesforce. I think, in a week, they can find out which of our existing customers use products we could make. They can also take their temperatures to see if they'd be interested in buying from us."

"Good," said Clark. "If you have ideas how we can grow our market by ourselves then let's check them in the way we have developed and perfected over the last five years."

Robert timidly added, "However, if you get ideas like that for true line expansions, like crackers, you need to find a lot of demand. I don't want to have to make microscopic production runs. The changeovers would eat up tons of capacity for not so much sales, at least at first. That isn't a problem right now, given our free capacity, but a nice acquisition might make us sorry we took that approach."

"Yes," Clark said. "Thank you for that segue. I still want to invest the almost two million that is being wasted in the bank. So, what about acquisition ideas?" And with that, he brought the team back on task.

Raphael offered, "Well there is that cupcake bakery but, as I said, they might be too small."

Clark offered a guideline, "Let's don't run down any idea. I don't want to increase anyone's reluctance to throw out an idea, because they are worried their idea isn't worthy. There is nothing lost by suggesting something. So, let the rules of brainstorming apply. First, we get out as many ideas as fast as we can—no filters. Just spit them out. Afterwards, we'll go back and pick the best ones by developing the criteria of what is a good fit for us".

Soon, they had the following list written on the whiteboard:

- Fun Cakes – Cupcake manufacturer – small mail-order business.
- Desserts Now – Retail store providing finished desserts and wedding cakes.
- Kayrouz Bakery – Chain of 5 – selling cookies, sheet cakes, and pastries.
- Kroger Regional Bakery – Bakes for the company's local groceries.
- Heine Bros. Coffee – Chain of 17 coffee shops all over the city.
- Country Oven Bakery – large bakery supplying grocery chains over the eastern U.S.
- MTC, Inc. – large bakery producing taco shells and tortilla chips.
- Papa John's Pizza – Commissary producing pizza dough and other products used in their pizza – made fresh.
- Pillsbury Bakery – Huge plant making "Poppin' Fresh" dough for biscuits and refrigerated rolled pie shells.

"All right," said Clark. "How do we narrow this list down?"

Raphael stood up, went to the whiteboard and took a red marker from the tray. "Well, we have to take off Country Oven, MTC and the Pillsbury Bakery. Their plants would cost hundreds of millions. Our measly $2m won't even get us close to them."

Robert said, "That Papa John's commissary makes pizza sauce, cuts up all the toppings their stores use on their pizzas and shreds and bags cheese. We could do the dough for them possibly but that seems more like a potential customer for Linda than an acquisition opportunity. I bet they would be slow to convince that we could make a better crust than they can at an attractive price. Plus, I bet they'd want to keep direct control of their own quality." The others were nodding.

"Should I cross it off as an acquisition candidate?" Raphael asked. They all nodded again.

Clark leaned back in his chair and rested his head in his hands, elbows out—his standard contemplative pose. "The rest all have some aspect of a retail component. Do we want to get into retail? Would our customers see us as competing with them?"

"That's a good question," Linda answered. "I think the answer might be yes, for Kayrouz and Desserts Now. Not so much for Fun Cakes and Heine Bros. Fun Cakes mostly ships out of town and Heine Bros is like a restaurant. People come in for coffee or to talk and then they get hungry and eat something. I don't think our customers have a chance at either of those sales."

Clark responded: "We could add our products to those out of town shipments for virtually no added OE, plus offering Fun Cakes' products to our customers. That could work!"

He went on, "Heine Bros. is also an opportunity to sell to end users and get feedback, and even promote Heine Bros.' reputation through our wonderful bakery products. Together, we can develop new products and then they can test the new products in their coffee shops. When successful, we use their successes to convince our regular customers, including Events to Remember, to buy them."

Clark added, "On top of that, Heine Bros. is well run. I know the President, Mike, very well. He is a great guy. They really do their best to give their shops an authentic local flavor. It's like Starbucks without the burnt bean flavor. All their coffee is fair trade. They prefer to offer local products in their stores. We'd have to bake more sweet pastries to serve them properly but they have enough stores to make that worthwhile."

"Regarding Kayrouz and Deserts Now, I feel that this is too risky, broadening our product lines in a very big way to cover them, with the chance of offending our customers."

Linda piped up, "That leaves the Kroger bakery. Here is what I know about them. They mostly make bread, cakes and pastries for sale in their groceries' deli departments. All the product goes into their local distribution center and gets pushed out to probably 100 of their grocery stores from there. I have no idea how to buy it from them or why they'd want to sell it. But, those are the same type, if not exactly the same products we already make. I shop there. It seems to me that some items come in baked and some, like bread, are fresh baked in each store. Sometimes you'll smell the fresh bread baking and people line up to buy it. I remember thinking that it was smart marketing!"

"That's a good one!" Raphael was scribbling notes. He was an inveterate note taker. None of the others bothered when he was in the meeting.

Clark said, "I suggest we first check Heine Bros. and then see where it takes us."

Raphael asked Clark, "What is their financial situation?"

Clark answered, "I don't know the details. My impression is that the company has been growing profitability as they progressively open more shops. Mike does have a silent partner who bought in a number of years ago. In fact, the guy is Papa John, the pizza guy's brother, Chuck, believe it or not. He used to their corporate council and must have made a pretty penny, as Papa John's grew. I wonder if Chuck, the silent partner, might like to be bought out."

Raphael then followed up, "Can you contact Mike and see if he has any interest?"

"Yes, I'd be happy to." Clark responded, "I bet they could accelerate the rate at which they add shops with our money and we'd capture a bunch of business we don't have now. The products would be somewhat different than what we sell our current customers but that is good, as some of the new products could also be sold to our current customers. I think, as a merger, this one has more potential than Fun Cakes."

"I agree," Linda said.

"Me too," Robert agreed.

"Let's go for it!" Raphael laughed.

"Alright," Clark said. "Let's conclude the meeting, then. I'll reconvene us when I know more. Thanks everybody and stay tuned!"

As it turned out, when Clark approached his friend Mike, there was no interest in an acquisition, even after Clark explained how he thought the Heine Bros. stores could sell Daily Bread's existing and imagined products. However, what did happen was Daily Bread picked up a large and growing new customer.

Of course, Raphael, Robert and Linda had carefully examined projections of the additional sales on capacity before closing the Heine Bros. deal. Both the pessimistic and the optimistic alternatives showed nice increases in EBITDA, so there was no doubt from the start that it was a great deal.

The deal with Heine Bros. ended up requiring 4.4% of the three ovens current daily capacity, which meant an additional three hours of Oven #3 each day. This still left 13 hours available of the Capacity Buffer. From a manpower perspective, Robert added just a few percent in overtime to support the smooth flow through the ovens.

As good as it was for Daily Bread, Clark found himself back to square one on finding an attractive way to invest his company's growing cash hoard.

Clark concluded that acquiring Heine Bros. as a client, rather than buying them, was absolutely the better choice. Running a chain of coffee shops is based on very different set of capabilities, especially managerial capabilities.

He wondered why they hadn't realized that Heine Bros. would be a better customer than an acquisition target. The advantage of an acquisition now seemed even greater, in view of the smaller Capacity Buffer available for new opportunities. This thought meant they needed a formal list of criteria that would help them recognize a great acquisition target. He decided it was important enough to get the gang together to consider it off-site, at the hotel.

Clark checked his watch as he clambered out of the Uber in front of the usual hotel. A week had passed. He and his wife had taken a quick trip down to New Orleans for a long weekend to visit greying college friends and enjoy a taste of the local cuisine. Ironically, their favorite restaurant had been Shaya, a new restaurant featuring Israeli cuisine in the Garden District. His flight back had been delayed but Clark was right on time for the meeting but without a minute to spare. All his time buffer was consumed by the tardiness of the flight. He hurried past the reception desk, to the left towards the meeting rooms. He opened the door to the now familiar Magnolia Room and found the rest of his top staff already there engaged in animated conversation, which did not miss a beat when he walked in.

Clearly, they had started early and felt no need to wait on him. He realized that he felt pretty good about it too. He didn't want robots that did his bidding. He wanted people with a common goal and different perspectives, to make decisions that were considered multi-dimensionally. Standing for a moment there in the doorway, he smiled as he realized they had integrated organically into a team that got results by depending on the others' various strengths to shore up their individual weaknesses.

Linda glanced up at him and waved him over. She said "You missed it, boss. We got here a few minutes early and already have a pretty good list of acquisition criteria." She pointed at the whiteboard where the following words were written:

1. Enhances Daily Bread's brand through cross-selling attractive products
2. We can operate out of a combined facility
3. We are close enough to deliver fresh products to all customers
4. Neither company's employees have to learn major new skillsets

Clark crossed his arms as he slowly read through the list. When he finished, he said, "Guys, this is a great list. Is there anything else you are working on that needs to be added?"

Linda, Robert and Raphael looked back and forth between themselves and shrugged. Linda said, "No, sir. That's about it!"

Clark smiled at them and said, "I have two things to add. The first doesn't even need to be a criterion, because it is so critical we can't even get started without it. **We must have enough money and financing to close the deal.**"

"The second ought to become the fifth criterion." He walked up to the white board and wrote:

5. The employees of the purchased company must be willing to work under our culture that embraces change, as well as other employees' differences, if they choose to stay on at the combined company

There were smiles and nods all around the table. It was obvious that nobody was willing to give up their culture which was a critical element behind the success of Daily Bread's rapid growth over the last five years.

Clark pressed on, "Guys, we all know these five criteria are important but, before we go on, let's articulate exactly why they are important. Starting with the first one, why do we want to be able to cross-sell each other's products?"

Linda erupted, "Clark, you know this! We are looking for a way to expand the markets for our products. It is far easier to grow existing relationships with customers who trust you. Presumably, their customers already trust them. Once we buy the company, their website and salespeople, they will be able to inform their customers about our products by just picking up the phone. Likewise, our customers would love to hear about the acquired company's products. The synergy between our company and the purchased one is built upon the mutual attraction of each company products to the other company's loyal customers. This is the crux of what we want to achieve."

Raphael volunteered, "I completely agree with you, Linda. Finding such synergy through cross sales is the obvious way to increase the sales of the combined company. We do it by utilizing as much of the spare capacity of both companies. In other words, cross-selling should grow T much more than OE. This is exactly the objective we strive for in any opportunity." Linda was nodding her head vigorously, as he spoke.

Linda added, "Yes, we'd have more products to offer to wider scope of clients. It solves our current problem: we are running out of ideas to sell more of our current products within the geography that permits fast enough delivery to protect freshness."

She continued, "I just want to emphasize that, to benefit from cross-selling, we need to make sure the products of one company do not compete with the products of the other company—so, we'll get more sales not just different sales. As much as possible, we should ensure that the other company's products are basically different – not replacements for ours."

Clark moved to the next criterion: "What about operating out of a single plant?"

Robert cleared his throat and said, "We've already discussed this criterion. I want one plant. I don't care if it is ours or theirs. One plant that produces all the products sold by both companies and has enough room for expansion to handle the expected growth. Operating from one facility utilizes resources better, definitely the building, and that reduces operating expenses as a percentage of sales. The logistics of raw materials, packaging and transportation to clients is much smoother to do from one facility."

Robert continued, "Another thing is a consolidated plant, using equipment and staff from both, will have more flexibility to make different products, because the combined protective capacity of both plants is more effective than protecting the performance of each plant separately. The purchased company will enhance our available capacity. Our operational methods are very effective in revealing hidden capacity. So, from both angles, operating expenses and delivery performance, there are powerful benefits to merging the facilities."

Clark asked his team, "Why it is important to us that the plant of the purchased company is close to us?"

Raphael responded, "If I can speak for you Robert and correct me if I don't get it right, once we close one of the plants, we want to be able to make deliveries from the remaining plant to the customers of the closed plant as responsively as they have grown accustomed to. It makes it simpler and cheaper to deliver the combined product line from one location." Robert gave him a mock bow.

Clark asked: "Is learning new skills a true obstacle?"

"Clark, we have to protect the time we managers have to devote to making decisions – what we've been calling management attention. We have learned this valuable insight from you." Raphael explained.

Clark smiled and innocently inquired, "And, why do we need to protect that?"

"Because the wheels can fall off without it!" Raphael answered. "But, it's more than that. We want to be able to work on growing and protecting our flows of Throughput."

Robert added, "Don't forget, there'll be a period of declining chaos, after we make an acquisition. It behooves us to make that Transition Period as short as possible. We need managers' attention to not only make the required changes but also to stomp out the inevitable fires."

"What about my cultural concern? What do we get out of that?" Clark inquired.

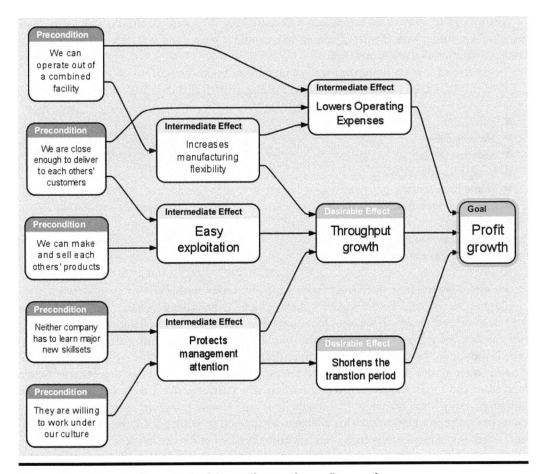

Figure 17.1 How the five criteria drive Daily Bread's profit growth.

Linda smiled and said, "That's easy, it protects management attention again, which speeds the transition and helps us focus on growing the business, as somebody (I can't remember who) already mentioned."

Robert volunteered that he had captured their comments into a cause and effect chart.[2] He said, "The point is to establish the benefit from the five criteria. This logical flow is generic, even without a detailed financial analysis. That can be done later, after finding a specific candidate and the pertinent quantitative data." He pulled the HDMI cable out of Raphael's laptop and plugged it into his own computer. In seconds, this logical map, Figure 17.1, appeared on the projected screen.

They scrutinized it. Some conversation and pointing ensued. In the end, they nodded and agreed that this was why they had listed the five criteria. Robert pointed out that technically it was necessary to either increase Throughput or decrease expenses in order to increase profit but they all accepted what he meant by connecting the causal arrow directly from shortening the Transition Period to profit growth.

---

[2] Flying Logic is a software package available for building just such diagram. www.flyinglogic.com

Then, Raphael cleared his throat and said something they were all thinking about in some fashion. "I'm happy with the list of criteria but, candidly, what good is it, if we can't agree on a company that meets these parameters?"

Linda reacted, "What about the list of companies we brainstormed?"

Robert, who was still projecting, switched the display to the list they had come up with earlier.

- Fun Cakes
- ~~Desserts Now~~
- ~~Kayrouz Bakery~~
- Kroger Regional Bakery
- ~~Heine Bros. Coffee~~
- ~~Country Oven Bakery~~
- ~~MTC, Inc.~~
- ~~Papa John's Pizza Commissary~~
- ~~Pillsbury Bakery~~

He said, "We still have the Kroger Bakery and Fun Cakes to check."

Raphael interjected, "Before we check them, which I'm not saying isn't worthwhile, I'd like to propose another direction. If we went four hours down the road to Humboldt, we'd have a whole new market that is bigger than our current one. I know that this means violating the first two criteria list and losing some of the value from meeting them all. But, isn't it a natural way to find a new market for our own great products? I'm aware that if we go there, we'd eventually need a local plant and Linda would have to find a whole new salesforce. We'd use our cash to invest in building a Daily Bread branch in Humboldt. That's the kind of things other companies do. How do we judge the pros and cons of this direction, as opposed to looking for a nice local company to buy, which might require very high price, because they are not for sale in the first place?"

Clark had been waiting for this sort of suggestion. He responded slowly to clarify why he preferred to look for a nearby company that together would generate real synergies, "Doing a start-up means either starting small and growing – which takes time – or dumping a lot of money right off the bat and losing money at first, then less and less over time. Under either scenario, easing in slowly or making a big splash, in Humboldt or any other different market, there will be no cross-selling. We'll have to produce and sell our products in the new market. It costs more than running one plant and doesn't give us any immediate synergies."

"The difference in buying a company that fits all or, at least, most of our criteria is producing a new cash flow immediately, both from their Throughput, plus the Throughput from cross sales. You can add to that any operational savings, plus anything we get from reducing their assets, including selling their equipment that becomes redundant. If we put together a pessimistic scenario for expanding into another market, it will certainly include losses that might go on for, who knows how long!"

Linda spoke up: "Wait a minute, we have established great reputation here, I can capitalize on our brand. If we opened a branch in Humboldt, it is not exactly like opening a new bakery from scratch. We can organize marketing events and start selling before we open the new bakery, by shipping from our plant here. Four hours of shipping is not something we'll want to do forever, because it will be quite expensive, but for a while we can do it."

Robert intervened: "Having a bakery in Humboldt is a complication that would take its toll, especially on our management attention capacity. On top of the investment we'll face high Operating Expenses, several local managers that we'll have to hire and train on our style of operation and culture. The Transition Period is going to be long. During that time, we'd have a lot of travel between the two places, which burns up more of our managerial capacity. While this direction is a valid option, I find it too risky."

Eventually, after more discussion, they all agreed with Robert about the risks. Linda expressed her conclusion from the discussion, "If we don't want to wait, it seems better to make sure we get a good company. So, to get back on point, do you all like the Kroger bakery better or Fun Cakes?"

Clark asked the room, "Do any of you all have a contact at Fun Cakes? I don't."

Dead silence. They looked around at each other, shrugging and shaking their heads, no.

Clark asked her, "Linda, you seem to know something about Kroger's bakery. Do you have a contact there?"

She answered, "John Harrison is my neighbor. He is retired now but he used to be the President of this region for Kroger. I bet he'd know all the players and the politics" she said, with a wink. "I've got his cell right here. You want me to ask him for you?" She was holding up her cellphone.

"You betcha! Thanks, Linda." Clark answered her. "Why don't you try him right now? Maybe he'll answer."

She pressed some buttons and held the phone to her ear. After a short delay, they heard her say, "Hi John, it's your neighbor Linda. ... Fine, fine. How about you? ... That's good. Say, John, I have a Kroger question. My company is looking for an acquisition. Do you think Kroger would sell us the bakery and let us supply the stores in this region? ... uh, huh ... uh, huh ... oh, I see. Oh, really? They would? ... uh, huh ... oh, that'd be great. Thanks, John. Talk to ya later." And, she hung up the phone.

They looked at her intently. They couldn't tell from her side of the conversation if it was good news or bad. She reported that he had indicated it was very unlikely that Kroger would divest its bakery. Their management was looking for more acquisitions, just like Daily Bread. However, they had a standing policy of considering outside vendors, if they were price competitive.

As they discussed it, they realized that another potential acquisition had converted itself into a possible customer. Linda shrugged. They all had a chuckle. Linda promised to get an estimate of the annual volume and whatever they'd be willing to share about their production costs.

Clark made her promise to bring that information back to the team before she moved ahead. He explained that the timing was critical. Unless they were unable to work on an acquisition, he planned to ask her to freeze the project, simply because of the impact on management attention. If the acquisition was way off in the future, he'd permit her to get Kroger out of the way first, assuming they had the capacity to do both.

That left Fun Cakes.

The Dance

It troubled Clark to have just one candidate that seemed a viable target. They knew almost nothing about the company. Even without any data on Fun Cakes sales and capacity, the chances that purchasing the smaller company would significantly boost Daily Bread's profitability both today and in the future was far from guaranteed. Two different scenarios could derail the deal:

1. Fun Cakes wouldn't allow enough synergies.
2. Fun Cakes' owners wouldn't part with the company or would demand a price that made it a poor value to Daily Bread.

At his request, each of the team had scoured their LinkedIn connections to look for people who worked at Fun Cakes that they knew. They searched the Fun Cakes' website, which included lots of information on each of the products and their quick delivery promises. Ordering from the site seemed very customer-friendly. The site included contact details for customer support. However, there was minimal information on the management team.

The owner and CEO of Fun Cakes was a woman, Bernice McNamara. Unexpectedly, none of them had any connections to her either direct or indirect. When they found her LinkedIn page, they found out why. She only had seven connections, no picture and no further information. She was either not a computer savvy type or quite private.

Linda discovered an online picture of her on the Voice of St. Matthews site, an online pictorial magazine that covered the area's social scene. She looked to be in her 60s or 70s. She was standing in a group at a charity event next to her husband, Sean McNamara.

As they had no connections to either Sean or Bernice, Robert suggested that he would try to connect with the operations manager of Fun Cakes and ask for a meeting. Robert felt that somebody in operations might talk more openly to a colleague from a similar company than marketing and sales people who are naturally suspicious about talking about their companies. Robert assumed that Fun Cakes' head of Operation would, at the very least, be familiar with Daily Bread as a well-known and similar business in the city. Clark gave him the green light to try.

Raphael spoke next, saying, "What I'm worried about is they are not for sale. We will have to offer enough to motivate them. That will almost certainly mean overpaying. Plus, the economy is growing rapidly right now. Everybody has money and is looking to invest it. This is driving prices up too. The economy will certainly go into a recession before long, how do we know that we won't be wiped out due to paying a premium?"

"I'm crushed you needed to ask," Clark replied. He feigned being seriously insulted by dramatically dropping his head and shoulders. "I once knew this brilliant CFO. What he said to do was to translate our best intuition into numbers. First, get the appropriate financial, marketing, sales and capacity data in place. Then, run the reasonably pessimistic and optimistic scenarios and see whether we like them."

"Oh, fine," said Raphael. "Embarrass me in front of the whole group."

"Welcome to the club," Robert quipped.

He carried on, now addressing Clark, "I don't think I should try their operations manager so late in the day," he said, checking his wristwatch. "Let me try to get in touch with him tomorrow and I'll report back."

"Good," Clark responded. "Well, guys, since Fun Cakes is the last possibility, at least at the moment, let's close the meeting and head home. Thanks for your good work today!"

Robert called the Fun Cakes' office after he finished his early morning missions of making sure all the deliveries were out and all production planning for the day was complete. He guessed that his counterpart at Fun Cakes would also have popped up for air by this time of the day. The call was answered by a receptionist with nice friendly voice. Robert introduced himself as the VP of Operations of Daily Bread and asked whether he could speak with the operations manager. The receptionist said that would be Mr. George Raney and that he had just stepped into his office. She asked Robert to hold the line while she checked if George was available.

In few seconds, George came on the line. Robert just introduced himself again and said he would like to meet to discuss general business issue that are of interest to both Daily Bread and Fun Cakes.

George responded, "If you were the operations guy of Daily Bread two years ago then I believe we already met at an exhibition for bakery equipment manufacturers in St. Louis. We had a nice discussion on how to improve the flow of products through our ovens."

Then, Robert remembered George: "Wow, what a memory. Now that you remind me, I remember you too. You have a short beard and red hair, if I remember right. You told me about the enormous variety of products you have to deal with. That was a very interesting discussion."

"Yes," George confirmed, "We chatted about subordinating manpower and set-ups on other equipment to the flow rate of the oven, trying raise daily plant capacity."

Then, they set a meeting at one of the Heine Bros. shops in town for the following morning, at about the same time.

The next day, after greeting each other, they both sat down with big cups of coffee and Robert came to the point.

"At Daily Bread, we have made quite a leap ahead over the last five years. To maintain our growth, we need to expand both our market and probably also our capacity. The best way is to purchase a good bakery, especially one with different products and customers and merge operations. From the outside you look like a good candidate for us. To my knowledge, we don't compete, which means we have different customer bases. So, such a merger could be good for you as well – having access to our products and customers. What do you say, is there any chance Fun Cakes owners might be interested?"

George kept quiet for some time, while eating a cinnamon roll and sipping his coffee. Robert could see George was running through many thoughts in his mind.

Finally, he said, "Let me ask you this – if you take over Fun Cakes, what will happen to the workers?"

"We'll keep everyone who wants to work for us and accept our culture, which is a good one that we are all proud of. That also goes for the whole management team. What we have in mind is a true merger. We'll need your and your people's knowledge of your products and market. Look at it from our perspective, George, we want to grow. We need a partner to do so quickly and we want to continue to grow. The merger is just the initial enabler, we won't stop there. We'll need you and everybody, assuming they are good workers."

George seemed troubled by the unknowns. Still, he responded with care, "Let me check with my boss, Bernice. She is an open-minded person, but she also has very strong principles. Personally, I'd welcome such a challenge, especially if you are serious about creating a new base for further growth. I'll call you in few days and let you know whether there is a chance to proceed with the idea in general."

Robert earnestly thanked him. Then, the two went head-to-head, talking flow theory in relation to their plants.

Three days later George called Robert. He announced, "I think might be good if you invited me over to visit your plant. Bernice did not reject the idea out of hand but she is not ready to move ahead yet. I have researched you and Daily Bread online, as much as I could, and I'd like to see your operations with my own eyes before going back to Bernice."

During the plant tour the following week, George was very impressed with the new and modern equipment at Daily Bread. He and Robert were thick as thieves – excited about what new things they could learn from each other. It seemed that George was very encouraged about the idea of merging the two companies. Both men thought that, other than preparation and decoration, the Daily Bread plant was quite capable of baking the various cupcakes which comprised Fun Cakes' primary product line.

They parted amicably. George said that although, he couldn't promise anything, he would share his favorable impressions with Bernice. It would be up to her to contact them. Robert wrote Clark's name and cell phone number on the back of his card and handed it to George. They shook hands and George walked out to his car.

A day passed and then two. Clark and Robert were worried when the weekend came and still nothing. Although they talked about it, they didn't see how they could re-engage without seeming pushy. It seemed like they might have hit another dead end.

Finally, Bernice called Clark on Monday morning. She said she had spoken with her husband over the weekend and they might agree to sell Fun Cakes to Daily Bread, provided they could agree on the price and several other absolutely necessary conditions.

She said she had heard good things about Daily Bread but she definitely needed to know more specifics about Clark's intentions.

Clark suggested that, first of all, they should sign a mutual non-disclosure agreement (MNDA) to protect either of them from taking advantage of the other, regardless of whether they proceeded with a deal or not. After that, he suggested that they both visit the other company's facilities to get a feel for things. If those visits went well and both sides wanted to continue exploring a merger, then he would want to see Fun Cakes' last three years of financials, plus the current year to date income statements and balance sheets. At that point, he'd provide her with a letter from his bank confirming that Daily Bread had the necessary finacial strength to complete a deal. This would allow both sides to decide whether there is enough of match up between the two companies, before they met to negotiate a deal.

A few days later, Fun Cakes and Daily Bread had exchanged signed MNDAs and dates were scheduled for both tours. The Fun Cakes folks were to come to Daily Bread first. If they didn't like what they saw, there was no reason to continue. Clark looked forward to hosting Bernice, George and Irene Lampton, her marketing person, web designer and office manager the following Thursday morning.

When Thursday came, Bernice McNamara and her team arrived a little before the appointed time of 9:00 in the morning. Clark was already waiting for them in the lobby with Linda and Robert. He had instructed his ambassadors to show their counterparts anything they asked – to be open with them.

As he walked towards Bernice, here was a tall slender woman with her grey hair tightly wrapped in a bun. She did not look like she had ever swallowed a cupcake in her life. She was forthright, putting out her hand and shaking Clark's firmly. She had a slower pace than Clark and was naturally reticent. Clark, who was a student of human nature, noticed this and instinctively slowed his speech and even his gait. He asked her what she'd like to see. She was interested in seeing the production floor. Evidently, they had all requested to see different areas, because the pairs had all headed off in different directions, talking together.

As they strolled in the direction of the plant, Clark pointed out the various departments along the way. They had a superficial tour, paying more attention to each other and speaking quietly together.

Clark inquired how she got into the baking business. Bernice told him that her father had been a baker, out in California. So, baking was in her blood. After she married, right out of college, both she and her husband went to work for her father's bakery.

Her father had passed away about 15 years ago, leaving her and her husband half the shares of the company each and he had named her husband president of the bakery. Right away, she began seeing things that she didn't like. Her father's culture was being replaced with more of a command and control style. She cautioned her husband about it but described him as changed – not the same person with whom she had spent her life. She appreciated that he felt his responsibility to the company strongly. Yet, she didn't agree with his approach. This drove a wedge between them. Their marriage eventually collapsed. She wondered out loud if it had been some sort of a mid-life crisis.

She explained that, after their divorce, she had quit her job and triggered the company's buy-sell agreement which required the company to buy out a motivated seller at book value. She had been bitter about it, both because the company was worth much more and also to have her ex-husband effectively "steal" her family business. Eventually, she tired of self-pity and sought a fresh start. One night she had called Sean, who she dated in college, before she met her husband. They rekindled their old relationship. After a time, she had moved to town and started Fun Cakes. A few years afterwards, she and Sean had married.

Clark was empathetic. He thought he knew but, to be sure, he asked her what her concerns about selling were.

Bernice revealed that her biggest concerns were for her employees – that they would lose their jobs. Clark related that Daily Bread was having trouble finding the employees they needed to support their growth. If combining the two companies provided some synergies, that could mean they would have some people who would immediately become available for the new positions for which Daily Bread was trying hire. Bernice seemed visibly relieved.

He appreciated Bernice's quiet bearing and kind smile but he was most impressed that her eyes were always in the right place. Bernice tried somewhat unsuccessfully to hide that she was impressed with the smooth flow of operations of Daily Bread. She even asked Clark's permission to talk privately with two or three of the workers. Clark fully understood that Bernice wanted to informally verify the culture at Daily Bread, so he permitted it, making it clear that he would not quiz them later about what they had told Bernice. He stepped away to give her privacy and to relieve any pressure his staff members might feel from him hovering.

Clark's, Linda's, Robert's and Raphael's visit to Fun Cakes took place the following day. In spite of George's efforts to show Fun Cakes in a favorable light, they all could see some problems. The heat on the floor was almost unbearable. Daily Bread had an effective heat evacuation and air conditioning system that made the heat coming from the ovens less oppressive to employees. In Fun Cakes, this was not case. Except for the oven, which seemed relatively new, their equipment was definitely old but the people seemed to be happy and dedicated to their work. Clark was quick to ask for Bernice's permission to speak with some of her employees, which she immediately gave – turnabout being fair play.

Clark chose to talk with two employees, one older woman, who looked to be about retirement age, and a relatively young man. Rebecca, the woman, told Clark she lived in the neighborhood and had worked at Fun Cakes for over eight years. "I like it here. The people are nice and the salary is as good as I could get anywhere else. I like the cakes very much. In fact, every weekend each of us gets a good sized basket of product and we love it! Even after I retire, probably sometime next year, I'll try to get some temp work here. I've got a lot of friends who have already retired who still work here off and on. Other than the heat, particularly in the summers, it is a great place to work."

Alan, a twenty-something, said he liked it at Fun Cakes too. "I've only worked here for three months. I told Bernice that I wanted to learn more about the bakery business, because I'd like to open my own confectionary shop. She was cool with it and even told me I could ask her anything about baking. She is a way nice lady. What are you all here for?"

Clark just shook his hand and said, "Just visiting." He thought to himself, "that's sure to spin up the rumor mill."

As he and Bernice walked back up towards the offices, Clark casually asked how she and her team made decisions. She shared that she usually didn't include her staff in major decisions at all, she wanted to protect them from the stress. She asked Clark how he managed big decisions. He related the essence of their approach and use of the Magnolia Room. She was fascinated. She became quite animated and wanted to know all about it. She was thrilled to know that, not only was the management team not stressed out by being included, they thought the meetings were fun. Bernice asked if, assuming an agreement was reached, she would be able to attend such a meeting. Clark had chuckled and responded that they would need her, George and Irene in future sessions.

Then, Clark had a brainstorm. He inquired if Bernice would be comfortable joining such a meeting devoted to the process of coming together and working to construct a deal with the Daily Bread team. Bernice was to bring George, Irene and anyone else she liked. She was clearly excited.

She said she looked forward to seeing the group decision making process and asked, what she should do to prepare.

He said they would need her financial statements for the current year and the previous three. He reminded her they already had a MNDA in place. He explained that they'd need that history for their preliminary analysis, so they'd be prepared to decide about the deal in the joint meeting. Clark asked her to decide how much she wanted for her company and bring that number to the meeting, they'd work together to see if they could say yes. In the meantime, he told her that he would prepare a formal Letter of Intent to give her at the meeting, presuming they had a deal. She had nodded.

As they ambled back into the reception area, Clark tactfully explained that he didn't want her to feel rushed. After she had a chance to speak to her attorney, if she wanted to share her financial statements, they would then schedule the group meeting. She thanked him and promised to call.

The Daily Bread team headed back to the office and immediately crowded into Clark's office.

Clark was eager to hear Robert's impressions of Fun Cakes operations and equipment. Clark asked Robert what he thought about how Fun Cakes operated.

Robert leaned back in his chair and closed his eyes. "The production floor is too congested. Most of the equipment simply unfit for the job. I wonder how they get production out. I also noticed that their software isn't much help to them in running the operations and managing raw materials inventory. I'm going to scour Google for customer complaints – if any. George says their performance is around 90% on time, in full (OTIF) – which I find incredible given the circumstances. I looked at their shipping department. Their average order size is about a sixth of ours and the flow through final packaging looks smooth enough."

"The oven is similar to our Oven #2 and they use it 24/7. However, they are unable to exploit its full capacity due to the lack of any kind of staging area and proper supporting equipment. They seem to have plenty of workers on staff but they are inefficient, because their software has no prioritization algorithm. All open orders are dumped into production. The folks that load the ovens don't know which orders are hot or how old they are. They just pick items with similar baking times and cook them together. It requires overtime just to hit 90% OTIF."

"If we move them to our plant and give them the right tools, then I'm pretty sure we can free up 30% of the capacity of the oven using the same manpower and without overtime. I actually think that, given the tough conditions, George is doing an impressive job. Anyway, it won't be a problem to produce all their products and gain more capacity for cross-selling."

He had asked Linda to get a sense of their marketing and sales people, especially how well they know their customers. He also wanted Linda to taste the cupcakes to get an impression of whether Daily Bread's distributors and possibly Events to Remember would want to add them to their purchases.

Linda shared her impressions: "What struck me as a great opportunity is their internet program. Irene is very impressive. They get 95% of their orders just through the website, and the photos and information of their products look great. I wonder, what could we do with it? They go directly to the end consumer, while we sell mainly to distributors. Well, they do supply events for various organizations. We'll want a strategy for exploiting both markets, paying particular attention to how our clients might feel."

She asked, "Did any of you taste the cupcakes?" Hearing No's, she continued, "They are out-of-this-world. So light, moist, and not too sweet. I could have eaten ten of them. If we buy them, I'm going to need hypnotherapy or else I'll have the biggest butt on the planet! Can I sell them to our customers? In a heartbeat!"

Clark had asked Raphael to keep his eyes and ears, and mainly his mind, wide open.

Raphael added his observations: "They produce far fewer units than us but selling directly to consumers and offering specialty cakes in a high variety, allows them to generate higher T per product unit, than we get. To an outside observer, their facility looks terrible. They must be surviving based on their product quality and taste. Customers never see the factory and I'd guess they are paying enough to cover the costs of the inefficiencies. I'm very curious to go over their financials and their capacity profile."

Clark said: "OK, that is the next step – check their financial statements carefully to see what synergies we can create. That's assuming she decides to send them. Raphael have you gotten that letter from the bank?"

Raphael answered him, "Yes, sir. I got it last Friday. For the rest of you, the bank certified that we have cash and credit to be able to immediately fund a deal up to $4 million plus 80% of Accounts Receivable and half the inventory of the acquired company. An additional $2 million could be made available with 120 days notice from a mezzanine fund that has- pre-approved Daily Bread. That should satisfy them that we aren't just tire kickers. I can't imagine this acquisition would require that much.

Clark said, "Well, when their financial statements arrive, we'll meet again. I'm pretty optimistic here but let's see. Thanks everybody!"

They all filed out of his office buzzing with excitement.

A few days later, Clark was packing up his briefcase and getting ready to go home for the weekend. The first shift had been trickling out and the second shift wandering in. Some stopped by his office to wish him a nice weekend on their way through. He stopped packing up for a moment and thought about how positive the culture was these days. Although Daily Bread had always enjoyed a good atmosphere, the improvements in their results over the last few years had really galvanized everyone. He felt like they were ready for a big step but worried about a possibility for a culture clash between his high energy group and the Fun Cakes people. He thought back to noticing Bernice's much more deliberate pace. Would the Fun Cakes staff enjoy being more action oriented? Would her folks become more timid? He just didn't know.

His revery was interrupted when his desk phone rang. Their receptionist informed him that she had Bernice McNamara on the line. He though to himself how strange it was to get a call at the same moment he was thinking about her. He thought it strange but these kinds of coincidences seemed to happen to him a lot.

When he picked up the phone, Bernice apologized for calling so late and explained that she had spent the last day and a half reading everything she could about mergers and acquisitions. She also spoke with her nephew, who was her attorney. The nephew had introduced her to a partner in his firm who was an expert on mergers and acquisitions. She had driven down to their office and spent much of the afternoon there. Her tone was decidedly upbeat. This excited Clark.

She told Clark that she had just emailed him the financials he had requested and was looking forward to joining them for the group meeting. Lastly, she asked if she could bring her nephew and husband as advisors. Clark had agreed instantly.

What Bernice kept to herself was why she had decided to move ahead to the next step. She had been feeling guilty that she had been avoiding working on a succession plan for her company. She was well aware that this was a serious obligation that she had neglected. There were so many things she was unsure about and she really dreaded even starting on it, all alone. She honestly felt that Clark and Daily Bread were a Godsend. But, she didn't tell him any of that!

Somewhat tentatively, she next voiced a concern that the mergers and acquisitions (M&A) partner at her law firm had raised, regarding Daily Bread's financial position. The partner had asked her how she knew that Daily Bread was in a position to make the acquistion and asked her to request Daily's Bread's current year to date financials. Clark responded that, even better, he had asked his bank and another financial resource to document the amount of money at his disposal for acquisition purposes. He proposed to give her that letter at the group meeting. If they needed more, he'd comply. She seemed relieved at his openness.

They set up the following Wednesday afternoon at 2:00 for a combined group meeting at the Magnolia Room in the usual hotel. Both promised to notify the other if that timing wasn't good for all the people on each of their sides.

As he hung up, he thought to himself that the person on the other end of the line did not sound like she was in her seventies.

The next afternoon, Raphael called another meeting back at the hotel to go over the financial and capacity situation of Fun Cakes.

They were all seated and talking amongst themselves incessantly. Raphael stood up and clicked the projector on. "Here's what we got, in summary format." Slowly, the conversation died and he was able to continue. "I have converted their statements to match ours, meaning cost of good sold (COGS) is just what we call TVC, and thus we can compare the Throughput numbers and percentages with ours. The company generates more Throughput than I thought and they do it with just one oven. That's good from our point of view. Fun Cakes has been doing a good job of steadily increasing their Throughput at seven to ten percent per year."

"On the other hand, their operating expenses have been rising faster than Throughput. My assumption is that overtime, repairs and underutilized capacity are driving that. It is probably due to how they load that oven. As their sales keep growing, they are forced to waste more and more people, time and utilities."

He displayed the chart labeled Figure 17.2. "To be clear, this means that the only reason net profits are up this year is because of the company's growth. Proportionally, Net Profits are consistently dropping, relative to Throughput." After they had the chance to see it, he switched back to the table shown in Table 17.2.

"Their bank debt is consistently dropping, which is good. I then calculated their borrowing base at 75% of receivables and half of inventory, excluding equipment."

Linda interjected, "Why would you delve into such details? How can that possibly help us?"

Raphael smiled back, because she had given him a chance to show off a little. He said, "They are currently borrowing twice their borrowing base. Given the age of their equipment and the fact that no bank would want it, regardless of its age, it looks to me like the bank has extended more credit that they would have normally be comfortable lending. The situation has been improving a little each year. On the other hand, you can notice that the company's debt to the family is regularly rising. My conclusion is that the bank is working with them to get their bank debt down. The McNamara's certainly have personal guarantees in place, since the company doesn't have enough

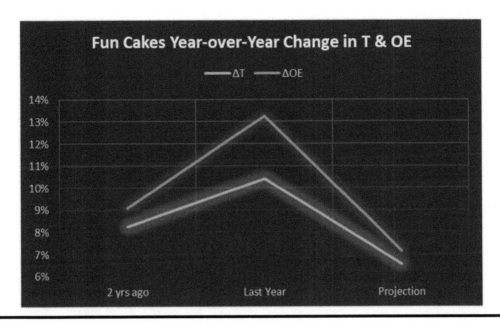

Figure 17.2   Fun Cakes' operating expenses are consistently growing faster than throughput.

liquid collateral. There is probably some term debt mixed in but it would have to be collateralized by other assets, not on the company's books. Either way, the company is picking their pockets. As it grows, they are being forced to invest more.

"As I looked further into how they manage their assets, I notice three things: one, they are being paid slower; two, their inventory turns are deteriorating and, three, they are paying their suppliers more slowly. It seems that, as the company grows, its internal processes are becoming more strained. They are slowly losing control."

"I'm guessing that Bernice and her husband are willing to sell the company for a number of reasons. One is, both are elderly enough to retire and they'd need the money. So, they want to get their investment back plus whatever they can get. The second reason is because it must feel scary to have to lend your company more money every year, even when you are making a profit. The company needs taking care of, instead of taking care of them. Lastly, they need an investor, like us, to help them upgrade their processes, the facility and get them access to modern equipment."

"Overall, I think we have a good investment here, based on the consistently growing Throughput and inefficient operations which I assume we could fix. Is that right, Robert?"

Before Robert could open his mouth, Linda gave Raphael a polite round of applause and the others soon joined in. It was a pretty damn good guess at the circumstances of Fun Cakes and the McNamara's, all from just understanding the numbers. He had impressed them all.

As the clapping subsided, Robert leaned forward in his chair and said, "I'm excited for the opportunity. I like George and am amazed at what he has been able to do on a shoe-string-budget and with outdated ineffective systems. I agree that, not just financially but operationally, as they load the plant more heavily, it is becoming ever more chaotic. I can bake their cakes right alongside our rolls and bread in our plant. We can easily smooth out their flow through the oven. I'd want that oven! Don't get me wrong, consolidating our facilities will be a significant project, lots of work and it'll cost some money but there is nothing conceptually or financially difficult in getting great outcomes."

Table 17.2   Fun Cakes' Year-over-Year Financials

Fun Cakes (thousands)	Actual			YTD Projection
	3 yrs ago	*2 yrs ago*	*Last Year*	
Sales	$1,897	$2,140	$2,283	$2,416
Truly Var. COGS	334	448	415	426
Throughput	1,563	1,692	1,868	1,990
Op. Expense	1,301	1,419	1,607	1,722
EBITDA	262	273	261	268
Tax, Int. & Depr	156	166	164	153
NP	$106	$107	$97	$115
Cash	51	47	58	60
A/R	47	64	75	99
Inventory	38	55	55	61
Other Curr Ass	18	25	31	16
Fixed Assets	1,336	1,518	1,586	1,660
Accum Depr	523	575	635	674
Fixed Net	813	943	951	986
A/P	32	45	43	43
Other Curr Liab	5	11	8	12
Bank Debt	371	385	297	210
McNamara	150	178	210	230
Net Worth	408	515	612	727

Clark commented: "Raphael, it is interesting to me that you mention the increase in T not the Sales. Why?"

Raphael smiled, "Well, this is the lesson we have learned over the last four or five years. An increase in sales might be caused by reducing the cost. This didn't happen at Fun Cakes. The adjusted COGS I'm showing here, being just the cost of raw materials that went into items sold, is less than 18% of sales." He showed the chart in Figure 17.3. "Ours is around 23%, which is better than most bakeries. This means they have a good product for which customers will pay relatively high price, plus the fact that they sell directly to the end consumer, capturing some of our distributors' margin. It is true that TVC did spike up to 21%, two years ago, but they seem to have it nailed back down again. Remember, we saw a temporary spike in the cost of flour and sugar back then too, due to the drought the summer before."

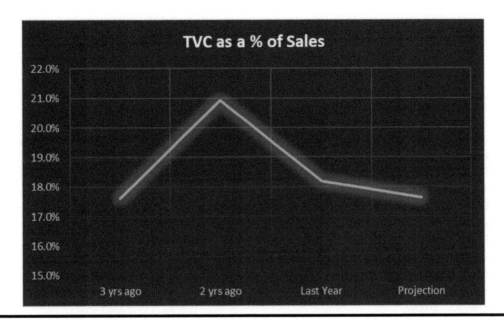

Figure 17.3 Totally variable costs as a proportion of sales.

Clark asked Robert: "Did you look into their capacity numbers? Can we know how much hidden capacity we can get from operating in our facility with better equipment and software?"

"No, their capacity data is awful, like other bakeries I have seen. Measuring the potential capacity of an oven is not simple. How long it takes to bake a certain product-mix isn't straight-forward. When the product mix changes you need to know how long it will take to finish all the baking. As you are all aware, we model all our products by creating an equivalency factor relative to a regular donut. They have many different end-products and no idea how to measure capacity. My rough estimation is that we'll be able to get at least 35% additional capacity, eight to nine hours, from their oven. They have more than enough manpower to make it happen. If you insist on a range between pessimistic and optimistic of excess capacity, 30% is quite pessimistic, it could go up to 45% free capacity of their oven but that is starting to stretch it, even with more than enough manpower."

Clark asked: "If we merge both companies at our plant, how much potential capacity would we have together?"

Robert was ready to provide the numbers, "After adding the demand from Heine Bros., we still have 13 hours of Oven #3 as capacity for growth, the two others are fully exploited. When we add the expected range of free hours from Oven #4 (that's what I'm calling their oven), we'll have the equivalent of 21 to 25 hours of oven time as a Capacity Buffer. This means from 28%[3] to almost 35%[4] of potential capacity for more demand. However, this is also the definitive limit of how much we can grow, without commissioning yet another oven."

He took a breath and continued, "If our cross-selling requires more capacity than that, we could consider giving up some sales to free capacity. I know Linda hates this idea but it's an

---

[3] 21 hours free/(4 ovens × 24 hours capacity − 21 hours free)
[4] 25 hours free/(4 ovens × 24 hours capacity − 25 hours free)

option, when you have an active constraint and you are not ready to elevate the constraint or the elevation takes more time. If we run out of capacity and Fun Cakes products yield more T per hour of the ovens, we might have to reduce some sales of our current products. Okay, maybe that won't happen but don't we all hope it does? I just want you all to be aware that there is an absolute limit to the combined plant's production capacity. As we get closer to it, the situation will become clearer."

Clark summarized, "Well, our conservative assessment is 28% growth potential in T. For ΔOE it is energy plus the need for some overtime, possibly. I don't want to rely on finding more potential capacity from exploiting Fun Cakes' oven to a greater extent. We should consider various options to elevate future capacity – maybe even revisiting the idea of opening a bakery in Humboldt. We are not there yet. Meanwhile, let's go over pro forma financials of the merger from pessimistic side, holding the potential capacity to 28%. Raphael, would you be able to prepare the information by tomorrow afternoon?"

Raphael responded, "I can do better than that. I already met with Linda and Robert. I can show you now, if you have the time."

Clark checked his wristwatch, settled back in his chair and said, "Sure, this is my one and only top thing. Can the rest of you all spend a few more minutes today?"

They all agreed.

Raphael projected information shown in Table 17.3 and said, "This is the income statement for the two companies combined, just the current year-to-date projections added together – no changes.

Raphael continued, "If the pessimistic side looks good, we'll know that we are interested in moving ahead, for sure. After we come to that conclusion, if we come to that conclusion, we'll want the Fun Cakes team to help us come up with the optimistic scenario and confirm our assumptions on the pessimistic side. Now, I want us to check the conservative potential of cross-selling that would start in earnest next year."

The Daily Bread group was nodding their heads. They got it.

Robert added: "For perspective's sake, let me remind you about the capacity profile." He displayed the chart shown in Figure 17.4. "Oven #1 and #2 work 24/7 and, with Heine Bros., Oven #3 now works eleven hours a day, seven days a week. With Oven #4 installed here, the

Table 17.3 Combination of Fun Cakes and Daily Bread - No Changes

Combination (thousands)	YTD Projection
Sales	$10,257
Truly Var. COGS	2,313
Throughput	7,944
Op. Expense	5,558
EBITDA	2,386
Tax, Int. & Depr	1,323
NP	$1,063

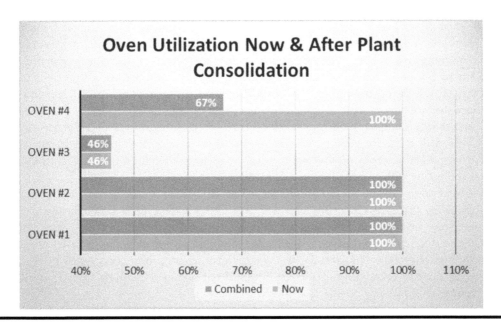

Figure 17.4   Oven utilization immediately before and after the merger.

Fun Cakes staff might need as much as two full shifts to cook their current orders – leaving eight hours of Oven #4 free for baking any demand on top of the 13 hours that is available from Oven #3.

Therefore, the combined daily oven load, expressed in oven-hours, is 24 hours on Oven #1 plus 24 on Oven #2 plus 11 on Oven #3 plus 16 on Oven #4, which comes to a total of 75 oven hours daily. This is what is required to smoothly deliver the combined demand. We'll have the potential to handle additional load that requires up to 21 extra hours every day, conservatively speaking.

Robert was on a roll, "I made approximate calculations of the cost of operating one additional hour of any oven per day. It comes to a range of ΔOE of $90 to $100 per added hour per day. The difference depends mainly whether we'd need to pay overtime or we have enough manpower on regular salary for those extra oven hours. With the new manpower I think it is safe to assume $100 in ΔOE, so the yearly ΔOE of one extra oven-hour is $36,500 per year for each oven-hour."[5]

Linda raised her hand like a demure schoolgirl and Clark nodded to her. "I hope I can use up every bit of that capacity!" She said with a big grin.

Robert came back to her, "That's what I'm worried about! I need to know before that happens. How much of my capacity do you think you can sell and how soon?"

Linda responded sheepishly, "How should I know? I barely understand what you all are talking about. I mean I get the calculations but, when I get a new customer, I don't think in terms of oven-hours."

Clark said, "However, Linda, you have an uncanny knack that none of us share. It's what we need most from you. Nobody else has your skill to think about product value in the customer's mind. If you can tell us how much you guess customers would buy of the new products made available by the merger, Raphael can translate that into money and Robert can translate the money into the extra TVC required, which should be proportional to ovenhours."

---

[5] $100 ΔOE per hour per day × 365 days per year

She then shared her expectations of the cross-selling opportunity. "I've thought about this a lot. I think that it will be tougher to sell Daily Bread products on the Fun Cakes website, because people are going there to buy a treat that satisfies their sweet tooth. Their customers are more likely to be buying for special occasions, like graduations, birthdays and retirements. Our products are daily staples. On the other hand, donuts might be seen as an appropriate special occasion treat and, once they are buying some cupcakes, why not get some rolls too?"

"Once shoppers find our products available on their site too, I expect it will add at least 25% to Fun Cakes' daily sales. The good news is that will be at retail prices for our products. We'll want to hike our normal prices by 40% when we advertise them on the Fun Cakes site, to avoid being seen as competing with our distributors and retailers."

She went on to explain her projections for selling Fun Cakes' to the Daily Bread customers, "I'm optimistic that Fun Cakes products will be a hit with the typical Daily Bread customer. However, there are two buts. First but, our customers are buying those types of products already, meaning we'll have to win them over one by one. Second but, we are going to have to discount their prices to our resellers by 20% to 30%. So, for a conservative projection assume 30% off of their website prices. Even with the discount, I expect our sales will climb by 15%. That is really conservative."

Raphael looked up from pushing buttons on his computer and took over again, "Okay, that means our combined annual sales will increase at least $1.78 million.[6]"

Clark got excited and blurted out, "And, about three quarters of that goes straight to the bottom line! Wow. This is big!"

Raphael held up his hands and said, "Whoa, boss-man. You're thinking from the standard Daily Bread point of view, where we convert about 76% of each dollar in sales into T. This is more complicated, because of the discounts and premiums Linda mentioned. Plus, I've got to figure how much capacity those sales would use up on the ovens. If, we need to add equipment and people, it will reduce the contribution to earnings."

"Why don't you all toddle off to the coffee shop and have a potty break and let me figure out how much TVC would be necessary for that much new sales. Give me fifteen minutes, then bring me a mocha latte. When you get back I'll have the ΔT for Linda's low-side estimate."

The room was quiet like a funeral parlor, even after they had all shuffled back in the room fifteen minutes later, given Raphael his fancy coffee and taken their seats. They were all pretty upbeat about what they would hear and anxious too, in case their intuitions were wrong.

Raphael cleared his throat, aware that he had their focused attention and began to explain, "Let me start with Daily Bread ΔTVC. Remember, Linda said plus 25% for Fun Cakes' sales of Daily Bread products. We don't know which of our products will sell yet, so I'll use the average % TVC for all our products which is 24.07% of our current sales. The Fun Cakes sales increase is $604,000 per year[7] but those sales are not equal to our sales, because we'll be marking up our prices 40%. Converting back to equivalent Daily Bread sales we need to shrink them back down to our normal prices by dividing by 140%. That means, if we had sold that same amount of TVC, at our normal prices, it would have been $431k. Since our % TVC from normal prices is 24.07%, multiplying gives us $104,000 of ΔTVC[8] required to sell enough of our products through their website to be worth 25% of their current sales! Now, taking their ΔSales minus the ΔTVC gives ΔT and that's half a million per year."

---

[6] $2,416,000 Fun Cakes sales × 25% + $7,841,000 Daily Bread sales × 15%

[7] $2,416,000 Fun Cakes sales per year × 25%

[8] 431,400 Daily Bread equivalent sales lift per year × 24.07% average TVC per sales for Daily Bread

"Now, watch me do the same thing with our sales of their products. Linda said to expect a 15% lift on our side. That works out to new sales of $1,176,000[9] on our side. Except, that's at a discount to their current prices. So, using the same method, had they sold at normal prices, they would have gotten a whopping $1,680 in sales.[10] Now, that the price is corrected to their levels, we can apply their % TVC of 17.63% to calculate that they would need to produce $296,000 more TVC per year.[11] The new sales of $1,176k less the ΔTVC of 296k gives us a ΔT of $880k!"

Raphael announced, looking very proud, "Overall, ΔT is $1,380k, from cross selling on both sides."

"Crap!" Linda spat out. "That's more than half again their annualized production! There's no way they can make that much."

"Hold on, Linda," Robert calmed. "That would surely tilt them into utter chaos, *if* they tried to make that much more in their rickety old plant. But, keep in mind that I already told you we can bake their products right alongside of ours. In a consolidated plant, any available capacity can bake it. We certainly wouldn't keep Oven #4 making their products full time. It would be a blend."

Robert carried on, "Let's convert the load into oven-hours. On our side, the $104k TVC increase is only 4.5% of our combined TVC of $2,313k. I broadly assume that the TVC is proportional to the oven-hours. Since we currently use 75 of oven-hours each day, that would be 3 hours and 22 minutes more oven-time that we need. The bigger load is 9.6 oven-hours.[12] The total is almost 13 hours. We have a total capacity of 96 oven-hours per day. We use 75 oven-hours now. The minimum load would add almost 13, bringing us to nearly 88 total oven-hours used out of a theoretical capacity of 96, which is in the range of 91-92% of the ovens' capacity!" He showed them the chart in Figure 17.5.

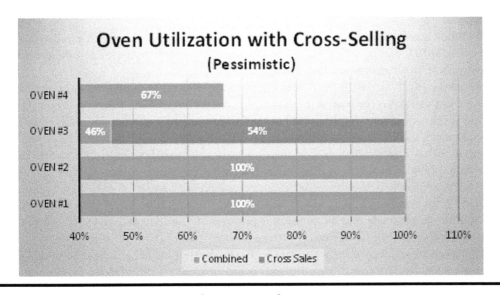

Figure 17.5 Expected load on ovens due to cross sales.

---

[9] $7,841,000 Daily Bread sales × 15%
[10] $1,176,000 Fun Cakes TVC per year / 70% after discount
[11] $1,680,000 sales at Fun Cakes' prices per year × 17.63% average TVC per sales for Fun Cakes
[12] $296,000 new TVC per year / $2,313,000 TVC now × 75 oven-hours/day

"You can see that Linda's bottom end cross-selling estimates wipe out the capacity of Oven #3. That leaves only a third of Oven #4 available. I can tell you right now, if you are serious about this deal, you better order another oven!" Robert was dead serious. He finished up by saying, "I've got to have spare capacity. It'd be enough that actual sales would rise by 3-4% and we'd have real problems with reliable delivery. After all, this is Linda's low end estimate, without considering which products are sold more than others."

Raphael said, "Let's see how much money this merger generates. If it is a bunch, then we can figure out how much protective capacity we need, which will help us decide whether or not to push the panic button and call the oven manufacturer. I assume that we'll have enough time to make this decision, as cross sales actually materialize."

Raphael continued with his own math. "The last thing we need to find is the cost to run the ovens for 13 hours. Robert already calculated $36,500 of ΔOE per extra oven-hour, so we just multiply by 13 which gives us $475k in ΔOE. If we subtract that and the needed TVC from the new sales we get ΔNP of $905k.[13]"

Robert chimed in, "Guys, I've got more! Operationally, there is no question that the merger would reduce the OE of Fun Cakes, even if we employ all their current manpower and promote several employees to assist in the managing and coordinating the bigger and varied flow of products. The reduction in OE would be a consequence of less overtime for Fun Cakes employees, the elimination of rent of that facility, combining the shipping, purchasing, accounting and human resources departments."

"We'd also reduce scrapped materials in Fun Cakes production process due to better handling and having the space to smooth operations. I checked George's costs on flour, sugar and butter, there's 2% to 4% there. And, don't forget external savings, like the accounting firm that does our taxes, bank fees and the cost of their legal advice. All would be combined and about equal to what we pay now."

"I think it is conservative to assume all these savings would easily exceed half a million dollars, maybe even $650,000 is possible. If we do have to add another oven or more lines, there would be some new ΔOE to offset some of these savings."

He continued, "However, those figures assume an investment of $300k, which is our current high-side estimation for the cost of the move plus making Fun Cakes' line work in our facility with the proper equipment. Raphael and I are still fine tuning that number. I'll need to buy some new equipment. Luckily, it will be only about $30,000. The best news is, there will be a significant portion of their equipment that we won't need. We can sell it to offset the purchase price. Expect to get back $290k to $340k from those sales. That will pretty much cover the transition, equipment and moving costs."

"Thanks for that, Robert," Clark said. "I can handle the math from here. Half a million ΔTVC and ΔOE to the good side plus $905k ΔNP is just over $1.4 million dollars a year, before taxes, right?" He looked around the table.

They were all nodding, except Raphael, who was shaking his head no and he said, "You're forgetting what they are already earning now, which is $268k of EBITDA less $22k in interest less $39k in depreciation and then you'll have the whole benefit of buying them, pessimistically, of course. That is at least $1.656 million per year, before taxes!"

Linda asked, "As great as that seems, the actual will be even better. But, how do we know whether it's worth what we have to pay, when we don't know what we have to pay?"

---

[13] $1,780,000 new sales − $104,000 increase in Daily Bread's TVC − $296,000 increase in Fun Cakes TVC = $1,380,000 ΔT. $1,380,000 of ΔT − $475,000 in ΔOE = $905,000 in ΔNP.

Clark responded by saying, "Great question! That won't take higher math to answer, Linda, which I know you'll be happy to hear. Companies, like Fun Cakes, and, by that, I mean companies that don't have huge cash reserves or some highly appreciated asset or massive growth expectations due to some breakthrough technology – regular companies that just have their profits to offer a buyer, get valued by a multiple of EBITDA. That's earnings before interest, taxes, depreciation and amortization, in case you forgot."

"What a buyer must decide is, how long am I willing to wait to get my investment in this business back? For a given deal, they compare their time horizon with the deal's by dividing the purchase price by the expected Net Profit, after taxes. This is a calculation that each buyer must complete for themselves, because every buyer is different. Only the buyer can know what the balance sheet will look like after the sale. It depends on how much cash the buyer wants to contribute into the deal. The more cash they inject the less interest is and the closer EBITDA is to net profit."

Linda asked him. "What multiple of EBITDA would make sense for Fun Cakes?"

Clark thought about it for a moment and answered, "Four, from our point of view and six, from theirs. Five is probably fair, for a company their size in the current strong economy. The point is that they have EBITDA of $268k. We can make an extra $1,405k of EBITDA on top of that from cross-selling, which is …" He reached for his iPhone to add it up.

Before, he could turn it on, Raphael shouted, "$1,673,000 of additional EBITDA on top of the $2,118,000 we are making now."

"Right." Clark said. "And that is …"

"Six and a quarter times what they make on their own." Raphael finished for him.

"Right," Clark said, again and turned to his CFO. "News flash! I *can* work a calculator!" Laughter all around the table interrupted them again. Finally, he got to spit out. "That damn company is a bargain to us at 25 times their current EBITDA[14]! On the other hand, it isn't reasonable for them to imagine that they could get any more than six times their current EBITDA, on the high side."

"Ooh, I like it," Linda cooed.

After he let this sink in for a few moments, Clark followed up. "Guys, we haven't even gone through the optimistic scenario yet. What we know now is that this purchase is our top priority. Everything takes a back seat to make sure we move ahead." Then he warned them saying, "At the same time, don't let any of the Fun Cakes people see our excitement. Play it cool. Always discuss the deal from their point of view. Show them we earnestly want to be fair. Bernice will bring her asking price for Fun Cakes to the meeting next Wednesday afternoon."

Raphael was quick to retort, "Well, the book value of Fun Cakes, what is called the Net Worth, is $727k. That is the minimum price, which is the difference between the cost basis of their assets less what they owe. It gives no value to the business, its profitability, its reputation or future opportunities. Their EBITDA is $268k. Fun Cakes is a small company, too small to attract the attention of private equity funds. The only buyers are other small companies, like us, or an owner-operator. Therefore, I assume that the absolute best they'd get in a hot market like we have

---

[14] Clark has said that a bargain price for Daily Bread would be 4 × EBITDA. However, the Daily Bread management team has just calculated that they expect the EBITDA increase from doing the deal to be 6 ¼ × Fun Cakes' current EBITDA. Therefore, from the point of view of Daily Bread, 4 × the expected EBITDA is the actual value of Fun Cakes to them. That is a 4 multiple × 6.25 × Fun Cakes' EBITDA = 25 times Fun Cakes' EBITDA or 25 × $268,000 = $6.7 million. Clark is establishing Fun Cakes' reasonable value to them. He goes on to say that he expects their price to be no higher than $1.6 million, a bargain.

now, is a multiplier of five. That works out to a price of $1,340,000.[15] That seems fair. Maybe a little more is possible."

Clark smiled, "Let's wait to hear her asking price and we'll work from there."

Linda shared her worry, "I'm afraid the McNamara's will ask for significantly more, because they weren't looking for a buyer in the first place. Anybody would. I would! I bet Bernice is well aware how much we'd like to get her company. She could figure out what the synergies would be. She's been around the block a few times. I bet she'll ask $2 million."

Raphael looked alarmed and shouted, "No way! That's much too high a price. Fun Cakes is *not* worth it!"

Clark responded: "Now, we are just going around in circles with hypotheticals. Let's close the meeting and wait for news from them. Again, as I promised you, Raphael, we won't do the deal, if you don't approve of it."

Clark wanted to clarify a point: "Guys, let me reiterate, don't communicate how good the deal is for us to any of the folks at Fun Cakes. It could drive up the price we have to pay. The way deals happen is when the company isn't worth the price to the seller and is worth more than the price to the buyer."

Raphael nodded and commented, "That's exactly right. Thanks for saying it, Clark."

With that, Clark stood up, smiled and started to walk out of the room.

Robert stopped him by saying, "Hey, wait a minute. I know everybody is all excited but Raphael promised we would agree on when to add another oven. We need a mechanism."

Clark said, "Oh, yeah. I forgot. Sorry." He sat back down. Then, he added, "Well, it can't be a cut and dried formula. It depends on what we expect for the future, how optimistic we are."

Raphael said, "Agreed. It also depends on how long it takes to get a new oven. Are there used ovens out there that we can expect to be able to find, Robert?"

Robert said, "Friends, we use the heck out of our ovens. I'd want new, not used. In answer to Raphael's other question, I think we can get a custom oven delivered, installed and running in 120 days. The cost of such an oven is $180,000. It would be considered an investment but operating it would also add OE for energy, maintenance and manpower. A bigger consideration is the variability in the demand. I'm certain Fun Cakes faces significant fluctuation, more than our current sales do. Then, whenever we expand our markets, we face uncertain fluctuations until the demand stabilizes. This means you need me to be able to catch up quickly, if we get slammed."

Raphael asked him, "What does that take, in your mind?"

Robert turned to Linda, "Linda, how comfortable are you squelching demand by raising prices?"

She answered right away, "I can always do that a little bit, by that I mean a price increase of less than 5%. More than that would be perceived as gouging and I'd expect the customers to take their revenge later. I don't want to be like those jerks at the airlines, who jack up their prices around holidays. However, when it comes to selling new products or selling new customers, we can be more flexible in our delivery. If a distributor asks for a huge quantity of Fun Cakes' products then I'll be able get them to agree that we start slowly and build volumes over several months. This is quite different from what I can get away with on products we sell now to our regular customers."

"Okay." Robert answered and then he turned to Clark. "Clark, do you think you can keep adding products and making acquisition into the future? I mean finding ways to use spare oven capacity?"

"Yes, I do, Robert. At least for the foreseeable future." Clark replied.

---

[15] $268,000 in EBITDA × 5 multiple

"Okay then, I think we better be placing an order for a new oven as soon as we penetrate the 10% remaining protective capacity level. And, given Linda's projections, you better order one *now*!" Robert concluded.

Clark asked Linda, "Do you expect all the new business in one surge?"

She thought about it for a minute and wrote some notes on her pad of paper before saying, "No. The sales of our products through the Fun Cakes site will probably build over a calendar quarter. I'd expect most of their customers would have gone on-line to buy something and discovered our products after that much time. On our side, it is tougher. We have to introduce the products to our existing customers one at a time. They'll have to taste then and decide if they want to add Fun Cakes stuff to their orders or whether they are going to use us to replace an existing supplier. That will be slower. The numbers I gave you is what I expect the run rate to be after the Transition Period. It will take at least six months."

"Oh, one more thing. It doesn't get me in trouble with customers not to tell them about new products. They are happy to hear whenever they do. So, I can slow down approaching customers, if we run too low on capacity."

Clark concluded for them, "Good. If we feel optimistic and break through a 90% utilization barrier, we'll order another oven and any other equipment necessary to utilize it. During the subsequent four months, before the oven is operational, Linda will slow down her presentations to add new products to existing customers. Only if that doesn't work will we raise prices. All for that plan say, Aye."

After a chorus of Ayes, they headed back to the office.

The following Wednesday found the combined teams of Fun Cakes and Daily Bread sitting around the conference room table chatting cordially, drinking their waters, soft drinks and tea, while munching on cookies, M&Ms and salted nuts.

In the previous few days, Clark and Raphael had looked at the deal inside out. Clark had asked Raphael to try and talk him out of it. No matter what Raphael threw at him, the Kroger Bakery possibility, even all the other opportunities Linda had in PipeDrive, their CRM system, combined using the most optimistic scenarios, the Fun Cakes deal was the most accretive to earnings. It wasn't even close.

Clark stood up, reintroduced himself and thanked Bernice for coming with her group. He introduced the people on his side, one by one, first Raphael, then Linda and finally Robert. He had decided to leave out anybody from their CPA and legal firms to avoid any potential for argument with the professionals Bernice brought along. He knew that these detail-oriented types of folks tended to see things in black and white, in favor of their clients. If anything, he wanted Bernice to feel like she had the advantage in today's opening talks. He hoped that would make them comfortable sharing information.

Next, Clark sat down, asking Bernice to introduce her people.

Bernice stood and said, "Thank you Clark and thanks for your interest in my little company. We are happy to be here. She pointed to Sean and said, "I'd like you all to meet Sean McNamara, my husband." Looking at George and smiling she continued, "I know most of you have already met George Raney, our production superintendent." George briefly bowed his head to them. "This is Irene Lampton, who is our web designer, office and marketing manager." They all looked at her and she smiled and waved back enthusiastically. "And, this is Sam McNamara, Sean's nephew and our attorney. Sam is here to make sure I don't fall into the deep end and drown." She winked at him and he grinned back.

Sam said, "Good to meet you, Clark. Bernice mentioned that you were bringing a letter of financial capacity from your bank. Would you mind if I saw that now?"

Clark nodded to Raphael, who passed over the letter. Sam's head bent over the letter. After a short review, Sam said, "Very impressive. Thank you." And, he nodded to Bernice.

Clark asked Bernice, "Where would you like to start?"

She came right back with, "If you bought my company, what would you want me to do? Do you have a place for me?"

Fortunately, Clark anticipated this question and had prepared for it. He responded, "One of the commitments we make to our employees is that we will only give them jobs that suit them. The way we do that is to look at every position and figure out what personality it requires. We use Predictive Index (PI) to assist us in making that psychometric assessment. PI inventories the personality traits of those employees who are interested in the job, as well as outside applicants. We match people to the job. We consider the functions we require to accomplish the work our customers will gladly pay for and limit the organization chart to those positions."

"That sounds like fitting a job to a person is something you would never do."

He hadn't expected her to be so insightful. Her question pushed him into dangerous line, one that could end up scuttling the deal before it ever got started. Nevertheless, he felt he owed her an honest response. Regardless of whether they had a spot for her, he needed her trust. "Yes, you are right. Fitting jobs to people ends up wasting resources by creating capacity that doesn't generate Throughput, thus, reducing the company's profit. That eventually puts us in a worse competitive position vis à vis our competitors. Worse than that, it wastes the person in a way which undermines their need for a strong sense of purpose."

"I understand that and it makes sense to me," Bernice replied. "So, since you have a successful company, built on a functional organization, that implies that you have people in all the necessary roles. But, I'm not ready to retire yet. What role is available for me in the combined company?"

Clark was ready for this one too. What he didn't know was how it would be received by Bernice. From what he could tell, she just might be a fit for what he had in mind. "Bernice, there is a new role we are going to need at Daily Bread that we haven't needed in the past and which will be increasingly important as we expand through acquisitions. We need someone who can handle the long-term function of integrating the staff of the companies we buy into our culture. We must be one team, with no us and them. The first duty of the person in this position will be to understand our culture well and get the Fun Cakes gang integrated."

Bernice smiled broadly and said softly, "Oh, that sounds like something I'd really enjoy!" And, then added, "how do you know if I'd be any good at it?"

Clark retorted, "Easy. With your permission, we'll get your PI[16] and compare it to the pattern that would be perfect for doing that job. Would you mind taking a PI?"

"No, not at all. I'd be happy to. The last thing I want is to be miserable for the last years of my career." Then, she added, "Do I get to know what all of your personalities are?"

It was Clark's turn to beam. He explained, "Absolutely, that is another of our core beliefs about how to treat employees. We share all our PI patterns with each other. After all, there is nothing so unfair as treating different people the same. Anybody can go on our intranet and review or print out any employee's picture, job description and PI. That's how new people get to know their co-workers and vice versa."

"I love that!" she said. You've mentioned two of your core beliefs so far. Are there more?"

"We have ten of them," Clark said.

---

[16] https://www.predictiveindex.com/. As mentioned earlier, PI is one of a number of available psychometric personality inventory tools.

10 Steps to Breakthrough Results

1. Pay a fair wage
2. Educate employees to understand how they help the whole
3. Give employees autonomy
4. Only give employees jobs for which they are well suited
5. Encourage non-constraint downtime
6. Gate initiatives to reduce bad multitasking
7. Treat mistakes as learning opportunities
8. Provide training to understand coworkers
9. Make relevant metrics public
10. Ask employees for their ideas

Figure 17.6   The printed business card carried by Daily Bread staff.

With that, Robert, who was sitting next to Bernice, reached into his breast pocket, right behind his pocket protector, and pulled out what looked like a business card, shown in Figure 17.6. He handed it to Bernice.

She looked at the card and read through the ten steps. Then, she handed the card to Sean, her husband. With an arched brow, she asked Robert. "Do you live by this?"

Robert blinked, not understanding, "Yes, ma'am, these ten have become habits with us all."

Linda pulled one out of her organizer. Raphael withdrew one from his shirt pocket and Clark produced the same card from the pocket of his sport coat. They all held them up. Linda explained, "Clark came up with this list a few years ago. We found ourselves talking about it all the time with applicants, the employees, customers, suppliers and our service providers. So, we decided to print them up in one handy format. Since the economy has gotten so strong, it became harder to find employees for our open positions, we use them to recruit new people."

"For recruitment? I don't understand," Bernice said.

Linda continued, "When a waitress does a good job or the usher at a concert or somebody at a store, we give them that card. You can see that the other side says, *'You've given me really good service. Thank you. We are always looking for people like you at our company. The other side of this card shows what we believe in with regard to treatment of employees. Please contact us if you ever consider changing jobs.'* You wouldn't believe how well it works. Many places treat their employees like chattel – you know, like property or chess pieces to be moved around or sacrificed, as needed."

As she listened to Linda, Bernice looked around at the other folks from Daily Bread and saw them earnestly nodding in agreement. She had never heard of a company being so intentional about their culture. She felt like she did a good job with culture, at Fun Cakes. Still, her people had to figure it out on their own as time passed. She wondered briefly how much of her turnover was due to people coming in not trusting employers in general, based on their previous experiences. Maybe if she had expressed what she believed, some of those employees would still be working for her now.

Clark noticed that his people had scored a point with that little exchange. However, he elicited no sign.

Bernice said, "What other little tricks do you have?"

Linda answered her. "They are not tricks. We believe in this stuff. In fact, we have a series of one-liners we use in various circumstances. They are basically our rules of the road. Like, *'Never do today what you can avoid forever.'* Having them all agreed on in advance means there is nothing impolite about bypassing the normal social morays that might make someone reluctant to make a useful and necessary comment."

"But, what does it mean?" Bernice asked her.

Linda answered her. "It sounds lazy, huh? Not like something an employer would ever say, right? We use it to stop people from doing busy work. Work that doesn't help customers also doesn't satisfy people's desire for a sense of purpose in their lives. We let them know it is okay to be idle, that we don't expect them to try to look like they are working all the time. It supports Step 5 on the card. We know that, if they get to charge up their batteries, they are ready for a sprint, should we need one. If they do have some slack time, we'd rather they work on their education, reading or helping somebody else on something important. That way, we don't end up spending money to accomplish something no customer will pay for."

George wanted to know if there were more one-liners. Linda laughed and said, "Sure, plenty, like Clark's Law which says, *'When in doubt, choose the less efficient route.'* Clark hates it when people put efficiency over effectiveness. He's right too." She glanced over at her boss. "I've never found a time when it wasn't true. If you are getting rid of pure waste, you are both trying to be efficient and you are not in doubt. That is good. But, when you're at risk of trading inefficiency for ineffectiveness, you are always in doubt – you just know. Why would any company ever want to be ineffective?"

"Ha," blurted out Sam, the lawyer.

Everybody turned to look at him, as it was the first sound he had uttered since asking for the letter. Clark said, "Ha, is right. You just thought of a circumstance in which my Law applies didn't you?"

Sam nodded minutely. He had a smirk on his face but he didn't say another word.

These one-liners are approved by all of us. They give us a way to correct a person's wrong thinking without attacking them personally or being rude. These are company authorized statements. We are all expected to quote them, under certain contextual circumstances. It isn't personal. It's how we roll. It is a socially acceptable way to get someone to think about an alternative approach – the right one!"

Sean, Bernice's husband, asked, "Do you print them out on a card too?"

Robert answered this question. "No, we have Word documents out on our shared drive for each of them, including usage suggestions and the explanation of their logic. We have found that when somebody is interested, because a particular circumstance is floating around in their head, they are much keener to learn. They go looking for these one-liners. It is a pull process. Like a box of Kleenex, they grab one when they need one."

Bernice declared, "Well, that is remarkable. I can see culture is important to you all and you didn't just try to snow me with a flowery speech. That makes it even more impressive. I can't wait to take that PI thing. I'd love to be the 'culture police' and help my folks adopt this win-win culture. I just hope I match the personality needed for the job!" She paused and then said, "What would I do after that?"

Clark answered her, "Bernice, this is going to be a never-ending process. As soon as we adopt one company, we will look for the next one. As we grow, we'll hire new people. I don't see us ever outgrowing the need. Of course, in the early going, we'll need your expertise to get us on track operationally and with your customer knowledge and relationships. My biggest worry is what to do after you do decide to retire!" She smiled at that.

Raphael stood up, clicked the projector on and displayed the information in Table 17.4. "Here's what we got from you all in summary format. The company is bigger than we thought. That's good from our point of view. You have been doing a good job of steadily increasing your sales."

Bernice interjected, "That's thanks to Irene's web design. I'm gratified that our customers love our products. However, even though we have been adding new equipment, or at least new to us, George has to struggle with breakdowns and work the guys overtime to catch up. It's crazy sometimes."

"I wondered about that." Raphael remarked. "I noticed that Operating Expenses have been rising faster than Throughput."

George asked him, "What is Throughput? That's the second time you've said that. I'm not familiar with the term."

Table 17.4 Fun Cakes Summary Financial Performance for Recent Years

Fun Cakes (thousands)	Actual			YTD Projection
	3 yrs ago	2 yrs ago	Last Year	
Sales	$1,897	$2,140	$2,283	$2,416
Truly Var. COGS	334	448	415	426
Throughput	1,563	1,692	1,868	1,990
Op. Expense	1,301	1,419	1,607	1,722
EBITDA	262	273	261	268
Tax, Int. & Depr	156	166	164	153
NP	$106	$107	$97	$115
Cash	51	47	58	60
A/R	47	64	75	99
Inventory	38	55	55	61
Other Curr Ass	18	25	31	16
Fixed Assets	1,336	1,518	1,586	1,660
Accum Depr	523	575	635	674
Fixed Net	813	943	951	986
A/P	32	45	43	43
Other Curr Liab	5	11	8	12
Bank Debt	371	385	297	210
McNamara	150	178	210	230
Net Worth	408	515	612	727

Raphael gave him a simplified answer, "For your company, gross profit is sales, less raw material costs, less direct labor costs and less plant overhead. We believe such a calculation makes you less interested in additional sales and protecting sales than you should be. Embedded in your gross profit calculation is the assumption that adding one more cake will require a little more plant overhead and direct labor. This is the opposite of the truth. Intuitively, you know it. The same staff and plant you already for can make one more cupcake. Throughput is sales less Truly Variable Costs only. Think of it as the money you get a chance at that comes in from sales."

"Before you ask me, because I know it's coming, Truly Variable Costs are those raw materials you buy without which you could not sell another cupcake. Another way to think about it is a cost that increases proportionally with every single sale you make, no matter how small." That seemed to satisfy George.

George asked, "But, what about when the extra sales do require an expansion of the support staff or new equipment?"

Raphael said, "Then we consider whether the extra Throughput from the change exceeds the extra operating expenses and the future benefit of the extra capacity." George seemed to be digesting this. Like most people who are exposed to TOC, it makes sense to them and even seems better than their old ways but those old ways are in their comfort zone, where their intuition works. Thus, old ideas are difficult to abandon.

Raphael then asked George, "Are overtime and repairs continuing to be a factor?"

George came back with: "Yes, it has gotten even worse this year and I've had to skimp on raises for the last few years. Our staff has been rolling with it, mostly. In this economy, we have lost a few good people to less demanding, better paying jobs. Then, we struggle to hire more and those we do hire require training. The overtime just keeps rising. I'm a little worried about a few people; they just seem to be wearing down. They have a home life too – kids to raise – you know." His brow was furrowed.

Raphael commented, "Bernice, I see you have been able to knock down your bank debt but not what the company has borrowed from your family."

Bernice answered that by saying, "Yes, Sean and I decided to pay off the bank first, even though we pay ourselves the same interest rate as the bank charges. His point is it is better to pay interest to ourselves than to an outside party."

Raphael asked her, "How did the company do during the recession?"

Bernice responded, "It was challenging. Sales dropped. Our employees pulled us through. They agreed to a 10% pay reduction across the boards. That was when Sean and I started loaning the company money. The money I got from my father's business was enough to pay cash for our house and start Fun Cakes with Irene."

The Deal

Raphael nodded and looked at Clark. Clark asked her, "Bernice, have you a figure in mind that you feel would be fair for your company?"

Bernice looked at Sam and nodded to him that he should speak. Sam said, "Bernice and I have discussed this. We talked it over with our M&A expert at the firm and reviewed current multiples of EBITDA on similar deals. We think that, if you adjust out half the overtime they have been having to use lately, EBITDA should be more like three hundred thousand per year. Bernice and Sean would like six times that plus an extra half a million to fund their retirement. Bernice wants an employment contract for five years at her current salary of $90,000 per year plus continued use of a new company car, similar to the Honda Accord she is driving now."

Raphael, ever quick with calculations, sputtered, "That's eight and a half times current EBITDA! For such a small transaction, that's double what is typically paid. Why …"

"Hold on Raphael." Clark interrupted. "Bernice would you and your team mind answering a few questions and then leaving me and my team to discuss your number?"

"That's perfectly fine." She said.

"There is a coffee shop out in the lobby, where you all can be comfortable. Now, George, what would it take equipment wise to get rid of that overtime?"

George started to write a list on his legal pad. Then, he wrote numbers next to the items on his list and added them up. When he finished, he looked up and said, "It would cost about $250,000 to be safe."

Clark followed up with, "How much of that is for equipment we already have?"

George looked at his notes, "Looks like around $220,000."

"And, how much overtime did you pay last year?"

"We just looked at that. As I recall, it was right at $70,000."

"Fine. Irene, what do you need for the website?"

Irene cleared her throat and responded, "Nothing, sir. We have what we need."

"How much business have you been losing due to the plant's inability to deliver fast enough?"

"I keep track of cancellations. They are running just over $1,000's worth a week," Irene responded.

Clark nodded. "Sean, would you be happy with that number, which I think is $2.3 million dollars?"

"You betcha!" Sean responded.

"Do you need all that money upfront?"

Sean responded for the McNamara's. "No, if you could pay us $1.3 million down and give us an attractive interest rate on the remaining million, we'd consider that. But, you can't string it out over more than five years. We're not spring chickens anymore, you know."

"Okay." Clark said. "Let me and my team discuss it alone for a few minutes."

With that, the Fun Cakes group filed out of the room and set off in the direction of the coffee shop.

As soon as the door closed, Raphael said in a loud whisper, "That's a load of crap, Clark. They'd never get so much for the company in a million years. They're asking nine hundred thousand dollars more than possibly makes sense. That's a 70% premium! If they put that company on the market, the most they'd get is $1.4 million and that'd be lucky!"

Clark responded somewhat cryptically. "They didn't put Fun Cakes on the market."

Raphael threw his hands up in the air and slapped them down on the table in exasperation. "Well, we're going to want to buy assets, not stock. We don't want any contingent liabilities from some health nut who got fat eating their cupcakes."

Clark wanted to calm his CFO down and he knew logic was the best avenue, so he asked him, "We can either have this conversation about price and deal structure among ourselves or we can have it with the Fun Cakes gang involved. Which do you think is better?"

Still obviously exasperated, Raphael answered, "Together is always better for making decisions. We've proved that. It means we can see other's reactions. It sets the tone for sharing. But, it exposes our hand!"

"What's such a big deal about that?" Robert asked him.

"I'm worried that you'll try to talk me into paying $2.3 million dollars for a company that worth half that much! Hell, if they clearly see what's in it for us, they may increase their price!"

Clark nodded. "That's what I thought. If I block that avenue, do you think you can control yourself in front of them, even if you worry they are getting much more than any other buyer would offer?"

"Yes."

"Okay, go bring them back in then."

"Me?"

"Yes, you. I don't want them to see you as an antagonist – someone who might hold a grudge."

Raphael left the room and soon returned with the three McNamara's, Irene Lampton and George Raney.

Clark smiled and said, "Thank you all for giving us a moment. We believe in win-win deals. As my mentor once said, *'win-lose deals eventually devolve into lose-lose deals as soon as the loser gets the opportunity.'* I know how the negotiation game works. One side tends to make an optimistic ask and hopes it won't have to give up too much in future compromises. The private equity world is full of wolves who'll say anything to get a deal. Then, they start their due diligence process. They claim to have discovered something they weren't aware of before and then adjust the EBITDA or the multiple downward. They rely on the seller's fear of losing the deal and their desire to receive something in return for months of hard work. In the end, they steal a few companies and lose so many more deals that could have been mutually beneficial."

Sam was nodding, as Clark was talking. Bernice and Sean McNamara noticed it too. Clark continued, "The thing is, good deals are good on both sides. Raphael tells me that if you wanted to sell your company, most buyers wouldn't accept your adjustment from $268,000 of EBITDA up to $300,000, because of overtime. They'd say, *'if you can't get rid of the overtime, why do you expect us to pay you as if you had?'* Even in this overheated market, Raphael tells me that five times EBITDA would be pretty good considering your size and financial performance. That would be $1.34 million or almost 12 years' worth of your current net profits – the money you receive each year. But, you suggested a price of $2.3 million dollars, hoping it would be worth that much to us. Your price is 20 years' worth of your best net profits over the last four years. I'd like to know, is $2.3 million something you're starting with, hoping to actually agree on something less?"

Sam glanced at Bernice in alarm. She motioned him and her husband over. They whispered back and forth together for a minute. Then, Sam spoke for them. "We agree that the price is higher than what we'd be likely to get from placing the company up for sale but we didn't do that. You approached us. We think you did so because you saw an opportunity. Sean has already offered to owner-finance almost half of the deal. Bernice would like to see the deal to happen but she has had a number in her head for years. She has been driving towards that number. She doesn't want to quit before she gets there. If you can get her there sooner, she's all in." Even Raphael appreciated such a gutsy unyielding stance.

Clark nodded and said, "I understand driving for a goal. Let me ask you this: will you agree now, as we work together, that you will consider dropping your price, if we discover together the deal is not win-win and, under no circumstances, will the amount you ask for ever be more than 2.3 million dollars?"

Bernice answered immediately, "You have my promise."

"Thank you. Okay, let us show you how our team makes decisions! Raphael, do you have our criteria handy?" Clark asked, knowing that Raphael would have complete notes.

"Uh, let's see." Raphael said, flipping pages vigorously in his black leather-bound notebook. He was still all fired up. "Criteria … criteria … where are you? Ah, here!" His finger stabbed the page.

> 1. Enhances Daily Bread's brand through cross-selling attractive products
> 2. Neither company's employees have to learn major new skillsets
> 3. We can operate out of a combined facility
> 4. We are close enough to deliver fresh products to all customers as well or better
> 5. The people who want to stay with us are willing to work under our culture that embraces change as well as other team members' differences

Figure 17.7   Criteria for a good acquisition.

He read them off. Meanwhile, Linda typed them up on her laptop and soon, they were projected on the screen for everybody to read. Figure 17.7 reproduces their criteria.

"The first one is a check," Linda said. "Irene and I agree we can sell your products to our customers and vice versa, at least to some extent. Maybe few people would come to your site just to buy loaves of plain white sliced bread but some that are buying cupcakes will add it on."

"Right," Irene said. "Also, more and more people are 'cocooning' – staying at home reclusively – I think we could capture even more business using a different url from our standard Fun Cakes site. We have the rights to several inactive domain names already."

"The second one is also a check," George added. "Both sets of employees could do a counterpart's work with minimal cross-training."

George continued, "Robert, what about the third criterion? We could operate out of a combined facility, right?"

"Most assuredly," Robert confirmed.

George nodded his agreement and added, "As long as it is yours! It would take an act of God to get our plant to produce all that bread." He said with a rueful chuckle.

He continued, "I can vouch that the fourth criterion is also met. Your drivers can certainly add our products to your deliveries. We use UPS to get our products out – no problem packaging yours for shipment and sending them along in the same cartons."

Raphael pointed out, "And, that just leaves the boss man's requirement that their people must be willing to work under our culture. I think so, what do the rest of you think?"

Robert nodded. Linda shot back, "I don't think Bernice would have been so excited about being the culture maven unless she knew her folks would love it. I mean, what's not to like? Really!"

"Yes," Bernice confirmed. "You all have impressed me on that front."

"Good." Clark sighed. "That's five for five on the criteria. How many of those have we seen?"

"None!" Robert and Linda called out in unison. Raphael just nodded his head and shrugged.

"How often do you expect to see a five-for-five match, Raphael?"

Raphael knew exactly what Clark was doing. He was trying to get him to go along with the deal that he thought was overpriced. However, he had to admit that hell could freeze over waiting, so he responded, "Not very often. Still, I think the price they ask is too much."

Clark asked him, "Did you do a comparison of what we'd earn one year later if we did buy them?"

"You know I did!" Raphael shouted back, annoyed.

"Would you take us through it?"

"Sure, that's the next slide. What do you want me to put in for the acquisition price?"

"$2.3 million, just for the sake of argument. What did you budget for one-time expenses for combining the two facilities?"

"Let me see. ... Here it is. $311,000"

"Not $300,000, like you said before, or $320,000?"

"I rounded it to the nearest thousand, didn't I? That's our latest pessimistic estimate."

"Okay, okay. It's fine. So, make the acquisition cost $2,611,000, including the extra working capital we'll need," Clark said. Turning to Robert and changing the subject, he asked, "Robert what does the Transition Period look like and how long do you project it will last?"

While Raphael was working on his laptop, Robert stood up. He looked at George almost apologetically and said, "It will seem to go on forever and it will be hell. We'll have to figure out how to bake all Fun Cakes products on our equipment. Although, I calculate we will have plenty of capacity, especially with all your staff and adding your equipment into our plant. Even without all your resources, we have room to make maybe 25% more with only a minor increase in OE for labor. That leaves only a small cushion for unexpected Murphy strikes."

"There may be some spot scheduling difficulties. Once we can make all your products, we'll have to uproot everything and move what's coming over here, including all the people. I've budgeted for a dozen temps for a month plus a crane and rigging company to do the heavy lifting. Then, we drop down to half a dozen temps for a several more weeks. We'll have to find everybody permanent a position, figure out who reports to whom and start a fast-track training process. It will probably be near chaos and all-hands-on-deck, no matter how much we plan, for the duration, which I estimate we should be able to complete in three months but it will probably take four somehow. It goes without saying that we'll kill or temporarily freeze every other project and initiative, anything to protect our management attention. Are you game George?" George smiled back at him and nodded. Bernice thought George looked concerned.

She asked, "What do the companies look like merged? I mean from a financial point of view."

Raphael went back to his laptop, clicked a few keys, stole a glance at Bernice and then looked up at the projected screen. A second later Table 17.5 appeared.

Raphael went on to explain, "This is just the sum of your sales and our sales and your expenses added to ours. There are no changes in these figures yet. We made some preliminary estimates but it would be silly to assume we know your business as well as you do."

"That's right," Clark said. And, he added, "The big assumptions we need your help with are what are the benefits we should expect due to cross-selling each other's products. Also, what prices

Table 17.5   Combination of Fun Cakes and Daily Bread - No changes

Combination (thousands)	YTD Projection
Sales	$10,257
Truly Var. COGS	2,313
Throughput	7,944
Op. Expense	5,558
EBITDA	2,386
Tax, Int. & Depr	1,323
NP	$1,063

will be necessary." He looked at the Fun Cakes group. They were nodding. He continued, "Linda will you handle the discussion about sales lift and pricing?"

"Sure," she replied. "Okay, first of all, imagine that all of our products, which you saw on the tour, are on your website, right alongside yours. Imagine too that you have opened your other url under the new name, which you mentioned you already had dormant. Irene, what is the reasonably pessimistic and optimistic expectations you have for how much those sales of our stuff would add to your sales in the first year? Now, that's after the consolidation period is over."

Irene asked for some clarity, "How pessimistic and optimistic do you want me to be?"

Raphael answered her, "Let's say there is only a 5% chance that the actual result is worse than the pessimistic projection and the same probability for being higher than the optimistic one."

"Irene made sure she understood. "So, your saying 90% of the time the outcome would be between my low and high guesses?"

"Just about. Take the 90% as a general guidance," Raphael confirmed.

"Hum," came from Irene and then she paused. "I can't imagine our sales of your products being less than 30% of our total sales but it could be as much as 100%! I mean, our products people buy occasionally. Your products, they buy daily. Even if we don't attract as many customers, it should be offset by return business from those we do attract. We think we have the freshness angle covered with shrink wrap. That way, we can keep the air off your products, so they don't get stale as fast. Our tests indicate that individually shrink wrapped bread and rolls might be fresher than what folks see in their favorite store. Frosted donuts we are still working on." Raphael was typing on his laptop.

Linda continued, "We think we'd have to offer our products at a premium of 40% to avoid undercutting our current customers. What does that do to your projections?"

"Nothing," Irene shot back. "I expected that you would go up by 50%. Although the lower markup is good for sales, for our customers, I don't really think it will be about price. They want good product and the convenience of direct-to-their-door delivery. What do you think?"

Linda explained, "I estimated 25% at a minimum. Which figure do you like better?"

Irene said, "Let's go with your number. I think that's about right. What do you think you'll get as a sales lift by adding our products to the price lists your customers consider?"

Linda surreptitiously glanced at Clark, who nodded almost imperceptibly to her. Then, she shared, "We expect the sales lift to be between 15% and 30%. We think our customers are going to love your products! However, since most of our customers are distributors, who mark up our products, we expect to have to discount 20% to 30% off your prices." Irene nodded. That obviously made perfect sense to her.

Linda then brought up an old idea and voiced it to the group. "Years ago, I don't exactly remember when, Clark had an idea for making daily home deliveries. I think, at the time, he was thinking of using our trucks to make milk runs." Clark was nodding. "With your shrink wrapped versions of our products and the ability to ship daily, without loading up our trucks, we could look at that seriously again."

"Not until after the Transition Period." Clark added with finality.

Bernice looked at him and asked, "Why wouldn't we jump right on that? It seems like a great idea to me."

Clark explained, "We are simple minded people. We believe in doing one thing at a time. Every move stirs up the unexpected. As we've already discussed, we call that the Transition Period. We like to wait and take the next move after the dust has settled. It keeps us from going crazy, first, and, second, it ends up being faster in the end, believe it or not."

Raphael turned to Irene saying, "George, mentioned cancellations of $1,000 per week. That's people who ordered something not in stock and then decided they couldn't wait, right?"

"Yes," she replied.

"I noticed on your site that you show the quantity in inventory and expected availability waits for those products that happen to be out of stock. How much of the time do you expect that a shopper substitutes something else when the item they want is out of stock."

She answered without pause, "I studied this and even did some surveys. The best I can tell, substitutions happen about half the time."

"What's your sense of the number of orders that you miss, due to shortages?"

"That one keeps me up at nights, because we just don't know for sure. I track the number of orders for which the shoppers load a cart but just abandon it, like they chickened out. Much of that simply has to be because of a shortage of a critical item for which they are unwilling to accept a substitute. My best guess is that those shortage driven lost orders are many times the cancelled orders."

Raphael clarified, "You're saying that lost sales, due to being out of stock, are more like $6,000 per week?"

Irene answered, "That's my optimistic guess that lets me sleep at night but, honestly, it could be twice that much!"

Robert said, "Based on our OTIF being almost 98% versus your 90%, I'm going to guess that we can recover 80% or more of those lost sales estimates, using our Simplified Drum Buffer Rope production system." Again, Raphael was typing on his laptop.

Robert continued, this time looking at George, "George, we were talking a few days ago about your oven loading. Our guess was that you can't load the ovens completely due to insufficient staging space. Is that correct?"

"Yes. Our oven is never full, like yours. We don't have the space to fully load it, even with extra people thrown at the job. I was very impressed with how you load. I tried to copy you but there just isn't enough room. It drives overtime too. The more we sell the worse it gets. Sadly, we don't have the profits to get a payback on an expansion."

Next, Raphael asked Bernice, "Do you work off a line of credit or is there some term debt in the mix?"

Bernice said, "Yes, we have some term debt. On our line, the bank is working with me to pay it down, because we don't have enough collateral in our borrowing base report to suit them. They have been a good partner. As Sean and I have the money, we lend some to the company. That makes the bank more comfortable. It will take another year or two to get to the debt to worth ratio they are looking for us to have."

Then, she asked, "How are you looking on capacity? Could you make enough to deliver the cross sales we have been discussing?"

Robert answered her, "We can do the pessimistic side, with the addition of your equipment, with over 8% to spare. We'd have to add two more lines and another oven to hit the high side targets."

"Can you afford that and buy us too, including the one-time moving costs?"

"Absolutely!" Clark answered. "Raphael, will you show the combined profitability figures, along with the integrated balance sheet?"

Raphael sounded off, looking straight at Clark, "You know, I think you're crazy, right? You said you'd only do the deal if I liked it, remember?"

"I remember. Quit worrying. Just put up the financial slide."

"Sure," Raphael said. "Give me a second. … Okay, here we are." The information in Table 17.6 flashed up on the screen.

Table 17.6 Full Comparison with Next Year's Reasonable Pessimistic and Optimistic Assumptions

(thousands)	Fun Cakes YTD Projection	Daily Bread YTD Projection	Combined YTD Projection	Pessimistic Changes Next Year	Optimistic Changes Next Year
Sales	$2,416	$7,841	$10,257	$12,082	$16,037
Truly Var. COGS	426	1,887	2,313	2,711	3,423
Throughput	1,990	5,954	7,944	9,371	12,615
Op. Expense	1,722	3,836	5,558	5,529	6,271
EBITDA	268	2,118	2,386	3,842	6,343
Tax, Int. & Depr	153	1,149	1,323	1,965	3,108
NP	$115	$970	$1,063	$1,877	$3,235
Cash	60	2,042	251	1,402	1,981
A/R	99	902	1,002	1,242	1,869
Inventory	61	130	191	226	236
Other Curr Ass	16	207	223	245	269
Fixed Assets	1,660	10,650	12,310	11,822	11,972
Accum Depr	674	7,114	7,788	7,981	7,951
Fixed Net	986	3,536	4,522	3,841	4,020
A/P	43	98	141	223	281
Other Curr Liab	12	81	93	102	105
Bank Debt	210	0	0	0	0
McNamara	230	0	1,200	0	0
Net Worth	727	6,638	4,754	6,631	7,989

"Whew," said Linda. "That's a lot of numbers for a girl with personality." She smiled and batted her eyes at Raphael.

"Aw, quit it!" Raphael shot back, pretending offense. Bernice was giggling quietly to herself. "For those of you with personality and no real skills, the top section is the income statement and the bottom part is balance sheet information."

"The first columns are obviously Fun Cakes projection for this year. The second pair are our projected results for this year. The next group of columns is what you get if you simply add them to us without any changes. I already showed you the income statement part earlier. The last three columns are where it gets interesting. They show the reasonably pessimistic and optimistic scenarios for next year, assuming the outcomes of obvious changes."

Sam McNamara spoke up. "So, you're showing a range? I like that. It seems more realistic."

Raphael responded, "Thank you. We are trying to be pessimistic but reasonable to see if it scares us off the deal. Then, we look at an equally reasonable but optimistic option. If we haven't fooled ourselves, the implementation should come in somewhere between those extremes."

George remarked, "And, you have a clear stretch goal for the people who are doing the work of getting the results. I like this. We should do this." He said looking at Bernice.

"I think that's the idea, George." Bernice said with a smile. She turned to Raphael, "Excuse me. Why are the sales up so much? Are you expecting organic growth on top of the cross-selling opportunities?"

"Good question. Yes and No. Wait just a minute while I show you my assumptions. Then, we can talk about them." With that he showed his assumptions (Table 17.7) on the screen.

"Look at Organic Growth. Pessimistically, we assumed that we both lost 2% but optimistically we gain 5% due to customers seeing us as a marginally more important supplier. Most of the sales increases are expected from cross-selling plus lost sales recovered due to improving availability. We assume we will be focusing on how to work together."

"I also assumed that there will be from 2% to 4% lower TVC for your products. We buy a little better than you do now. We hope to leverage your additional volume to buy better still! That's captured in the OE & TVC savings line."

Table 17.7 Summary of Assumptions behind the Combination of Daily Bread and Fun Cakes

	Optimistic	Pessimistic
Interest	0	0
Turns	12.0	14.5
CrossSell FC>DB	15%	30%
CrossSell DB>FC	25%	100%
CS FC>DB Disc.	30%	20%
CS DB>FC Prem.	40%	50%
Availability @ FC	250	499
Extra OE	471	1363
OE&TVC Savings	500	650
Sale of Assets	290	340
New Equipment	0	234
Organic Growth	−2%	5%

"Wait a minute," Linda spat out. "You have Extra OE and OE&TVC Savings. Which one is it?"

Raphael laughed, "Yeah, I guess that does look weird, don't it? Okay, it is both, Linda. Extra OE is new expenditures for expanding our capacity, raises and the like. OE&TVC Savings are synergies from eliminating duplicate efforts in both companies. Most of those savings are the elimination of Fun Cakes plant and its operating expenses and, like I just mentioned, the improvement in our buying power."

George commented, "I see your optimistic on expenses is that there will be a huge increase in total? Where does that come from?"

"Yes," Raphael answered, "The assumption is that we keep all your people and promote some of our combined staff to middle management. Remember, George, you indicated you wished you already had more managers. We will have to man more shifts of ovens, in the optimistic scenario. With the optimistic volumes, running more lines and ovens means we add about $700,000 of operating expense."

Clark followed up, "One of the advantages of this acquisition is that it gets us proven, tested employees with baking skills. That is very important to us. We don't want to lose anyone." Bernice put both thumbs up and shook her fists.

George was having trouble digesting something that he had heard from Raphael. He finally articulated his concern, "How do you pay for the new lines and oven? I don't see any bank debt."

Raphael answered him, "Easy. Out of cash flow." And, he flashed a proud smile. "Even on the negative end, our combined Net Profits after taxes are over $1.8 million. We just write a check for the $234,000 of new equipment and installation we will require. Of course we won't need it unless the outcomes are more positive and our earnings are much higher." George seemed to be struggling to imagine just writing a check for a major expansion.

Raphael carried on, "Let me discuss the balance sheet with you, because it is less obvious. If you look back at the combination year to date projections for this year. Those balance sheet numbers are the worst point of the year, not the end of the year, which would be normal. I did that to show our worst cash position, the moment after the acquisition. I used our cash to pay the McNamara's the $1.3 million down payment we'll owe them. The remaining cash is plenty to pay the $311,000 in one-time merger expenses plus a nice cash buffer. On top of that, our line of credit at the bank is unused and together we'd be able to borrow about $900,000, if need be."

"Other than those accounts, you can see increases to the other assets and liabilities due to combining the two balance sheets. You'll also notice the drop in our net worth to $4.75 million. Any questions?"

Sean McNamara asked, "This may be a silly question but shouldn't the net worth of the two companies together be more than they were apart?"

Raphael loved being the man with the answers and smiled in spite of himself. "Practically speaking, you are right but accounting-wise the net worth could only have gone up, if we didn't have to pay for your company." He winked at Sean. "If we only needed to pay you your book value of $727,000, our old net worth would have been maintained. This scenario shows what paying a premium of $1.6 million over your book value does to the combined companies." Clark thought his answer was pretty good, considering it had come from Raphael, who is worried about the price.

"Well, if there are no more questions, I'll move to the projections for next year." He paused and then continued. Under either scenario, we pay off the McNamara's completely. Optimistically, we accumulate almost $2 million in cash and pessimistically about a million four hundred thousand." Sean whistled at that.

Linda asked, "Is that just because we make more profit in the optimistic side?"

"Not entirely," Raphael answered. "There is the new equipment, don't forget. I also made some assumptions that we could collect A/R a few days faster and inventory turns going back to what is normal for us, using Dynamic Buffer Management."

"What is Dynamic Buffer Management?" Bernice wanted to know.

"Oh, sorry. I should have explained. We use a software we developed called Dynamic Buffer Management.[17] It is an implementation of Eliyahu Goldratt's Theory of Constraints replenishment solution."

"Who? What?" Bernice was sitting on the edge of her seat.

"Eli Goldratt was a brilliant Israeli physicist who turned his mind to business. TOC – the Theory of Constraints – is a very simple idea that I discovered and brought to Daily Bread a little over five years ago. Basically, it guides business managers on where to focus to get fast bottom-line results. Before we found TOC, our profits were at a similar level to yours."

"You mean to say five years ago Daily Bread only earned $100k per year?"

Clark answered the question, "Our average was less than that. Our earnings were not nearly as stable as yours. It fluctuated all over the place. How do you manage such stability?"

"Oh, that's easy. You just cut your salary as necessary to keep the net around $100 thousand per year." Bernice quipped. "What does this Dynamic Buffer Management do?"

Raphael explained. "Dynamic Buffer Management does two things. First, it automatically replenishes raw materials which are consumed by our operations and places new workorders in the production schedule as inventory is sold. Secondly, it automatically adapts to changes in the supply chain, so we (almost) never run out of anything, while holding less inventory. That is how we can easily do over fourteen inventory turns – twice what you get."

"Wow! Never running out! That would be a change of pace." George shot back. "When you asked me before what I needed? I NEED THAT! It never occurred to me to ask for the impossible. Boy, do I ever need that." He sat swinging his head back and forth at the very idea.

Sam asked, "Why are fixed assets lower in both scenarios?"

Raphael responded, "Oh, that's because we would have the opportunity to sell off many of your assets that we wouldn't need together. I did some preliminary work with Robert. As you know, we are desperate for your oven, which would become Oven #4. That will give us some scheduling flexibility. Fun Cakes batch sizes are smaller than ours and the items are generally smaller as well, which means shorter baking times. We'll want all your conveyor, preparation, decoration, packaging and office equipment, some dollies, carts, and all your cooling racks.

"On the optimistic side, with five ovens having the potential to run 24/7, that gives us 120 oven-hours per day. Robert calculates that he'd have about 10 oven-hours to spare in the optimistic scenario. He is determined that if we hit that level that we'd have a sixth oven on order, both to anticipate growth and be able to meet demand, even if something breaks down. It is fantastic that we even have enough space even for six ovens! At the time I didn't appreciate Clark's decision to settle for such large space. He was convincing in his vision of growth and the difference in price from another facility was almost negligible. You were right again, boss!"

Bernice looked straight at Clark and said, "Clark, you are a dirty rat! First you tried to make me feel guilty for asking so much. Then, you made me agree not to raise my price, before you showed me that you expect to pay off the whole acquisition in less than one year!"

---

[17] There are several real software products on the market today. Readers should feel free to contact any of the authors for suggestions of alternatives, all manage inventory according to TOC. If you manage a combination of more than 50 raw materials and finished goods. The software makes life much simpler and more profitable.

"Furthermore, if my math is in the neighborhood of being correct, using what I've learned, one year later, your company will have increased its value to an outside buyer by $10 to $30 million."

Clark and Bernice just grinned at each other. Sean joined in on the grinning, as he realized that he was getting both the money and more of his wife back. Linda crossed her arms with a satisfied air. Sam shrugged. Irene, Robert and George looked slightly left behind. The only one who looked shocked was Raphael.

It had just hit him that $2.3 million wasn't a bad price for something that boosted the enterprise's value by ten times as much. What would be bad is not making the deal. He thought to himself that Clark was indeed a dirty rat, a pretty damn smart rat too. He hadn't argued for paying that much. He had left Raphael explain it to himself. Rat! But, then he too smiled and thanked his lucky stars he was a part of this company. About the time he finished mentally patting himself on the back for bringing TOC to Daily Bread, he realized that his thinking was still stuck in the past because of his old intellectual habits. He smiled, leaned back in his chair and gave Clark a thumbs-up.

Bernice stood up and walked over to Clark. She stuck out her hand and said, "Do we have a deal? My company for $2.3 million dollars?"

Clark responded, "DEAL!" and they shook hands on it. "To make it formal, I have a Letter of Intent right here."

He wrote in $2,300,000 in the blank, signed his name and handed it to Bernice, who threw her arms around his neck and kissed him squarely on the cheek. Clark thought to himself that TOC was really something. He had never made a more satisfactory deal in all his life, other than marrying his wife, his conscience amended for him quickly!

"Oh, Clark?" Bernice whispered. "I'm sold on your group pessimistic/optimistic decision-making process."

Chapter 18

An Analysis of Acquisitions

The Daily Bread example in Chapter 17 is one stylized example of how an acquisition might happen. There are thousands of real cases and far more reasonably possible cases that one might imagine. Companies are complicated. Combining two complicated companies is complex. Because of this, there is enormous uncertainty regarding any acquisition. According to consulting giant McKinsey and Company,[1] 66–75 percent of mergers and acquisitions fail to result in transformational value–annual returns on the acquisition of 30 percent or more. If you don't expect to create transformational value, don't bother making an acquisition—too risky.

A consequence of both the natural human fear of loss and the widespread knowledge of the M&A failure rate is that acquisitions often fail to occur, even when there is both money available and the intention to invest it. Investors are correct to be cautious. Yet, done well, the returns from M&A activity can be remarkable, especially compared to the average yields from commonly available investments in stocks, bonds and real estate.

The conflict diagram, Figure 18.1, starts with a real conflict, depicted in the red and blue conflicting actions, that trouble all investors. Each action is required to satisfy need in either B or C. The problem is, we require both needs but the action that is required for one need spoils the other. We seek an action that satisfies both needs without compromising. In other words, making investments that even in the worst reasonable case would still get a good return without losing any capital. Identifying very promising opportunities, while validating that there is very low risk, is one of the central messages in this book.

Many experienced buyers of businesses will tell you that trying to buy a company is a trail of tears. The story in Chapter 17 clearly exposed Clark's difficulty, not just in finding a suitable target but also in getting targets interested in a sale. One can expect to be lied to, cheated, blocked by indecision, "left at the altar," and blown off, even by a seller whose best interests would be served by selling. At the same time, buyers too often behave badly, are distrustful, lose the sellers' trust, take offense, stand on ceremony, are too greedy and suffer from the same counterproductive behaviors as sellers.

As they say, money does funny things to people.

---

[1] Deutsch, Clay and West, Andy: *A New Generation of M&A: A McKinsey perspective on the opportunities and challenges*, June 2010.

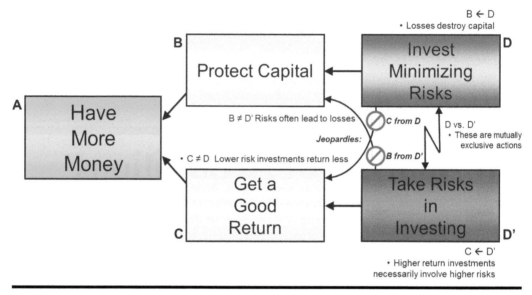

Figure 18.1   An investor's conflict diagram.

The point that it is difficult to come out of the closing, in control of a new company, is the reason the authors dragged you good readers through many pages of Chapter 17 before the final target was even identified. Expect to go through many times as much work in real life, unless you are willing to overpay for a target. Keep in mind that you had better be pretty sure you are going to produce some of McKinsey's "transformational value," if you consider paying more than market multiples.

Based on the authors' experience, TOC provides just the sort of strategic focus necessary to both develop and implement plans that create breakout value and at the same time are reasonably safe. It really doesn't matter what type of company or line of business. However, there are caveats to that last statement.

Before delving into these caveats, let us just clarify that all business races are run against time. It is not how much you make in absolute terms but also how long it takes. You may have heard the joke regarding the savvy negotiator who offered his opponent the opportunity to name his price, while he would only set the terms. The price demanded was $1,000,000. The man nodded his acceptance, even though the price was unrealistically high. He responded that his payment terms were $1.00 per year for 1,000,000 years. Suddenly, the context became more important than the price.

So, let's contemplate caveats to consider when buying a company:

Looking for a Bargain

A major perceived obstacle to buying a company is not having enough money. If you aren't already very wealthy, your first inclination may be to look for what you can afford. What types of companies can be bought cheap? Small companies, startups[2] and companies in trouble.

---

[2] If a customer wants a product or service enough, it is possible that this customer will finance someone they trust to start a new company to provide it. One of the authors received payment from a major corporation for a planned service in which he was expert for six months before actually being expected to provide the service. There are other startups that do not require any more capitalization than what's in the average person's bank account.

Let's consider **small companies** first. The advantage of a small company is that there is less competition to buy one. A private equity firm that raises half a billion dollars in investment capital each year is not attracted to companies with enterprise values of $1,000,000. They would have to close on two per weekday to invest the funds; that would be too much due diligence and legal fees to make it a reasonable strategy. They would be far better off with eight to ten deals per year, meaning they want companies exceeding $50 million in value.

This is the common practice, but is it correct? While from the perspective of spreading risk, buying several companies is a good move for big private equity funds. The question is do they buy high growth potential? Could be that such private equity firms have a constraint in their due-diligence capacity, thus they like to focus on larger companies, which relative to their size takes less time. But, should they change their approach? If it is possible to recognize high potential very quickly and be able to substantiate it quickly, then a different exploitation scheme should be in place—making more while spending less.

Smaller family offices typically complete fewer deals infrequently. Consequently, they are also unlikely to look for companies in this price range.

Small companies might have high potential for very fast growth. What they need is a new insight or vision, the capabilities and management attention to make it happen. Thus, such small companies could attract investors that have the vision and capability to turn the small company into a goldmine. The problem is most investors interested in purchasing small companies are not aware of this insight.

Thus, appropriate buyers for small companies tend to be owner-operators. The buyer is purchasing a job from which he or she cannot be fired. Sellers often are forced to finance some or all of the purchase price—that means they take a promissory note from the buyer which pays them interest and principal on the debt over time (they hope!)

Instead, let's say you are the buyer and you are both clever and lucky. Under your guidance, the company develops the idea for some sustainable competitive advantage. Customers are interested; it solves a significant problem that they have been forced to work around. And, now, you need to build the capabilities to deliver this great solution. Next, you'll need a way to capitalize on it. Who helps you?

It is a small company you bought. There are few managers in a small company. Since there are fewer managers in a small company, there is less management capacity to attend to the changes which are mandatory to achieve your vision. As a consequence, either the buyer has to put additional managers into the small purchased company or the changes take more time.

(By the way, what is the difference between an effective manager and an effective subordinate? According to Elliot Jaques[3] it is their time-span of attention. Simply stated, the manager looks out further into the future.)

There it is, *time* again. If you buy a small company, you have three difficult jobs instead of two. You must not only build the capabilities to deliver your competitive edge and develop the skills to capitalize on it, you must also build the management team necessary to achieve it. All these three must be done without considerable funding! Remember, you most probably didn't have lots of money and your company doesn't either, that's how you came to consider a small company in the first place. So, buying a small company means making improvements, waiting for after-tax profits to accumulate and then spending that money to do a little more.

---

[3] Jaques, Elliot (1989) *Requisite Organization: The CEO's Guide to Creative Structure and Leadership* Cason Hall and Co. Publishers, Gloucester, MA

It's usually a slow process to improve a small company. If you have no other option, fine, wait. There are other options though.

Startups are a special subset of small companies. They are often built on a far-reaching vision. The idea of fast growth is ingrained in the minds of everybody in the startup. However, quite a lot depends on the specific vision of the startup, is it that great? Startups often spend a lot of money before they get revenues enough to generate the T necessary to offset the OE they must spend for their capacity needs. So, they frequently need more money to continue the tricky route to the sky. Startups attract venture capital funds that look for one or two nice successes and are prepared to tolerate 80-90% failure rates. Consequently, these risk-funds might not be the preferred choice for companies and investors with limited money looking for something pretty safe that still yields nice returns.

That brings us to **troubled companies.** Of course, troubled companies can be small or large. The important point is that their price is low and thus affordable. Losing money is an obvious category of trouble. However, it does not always allow you to steal the company. The balance sheet must be figured into the equation. In Chapter 17 we discussed a multiple of EBITDA as a means to arrive at a price. If the company has negative EBITDA, that does not imply that the owner will pay you to take it. Losses simply mean that the company cannot be valued based on its earnings. What else does the company own? If the company were closed and liquidated, does it have valuable real estate? Is there equipment that could be sold?

From your point of view, as a prospective owner of the company you intend to buy, can the company be turned around, back into a profitable entity? Are there mistakes that the previous owners made that you recognize clearly, as well as an improved approach? Or, is the company a dinosaur that provides products and services that are no longer appreciated by its marketplace?

Let's say the sellers have been making an error, you recognize their mistakes and know exactly how to correct them. Lovely. Now, imagine for a moment the recent history of this troubled company. Profits are low or the company is losing money. What actions can you expect from managers of such companies (those who do not utilize the TOC)? We can hear you answering, "selling assets and cutting costs."

Exactly. And, what did those assets which were sold and those costs which were cut provide? You better have immediately thought "capacity." There is less capacity in a weak company. Where did they cut capacity? Presumably, they cut it where it mattered the least and reluctantly worked upwards to more important capacity. This seems logical, previous management, although mistaken, probably knew a thing or two about the business. In constraint management terms, they cut protective capacity of non-constraint resources. As they ran into trouble or realized they had come close, from this paring of OE and I, they would be forced to move to the next non-constraint and cut there.

As the process continued, they would have gotten ever closer to balanced capacity. A situation where nearly every resource is utilized to its limits. The difficulty with these circumstances is there is no spare capacity to handle the normal fluctuations in demand and supply which are always occurring. Chaos ensues, service levels drop and customers choose competitors, which triggers more cost cutting and selling of assets, more chaos and around the death spiral they went.

Here you arrive on the scene with your savvy and general brilliance. You bought the company, because it was cheap and now you must fix things. What capacity do you utilize to make these improvements? There isn't any. Do you hire the capacity before you have the profits to pay for it? Risky. So, like the small company, you make important but easy changes and wait for after-tax profits to accumulate so you can repair some more, just like in a small company. This process can be accelerated, it is true, by improving the flow of inventory, assuming the company holds some, but that only works once.

There is one more negative to troubled companies. The culture has taken a hit. Employees who remain fear for their jobs. They are in a self-protective mode, not a giving trusting mode. Good people, who can easily get a job anywhere, have already abandoned ship. Rebuilding a good culture and attracting a more capable staff also take time.

Again, we come back to *time*. Bargains come with embedded time penalties. Caveat Emptor. Buyer beware.

Buying a Good Company

If you find the arguments above convincing, the alternative is to find some way to buy a good healthy company that hasn't cornered its market to the extent that its ability to grow is impaired. Let's define that quickly. A good healthy company:

- has a culture of trust,
- makes a nice profit and
- has the capacity it needs to both improve and handle the uncertainty it experiences.

Good companies also make mistakes. However, their market allows them prices satisfactory to make money despite them.

A constraints mindset is a strategic advantage in that it allows the manager to envision the flow as well as blockages and disruptions to smooth flow. The power of this approach is being able to recognize the mistakes. What we are saying is correcting errors in a good company results in rapid improvements. The company's ability to finance the required extra capacity is intact. Management attention is available to oversee the necessary improvements. There is also enough protective capacity already in the company's various systems to handle the initial load of increasing demand. The advantage is obviously *time*. Better outcomes are more quickly realized by good companies.

Everybody likes a good company. So, what are the problems? Good companies are

- expensive,
- considered less risky by other buyers, meaning they get snapped up so fast that they may never go on the market or, if they do, you may not get enough of a chance to notice or
- not for sale – there may be no desire to part with a good company, because when a company is growing consistently, any price that might reasonably be offered may be perceived as too low by its owner, based on the company's expected value a few years hence.

How to Afford your New Good Company

Starting with the high price tags on nice companies, there are a few ways to overcome this seeming obstacle. Before we approach mechanisms to hurdle the price bar, just a short paragraph on why it is intrinsically an obstacle. Human beings come with a fear of loss bred into their bones. This fear is two to five times more influential than the desire to gain, depending on which studies you read. So, the first obstacle is making the decision to part with money you already have and spend it on a company, given uncertainty in the future of the economy and the company, especially considering the documented failure rate of acquisitions. This, each investor must wrestle alone.

The most obvious work-around, is to buy less than all of the company. Buying 55% of a company is less expensive than buying all of it. Why would sellers want to remain partners? The answer could be to learn something new, to bring in new ideas, avoid loneliness or reduce stress, and the like.

Another reason could be that the owners want to make more money from the company. What if the part the current owners didn't sell became worth more than the whole company's value today? Financially motivated owners would be crazy not to go for such a deal. If the upside potential is strong and you need partners to afford the purchase, it can pay to include the current owners in your plans and share the potential of what the TOC perspective or the buyer's special capabilities reveals. The necessary condition for a fractional sale to materialize is that the seller trusts the buyer's ability to grow the company in a way the seller could not accomplish alone.

For instance, assume you buy 55% of the company, to gain the control necessary to ensure that your envisioned changes are implemented. If the company responds by steadily increasing its value, it is quite likely that the sellers, now your 45% partners could see the value of the part of the company they retained grow to be higher than the value of the whole company, a few years later. (See Figure 18.2).

Was there no other way? What if the seller doesn't want to remain an owner? Perhaps they prefer to avoid signing a personal guarantee of the company's debt.

What if the sellers had instead accepted a promissory note for the part of the deal you couldn't afford? Using the above growth scenario, assume you agreed to pay them 10% interest, and equal monthly payments over three years. The interest would have cost you $1,616,187.39 over those 36 months, around five times less than sharing the appreciation on 45% ownership with the sellers.

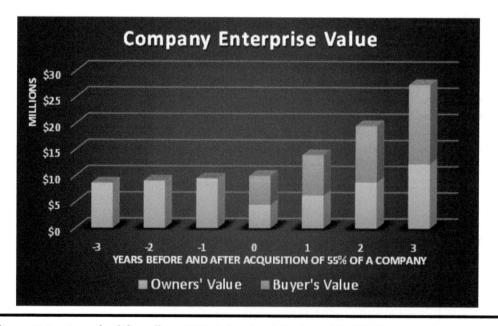

Figure 18.2 Growth of the seller's 45% stake after injection of the TOC perspective.

Under the buyer's promissory note financing approach, you would be wise not to share with the sellers too much of your expectation for the appreciation of the company's value. However, you must convince the sellers that you can run the company well enough to earn the money you promised to pay them. That might require a little peek under the kimono that covers your plans.

What would gain seller financing? Recognize that different people have different motivations. It is incorrect to assume that because you value something at X, that someone else doesn't see the value as half of X or twice X. It is equally true that reasons to sell are as numerous as reasons to buy. If an owner or owners are motivated to sell and don't have full cash alternatives, they have a reason to provide owner financing.

Likewise, if seller financing means a higher purchase price, that is another powerful seller motivator. Using the deal contemplated above, what if you offered to pay not a reasonable $4.5 million but instead an unreasonable $5.5 million for the same 45% of the company you can't afford, in return for the sellers accepting your note? The answer is that it would be a mechanism to make you far more money than keeping the sellers on as 45% partners. All this assumes you know that you can safely make more money than the owners previously did, to the extent that you are confident that you will recover the extra million you paid and didn't have a less expensive alternative at your disposal.

We've discussed seller financing but there are other ways. The first should be friends and family. Again, review the assumption mentioned at the end of the previous paragraph. You don't want to let down your friends and family. This group should be approached before banks. That does not imply that you should offer them lower interest rates. The bank rate is fine. Banks charge much lower interest rates than we suggested for enticing the owners to accept a note.

A reason to prefer loans from friends and family is because wouldn't you rather pay your friends and family than a bank? Secondly, the agreement between you and the people you know can be written on a single page. Banks will require thick inches of paperwork, dozens of signatures, all the collateral you have and don't forget the fees for closing costs and their attorney's time to draft the inches of paper and watch you sign each in just the proper spot. But, best of all, money you borrow from friends and family looks to you like equity in the deal.

Friends and family lend on trust. Friends and family who have cash on deposit are paid much less interest than banks charge on loans. That's how banks make money. Paying them bank rates on loans cuts out the middle man. After all, banks are borrowing from your friends and family and lending those deposits to you.

Banks lend based on trust plus collateral. The company's assets are great collateral. Don't get the idea that we are down on banks. Banks are wonderful for three reasons. 1.) They have the money you need. 2.) They don't want to be your partner. 3.) They just want their little bit of interest repaid with what they loan you.

When you are still short after you have borrowed from friends, family, banks and the sellers, there is another source of loans. There are hundreds of mezzanine lenders around the world. Many business deals have a component of mezzanine debt. If you think about how much you can borrow in total, it makes sense to express that amount in terms of multiples of EBITDA. That way deals are comparable across industries and sizes of the companies. Mezzanine lenders are the main component of non-bank lending. (See Figure 18.3).

Heavy regulation on banks has created opportunities for alternative lenders to charge much higher rates, 2 to 3 times higher than banks. The good news for a potential acquirer

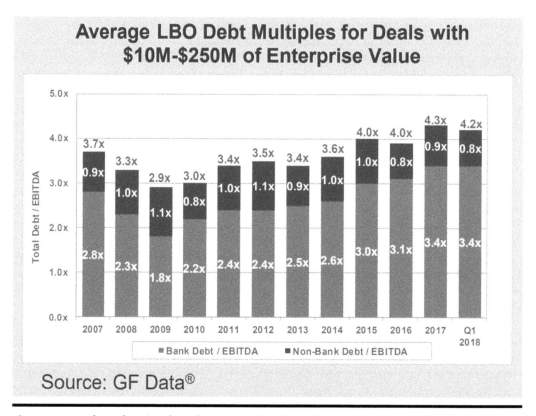

Figure 18.3 Chart showing the reluctance of lenders following the recession of 2008–2009.

is that these funds are lent not on what is demonstrable yesterday but by what is expected in the future. Additionally, Mezz funds are often willing to delay some of their payments until the company is projected to be able to afford to make them. Some part of the interest may be payable in a lump sum years later, when the company is sold or flush with cash. However, these Mezz funds protect themselves not only with higher interest rates but with guarantees backed up by the right to demand ownership in your new business, if you fail to pay them as agreed.

Looking back at Figure 18.3, you can see how much of a deal can be financed with borrowing on average. Individual deals will be much different. Remember, buyers with plenty of capital avoid mezzanine funds because they charge such high interest rates.

Looking ahead to Figure 18.4, you can see historical average deal values in terms of multiples of EBITDA, before and after the 2008 to 2009 world recession.

The difference between the multiples in Figure 18.3 and Figure 18.4, expresses the amount of money put into deals by the buyers, on average. Bear in mind that some deals were all equity and others were all debt. Again, these are just averages.

Generally speaking, smaller companies are sold for smaller multiples. For instance, a fair arm's length price for Fun Cakes, which is too small to be included in the data collected in Figure 18.3 and Figure 18.4, might have been 5 × EBITDA. Nevertheless, prices on smaller companies both vary across a wide range and the average multiples fluctuate up and down with the market.

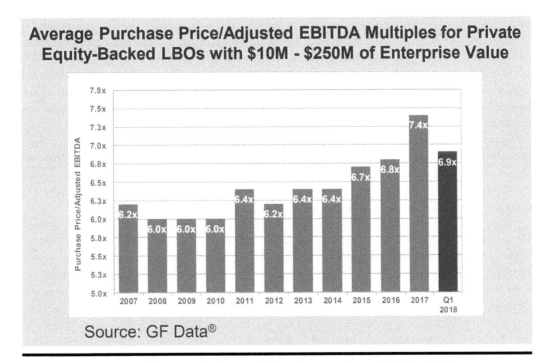

Figure 18.4   Leveraged buy-outs before and after the recession of 2008 to 2009.

The last alternative we haven't yet considered, if you don't have enough money yourself, is to join with partners to buy the company. It is just as expensive as being partners with the previous owners. The advantage is you get to hand pick the people who are your partners.

As much as you may like your partners and as wonderful as their skills may be, unless you personally own 51% of the company, there will be times that management fails to act as decisively as a single majority owner is capable. That can be crippling, especially when you know what to do and others don't agree. You think they are caught in mental inertia; they think you like to gamble too much. However, it may also be good, particularly when the majority owner's would-be decisive action is wrong!

Rich friends and family are obvious choices. Some may prefer ownership to lending. However, when you are an owner you can lose more than your investment, while a lender's downside is limited to the amount lent. But, what happens when you don't know anybody or they are invested in something else or they don't care to invest using TOC, which is a strange concept to them?

There is too much money in the world. Literally. An article in PitchBook[4] suggests that $1.1 trillion dollars is sitting in the hands of private equity and venture capital funds. A year earlier than that, corporations, in America alone, had amassed more than twice that amount according to a 2017 article.[5] And, don't forget about banks. Bank deposits have risen to over half

[4] Garrett, J. B. 2018. 'The trillion-dollar question: What does record dry powder mean for PE & VC fund managers?' PitchBook, <https://pitchbook.com/news/articles/the-trillion-dollar-question-what-does-record-dry-powder-mean-for-pe-vc-fund-managers>

[5] Abramowicz, L. 2017. 'The Great Corporate Cash Shell Game' Bloomberg Opinion, <https://www.bloomberg.com/gadfly/articles/2017-09-22/corporate-cash-isnt-doing-much-but-hiding-debt>

of world-wide GDP. World-wide, the loan to deposit ratio is about 20:1. In the U.S. that ratio is only 72%, while in China it is just over 60%.[6] Speaking of the U.S. alone, deposits are over $12 trillion. And it might be reasonable that U.S. banks wish they were able to loan out 90% of their deposits, rather than just 72%. The difference is another $2.2 trillion dollars that banks wish were loaned out and producing interest. I have shown that there are about $5.5 trillion just in the United States seeking investments that are safe enough and return enough. See? Too much money!

Many people would be business owners but for lack of funds. So, all you have to do is convince part of that $5.5 trillion that your deal is safe enough and lucrative enough. They are so desperate to invest, either safety or a high ROI, one of the two is probably satisfactory.

Wouldn't it be nice if you weren't required to invest any of your own money at all? That would open the opportunity to many more would-be business owners.

How to buy big enough companies with no money down? Well the chart above, labeled Figure 18.3, gives the answer. You can usually finance four times EBITDA, combining funds from a bank and mezzanine financiers. How you ask? Well, Chapter 17 provided a template of how to combine companies well enough so that four times projected EBITDA is enough money to fund an acquisition. Pessimistically, the added EBITDA due to the combination of Fun Cakes and Daily Bread was $1,456 million. That's over 5.4 added Fun Cakes' EBITDA turns.[7] That could be financed fully by a mezzanine fund, without any funds from a bank. Of course, you wouldn't do that, because bank financing is so much less expensive.

It is easier to buy two or three companies than it is to buy one. Particularly, if you can reasonably expect them to be synergistic. The main synergy benefit is cross-selling the various companies' products to the other companies' customers. This strategy suggests a main platform company with other companies bolted onto that central platform.

In case it isn't obvious, such synergies are only available within a common geography. If the companies to be combined serve a local area like Charlotte, North Carolina and sell to the same customers and same types of customers, that is wonderful, just like the example in Chapter 17. Having one company in Charlotte, one in Nashville, Tennessee and the other in Indianapolis, Indiana is much less attractive. Companies in those different markets will have few if any overlapping customers. Likewise, you want a shared facility, a shared delivery fleet and, if applicable, combined service capabilities. Now, if the three companies all sell via an internet store, they have a common geography. However, if the Indianapolis company will become the hub (there should be just one) that is not so good for the people working in Charlotte and Nashville. Keep the best interests of the people in mind. They are the most important part.

A small warning: while the synergies described above are quite real, combining companies in the same market with the same customers exposes the owners to a downside risk, if the region or industry is hit by a recession. One way to mitigate such a risk is to own different types of consolidated companies in different geographic markets.[8]

Let me reiterate that banks look backwards while mezzanine funds look forward. The multiples of EBITDA in Figure 18.3 are looking backward–last year's EBITDA.

---

[6] https://www.statista.com/statistics/276285/loan-to-deposit-ratio-in-the-global-bank-industry/

[7] An EBITDA turn means a multiple of one times EBITDA. If you were to buy a company for five times EBITDA, you would have paid five EBITDA turns. Think of EBITDA turns analogously to inventory turns.

[8] Just when we try to tempt you to get started, we now suggest a bigger broader and more expensive scale. Shame on us!

That means banks will lead from 2.4 to 3.4 times the last year's total EBITDA of the combined companies. If you expect EBITDA to grow by 50% next year, because of TOC improvements and cross-selling, you can probably make a deal without putting up your own money. Here's the math:

> *Company X EBITDA = $2.5 million*
> *Company Y EBITDA = $1.5 million*
> *Company Z EBITDA = $1.0 million*
> *Combined Companies Last Year's EBITDA = $5 million*
> *Average Negotiated Price* $5 \times$ *EBITDA = $25 million*
> *Primary Bank Lending* $3.0 \times$ *EBITDA = $15 million of Secured Loans*
> *Expected Increase* $150\% \times$ *EBITDA = $7.5 million*
> $1\frac{1}{3} \times$ *New EBITDA = $10 million of Mezzanine Financing*
> *Total Funding $15 million Bank + $10 million Mezz = $25 million*

Although it may seem counterintuitive, if you don't have much money, it is easier to buy three synergistic companies than one, from a purely financial perspective. Remember, synergies are known to people who haven't read this book. A simple plan to quickly double a company's sales may be unbelievable to prospective financiers, even though one author consulted with a company that doubled sales within one month.

Still, there is an art to blending the cultures of multiple companies that is quite easy for some and so impossibly complicated for others that they often disclaim culture is important at all. Make no mistake, culture is critical.

Culture Matters

First, people need to be good citizens. It is fair and reasonable to expect that they bring honest trustworthy behavior with them when they become an employee. And, if they lie cheat or steal, it is proper to fire them for it. However, it is up to management to create an atmosphere in which each employee can flourish and isn't pressured or taken advantage of to the point that they resort to imperfect behavior. Trust them first and see if they won't trust you; it may take a while, considering what they've seen elsewhere.

In an acquisition, don't be passive with respect to culture. Get out in front and lead. **It is not okay to ignore culture.** Say what you believe in. Share it with people. Then, you must walk the talk, as they say. Make your actions congruent with what you said was important.

Allow no excuses. Excuses are cultural poison. Particularly, new employees may be unable to avoid mistakes. Folks require mistakes to learn. You can't avoid that unless you can afford to train them for years before getting any work out of them. To protect trust, employees shouldn't find mistakes to be fatal to their employment. What you want is accountability. When an employee blows it, you want them to be able to admit it and make it right. It is about integrity.

People who can't be honest about their part of a failure should be coached back towards reality. If they refuse to doff their Teflon® garments and continue to blame others and justify their own mistakes, warn them once. After the second time, release them to industry for their third chance. We are advising that it is not the mistake that gets you fired, it is not admitting it and taking full responsibility.

It is a lot easier for people who are of good character to consolidate two or three companies than it is for people with weak and fraudulent character. Once the combined staff sees what isn't tolerated, they simply decide whether they like having a team of co-workers they can trust enough to decide to live being personally honest or they don't and then you can work with them to find a new place to work that they prefer.

Let us quickly clarify that being unable to embrace the company's culture in word and deed is not grounds for immediate termination. After all, people can have different opinions. When employees opt into your company, they must accept your priorities. If they don't or can't live under them, it is time to plan, with them, their outplacement. Many employees who fail to buy in initially, eventually do decide to embrace the culture, rather than be eased out. The ones who initially struggle but eventually are won over become the strongest cultural proponents in the end. Those who can't or won't leave as soon as they find another job.

The people who you were worried might be angry when one of their co-worker buddies is fired or eased out always ask, "Why did you let that guy stay around so long?" Then, they'll follow up with, "He didn't fit in here." Who wants to work with somebody who blames others for his or her mistakes?

The main point is, it isn't as important what culture you choose, as it is important that you populate the company with those who share an agreement about what the organization stands for. Why is that important? Because you are about to enter the Transition Period but, before we get to that, let's address risk.

Evaluating the Potential and the Risk of Purchasing a Company

No matter whether your ideas for purchasing a company and dramatically increasing its value are based on TOC, cross-selling with your current company or a brilliant idea you have, there is always the possibility of a worst case outcome. The fear of losing is always there. If you succumb to your fears it could mean losing everything!

Practically speaking, this is probably a gross exaggeration. You might lose everything, if something very rare happens. Every time you fly in an airplane you may wonder if it might be your last. But, most of us still fly and live with such fears that are truly rare. We adopt a reasonable approach – assessing risks and choosing not to let extreme and very rare possibilities to impact our behavior. To remain sane, we construct a pessimistic scenario represented by a chain of events that could happen from time to time, say one in a hundred. When you look at the pessimistic scenario, like we have throughout the book, you understand the degree of risk. If that risk means only earning 15% on the equity you invest, then the downside is actually not risk, just a less preferable result.

Going through both pessimistic and optimistic assessments of the future is key advice we offer every investor, actually every decision maker to seriously consider. Taking out a loan can be low risk when the reasonable worst-case scenario is better than your current state. The other side, the optimistic scenario, is what you truly strive for, even though you know you'll probably achieve somewhat less.

Purchasing a company means having a clear idea how so much more could be realized. Only when the optimistic scenario looks almost too good to be true then it is a truly worthy purchase. And, inquiring into the pessimistic side must be done to reveal the reasonable downside. Failing to do assess both is a huge mistake, meaning after you do it once, learn the lesson and move on making much better choices.

The Transition Period

After any merger of companies there will be a time of hardship. No matter how well organized the companies were previously, the integration process will disrupt existing processes and call for new ones. During this Transition Period, some of the old rules no longer apply, while new rules are not fully defined or used and there will be added pressure on the affected people. The pressure does not abate simply because all the new rules are in place, it requires building new habits and the time to do that depends on how much emotion each individual puts behind adopting the changes. Learning not to lean your palm on a hot stove is learned instantly in one go but how much emotion can you muster for stopping production?

It is wise to plan for extra management attention during any Transition Period. Employees will be unsure, under certain circumstance but not all circumstances, of exactly what to do and how to behave. All other major initiatives should be completed before the Transition Period starts. If that can't happen or doesn't happen, freeze major initiatives until after the Transition Period.

Every manager should have one-on-one meetings with all new direct reports. Do this as immediately as you can. Ask what they liked about what they have been doing. Find out what they didn't like, more importantly. Find out what tools they lack which would allow a better job. Ask them what they would change and write down those ideas. Give them an idea of what expansion efforts will be undertaken. They will be hungry for a brighter future. Lastly, ask for their aspirations five years out. The answers will tell you which want to grow and improve.

Recognize that people worry about changes. They will ask themselves, "Will it be good for me?" If they decide the answer is no, they may look for another job. Some turnover is positive but you don't want it to be immediate, unless the person really behaves badly.

During the transition, expectations will be too high in some areas and too low in others. When expectations are different from the observed reality, frustration is a natural consequence. Folks who are frustrated behave worse than folks who are not. Forgiveness is critical at these times. Yet, at the same time, a commitment to improvement is not less important.

From a very successful software provider in Australia[9] comes this simple adage, "If it's worth doing twice, it's worth never doing again." This statement legitimizes stopping the current course of action and building necessary content and processes. Whenever a conversation is occurring for the second or third time, it is a signal that the process is not yet robust enough to occur without conversation. Failure to establish the requisite guidelines leads to repeat conversations and eventual misrepresentation of the original intent. Getting things right is more important than usual, during a Transition Period.

As the transition progresses, there should be fewer and fewer unexpected problems. Then, fewer problems whether expected or unexpected. Eventually management attention will become less exploited. Enjoy it for a few months, then get back on the improvement bandwagon by defrosting frozen initiatives or beginning new ones your new employees suggested. Remember that list? When you start the defrosting process, you are saying that the Transition Period is at an end. The quicker that happens the better!

---

[9] Wise Tech Global, a public company majority owned by Richard White, a fast-growing TOC company. By the way, such "one-liners" are an excellent way to make it socially acceptable to interrupt wrong-headed thinking. If the circumstances fit the one-liner's applicability context, employees and managers are required to state it. This approach removes any sense that the comment is a personal attack. Rather, it is just a necessary reminder that the whole company rolls in a different way. It is not only okay to disagree and to work to affect a change, it is lauded. However, it is not okay to disagree and behave out of synchronicity with the rest of the staff and management. That is what gets a person eased out.

Before declaring victory, look for the unexpected. Eli Goldratt used to call these "mysteries." Look for effects that surprise you. It doesn't matter whether it is something better than expected or worse. If you don't understand the cause and effect, that makes it a mystery. Seek to understand them. Mysteries tend to bite, particularly when you can least afford to be bitten. Some bites are minor others are fatal. Watch for them. They suggest that your understanding is more limited than you thought.

If you pay attention to culture, particularly avoiding making the deal work by saving money on people costs, you will have many helpers to make sure that the consolidation of your businesses happens quickly and without the loss of orders and customers. If you try to make the deal work through cutting costs, you can expect to receive some serious mysterious bites.

Your Team

Rarely, along comes a person who can do it all. What this person doesn't know, they easily figure out. Such a superstar does not need partners. They prefer to utilize employees and they can afford the best, regardless the required compensation, because people who can do it all have plenty of money or, if they are still young, will soon.

Let's assume you are not a superstar. You have strengths like we all do, balanced by weaknesses. There are holes in your knowledge. You don't have infinite stamina, the best education or natural attractiveness of the Pied Piper of Hamelin. If you are like us, you understand there is strength in numbers. Furthermore, strength comes from combining different personalities and skillsets.

If you want to own a company, you may have to share it with others—build an association of players to do what any superstar could do alone. It is far better to share than to go hungry. Ten percent of something big is better than all of something very small, which is, in turn, better than nothing at all. While employees are less expensive in the long run, if you become very successful, expensive partners are far better than never succeeding at all.

That being said, remember as we wrote earlier, a collaboration is very good for making good decisions that can be implemented well but poor for decisions quickly. Decisiveness is also important in the face of our adversary, time. If you require a collaboration, be very careful choosing the players and make sure that one person is the boss. It is easiest if one person owns legal control of the company. Such a person has the legal right to make decisions, even over the objections of all the minority owners. This sounds bad but it is just like a constraint—a focusing mechanism. It is also possible that one person can be given contractual control.

One of the authors is a partner in a private equity fund that owns three small companies. The fund bought 51% of one of the three companies. However, the fund bought less than a majority of the other two companies. Before we invested, we demanded a contract that gave us operational control. We wanted to make sure that the companies respected the Theory of Constraints. After all, aside from capital, this was the future value that we brought into the investments. The sellers had to decide they needed help and money, not just money.

In one case and after much discussion and time, we exercised our control to remove the founder and majority owner from operations of his own company and then worked to make him as wealthy as possible. The major owner's stake today is worth many times more than it was before we bought in as partners. Such actions are seldom necessary and can be done without hard feelings. Many of the owner's family worked at the company and we were able to retain all of them after removing him and did so without making the owner look bad to his family.

The moral of the story is that it takes a team. It is not enough to be on the right bus heading in the right direction. You must have the right people in the right seats on that bus. If you don't have the money you can trade for ownership. Sometimes this works well and sometimes not. So, be sure to have a well-considered buy-sell agreement between the partners which allows a partner to buy more ownership or sell some or all of theirs. At the same time, you want to protect the company from being financially emasculated due to buying out partners. It is a balancing act.

It is easier to be a superstar. Good luck with that.

Chapter 19

Management Attention as a Special Critical Resource

My Plate is Full

Formally, I'm the VP of Business Development of FriendlyVac, a medium-sized manufacturer of vacuum cleaners. Actually, my brother and I own 51% of the shares, so I'm quite aware that I have much more influence than my title suggests. My brother, Harry, and I nominated Denis to be our CEO, first of all, to settle the sensitive relationships between us but mainly to bring order and establish a stable structure within the company. He is doing an excellent job. Still, the future of the company depends mainly on Harry and me. Harry is the VP of Research and Development and I'm the one with the crazy business ideas for various ways to make more money. This management structure has worked very well so far. We grew from $20M in sales seven years ago to $150M last year.

Although the pace of growth has declined over the last two years, I'm looking farther into the future. Five years ago, we purchased an old plant in China and made it modern and productive. Now, we are covering our growing sales in Eastern Asia, including India, Japan and Australia. Last year, we opened a new plant in South Brazil. I still need to spend more time there to open new distribution routes in South America.

Denis is great at establishing the procedures for smooth operations. I still need to establish commercial relationships with many more, new, big, clients. This is the right timing because Denis raised an interesting idea of offering vendor managed inventory (VMI), for important and large distributors. Our VMI program would relieve them from the hassles of placing orders and, more importantly, all the work involved in avoiding and resolving shortages for all their branches, leaving that to us. Denis is influenced by Goldratt's Theory of Constraints, which helps him establish very effective ways to manage the flow. As a result, our delivery performance is now far better than our competitors. To my mind, our excellent performance in on-time delivery on top of offering truly great products, yields us about 30% more sales.

But, I am looking for so much more. The VMI idea is just a part of what I want to achieve. I'm going to give it a try in South America when I meet the key people in most of the large distributors and see how they respond to the idea. And, I also want to offer it to several of our key clients in the U.S. and Europe. I just need more time to do that. This is a kind of sale that only I can achieve, since I know how to get a meeting with senior executives in any giant distributor. Only high-level people can truly appreciate the holistic value of such an offer. Lower level people might feel threatened by an offer to relieve part of their duties and giving the responsibility to their supplier.

Harry and I are engaged in developing an idea that would combine robotic technology to enhance our vacuum's versatility. Well, Harry is leading the development project and we badly need the electronics to be developed by experts in that field. I have found a French high-tech company capable of developing the circuit boards for us and then also manufacturing them. I still need to dedicate a lot of time to establish the details of the commercial side of the collaboration. This is the one initiative that I have the highest hopes for to bring us to my target of one billion sales within three or four years. I feel pressure, because the project seems to be moving too slowly but we are moving ahead. I really enjoy doing this kind of work.

Also, I have a truly urgent project to manage. We must move our main plant in the U.S. to another region. Over the last ten years, we have been under pressure to do so. The ridiculously high transportation costs from the current location is one important reason. The difficulty to find reliable employees willing to work on night shifts is another. We now ship a lot of products from our South American plant to the U.S. This makes it much more expensive to sustain our trademark reliable delivery performance. Anyway, once I gain more market in South America, the plant there won't be able to support both markets. So, we have to move before we really get ourselves in a jam.

I, of course, plan to capitalize on improving our capacity, in addition to enhancing the capabilities of our critical equipment. Therefore, our new plant will be capable of serving 25% more demand in North America, which I think I can easily get, provided we have the capacity.

That project of moving our plant has been dragging for quite awhile. I need both Denis and Harry to be more active in pushing it ahead but they have their own priorities, while I have mine.

I'm quite frustrated about how things are progressing. I have three assistants helping me to move things ahead. One is stationed in South America; another is focused on the French collaboration project, while the third supervises moving the plants. They do their best but it is not enough.

This story touches upon several problematic points that are typical of the work lives of a truly senior executive. In the end, it is all about how a key person in an organization spends his own capacity for moving improvement ideas ahead. So far, we have dealt with the potential impact of lacking enough capacity of machines, even the potential lack of a critical material, in addition to cash as a critical resource. It is time to inquire more deeply into the role of management attention, especially the attention required to implement changes.

It is reasonably obvious that many organizations are constrained by the capacity of the management team to deal with important matters, especially new initiatives that require considerable managerial intervention, while also handling urgent issues that seemingly appear out of nowhere and demand immediate action. Every manager experiences the ongoing conflict between the important and the urgent. There is a natural tendency to prioritize the urgent but how soon their attention reverts back to the important depends on the manager's personality.

The topic of management attention requires us to consider the distinction between capability and capacity. The basic capability of a manager to deal with a complicated topic is an issue we do not address in this book. Our assumption is that the managers have the knowledge and intellect to handle all the issues for which they are responsible. If we are wrong about this, in your particular case, please admit it now and take action soon, otherwise you will suffer until you finally are forced to. A manager's capability has a certain impact on their capacity.

Capacity means how much work can be handled in a period of time.

Focusing on what truly matters is an integral part of the Theory of Constraints knowledge. The subject of this chapter is the concern that the load on the management attention capacity might be too high and the ramifications are almost always quite serious. We will not address improving the capability of managers to waste less of their capacity and, by doing so, free enough capacity to handle the load. Even for managers who don't waste their capacity, the possibility of overload is real and thus a serious concern.

The difficulty of measuring management attention capacity is clear. We don't know how long a person must think about an issue in order to come up with an appropriate solution. Dreaming up a new insight is a process. There is no way to guess how long it should take and how badly other issues might be delayed meanwhile. We also face a difficulty in categorizing the huge variety of managerial issues. We only know that some take just a minute, while others require many hours of full concentration. In the latter case, recovering from any small interruption can be quite difficult. Sometimes, we must start over to rebuild a novel train of thought.

We are aware, though, that management attention in general is likely to be a critical resource, so we should look for a way to estimate the relationship between the actual load and the capacity of every manager and for the whole management of the organization, in general. If we find such a way, then the analysis of new opportunities should include management attention capacity as one of the critical resources. The story above demonstrates a situation where the load of managing three major initiatives at the same time is simply too great for them to be handled effectively. The ramification is all three initiatives stall. And, it is not necessary that the projects be large, enough small projects can effectively delay a huge number of them from being completed in a timely fashion. Even if managers are powerfully capable, they can find themselves unable to move, just like Gulliver tied down by the Lilliputians.

When it comes to human beings, especially senior executives, can we draw a very clear line between the right load and being overloaded?

It is obvious that measuring "units of capacity" against a certain measure of available capacity in a month is not applicable for management attention. Hence, we cannot simply follow the procedure of calculating the cumulative load, compare it to the available capacity during the relevant period of time and present a utilization bar chart.

On the other hand, claiming "we don't have a clue" is neither a solution nor true. While our knowledge about the available capacity for attention is fuzzy, what we do know can be effectively utilized. We suggest overcoming the complexity of measuring human capacity by preferring to be "about right" rather than giving up, because it is impossible to be precise.

What we might be able to do is find a practical way to predict when a certain manager, or even a managerial team, might be overloaded when an additional significant task is added to their list. When such a critical concern is raised, then a shift of priorities or delay of some initiatives or freezing others should be analyzed and agreed upon, as an integral part of the high-level decision-making process. Other options include delegating certain tasks to lower level managers or expanding the management pyramid. The serious ramifications of penetrating into the protective capacity might yield very inferior business results relative to what were evaluated as very promising moves.

In order to better understand when management attention becomes a truly critical resource, as well as the negative consequences of management's becoming overloaded, we must make a distinction between two critical flows in every organization:

1. **The Flow of Value**
   This flow is critical in any organization. It consists of the current products and services and how they move through the organization to meet the current clients' needs. It is what was described in previous chapters as the reference sales profile, expressed by the list of all active

T-generators and the prediction of sales when no new decision is made. The capacity profile of the critical resources is what allows and maintains that flow as it varies.

Managerial attention, especially of operations and sales managers, is required to ensure the existing processes are maintained. This includes validating that every customer gets exactly what has been ordered, every potential customer receives good information about the offerings, the routine negotiations of price and other delivery parameters are all accomplished in an orderly manner. In other words, the management of the whole supply chain is under good control. Managers might face frequent "fires" in the ongoing activities. They have to dedicate their minds and time to identify every glitch and fix them before they disrupt the flow. This flow is what determines the current value of the ongoing activities of the organization. In the leading story of this chapter, it is the duty of Denis, the CEO, to establish and maintain law and order, ensuring high delivery performance. He is the sheriff of the Flow of Value, while the two brothers focus on initiatives to grow the company.

2. **The Flow of Initiatives** aimed at significantly improving the Flow of Value.

This is the flow of the activities undertaken to improve future profitability by smoothing and adding to the future Flow of Value. Such improvements could be focused on preventing chronic delays or poor quality. They could mean fixing ineffective procedures by using superior methodologies, such as implementing TOC's simplified Drum Buffer Rope (SDBR) in the plant or Critical Chain Project Management (CCPM) in the sales department. Other managerial initiatives might include developing a new Decisive Competitive Edge (DCE) capability in operations, implementing a way to capitalize on it in large enough markets in a way that no significant competitor can copy, without exhausting the company's resources or taking real risks.

Sometimes such strategic moves require a Proof of Concept (PoC) as the first phase of implementation, followed by a formal decision point to determine whether to continue or stop. Once a new concept is agreed upon, implementation expands according to a detailed planned timetable. The two brothers, who are the owners in the story, are fully occupied by the flow of these kind of initiatives, with very little, if any at all, of their time spent attending to the current Flow of Value.

There are some key differences in the use of management attention between these two critical flows.

The Flow of Value is mostly managed by operational, logistical and sales managers who are focused on the short-term performance. Some of the supporting functions like IT and Finance are also occupied mainly with the Flow of Value. Typically, those managers are responsible for the short-term planning and exert a lot of control over what is done every day. Ichak Adizes calls the two general areas these managers preside over Producing and Administrating,[1] the former being short-term effectiveness and the latter short-term efficiency. Such managers are occupied by handling daily emergencies that require immediate response. Yet, the higher-level management of those key functions have also to dedicate thought and efforts to improvement initiatives, which belong to the Flow of Initiatives, even though the horizon is relatively short-term.

Marketing, R&D, Engineering, Finance and Business Development are typical functions dealing mainly with the Flow of Initiatives. Adizes generalizes these long-term activities into what he terms Entrepreneuring and Integrating. Most of the actual attention of the CEO should be

---

[1] Adizes, I.C. 1987, *Corporate Lifecycles: How and Why Corporations Grow and Die and What to Do About It*, Prentice Hall, Englewood Cliffs, NJ.

dedicated to this flow of initiatives. Even with this type of flow, over its longer-term horizon, a considerable amount of attention is dedicated to urgent and semi-urgent issues that require immediate response. For example, signing a long-term contract with a new large client might suddenly require a lot of attention in a very short period, to evaluate new developments and sudden requests that have not been planned. New obstacles in product development could also call for a sudden review, leading to urgent actions to mitigate the situation.

When does the Load on Management Attention Become Problematic?

How does the Lack of Management Capacity Impact the Two Flows?

As long as the manager is doing all her duties with good enough response times and without harming the quality of the decision, then the load is not a problem and we should not consider the manager's attention capacity as a critical resource.

From the above, we understand that when allowable response times are too frequently stretched or too many mistakes are occurring, causing a variety of negative consequences, then the manager's capacity to pay attention is definitely constraining the organization from achieving more sooner.

The resulting effect of a manager being overloaded is unbearable pressure, causing mistakes and delays that can be seen in a rise in the number of urgent, but unattended, issues.

When it comes to the Flow of Value, the delivery performance of that flow is closely controlled by the clients. Through their complaints, clients establish an informal reference for acceptable performance, which is less than 100% on-time and in full but is drawn at a certain level that is not usually[2] disastrous to the organization. TOC and Lean offer much improved ways to run the Flow of Value, causing the informal perception of acceptability in delivery performance to rise – forcing all competing companies to improve their operations as well.

However, when management attention dedicated to the Flow of Value becomes an active capacity constraint, then there is real risk of chaotic delivery performance. Managers wrestle imperfect operational policies using whatever spare attention capacity they have to remove the blockages to the flow and to make sure clients won't be harmed beyond their tolerance. When all the spare capacity is gone and time pressures result in more mistakes in handling the flow, then the delivery performance becomes erratic and, in severe cases, even chaotic. Clients with other options are unwilling to tolerate such lousy performance. The only things that can restore order is the clients placing orders elsewhere or developing more management attention.

Because of the huge price paid as a result of allowing management attention to the Flow of Value to become a constraint, the simple solution is to provide enough protective capacity. This understanding may seem to clash with the fact that we rarely see operations or sales managers relax. The spare capacity of these managers is not visible, because human beings know how to be seen as busy all the time. Typical operations people are "action oriented" – they hurry to take an action, even before it is well thought through. So, keeping busy is natural to them. The real test that proves there is a management attention overload is when the many small "fires"

---

[2] We say "usually," because some true commodity businesses have so many equivalently priced competitors that a customer may change suppliers as soon as they notice any deterioration in delivery or quality performance.

are not quickly extinguished and a real "forest fire" situation seems to be developing. When this occurs, top management must interfere to resolve the paucity of management attention capacity.

The very different nature of managing the Flow of Initiatives impacts management attention in another way. These managers are not subject to clear, stiff and rapid judgments on their performance, like in operations or sales, where the clients are the ones to voice their dissatisfaction. On time performance is a prime measurement for some projects but not for many other initiatives. Executives and their mid-managers dedicate part of their time to evaluating new ideas, while simultaneously running formal initiatives, which have already been approved by top management. The formal initiatives, projects or major missions usually involve several different people from other functions and the attendant need for interpersonal and interdepartmental communication always slows down the progress. Formal initiatives have emergencies here and there but much less than in managing the Flow of Value. The executives and managers who deal mainly with the Flow of Initiatives frequently constrain the pace themselves and also the very quality of the plans for the future. While the sky is not a limit to what an organization can achieve, there is an internal limitation to the pace of growth. The resources that most commonly suffer from limited capacity are top management. It is quite normal that they are unable to give the appropriate attention to all the issues that would help the company.

The unavoidable result of too much load on executives and managers is a slow drag on all the current initiatives and ideas for future initiatives. It is identifiable, when the response from a manager to a request, from a colleague or subordinate, takes too long to be of any value. The term "bad multitasking," originally describing an observed characteristic of multi-project environments, is used to describe the cause of seemingly uncontrolled delays in most projects. When too many open tasks are attempted at the same time, the unavoidable negative result is that the progress of other people is delayed due to lack of necessary inputs. Another contributor to the delays is the loss of the train of thought that occurs when somebody switches from one task to the next and then back again. Getting one's mind back to the point where it was when it was interrupted consumes capacity.

When, on top of the delayed progress of important initiatives, the load on management goes up to the limit, things get considerably worse. The characteristic of a Bottleneck is that the rate at which new tasks are introduced is greater than the pace of completions. The psychological pressure makes matters even worse. Practically, it can mean there is no progress at all. People who are freaked out badly enough will just freeze. Yet, as the current Flow of Value continues uninterrupted, one might get the wrong impression of business as usual.

Thus, the number of initiatives undertaken by the organization must be limited, in order to avoid overloading any of the executives. Of course, the choice of the few initiatives to focus on is itself a worthy challenge. The analysis of the expected economic impact on the bottom-line, as we have already described in detail, is a good tool to provide the necessary information. While this is common sense, the temptation remains to add just one more initiative, because the current load seems to be, momentarily at least, under good control.

But, is the Load on Top Management within Good Enough Control?

As we don't have an effective way to directly measure management attention capacity, we need to institute a control mechanism that constantly checks for early signals of excessive delays. It requires monitoring all the important missions, their start and expected conclusion time.

Furthermore, managers would be remiss if they failed to segregate their initiatives in broad categories of complication and relative importance. Some very complicated and critical mission might require 40%–60% of the manager's daily attention. If we assume that that person's routine management of the Flow of Value already requires 20–30% of each day, then adding one such major mission as described creates a huge and, perhaps, dangerous load. Other missions could vary from 10%–40%.

This control mechanism need not include the many small routine issues with which the manager regularly deals. It should only consider the overall impact of the load on the manager without trying to closely monitor them. When, over a stretch of time, several simultaneous missions are identified, it should raise an alarm of the risk for too much load on the management team. In such a case, some of the missions should be formally killed or frozen and reintroduced in a staggered way, in order to allow focusing on what is truly required now! Then, finish each one as soon as possible before embarking on the next initiative.

The focus of this book is on being able to check new ideas, opportunities and suggested initiatives to bring the organization to much better state. A chosen limit on the number of major "strategic" initiatives should be part of the group discussion when the choice of competing initiatives is analyzed. This limit should be checked through the control mechanism and, when necessary, changed.

There is another aspect of the Flow of Initiatives and management attention that requires careful handling. Eventually, every initiative for the future is implemented into the Flow of Value. Depending on the amount of change the Flow of Value has to go through, there will be a certain Transition Period. During the transition some of the old rules do not apply anymore, yet the new rules are also not yet fully operational. During this period of time, all levels of management must deal with a very high number of urgent issues that fall between the old rules and the new. This means the load on many low and mid-level managers in operations and sales will grow considerably, with the concern of facing a temporary peak load.

The story at the head of this chapter mentions a plan to move a plant to another location. When the transfer does actually occur, a Transition Period will take place, during which the staff will have to get used to the new equipment and many other new issues, such as establishing new transportation routes. Other potentially urgent issues could be dealing with the relocation of key personnel, hiring and training many new workers, etc. This will undoubtedly be a tough period for Denis and his people to manage the Flow of Value in a way that maintains the same level of performance so that clients are not aware of any temporary difficulties, until the new Flow of Value is stabilized.

The simple advice is to plan the implementation of the finished initiatives into the Flow of Value to occur one at a time. In practice it means staggering the implementations into the Flow of Value so no two significant changes occur at the same time.

What Ways are Effective at Elevating Management Attention Capacity?

This is a critical strategic issue. It directly leads us to review again the five focusing steps defined by Goldratt and briefly mentioned in Chapter 6. At first, the organization should exploit the available management attention by setting clear priorities for focusing, while actively restricting the consumption of managerial capacity on other issues. Empowering lower level people with the appropriate capabilities is another way to exploit the limited managerial capacity.

Adding just one or two managers, usually just at the headquarters level, who are focused on specific areas within the strategic plan is possible as a temporary move. We also must take into account that adding managers requires an additional load on the existing managers temporarily due to the necessity for a higher level of communication.

Eventually, when there is a constant growth in the company activities, there is a real need to expand the managerial hierarchy. It means seriously going to the fourth focusing step of elevating the management attention constraint. But, this step, while being absolutely necessary at certain times, involves going through another Transition Period until the new hierarchy works well together.

As the reader can easily see, handling management attention capacity issues requires more experience, research and, eventually, the verbalization of more detailed rules and guidelines. So, this is an excellent topic for other authors to do the development and then write the next book to complement this one.

Chapter 20

The Critical Nature of Metrics

Hmmm, well what about measurements? This is a book about finance, numbers, and making better decisions. Why has there been so little discussion dedicated to measurements?

Our goal is to provide you a process for imagining, preparing and presenting your initiatives, targeted at improving profitability. Lasting profitability is impacted by what is holistically measurable, think overall T, I and OE. We also encourage you, through storytelling, that there are cultural intangibles that you should consider in your analysis.

The need for performance measurements is to have a clear picture of where the company is now and what it can do better. As a direct result of their importance in any organization, metrics tend to become embedded, locking in how they advise people to act and influence management's enforcement actions.

These actions include management's use of performance measurements to secure accountability by dictating targets, stated as clear numbers based on certain measurements. For example, the amount of sales or even T to be generated next month or quarter. These include the accountability of a specific salesperson to meet a quota. The imbedded assumption is that people fail to achieve their targets because of lack of motivation or skills. This assumption is usually wrong! The measurements do not identify the reason why they are under performing. Once management sees the full picture, then an analysis should be carried out to identify the core reason for not doing better, even without targets.

We want to encourage you to become a bridge builder. Let us explain, by way of example.

Say you use what you have learned in this book with your team and, after analysis, you make a significant go-forward decision for your company. Even though you altered your decision-making analysis to consider Throughput based accounting, there is a strong likelihood that existing measurements based on full-absorption costing are still in place.

Throughout the year, you are tracking acceptably well, within the range of expected outcomes, according to your new analysis process that led to the go decision. At the same time, you and others are hearing directly and indirectly from Finance who are reporting on your progress measured against all their traditional historical measures. Now, you may have a lot of defending and explaining to do to maintain support and even your job. There will be doubters.

This could have been mitigated if, as a part of the decision process itself you had reconciled your TOC inspired performance metrics, which led you to the decision to go ahead, with how those same results would be presented under normal performance reporting.

We suggest you develop a "bridge of understanding" between what will be measured traditionally and the Throughput-based performance metrics that led to your decisions to proceed with your initiative.

This is critically important, because, unfortunately, it is not at all uncommon for a good area of business to be eliminated, due to failing to pass muster according to traditional metrics.

If you are thinking along with us – *yes* – the metrics must dynamically adapt with the continually changing environment that your company experiences over time. Their content should be periodically reconsidered and verified as relevant. (See Appendix B.)

Measuring any environment by T and capacity profiles, plus the OE and I, gives a valid overall picture of the current performance. When impending changes loom, it is wise to be watching secondary metrics that signal advance warnings that your focus should change dynamically and specifically to the situation.

This suggests that you should be deciding what indicators to focus on to improve your future. And, that sounds like changing existing metrics to support superior decisions. You should be careful. When you make a change in what you measure, you should expect people will behave differently. However, such change, even when it is for the long-term betterment of the company, may cause problems in the short term.

We have thoroughly covered the concept of a Transition Period—a period after a change in which operations become abruptly more chaotic, requiring significantly more management attention to protect the Flow of Value, until new habits are formed enhancing performance (assuming the change was a positive one). A consequence of changing metrics is a Transition Period. You will be wise to ease into them or, when you don't think it prudent, be prepared for the Transition Period. Consider this as you read the next section.

What Not to Measure

Before we get to what should be measured, let's identify commonly used metrics that are likely to result in damage. Here is a list so you are clear on which measurements to abandon.

- First and foremost in general, any **local measurement** has the ongoing potential to undermine the global goals of the company.
- **Measuring sales.** Units of sales are not the same as units of your goal. Sales obscures the true added-value which is Throughput. Of course, your income statement always reports sales but management should direct themselves and their staff towards T to measure the value the organization has delivered to its clients.
- **Measuring the company against a fixed budget.** What if there is a wonderful opportunity to massively increase T that requires very little ΔI but substantial ΔOE? Under a fixed budget, it is less likely that the opportunity will be undertaken. The opposite can be worse; an opportunity that doesn't cost much OE and requires a massive ΔI can cripple a company, while improving profits. Performance to budget's only real use, with limited benefit, is for departmental management.
- **Measuring reductions in OE.** Be very careful. OE is spent to provide capacity. You require protective capacity in order to keep the commitments to the market despite considerable uncertainty.
- **Measuring labor productivity.** You want the staff to have protective capacity. Since you can't measure it directly, providing an incentive to reduce that capacity will soon cause chaos.

■ **Comparing the output of any worker to other similar workers.** We hope you understand, after reading this far, that you should be concerned about systemic performance and not the performance of an individual alone. We understand conceptually that you want strong contributors in your company. However, every metric an individual is measured by should be perfectly aligned with the performance objectives of the initiatives for which they are involved and with the company's best interests as a whole. Measuring people individually foments competition between them. You prefer them to work together against competitors. *"Tell me how you measure me and I'll tell you how I'll behave."* If you do compare one person with others, particularly if they are paid based on that metric, expect:
  – employees to see co-workers as enemies,
  – employees to do a poor job training new people,
  – any time a commissioned salesperson is under performing and at imminent risk of being fired, the rest of the salesforce will vie for the opportunity to 'help the company' avoid losing what customers their endangered 'comrade' currently has (a fear of management's that is leading to the impending dismissal) and their desire to gain commissions and status will be so great that they will be distracted from selling themselves,
  – backstabbing, to gain promotions,
  – sucking up to managers, to gain raises and promotions and
  – team members who are suspicious of each other's motives, making agreement, collaboration and effectiveness less likely.
■ **Measuring net profit per department.** The departments will become silos and
  – work against each other,
  – seek to increase their budgets at the expense of other departmental budgets and
  – improve their departmental metrics, even by reducing overall profitability.
  – Net profit per department is usually a distortion. Just question whether the department could have achieved that profit without any contribution from any other departments, including top management!
■ **Measuring the T produced by a department** can also be tricky. Does some other department buy the inventory that was sold, collect the bill, make the delivery and so on? If you must, the T should be allocated and we know that can't be done accurately. Please don't bother. Measuring T per department results in the same misalignments mentioned above with regard to measuring net profit.
■ **Measuring net profit per customer, product or product line.** It will result in distortions and errors in judgement such as those we discussed in Chapters 1 and 4. That is, unless you go all the way and calculate $\Delta T - \Delta OE$, including the impact on capacity. All other ways of considering net profit of a subsection of a company are problematic. Additionally, there are commodity-based relationships and there are value-based relationships. The point is net profit per product and per customer distort your understanding. If your intuition gives you doubts about a product, product area, customer or region, instead go through a full holistic check.
■ **Calculating costs using any kind of allocation.** If you feel compelled to allocate costs, just consider those costs OE, stop and think.
■ **Measuring two numbers divided together.** Be very careful. Most ratios are local efficiency metrics—how much of something is gained per unit of a resource. Employees often forget the purpose of a measurement or perhaps they never knew it. They do understand that they want to help by making the ratio look better. When they feel blocked from quickly raising the numerator, usually T (or worse) net profit, they try to adjust the denominator, which

is usually tied to capacity – OE or I. They may be unaware that the elements are interrelated. For example, in a call center, they may make calls per agent a primary metric. If the agents want to increase the number of calls they handle, they only need to reduce the time they spend on each call. This leads to concluding a call before the caller is fully satisfied. Dissatisfied customers may switch to a competitor, reducing the number of calls received. As the ratio declines, there is increased pressure for agents to complete calls quickly. There is also pressure for management to reduce the number of agents. The whole process devolves into the miserable service provided by call centers, which you have certainly experienced.

■ **Measuring too many things.** Don't focus on more than five key metrics. The more metrics you have, the more likely that different parts of the company will become misaligned. The guaranteed result of misalignment is lower profits. Since you want higher profits, measure fewer things.

What Should be Measured?

Well, that depends on what you want, doesn't it? Throughout this book, we have assumed that the people who manage their company want more of what the company exists to deliver. In the case of for-profit companies, the goal is more profit. Not-for-profit companies have a social benefit in mind, as their primary goal. However, they too will have to get good use from the money they generate, in order to better support their specific notion of charity. To keep matters simple, we assume the goal is profit. Not just a profit today but a growing profit over time.

A quick primer: Lagging indicators are typically historical metrics. Leading indicators are forward looking metrics.

There will be measurements in place, lagging and leading. Financial statements are the typical lagging indicators. Lagging does not mean bad; they are very important. Leading indicators may include metrics of your internal processes to support ongoing improvement. So, leading indicators are measurements that point in the direction of better performance in the future. Important process indicators would be in the sales and customer fulfillment processes. Metrics such as lead quality, the length of sales cycles and offer acceptance rates are an important part of any improvement efforts. For example, an important leading indicator of the strategic ability to grow is free capacity, etc.

Please understand, this chapter's goal is to help you establish conceptually how you should reconsider, develop, deploy and enforce metrics that will best support your initiatives and help your company thrive.

In the end, when fully implemented, this approach is much simpler to understand, because it reflects the reality you and your people live every day, on which your intuitions were built.

Here's to hoping for you that, someday soon, one plus one can be two again.

Epilogue: What We Have Covered Together

A well-known paradigm for a good teacher:

> *First you tell the pupils what you are going to teach, then you teach, then you tell them what you have taught.*

We think that a good teacher has to also include the question:

> *Why it is important for you to learn this?*

An underlying paradigm suggests that repetition makes the delivery of the key messages much more effective. This leads us to write an epilogue to summarize our important messages.

Throughput Economics provides the best available guide for decision making in an organization. It points to a different process from what is typically used today when decisions are called for concerning proposed new opportunities. There are ways to identify new opportunities or emerging threats but the focus of this book is not about how the ideas are surfaced. Rather, once someone dreams up an idea, how it can be judged as objectively and effectively as possible?

Currently, the common method to check ideas is using cost per unit, especially attempting to allocate every bit of capacity consumption into unit costs. This approach is based on assumptions so old, like when people got paid by the hour or by piece, you may no longer even consider their source. The conventional approach also assumes that improving local performance generally improves the global outcome. These are very poor assumptions, leading to many distortions.

So, we suggest ignoring "per-unit" considerations and go directly to answer the main question:

If the proposed idea is accepted how much will the performance of the whole organization improve?

Our simple logical approach adds the implied actions from a new idea on top of all the activity of the whole organization and checks the predicted bottom-line. This is, of course, conceptually simple but it looks daunting to actually do but we hope you have realized that, using the concept of Throughput (T) and Operating Expense (OE) and using the power of today's computers, this mission is quite possible and the required actions are far easier than it may first appear.

Here comes the other critical consideration, **uncertainty.** Seldom, do you know in advance how a specific action will impact market demand.

It is so easy to say "I don't know – the resulting demand could be anything".

Really?

In most cases, "I don't know" means you don't know the exact answer but, if you consider the intuition of key people and treat it as a legitimate input into the full analytics of the case, you will get something worth much more than "I don't know."

You must consider intuition, because without it all marketing and sales predictions are practically worthless. There are no scientific tools to determine with great accuracy the future success of a new product, the full impact of a price change or the effectiveness of a suggested advertising campaign. Operations are also required to state their intuition, estimating how much protective capacity is mandatory for meeting the delivery performance the market is expecting. Research and development people surely require intuition for estimating what can be done and over what timeframe. Management always considers intuition. The decision-making process is only possible by integrating and evaluating a variety of different intuitive inputs from various perspectives with analytics that combine the available hard data. Translate every intuitive input into numbers, usually a range, and come up with two reasonable scenarios that describe the plausible range of potential results. Then management, armed with the best information that is available at that time, makes the call.

Capacity and demand are the two major groups of interactive variables that impact financial results. The assumption is that the net capabilities are either already existing, along with their associated capacities, or can be achieved or purchased by an investment that is an integral part of the idea.

The three critical simplifying factors to come up with two realistic scenarios that are good enough:

a. There is no need and there is also no practical way to be accurate! The objective is to be able to make the decision, considering both risk and the potential gain. In the vast majority of the cases, the actual result will lie within the expected range. So, the two extreme results can guide the decision. Small improvements in the accuracy of the extremes of the range only impact the decision materially in rare cases.

b. The pessimistic and optimistic impact on the market demand can be fairly described by the key Marketing and Sales people. They take into account the probable reaction of the market to changes in the offerings, like the promotions of some T-generators[1] on the demand for other T-generators or the consequential impacts of limiting sales of other T-generators. In other words, you should assume the Marketing and Sales people have enough intuition regarding the subtle interdependencies that exist between the company's offerings.

c. Operations managers have a good idea of the overall requirements for protective capacity that allows satisfactory delivery performance. Using excess capacity without penetrating into the required protective capacity adds no new expense. That means that there are many truly profitable opportunities to be grabbed. Operations should be able to identify several resources which are critical because they might run out of capacity, should a moderate increase in market demand occurs. For these resources, good-enough data on capacity consumption should be available to support reasonable approximations of the capacity requirements, given detailed demand patterns and, by that, reveal the feasibility of serving more market.

---

[1] Reminder: T-generator is an offering to the market that consists of products, delivery services, and a price.

The strategic option to maintain Capacity Buffers, which are a means to increase capacities of specific vulnerable resources very quickly at a premium price, was demonstrated by the detailed analyses of our cases. Managing such buffers yields a strategic advantage by allowing more ways to accommodate more sales without always having to invest in permanent additional capacity. This is a safer way to check the true potential for growth in the market before investment decisions are considered.

The cases in the book give a deeper understanding of the huge value that can be drawn. The dialogue among the management team highlights the concerns and reveals the underlying assumptions of the executives. Eventually the numbers tell their story – how this process sheds light on hidden opportunities that exist in your reality.

The decision-making process can be aided by software which quickly calculates the entire scenario, including all the sales within the pertinent period of time, noting the Truly Variable Cost of every product and considering the capacity requirements of every critical resource. Then, the user benefits if the software has a good user interface that allows inputting changes easily and recalculating the T, I and OE and the capacity profile of the critical resources.

Technically, Excel can do all that but the user interface might require additional efforts to make it easy. The algorithms for such software are public and, thus, it can be developed by any organization wishing to do so without difficulty and without needing permission.[2]

The scope of the decisions that can be checked according to the logic described in this book is broad. This approach should open the minds of many people in the organization to understand that their ideas are needed and then will be carefully checked. The person who had an idea is not the one responsible for its outcomes, as the management team will carefully check the full ramifications and they will have the responsibility, as a group, if things work out poorly.

Management should encourage ideas from employees and executives, even though those ideas might be rejected. In too many cases, you cannot know a priori whether an idea adds value or not – you must check it from all angles and this must be done taking the global parameters into account.

Management attention is an area that calls for more research. This is a sensitive issue to many people, when the limitations of their capacity are measured. We think that actively looking into signals of managers being under stress due to overload is critical for the smooth and safe progress of the organization. Management under stress could be disastrous to the future of the organization. Further developments in this sensitive but also crucial area are welcome.

Our proposed decision-making process could open the way to much better decisions and support a much better flow of ideas. Some ideas will turn out to be great and, overall, less risky. This process allows confident management of the organization, while facing uncertainty with open eyes.

Feel free to share your suggestions, successes and ask any of us questions.

Eli Schragenheim	elischragenheim@gmail.com
Henry Camp	henrycamp@ideallc.com
Rocco Surace	roccotpe@gmail.com

---

[2] Vector Consulting Group from India has developed such decision support software, called DSTOC.

Appendix A

Modeling and Data Requirements for Performing the What-if Scenarios

General Organization

Every meeting should define time horizon that is relevant for the decisions to be checked. All the data regarding the predicted sales, the capacity consumption as well as the capacity available for all critical resource, have to prepared for that particular time horizon. The initial horizon could be a typical day, like most of the analyses concerning Daily Bread, a week, month or a year.

As some decisions might have an impact on longer or later time horizons it could happen that decisions that passed the initial time horizon check would have to be re-checked for a different time-frame. For every such meeting and timeframe both the current Sales Profile and Capacity Profile must be prepared and calculated by the supporting software tool. During the meeting, some of the data might need to be changed and then, the whole state must be re-calculated.

The total OE for the time period, covering all the costs required for the baseline Sales Profile, should be entered by the CFO or an experience delegate. The supporting software only calculates the ΔOE for additional capacity.

An example of a reference Sales Profile for one month, with just six T-generators is shown in Figure A.1.

And the monthly Reference Capacity Profile for the same example is illustrated in Figure A.2.

The rightmost column in the Sales Profile includes the forecast of the sales in units. Producing all those products for sale only requires 75% of the available capacity of the most loaded resource (MB). This, of course, leaves very big opportunities for further sales, for which all the additional T would go directly to the bottom line.

The description of the data elements required to produce the Sales Profile and Capacity Profile are given here:

	S.No	T-Generator	Description	Orginal	Δ Price/Unit	Δ TVC	Throughput/Unit	Total Throughput	Original	Δ Sales Qty
Existing T-Generator (6 items)										
I	1	TA1			350.00	0.00	240.00	13,920.00		58
I	2	TA2			400.00	0.00	170.00	15,130.00		89
I	3	TB1			275.00	0.00	165.00	18,315.00		111
I	4	TB2			325.00	0.00	215.00	24,080.00		112
I	5	TC1			350.00	0.00	160.00	12,800.00		80
I	6	TC2			400.00	0.00	210.00	23,520.00		112

Pricing Data (Scenario :Basic , Decision :Basic) — Search by T-Generator — Profit Details

Figure A.1   Reference sales profile composed of just six T-generators.

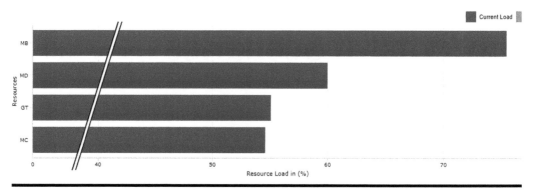

Figure A.2   Capacity profile for the baseline reference profile.

Describing the Critical Resources Available Capacity

The data requirements start with defining the critical resources. Suppose four resources, R1, R2, R3, and R4, are defined as critical. R1 might be specific group of skilled people. R2 could be a work center that consists of four similar but not necessarily identical machines. R3 is a dedicated production line producing a specific product family and R4 is an oven.

Each resource has limited available capacity over a certain period of time. The most common unit of capacity is a unit of time, like a minute, a millisecond or an hour. Sometimes, it is easier to describe the capacity as maximum quantity which can be produced per period of time. For instance, an oven could be broadly defined as being able to heat treat 200 units of standard products in an hour. When that oven works 16 hours a day, then the daily capacity limit for that resource is 3,200.[1] When you require full capacity for a whole month, assuming 25 working days, then the capacity limit for the oven is 80,000.[2]

There is no requirement that all resources use the same units of capacity. The software allows you to think in terms that are most easily comprehensible in your particular situation!

However, there is a requirement to define capacity limits for each resource. Suppose R2, the work-center with four machines, also works 16 hours a day. To define the capacity requirements for a unit of product, assume you want use minutes. So, the number of minutes in 25 working days a

---

[1] 200 units per hour × 16 hours

[2] 3,200 per day × 25 days

month for four machines is: 96,000 machine-minutes.[3] Suppose you have, on average, 50 hours of maintenance per month for all four machines, then you should remove 3,000 machine-minutes[4] from the capacity, reducing it to 93,000 machine-minutes.

Setup is a complicating factor. You might roughly assume, setup is about 15% of the total capacity required and this is a good enough approximation of reality. Remember that you cannot be precise no matter how you try and you cover for the imprecision by maintaining protective capacity – meaning you never plan for the full 93,000 machine-minutes of R2. You'll have to decide on the maximum utilization of R2 that you allow to be planned without having to use overtime or any other means of temporarily adding capacity. This is how you plan, by providing at least a certain percentage of protective capacity which is required to overcome the variety of fluctuations, like temporary peaks, breakdowns, missing materials and quality problems.

The alternative for considering setups is to assume all the 93,000 machine-minutes are available for planning but including the setup time for every product using that particular capacity. This could be done by allocating the setup time to every product unit produced, based on the average batch size of that product.

So, for every critical resource you need to define its capacity limit using the units you decide are the most appropriate.

Suppose you have a profile of capacity limits, as show in Table A.1.

Means for Increasing Capacity

Every means of increasing capacity has a cost. It requires increasing the capacity of, at least, one resource. In some cases, the capacity of several resources are increased at the same time. For instance, outsourcing of a whole product line would increase the capacity of all the critical resources that take part in the production of those products. Overtime of an operator might allow utilization of several machines.

Table A.1   Example Capacity Limits Profile

Critical resource	Monthly limit	Unit definition
R1 – Specially skilled manpower group that deals with manual work required for some products	20,000	Man-hours. There are 100 people, working 8 hours a day each (two shifts, occasionally three shifts), 25 days per month
R2 – Work center	93,000	Machine-minutes
R3 – Dedicated production line	2,160 million	Milliseconds. The production line is working 24 hours per day, 25 working days per month
R4 – Oven for heat-treat	80,000	Standard products treated per month

---

[3] 16 hours per day × 25 days × 60 minutes per hour × 4 machines
[4] 50 hours of maintenance per month × 60 minutes per hour

Increasing the capacity of R2 by one hour on one machine might require three operators for that hour. The financial impact, the ΔOE, is the cost of overtime of three man-hours, unless the cost of maintenance truly depends on every hour the machine is active. Most of the time, the cost of energy during the overtime is ignored but, when it seems significant, it should be included too. An hour of overtime may be the minimum overtime that can practically be used. If overtime can be delivered in minutes, adjust the unit of measure to minutes. Of course, we might need to increase the capacity of the work center by twelve hours during the month. If so, you need twelve times the basic unit of capacity increase.

Suppose, the overall cost, the ΔOE of one additional hour of one machine within the work center considering the overtime expense of three people plus the cost of energy, is $180. That one hour increases the capacity of the work center by 0.0645% of a month.[5]

Every possible means of capacity increase should be modeled to provide management with the full spectrum of possibilities to respond to optional demand. The modeling should include the minimum unit of capacity increase and the maximum possible units of capacity increase during the time horizon.

Products – Outputs from Production

The basic data for every product are the associated Truly Variable Cost (TVC) and the capacity requirements from the critical resources list.

The TVC at the product level is mainly the cost of materials. Part of the modeling is to decide how to enter the cost of materials. Is it the price that was actually paid for the materials or the price of buying the materials now? Using moving averages to calculate the cost of materials is usually good enough.

The necessary data, which is sometimes difficult to get, is good enough numbers on the capacity requirements for every product that is actively sold. Certainly products that are no longer in demand or their demand is so low that their capacity consumption is negligible need not be included in the analysis.

Capacity figures are stated in the same units as defined for the resource. For instance, Product A1 might require $2 of materials, 2 hours from R1, 85 minutes from R2, 0 from R3 (not produced by the production line) and 2.4 units of R4.

The basic capability of the software to calculate the Capacity Profile, based on the Sales Profile providing all the typical monthly sales, is a necessary tool to establishing good enough total capacity consumption numbers and the ratio of the predicted consumption to the total available capacity. The algorithm itself is trivial; the only obstacle is to calculate changes fast enough to provide immediate answers to questions that are raised during a meeting. The resulting typical load of the critical resources can be roughly compared to reality to validate whether there is a reasonable match. When this process is repeated month after month it should enhance the validation of the raw capacity data.

---

[5] (1 hour × 60 minutes per hour)/93,000 machine-minutes

T-generators' Data

Naturally this data set goes through frequent changes.

Every T-generator is built from one price for a product or products along with various quantities. Thus, every T-generator defines the specific products and the quantities per unit of the T-generator.

Every T-generator has a price and a forecast of its sales over the period management is considering. When the pessimistic and optimistic scenarios are discussed, the forecasts are normally quite different, reflecting an evaluation of both assessments.

Another data element for every T-generator is ΔTVC, the change in TVC means the amount on top of the baseline TVC stated for the raw materials included in that T-generator. There is a need to provide the flexibility to add elements to the T-generator that don't come from operations but are, rather, sourced from a supplier. For instance, when the shipping costs are part of the deal, then this is an additional TVC required to make the sale. A T-generator could be a whole package of products sent to the client. Another example is a purchased item added to a package as a bonus.

Changes and Additions to the Current Sales Profile and Capacity Profile

Every proposed idea means introducing some additions or changes to the sales or to the capacity or both. The additions require the same data as above. Changes can be made just to the relevant data fields within the applicable structure. The changes and additions and their impact on the sales and capacity profiles should be stored separately from the original reference Sales and Capacity Profiles. This allows comparison of the results and keeps a good log of the steps considered during the meeting.

Modeling Issues with Job Shops

Job shops are characterized by most orders being unique according to the detailed specifications and needs of the client. Job shops frequently have very flexible flow, where the sequence of the operations is highly variable.

As an example, JJS Corp. is a job shop offering a wide range of services for metal working. The company has available capacity of the following work centers:

Engineering, CNC1, CNC2, Sawing, Grinding, Heat-Treat, Welding, Plating, and Assembly.

Every order is built from materials that are either supplied by the client or purchased according to client directives. A planned order contains estimated hours of work of the relevant work centers. These estimations dictate the price of the order: cost of materials plus hours of every required work-center at the price of each particular work center plus the cost of shipping the finished product to the client.

Every client has its own characteristic orders. So, while the price per hour of each work center is fixed for each client, some clients get a certain percentage discount.

The JJS Corp. price list, per hour for each work center is given in Table A.2.

JJS tries hard to get additional customers. But, do they know which types of projects yield more Throughput without consuming too much capacity that might be required for more profitable orders?

Modeling such an environment, where every product is different from the rest, calls for looking at the building blocks of every order – hours of the resources. Suppose we model

Table A.2 List Price per hour for JJS Corp. Work Centers

Work Center	Price per hour
Engineering	100
CNC1	90
CNC2	110
Sawing	75
Grinding	75
Heat Treat	50
Welding	75
Plating	85
Assembly	50

products not as one time outputs detailed by the specific order but as hours of each of the above work centers. This way every order is translated into the estimated list of hours from each work center and that list defines the products that go into the specific T-generator, which is the customer's entire order. This approach massively simplifies the modeling of such a job shop, which should actually sell capacity on each of its various resources, rather than predefined products.

The real difficulty of modeling a job shop is the infinite variety of potential T-generators, because almost every order is different. Coming up with a typical sales profile can be simply based on actual orders received plus the baseline from the previous period. Predicting the impact of a marketing move, like winning a significant new customer wanting a different type of products seems complicated.

A simplifying idea is to categorize types of orders based on their capacity requirements from the work centers. Then, categories of orders that require similar capacity pattern from the work centers can be lumped together as a template. You can reasonably assume that averaging the number of hours per work center for the category, you will have a good enough approximation of the total Throughput and the capacity requirements of the key resources. The generic approach of creating pessimistic and optimistic scenarios helps to cover the range of natural variation between orders within a common template. This is close enough to forecast sales and understand the capacity required for the overall predicted demand.

Here is a simple example where all the orders for the above job shop, JJS Corp., were divided into three different templates, plus three more with the same capacity requirements but with prices that are 8% lower, for customers who are offered a special deal.

The current monthly sales of JJS Corp is shown in Figure A.3.

Based on the predicted sales quantities the Capacity Profile looks as shown in Figure A.4.

What can JJS do to improve their situation?

Right now, any additional order should be welcome, because even the weakest link, the Engineering work center, has excess capacity, at least until the 90% limit for protective capacity line is crossed.

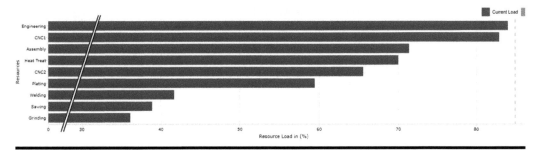

		S.No	T-Generator	Description	Orginal | Δ Price/Unit	Δ TVC	Throughput/Unit	Total Throughput	Original | Δ Sales Qty
Existing T-Generator (6 items)									
I	1	Template1			1,820.00	840.00	980.00	9,800.00	10
I	2	Template2			1,890.00	1,000.00	890.00	10,680.00	12
I	3	Template3			3,595.00	750.00	2,845.00	14,225.00	5
I	4	TemplateX1			1,674.40	840.00	834.40	25,032.00	30
I	5	TemplateX2			1,738.80	1,000.00	738.80	5,171.60	7
I	6	TemplateX3			3,307.40	750.00	2,557.40	12,787.00	5

Pricing Data (Scenario :Basic , Decision :Basic) — Search by T-Generator

Profit Details

	Throughput (T)	Operating Expense (OE)	Profit
Current	77,695.60	60,000.00	17,695.60
New	77,695.60	60,000.00	17,695.60
Delta	0.00	0.00	0.00

Figure A.3: JJS corp monthly sales profile.

Figure A.4 Capacity profile for JJS Corp.

But, some care needs to be given to the second most loaded work center: CNC1, where its protective capacity line is 85%.

All the rest have much more capacity, so selling more of their capacity is absolutely beneficial, until one or more work centers also penetrate into the protective capacity. We assume there are possibilities for Capacity Buffers but they were not modeled into the simple JJS Corp. example. Tables A.3, A.4 and A.5 specify the data required for building all the templates.

Table A.3   Data from which Template1 and TemplateX1 Are Built

Work Center	Standard hours
Engineering	7
CNC1	4
CNC2	1
Sawing	3
Welding	3
Assembly	4

Table A.4   Data from which Template2 and TemplateX2 Are Built

Work Center	Standard hours
Engineering	6
CNC1	1
CNC2	2
Welding	5
Plating	3
Heat Treat	4
Assembly	3

Table A.5   Data from which Template3 and TemplateX3 Are Built

Work Center	Standard hours
Engineering	6
CNC1	2
CNC2	4
Sawing	5
Grinding	8
Heat Treat	5
Welding	7
Plating	5
Assembly	4

Appendix B

Specifics on What Metrics to Use and When they are Applicable

We have discussed metrics in general and conceptually within the book, even devoted a short chapter to the subject. However, what we have presented herein is ultimately worthless, if not accepted by the people who work at the companies where the ideas presented here are first tried and then used.

Since all your authors are what might be characterized by some as "old people," we have seen a few things. We have observed that adding something new in the thinking arena inevitably means purging something existing, because behavior is more determined by habit than most of us would like to admit. Just because you think something is the right thing to do, doesn't mean you'll do it. Building new habits takes time. The amount of time required can be reduced, if there is enough emotion supporting the desired new habit – just a hint.

Dr. Goldratt often said,

> **"Tell me how you'll measure me and I'll tell you how I'll behave."**

Managers in all companies want good performance from their people. In order to see that they are getting what they want, they use measurements. Therefore, measurements are already in place. Most were put into place long ago – long enough to become habits that you no longer think about much. Furthermore, as mentioned in Chapter 20, they were undoubtedly based on the conventional cost-focused local efficiency mindset. That means your habitual metrics may be dangerous!

Unless you are already getting results like we have described in this book, you should consider removing your old measurements and choosing new ones. Otherwise, nothing will change – people won't follow you. If you change everything at once, you will have thrown the whole company into a Transition Period of some chaos. Because, the first thing every person does when a change is suggested is to run a simple test. They will ask themselves, "Is this change good for me?" If the answer is affirmative, they may begin to really listen and actually consider changing. If you leave inappropriate metrics in place, the answer to the first question will be, "No!" Consequently, your old metrics must go but ease them out. First show a big improvement that worked despite making a metric look worse. Then, agree with everyone to change that one. Show a willingness to open a dialogue about your company's measurements. Make it possible for your coworkers to reconsider them.

This Appendix shows what you should be moving towards and specifically what you should measure based on your company's financial situation.

Metrics

Eli Goldratt expresses the goal of a company as being "ever-flourishing." Henry Camp calls it "thriving and growing." Ravi Gilani[1] calls the goal "the 4Ms – Making More and More Money." They are different words for the same thing.

Once the goal is known, we can begin to think about appropriate metrics.

We have already introduced a few terms, all of which you apply holistically. Throughput or T is the flow of money that the company has a chance to turn into net profit. Operating Expenses or OE is the flow of that T back out of the company that is needed to maintain the capacity necessary to produce the T in the first place. Lastly, Investment or I is the pool of money that the purchased capacity converts into T.

A Simple Pictorial Financial Model

This is the first time we have used the word "pool" in the book and it refers to I. Think of I as a series of pools of money, representing Cash, Accounts Receivables, Inventory and Fixed Assets. If that money weren't invested, there wouldn't be any inventory to sell, no Accounts Receivable soon to be collected, no buildings from which to operate, no equipment within the buildings to accomplish work and so on.

From the point of view of the owners, the pool of investment seems smaller, because it is offset by or, if you prefer, leveraged by debts, like supplier invoices on terms that haven't yet been paid, lines of credit, term loans, and even the work provided by employees for which you haven't yet paid them. From the point of view of the company, which is how we think of it throughout the book, I is all the assets of the company.

The diagram in Figure B.1 was created to explain the concepts of flows and pools to non-financial people. The PowerPoint presentation linked in a footnote early in Chapter 15, builds this diagram step by step. However, let us explain it now.

Every company was started with an investment from investors in cash and property. From there, the cash was spent to invest in inventory. To keep things simple, the light green bucket represents inventory defined broadly to include furniture, fixtures, equipment, computers, buildings and land as well as raw materials, work-in-process and finished goods ready for sale. They all qualify to be called inventory because they can be sold and will be sold some day.

When inventory is sold, it "flows" along the yellow pipe. Stock or TVC shifts into a (usually) wider green pipe as it becomes sales. The green pipe is wider to show that the TVC was inflated to some degree as it was billed at selling price.[2]

---

[1] This chapter is dedicated to Ravi Gilani, who was mentioned earlier in the book in Chapter 15. Mr. Gilani is a TOC consultant in India. Much of the material in this chapter stems from his work and teachings. It is our hope that readers will benefit from our sharing his good ideas.

[2] If the green sales pipe is narrower than the yellow TVC pipe, that means you have decided that getting some money back for the inventory is preferable to having the cash it represents trapped in inventory. You take such an action when you don't expect the inventory to turn into cash with positive T any time soon.

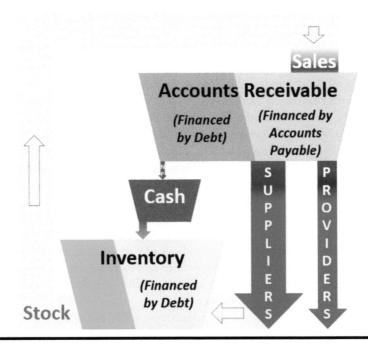

Figure B.1   The flows and pools of money in any for-profit company.

To remain competitive, most companies don't demand cash on delivery or in advance. So, their sales flow into a pool called Accounts Receivable. There sales languish until the customer pays.

Practically, payments are received every day and bills are paid every day. Therefore, Figure B.1 shows Accounts Receivable funding suppliers for TVC and providers for OE. Any money left over, trickles into the cash pool in the form of net profits.

$$Sales - TVC - OE = Net\ Profit$$

In a final nod to the owner's point of view, you can see in Figure B.1 that some of the pools of money are solid colors (Cash and part of Inventory). Solid colors indicate outright ownership. Pastel colors show the portions that are financed by some form of debt, identified parenthetically.

The relative proportions between the pools and flows of money will be different for your specific company. This particular example is for companies like importers, distributors and commodity manufacturers who have large inventory investments, more TVC than OE and a small net profit return on sales.

Enough with the diagram. Perhaps you can use it to explain the holistic financial aspects of the business to your co-workers who don't know accounting well.

Context for Metrics

There are better and worse times to calculate certain metrics. We stated that making more and more money is the goal. Is net profit always the prime metric, the most important thing to measure? No.

Ravi Gilani suggest there are six different levels of financial health and each of them demands a different prime metric to manage properly.

At all levels, he also recommends less than a handful of secondary metrics. Note that the secondary metrics are not something to maximize or minimize. They are things that management should watch to avoid being blindsided by knowable impending problems.

When driving your car through an area known for tight speed control by the police, the speedometer would be the primary indicator. This does not mean that the car shouldn't be stopped and checked out if secondary metrics get out of control, for examples, the coolant temperature gauge exceeds its limits or oil pressure drops to zero. However, these gauges might fluctuate within a range and not be the cause for any action at all. It works the same for the secondary metrics.

Here's a suggestion. Assign each of the secondary metrics to somebody in the organization. It is not at all necessary that it be a manager, in fact, it is better if they are not, since managers who are helping their company improve generically suffer from a lack of management attention. Train each person in what their one metric means and how signals trouble. Empower them to sound an alarm, if their secondary metric starts to head out of bounds. It helps involve more people in following the metrics. It saves harried managers from one more responsibility, while giving them an important role as a company protector. People love it. They like that you trust them. They like doing their part. They like making a difference.

You'll smile from ear to ear when the receptionist comes and pokes her head into the top management meeting where you are all deciding on the pessimistic and optimistic scenarios for some move. Instead of announcing an important call, she says, "Our Throughput percentage has been falling over the last four months. It was just a tiny bit in the first three months, so I didn't mention it, but this month it is down a half a percentage point. You asked me to inform you, remember?"

What Should be Measured and When?

Figure B.2 summarizes our advice about metrics required for different contexts. Following the table, we explain what you might need to know to properly use it.

Financial Level 1: Unable to Meet Financial Commitments

At Level 1, the company is cash constrained. What does that mean exactly? The company can no longer afford input materials or services required meet customer demand. Lack of necessary inputs means that the company's delivery performance will suffer. Bad enough delivery performance results in declining sales. Lower sales result in bigger losses, which further erodes cash. When cash goes negative, the jig is up. The company will soon be forced into bankruptcy by its creditors. Unless there is some new idea that gets court approval, it won't be a reorganization, it will be a liquidation. Assets will be sold or auctioned with the proceeds going to the creditors. If there is anything left, usually not, the remainder goes to the owners.

At Level 1, your primary metric is Free Cash Flow. It isn't that net profits have ceased to be the goal. Profit is still the target at which the company is aiming but it is currently of secondary importance to survival. If you don't survive, it doesn't matter that you earned a profit.

Free Cash Flow means receiving more money every period than what flows out. The best way to make good decisions to protect free cash flow is using the formula for Cash Velocity, which considers when you will get the cash as a priority over how profitable the deal is. The measurement

Constraint Identification:

Operations: Overall Equipment Effectiveness (OEE) > 90% for some Equipment on 24hrx365day basis AND On-Time-in-Full (OTIF) <95%

Market: > 50% World Market Share	Orders: > 95% OTIF	Cash: OEE < 90%, OTIF < 95% AND Shortages due to late payment

	Financial Level	Constraint	Recommended Metrics to Share					Measurements to Ignore
1	Late pay interrupts flow	Cash	Free Cash Flow	Months of Survival Cash	Overdue Receivables	Overdue Payables		Sales, T, NP, OE savings, OEE, Any ratios
2	Not making Net Profits	Orders	Net Profit	Free Cash Flow	On Time in Full	Protective Capacity		Sales, T, OE savings, OEE, manpower productivity
		Operations	Net Profit	Free Cash Flow	On Time in Full	Overall Equip. Eff.		Sales, T, OE savings, non-CCR equip. util., manpower prod.
3	Net Profits fluctuating	Orders	Net Profit Growth	Free Cash Flow	On Time in Full	Protective Capacity	T%	Sales, T, OE savings, OEE, manpower productivity
		Operations	Net Profit Growth	Free Cash Flow	On Time in Full	Overall Equip. Eff.		Sales, T, OE savings, non-CCR equip. util., manpower prod.
4	Net Profits continually increasing	Orders	Growth in T	Free Cash Flow	On Time in Full	Protective Capacity	Operational Productivity	Sales, T, OE savings, OEE, manpower productivity
		Operations	Operational Productivity	Free Cash Flow	On Time in Full	Overall Equip. Eff.		Sales, T, OE savings, non-CCR equip. util., manpower prod.
5	NP, ROI & ROCE continually increasing	Orders	Capital Productivity	Operational Productivity	On Time in Full	Protective Capacity	Growth in T	Sales, T, OE savings, OEE, manpower productivity
		Operations	Capital Productivity	Operational Productivity	On Time in Full	Overall Equip. Eff.	Growth in T	Sales, T, OE savings, non-CCR equip. util., manpower prod.
6	NP, ROI, ROCE & FCF cont. increasing	Any	Continue current measures without any changes					Outside Advice

Figure B.2 Recommended metrics and when they are pertinent.

of cash velocity is crucial to the life of the organization at Level 1 and may be nice to have at other financial levels. This parameter helps in making correct decisions on:

- accepting orders at lower prices
- accepting different credit terms
- procuring raw materials at different prices and credit terms
- setting minimum order quantities
- determining modes of transportation and
- determining production batch quantities

Beware, the results can seem counterintuitive.

The formula for Cash Velocity is:

$$Cash\,Velocity\,per\,month = \left(\frac{Sales}{TVC}\right)^{\frac{1}{n}} - 1$$

$$n = Cash - to - Cash\,cycle\,time\,in\,months$$

Our apologies, if you don't like math. Our advice, if this is speaking to you, is don't ever allow your company to get to Level 1! The good news is, this is the hardest math in the whole book. Let's work through a completely unrealistic example to give you a sense about alternatives you might ignore but shouldn't, when your company is starved for cash.

Example: You have two suppliers for a non-stock raw material. You require 100 units to fill a customer's order. The customer pays in 45 days. The sales from this order, should you manage to fill it, is $1,000. In addition to the raw materials you require $150 of other TVC. Here are the differences between the two suppliers in price and terms.

- Supplier A charges $1 per unit and has you on COD terms
- Supplier B charges $4 per unit and offers 30 day payment terms

Let's apply the Cash Velocity formula above to Supplier A first. Sales is $1,000 in both cases. For Supplier A, TVC is $250.[3] Now you need to calculate n, the cash-to-cash cycle time in months. The customer pays in 45 days. That is 1 ½ months. The supplier must be paid on delivery. So, assuming you can make the order right away and ship it, your cash-to-cash cycle time from the moment you pay the supplier until you get paid is 1 ½ months. Substitute these three values into the formula above and you have:

$$Cash\ Velocity\ per\ month\ for\ Supplier\ A = \left(\frac{\$1,000}{\$250}\right)^{1/1.5} - 1$$

$$Cash\ Velocity\ per\ month\ for\ Supplier\ A = (4)^{2/3} - 1$$

$$Cash\ Velocity\ per\ month\ for\ Supplier\ A = 2.52 - 1$$

$$Cash\ Velocity\ per\ month\ for\ Supplier\ A = 152\%$$

Let's repeat for Supplier B, who you probably haven't bought from recently, since they charge so much more. Luckily for you, they aren't yet aware that they should have you on COD too. TVC in this case is $550,[4] more than double using Supplier A! To calculate n, the cash-to-cash cycle, it is the same 1 ½ months to get paid but, with this supplier, you can subtract the 1 month you are given to pay them. Whatever you do, don't pay them late. You may need them again! Therefore, n is half a month.

$$Cash\ Velocity\ per\ month\ for\ Supplier\ B = \left(\frac{\$1,000}{\$550}\right)^{1/0.5} - 1$$

$$Cash\ Velocity\ per\ month\ for\ Supplier\ B = (1.818181)^2 - 1$$

$$Cash\ Velocity\ per\ month\ for\ Supplier\ A = 3.31 - 1$$

$$Cash\ Velocity\ per\ month\ for\ Supplier\ A = 231\%$$

As weird as it seems, if, and only if, cash constrained, you prefer the deal that increases your cash faster, even though it lowers ΔNP from $750 to $450! This proves that, if your goal is net profits, you must place Cash Velocity and survival above profits until you can graduate out of Level 1 to a higher financial level.

If you need a formula to help you calculate n, the Cash-to-Cash cycle time, here it is:

$$n = \frac{\left(Average\ Inventory - Average\ A/P\right)}{Average\ TVC\ per\ Month} + \frac{Average\ Accounts\ Receivable}{Average\ Sales\ per\ Month}$$

---

[3] 100 units of the raw material × $1 per unit + $150 of other TVC
[4] 100 units of the raw material × $4 per unit + $150 of other TVC

For companies that have settled into Level 1, there hasn't been enough money to pay suppliers on time. At some point they demand COD. When they do, remember, *Average A/P* is 0.

There are three other holistic metrics which are applicable at financial Level 1 and secondary to Free Cash Flow (See Figure B.1).

• **Overdue Payables**	This should be shrinking, after using the cash velocity formula to prioritize decisions for a while.
• **Overdue Receivables**	This is your source of funding. Stay on it. Collect in person, if need be; nobody does that these days, it may shake some money out of a slow paying customer. Camp's Law is never more crucial than at Level 1. "When in doubt, choose the less efficient route." Do whatever it takes to keep A/R collected on time.
• **Survival Cash**	This is how long you have to live. If you are following the advice above, you should see the company gaining months of life.

Let's dig into this a little more, shall we?

Let's use an example here as well. The company gets paid in one month and has to pay their suppliers in one month (it hasn't gotten too bad yet). If the inventory on hand is two months' worth, for this company, n equals 2.[5] A safe amount of survival cash is n times the expected monthly OE of $2 million, then safe survival cash is $4 million. Oops! They are nearly out of cash. The $200,000 they have in the bank is only 3 days of survival cash. Note: it is fair to consider any credit available to the company towards the safe cash target. At Level 1, however, the amount of credit banks are willing to extend is zero. If they have outstanding loans to a Level 1 company, they will be seeking to recover them.

Corrective actions to escape Level 1 and build a safe amount of Survival Cash:

■ Reduce inventory. TOC Replenishment is an excellent way to both improve availability, improving on time, in-full deliveries to customers, recovering sales that were previously lost. Simultaneously, it typically reduces inventory investments by one third to one half.

■ Collect A/R, use top executives as collection agents, if necessary. Offer customers a discount for quicker payment. This will reduce T and net profits but if you check the option using the Cash Velocity formula, you will find that it improves your situation.

■ Stop taking discounts from suppliers. This gives you longer to pay but is almost always already a moot point for companies at Level 1. Most have no more credit with their suppliers, because they didn't have the money to take discounts in the first place.

Every dollar of working capital that is saved is a dollar more in cash. If your bank still lends you money (you are lucky, if they do) your borrowing base report, where you calculate your collateral, will drop. That means you will be able to borrow less but you will have gained more cash than you will have lost in borrowing potential.

---

[5] ($5.7 million of Average Inventory − $2.85 million in Average A/P)/$2.85 million in TVC per month + $4.75 million Average A/R/$4.75 million of Sales per month.

Table B.1 A Company in Trouble - Financial Level 1

	This month
Sales	$4,750,000
TVC	2,850,000
T	1,900,000
OE	2,000,000
Net Profit	(100,000)
Cash	200,000
A/R	4,750,000
Inventory	5,700,000
A/P	2,850,000

Let's calculate what the poor company in Table B.1 would have to do.

First, they use TOC Replenishment to cut inventory to one month's worth instead of two. That reduces inventory by $2.85 million, which accumulates in cash. This also reduces their cash-to-cash time to one month.

Recalculating the safe amount of survival cash is now one month's OE or $2 million. So, this effort is enough, for now.

Now, there is plenty of money with which to buy the inventory necessary to welcome their lost customer back into the fold. They can stop being harried and feeling panicked. As, they feel more comfortable, they can start taking supplier discounts, one by one. They may choose to offer a discount to chronic slow paying customers. That way, if those customers stop taking the discounts, they will have a good idea that those customers may be approaching Level 1 themselves.

Level 1 is a special case where cash is truly a constraint. As such, it requires the special explanation above.

The remaining levels are much simpler and more straightforward to explain. You just need to know how to calculate the metrics properly and the logic behind changing them subtly as financial progress is made.

When a company is more financially healthy than Level 1, there are then two possible cases. You can't be constrained by cash or you'd still be at Level 1. Now, you are either constrained by a lack of orders from the market or you are internally constrained to the point that you can't fill all the orders customers are willing to place with you. (Technically, there is a third possible case but it is quite rare. That case is being market constrained. In other words, you already have over half of the world market for the products you sell and that very success constrains your growth. Unlikely.)

Let's take the orders constrained scenario first, since it is much more common. A company is orders constrained if its on time, in full (OTIF) delivery rate is consistently greater than 95%. This shows that operations can meet the current demand.

You are constrained by your operations when, even though supplier payments are on time and raw materials are consistently available more than 95% of the time, OTIF delivery is consistently worse that 95%.

Financial Level 2: Meeting All Financial Commitments But Not Profitable

At Level 2, you're losing money but not yet out of cash.

Primary metric for Level 2: **Net Profit**

There, are you happy? At Level 2, regardless of the constraint, the main thing you want to focus on is adding profits. The reason is, you are losing money. Anything you can think of to add profits – do it, to the extent that you have enough bandwidth and capacity. Like Level 1, there are only three secondary metrics. Everything else should not be measured and especially not shared with the staff. The first two of these secondary metrics is the same regardless of whether the company is internally or orders constrained.

Secondary Metrics for Level 2:

- **On time, in full** percentage (OTIF)
- **Free Cash Flow**

We have discussed OTIF and Free Cash Flow before now. It is time to get precise on how to measure them.

$$On\ time,\ In\ full = \frac{Orders\ shipped\ on\ time\ and\ in-full}{Orders\ shipped}$$

$$Free\ Cash\ Flow = Profit + Working\ Capital\ reduction$$

Looking at the Free Cash Flow formula, by now you are onto the fact that Profit is T - OE, for the whole company. Working Capital is reduced when there is a drop in Accounts Receivable, a drop in Inventory or an increase in Accounts Payable. When Free Cash Flow is positive, cash will be increasing month after month. You can see that assigning somebody manage Free Cash Flow will ensure that you don't slip to Level 1 without warnings.

The last secondary metric for Level 2 depends on the company's constraint.

Orders Constrained	Operations Constrained
• **Protective Capacity**	**Overall Equipment Effectiveness**

Protective capacity is important for companies with internal capacity at Level 2 to monitor, because you'll want a warning before the company's constraint shifts. Allowing the constraint to change by surprise is bound to cause chaos. Moreover, when the constraint changes, all the rules of the company which were enacted to get the most out of the constraint and subordinate to those decisions must immediately change. People would have to change their habits. They even have to change habits of which they are unaware. It is difficult. There will be a Transition Period of some higher degree of chaos. Even when worthwhile, changing constraints shouldn't be undertaken lightly and certainly not by blindly. It is so much easier to monitor and do nothing until one resource begins to be too heavily loaded. Before it happens, you can hire someone new or buy a new machine or invest in some more inventory – whatever it takes, even though you are losing money.

Overall Equipment Effectiveness[6] (OEE) is a term in common use in manufacturing. In this case, you are looking at the most loaded resource for the metric. Problems will become obvious long before this resource is loaded close to 100%. Recall, one piece of equipment or a resource can be loaded more than the others, as long as the others have enough capacity to catch up after an interruption. That is, the other resources are less loaded than the weakest link. Again, an appropriate warning level is when any resource is loaded above 90% OEE. In most circumstances, that resource will limit the T the company can produce.

Financial Level 3: Meeting All Financial Commitments, Not Losing Money but Profits are Fluctuating

At Level 3, you're making money but profits are not consistently rising. You make $500,000 one month, then $600,000 the next and $200,000 the month after that. Most companies are stuck at this financial level.

Ravi Gilani shares the results of a study on 3,000 companies in the Bombay Stock Exchange. Only 23 of those companies had profits that rose every year over a period of ten years. That means that, technically, 99.2% of the companies in the Bombay exchange are stuck at Level 3. Practically, there will be another handful who grew nine out of ten years with one year that had a small decline. Still, the point is clear, whether the correct statistic is 95%, 98%, or 99.2%. The vast majority of companies get stuck at Level 3. This is not limited to India either. The same pattern exists in any group of companies anywhere in the world.

There is a persistent notion that companies "mature" and then decline. Here is a quote from an article in Science Daily: "As companies reach maturity, their sales tend to level off[7]." There are reasons that companies begin to decline, however, declines are not an inevitability. Think of Eaton, DuPont and IBM. Together these companies are over 400 years old and not one is less than a century. When did these companies' sales "level off?"

Primary metric for Level 3: **Net Profit Growth** or ΔNP

We are hoping for bigger and bigger increases in profit, as time goes on. This situation is what Eli Goldratt called the Red Curve. (See Figure B.3).

Notice that red curve has a steeper slope with every change in time. At Level 3, this is what you're shooting for and your prime metric. If the change in net profit this period over last is 1%, subsequently you should no longer be satisfied, even if profits rise but by 1% or less. At Level 2, you were happy if profits rose. Now, at Level 3, that is no longer good enough. See Table B.2 for an example.

For this to happen, you simply need to grow T faster than OE. Notice that between "This month" and "Next month," the ΔT was a $40,000 increase. Then, the ΔT between "Next month" and the "The month after," was again a $40,000 increase. This wouldn't have been enough, unless ΔOE declined but, instead, ΔOE was $0, keeping ΔNP the same, month over month. This $40,000 increase in net profit would have satisfied the prime metric back at Level 2 but it is now a danger signal of slowing growth, portending a slip backwards.

---

[6] https://en.wikipedia.org/wiki/Overall_equipment_effectiveness
[7] https://www.sciencedaily.com/releases/2015/04/150401132856.htm

Results with Stability

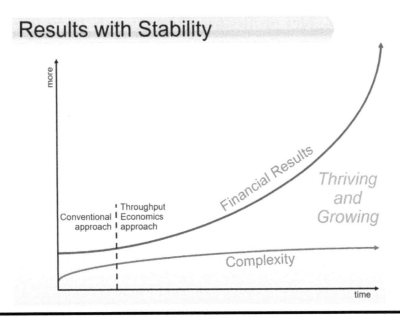

Figure B.3   Throughput Economics red curve financial results.

Table B.2   Examples of the Change in Net Profit Improving and Deteriorating

	This month	*Next month*	*The month after*	*The month after that*
Sales	$8,000,000	$8,100,000	$8,200,000	$8,400,000
TVC	4,800,000	4,860,000	4,920,000	5,040,000
T	3,200,000	3,240,000	3,280,000	3,360,000
OE	2,000,000	2,000,000	2,000,000	2,040,000
Net Profit	1,200,000	1,240,000	1,280,000	1,320,000
ΔNP		40,000	40,000	40,000
ΔNP%		3.3%	3.2%	3.1%

Slowing growth is a precursor to fluctuating profits. Much better, if profits keep squirting ahead by larger amounts, as shown in the Red Curve in Figure B.3.

The secondary metrics remain the same as in Level 2, with one addition and only in the case where your company is constrained by its operations. **T%** or Throughput as a percentage of sales.

Let's think for a moment about why a company that can't fill all its orders and has fluctuating profits would want to add T% as a fourth secondary metric. Now that profits are back, it behooves the company to be a little more choosey. It can't run everything anyway. Of course, the company could add capacity to its weakest link. However, that is Focusing Step 4 – "Elevate the constraint(s)." Before spending the money to do that, we have Focusing Step 2 – "Decide how to exploit the constraint." Your decision in this case is: "trade out lower T% business for higher T% business, as you can do it without causing ancillary problems."

Financial Level 4: Net profits are Continuously Increasing

At Level 4, you are pretty darn happy. The biggest worry is how to sustain it.

Without the TOC mindset, at some point, orders start coming in a little slower. Later, lost business grows to the point that it offsets new business. This is why we pulled the above footnoted quote "As companies reach maturity, their sales tend to level off" into the book. This phenomenon occurs because, in order to reinvigorate the growth of T, managers are forced to work harder. When they do, they accept greater complexity, such that OE typically grows faster that T. Figure B.4 is a clip from the graph in Figure B.3.

The Red Curve is net profits. The Green Curve is complexity. When the profit and complexity lines are moving closer together there is more stress, more chaos, more OE, diminishing returns and a tendency to slide down the financial levels. When the profit curve outgrows the complexity curve, companies ascend the financial levels.

Only at Level 4 there are there different prime metrics depending on whether your company is constrained by orders or operations.

Primary metric for Level 4:

Orders Constrained	Operations Constrained
• **Growth in T** or ΔT	**Operational Productivity**

The only way to get a company constrained by orders to Level 4 is to get operations and OE under control. There is less need for new OE relative to the T increases that come from every one of your initiatives, because your systems are lined out, trouble free and have protective capacity. You add less complexity as you grow. Once that is the situation (to the right of the dotted line in Figure B.4), the focus becomes how to add more and more T using templated and proven approaches. Therefore, the Prime metric for an orders-constrained company at Level 4 is ΔT.

What if your company is operationally constrained? Well, the question holds the answer. Systems within the company which would have been elevated had it be easy, quick or affordable are the

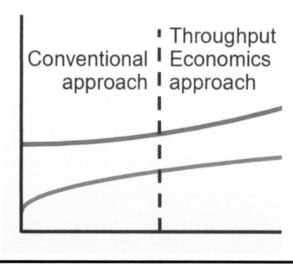

Figure B.4 Showing Complexity Increasing faster than throughput until the Injection of the TOC approach at the vertical dotted line.

limiting factors to taking more orders and generating more T. As you elevate the weakest link, more orders can be filled, increasing the overall Flow of Value, until the next most constrained resource usurps the weakest link title. If this doesn't occur, you have become constrained by orders and will be dealing with a whole new Transition Period in which all the subordination rules must change.

Since operations can't handle all the orders, you want to make the most of the orders you have. This means getting as much T out of the system as possible, obviously. Equally obviously, the prime metric at Level 4 reflects that means of making more and more money. Operational Productivity means getting the most T for the OE spent to produce it. Here is the formula:

$$Operational\ Productivity = \frac{T}{OE}$$

Throughout this book you have read warnings to avoid metrics which are ratios, because they are typically local efficiency metrics that drive employees to improve their silos, too often at the expense of company-wide performance. And, here we suggest a metric that is a ratio! Why?

First and foremost, Operational Productivity is a holistic metric. That is, it applies to the whole company, not a silo, department, customer or product line. Secondly, every company becomes more efficient as it climbs the financial levels. This is because efficiency is a consequence of becoming more effective, not a goal or a number to manipulate.

That doesn't mean that the Operational Productivity (and Capital Productivity, which we introduce next) isn't dangerous. There is a risk that somebody will fiddle with the denominator.[8] In this case, the denominator is OE. OE exists for a purpose – to provide the capacity to convert I into T. The risk is that some bright person, trying to help, will outlaw overtime, one of your Capacity Buffers that should be used when needed to get more through the weakest link. If the OE you spend doesn't provide enough capacity to process all the orders customers place, then why does reducing capacity make sense? There are only two good answers: a) there is capacity in some area that is in surplus to its reasonable protective needs and b) there is capacity that produces T but less T than it costs to maintain that portion of the capacity. If a) or b) apply then, by all means, cut that OE, as long as there are no risks of side effects more damaging than the benefits of the cut. If a) and b) are both false, you better make sure everybody is trained and retrained that they should instead be looking to increase T to make the metric improve.

The rest of the metrics at Level 4, are our same old friends from before and so require no further explanation, other than one thing:

Operational Productivity is useful at this stage, even for companies that are orders constrained. Keep an eye on it. Should its increases slow or start to drop, investigate. While, T% is no longer a secondary metric for companies constrained by their operations. Operational Productivity does a better job of factoring in cost to produce, which is important here.

Financial Level 5: Profits and Return on Capital Employed are Increasing Continuously

This is really good. Profits accumulate into capital over time. However, managers can run out of ideas for investing the accumulated capital, which we cover in Chapter 19. When there is a perception of "too much capital" companies often make distributions or pay dividends.

---

[8] That's the bottom part of the fraction, the part that is divided into the top part or numerator.

We suggest that any company's value is enhanced by using their capital to produce a return. That is why:

At Level 5, the prime metric is **Capital Productivity.**

$$Capital\ Productivity = \frac{T}{I}$$

In the case of the formula above, I requires a precise definition so the reader knows what numbers to substitute for it. We have already made the distinction above between the owner's point of view and the companies. From the owners' perspective, their investment is the money they invested in the company, plus any profits they haven't yet taken out. This is the Net Worth of the company. However, as stated, we are looking from the company's point of view. So, we use all the Assets that the company has on its Balance Sheet. From the company's point of view, these are the investments it deploys to earn its money.

$$Capital\ Productivity = \frac{T}{(Assets)}$$

The rest of the subordinate metrics at Level 5 have already been explained.

Operational Productivity remains but as a secondary metric to watch, in the operations constrained case.

Free Cash Flow dropped off, because if Return on Assets grows, cash should not run low and, if it does, there should be no problem borrowing the needed cash.

Finally, our old friend ΔT returns to keep people focused on the numerator of the Capital Productivity prime metric.

That brings us, at last, to the highest level.

Financial Level 6: Profits and Return on Capital Employed and Free Cash Flow are Increasing Continuously

This is the ultimate. Not only does the company enjoy the ever-improving results of Level 5, it also now throws off cash in surplus to its needs. When appropriate, deploying Focusing Step 4 is easy. The cash is already there. In fact, the company gains more money the faster than it grows. That funds reinvestment, expansion, acquisition and new start-ups.

What to measure at this level? **We don't know.** If you get to Level 6, keep measuring what you think is best, because you must have something special, expertise, experience, intelligence or luck. Keep doing what you are doing, call us and give us some advice!

Summary

We authors were enthusiastic about providing guidance on measurements. The rationale for performance measurements is to have a clearer picture of where the company is now and what it should do to improve.

A problem we see is that performance measurements are used to judge and compare people's performance. We believe this has disastrous results.

This book is about making better decisions. Without pertinent metrics it is too easy to make mistakes and cause damage. These metrics help you make better decisions. Changing them *alone* will almost always produce beneficial results.

Appendix C

List of Figures

Appendix D

List of Tables

Index

Note: *Italicized* page numbers refer to figures, **bold** page numbers refer to tables.

Testimonials

Boaz Ronen, Professor Emeritus, Coller School of Management, Tel Aviv University, Israel

Schragenheim, Camp, and Surace, three leaders of TOC community, are tackling one of value destroyers of corporations—the misuse and abuse of traditional cost accounting. This book develops a practical methodology for better decision making by looking at the impact of certain types of decisions on a company's bottom line. This well-defined methodology allows mid-managers, higher level managers, and financial staff to create real value by concentrating on what truly matters.

Andrea Zattoni, CEO of Antifragility, Italy

Throughput Economics reduces the stress of entrepreneurs and managers, allowing them to orient themselves in a nondeterministic world, full of uncertainty, complexity, nonlinearity, and asymmetry. The book guides the reader a step-by-step in the decision-making process even when the relevant information is not completely available. It gives a simple, effective, and practical way of checking all the ramifications of any proposed improvement idea, allowing an *a priori* evaluation of risks and potential gains. *Throughput Economics* is a must read for entrepreneurs and managers who want to make their organizations more and more antifragile.

Rudolf Burkhart, Business Development Director, Vistem Gmbh, Germany

There are a couple of ways I have used this book and have found it very useful.

1. Every once in a while, I am confronted with a particular (Throughput Economics) problem a client has that I cannot immediately answer or for which I don't want to give an immediate answer for fear of shooting myself in the foot. Throughput Economics may not provide the exact answer, but it has already led me to find a solution direction to follow.
2. A manager will often want to maintain the "old Cost World" way of doing things—it has been the common practice for many years and such common practices are difficult to give up. The book has again come in handy for finding the ways to show a customer the consequences of common practices and, at the same time, show them the magnitude of the benefit of taking the other (Throughput World) route to greater success.

One particularly important sentence in his book is as follows:

"Rules that were meant to bring consistency to financial reporting have been extended as 'rules' within companies' managerial systems."

These rules for consistency between organizations have compromised generations of management competence. Managers need to use this and similar books to change their management accounting to have a basis for considerably improved performance. I hope the readers get this message from the book—it is there, just listen to it!

Management accounting is a dry topic. Throughput Economics is not—managers can learn a lot they can apply to their company from it.

Pavel Vitovec, IT specialist—DCS support, Czech Republic

This book is for anybody who has heard about Throughput Accounting, or at least is able to admit doubts about the usability of cost accounting for managerial decisions. Starting with reasons for Throughput Accounting and its principles, it will guide you through simple example applications to more complex ones, until you get a feeling for how Throughput Economics is used for better decisions. And, even if you already know Throughput Accounting, you will gain new insights from the book through its careful explanations.

Stephen Roper, Founder: Value360 Solutions (Pty.) Ltd., South Africa

Throughput Economics makes a very meaningful contribution to the quality of management decision making by focusing attention on the causes of cost in an organization. The illusions and distortions produced by traditional cost and management accounting are replaced by insights that produce meaningful and tangible results. *Throughput Economics* has a worthy place in the growing body of literature focused on understanding and managing organizations as systems.

Bob Sproul, author and consultant, United States

This book focuses on making superior managerial decisions when the situation is both complex and uncertain. To do that, the authors explain that one must be aware of what prevents good managers from making the right decisions on behalf of their organizations. This is illustrated eloquently through a series of case studies. The authors also tell us that there is a common practice of differentiating between long-term decisions—so called strategic decisions—and short-term or tactical decisions, when in reality these two types of decisions should be closely related. The methodology presented in this book is targeted at both kinds of decisions by connecting them through understanding the relationships between short-term opportunities and their full potential over the long term. In my opinion, this book is a classic and should be required reading in all graduate programs! Well done!!

Kevin J. Clarke, CEO, Board Director, large-scale operations subject matter expert, United States

After reading this book the authors reinforced to me that "complex problems do not always require complex solutions. The solutions are often staring you in the face once you clearly define your objectives." This book will help you broaden your view of business from every angle.

For Product Safety Concerns and Information please contact our EU
representative GPSR@taylorandfrancis.com
Taylor & Francis Verlag GmbH, Kaufingerstraße 24, 80331 München, Germany

www.ingramcontent.com/pod-product-compliance
Ingram Content Group UK Ltd.
Pitfield, Milton Keynes, MK11 3LW, UK
UKHW050931180425
457613UK00015B/362